The First Credit Market Turmoil of the 21st Century

World Scientific Studies in International Economics

(ISSN: 1793-3641)

---

*Published**

Vol. 3 Risk Management and Value: Valuation and Asset Pricing
edited by Mondher Bellalah, Jean-Luc Prigent, Annie Delienne (Université de Cergy-Pontoise, France), Georges Pariente, Olivier Levyne, Michel Azaria (Institut Supérieur de Commerce, ISC Paris, France) & Jean-Michel Sahut (ESC Amiens, France)

Vol. 4 The Rules of Globalization (Case Book)
edited by Rawi Abdelal (Harvard University, USA)

Vol. 5 Institutions and Gender Empowerment in the Global Economy
edited by Kartik Roy (University of Queensland, Australia), Hans Blomqvist (Swedish School of Economics and Business Administration, Finland) & Cal Clark (Auburn University, USA)

Vol. 6 Globalization and Systemic Risk
edited by Douglas D. Evanoff (Federal Reserve Bank of Chicago, USA), David S. Hoelscher (International Monetary Fund, USA) & George G. Kaufman (Loyola University Chicago, USA)

Vol. 7 Fostering Monetary and Financial Cooperation in East Asia
edited by Duck-Koo Chung (North East Asia Research Foundation, South Korea) & Barry Eichengreen (University of California, Berkeley, USA)

Vol. 9 Globalization and International Trade Policies
by Robert M Stern

Vol. 10 The First Credit Market Turmoil of the 21st Century: Implications for Public Policy
edited by Douglas D Evanoff (Federal Reserve Bank of Chicago, USA), Philipp Hartmann (European Central Bank, Germany) & George G Kaufman (Loyola University, USA)

Forthcoming

Vol. 8 Challenges of Economic Development in the Middle East and North Africa Region
by Julia C Devlin

*The complete list of the published volumes in the series, can also be found at http://www.worldscibooks.com/series/wssie_series.shtml

10 World Scientific Studies in International Economics

The First Credit Market Turmoil of the 21st Century

edited by

Douglas D Evanoff
Federal Reserve Bank of Chicago, USA

Philipp Hartmann
European Central Bank, Germany

George G Kaufman
Loyola University, USA

World Scientific

NEW JERSEY • LONDON • SINGAPORE • BEIJING • SHANGHAI • HONG KONG • TAIPEI • CHENNAI

Published by

World Scientific Publishing Co. Pte. Ltd.
5 Toh Tuck Link, Singapore 596224
USA office: 27 Warren Street, Suite 401-402, Hackensack, NJ 07601
UK office: 57 Shelton Street, Covent Garden, London WC2H 9HE

British Library Cataloguing-in-Publication Data
A catalogue record for this book is available from the British Library.

World Scientific Studies in International Economics — Vol. 10
THE FIRST CREDIT MARKET TURMOIL OF THE 21ST CENTURY
Implications for Public Policy

ISBN-13 978-981-4280-47-1
ISBN-10 981-4280-47-X

Typeset by Stallion Press
Email: enquiries@stallionpress.com

Printed in Singapore by Mainland Press Pte Ltd

Contents

Preface

Credit markets in almost all industrial countries have been in substantial turmoil since the summer of 2007. This has resulted in the most severe disruptions to financial institutions, financial markets, and macro-economies worldwide since the Great Depression of the 1930s. What were the causes of the crisis? Why did it spread so rapidly and broadly across countries? How was it related to the bursting of the housing (real estate) bubble, particularly in the United States? Were the prudential bank regulators caught off-guard? How serious is the damage to the financial system and the real economy? What have been the public and private policy responses? What happened to market discipline? How will the regulatory structure be affected? Where should we go from here?

These and related issues were explored by leading financial experts from a rich variety of countries and professional affiliations at the eleventh annual international conference. The 2008 conference was co-sponsored by the Federal Reserve Bank of Chicago and the European Central Bank at the Federal Reserve Bank of Chicago on 25 and 26 September 2008. It focused on important issues confronting the international financial system. The conference was attended by some 170 participants from over 30 different countries and international organizations. The participants represented both the private and public sectors and included bank regulators, financial policymakers, bankers, other finance practitioners, trade association staff, and academics. This volume includes the papers presented at the conference sessions, comments by discussants and special keynote addresses. At the time of the conference the dynamics of the financial turmoil were changing almost daily. Indeed, September 2008, the month of the conference, probably marked the tipping point from primarily a significant market turmoil to a systemic financial crisis. Thus, the contributions in this volume were mostly prepared during the summer of 2008, before the change, on the basis of the information available at that time (with relatively minor updating possible in some cases through press time in early November).

Publication of the contributions in this volume is intended to share the ideas, analyses, and conclusions presented at the conference with a larger audience to further enhance our understanding of the important forces shaping the observed events in financial markets and our ability to adopt both public and private policies that will improve performance in the future and mitigate, if not prevent, such crises.

Douglas D. Evanoff
Federal Reserve Bank of Chicago

Philipp Hartmann
European Central Bank

George G. Kaufman
Loyola University Chicago
and Federal Reserve Bank of Chicago

Acknowledgements

Both the conference and this volume represent a joint effort of the Federal Reserve Bank of Chicago and the European Central Bank. Many people at each institution contributed to the effort. The three editors served as the principal organizers of the conference program. They would like to thank all the people who contributed their time and energy to the effort. At the risk of omitting someone, we would like to thank Julia Baker, Olli Castrén, John Dixon, Ella Dukes, Cornelia Holthausen, Hala Leddy, Rita Molloy, Loretta Novak, Elizabeth Taylor, and Barbara Van Brussell. Special mention must be accorded Helen O'D. Koshy and Kathryn Moran who had primary responsibility for preparing the program information and shepherding the book from manuscript review to final copy, as well as to Sandy Schneider and Blanca Sepulveda, who expertly managed the administrative duties.

I. SPECIAL ADDRESSES

Central Banks and the Financial Turmoil

José Manuel González-Páramo*
European Central Bank

1. Introduction[1]

It is a great pleasure to be here in Chicago on the occasion of the Federal Reserve Bank of Chicago's Eleventh Annual International Banking Conference. Since its inception, this conference series has aimed to gather prominent academics, policy-makers and market participants to discuss issues of major importance for our banking industries, financial systems, and economies at large, such as asset price bubbles, systemic financial instability, cross-border banking, or financial globalization.

Over time, a permanent concern of the organizers has been to focus on the implications for monetary and regulatory policies and, more generally, for public policies of such phenomena. It is fair to say that a great deal of knowledge has accumulated over time, thanks to this series of conferences. It is also reasonable to reckon that the foundations of this body of knowledge have been put to the test by the financial market turmoil over the past year.

When the Tenth Annual International Banking Conference took place in September last year, the market turmoil had already broken out and central banks were already engaged in interventions aiming to minimize the disruptions to money markets and to preserve the implementation of their desired monetary policy stance. While market data on future interest rates suggested that we were in for a rather protracted period of tensions in money and credit markets, it was not obvious at the time that the financial turmoil would turn out to be one of the most challenging events of the last century for our financial systems.

---

* Member of the Executive Board of the European Central Bank.
[1] I am very grateful to Cornelia Holthausen for her valuable contributions.

Indeed, the international financial landscape looks very different today compared to one year ago and almost every day new events contribute to re-shaping it further. In particular, over the past two weeks, adverse events occurred almost on a daily basis and led to increased uncertainty and significant financial market volatility. A large bank failed, while several financial institutions had to be partly or entirely taken over by others. In response to the renewed tensions, public authorities announced a number of measures and initiatives to address problems at both stressed markets and troubled individual institutions. In particular, central banks stepped up their efforts to inject liquidity in global money markets in order to guarantee their smooth functioning.

As I mentioned earlier, one of the main objectives of this series of conferences is to discuss the main lessons for public policies arising from developments in the international banking and financial sector. The continuation of the market turmoil does not allow me to talk to you with the benefit of detachment and the comfort of an ex-post assessment. However, I should like to take advantage of the occasion to share with you some considerations on the European Central Bank's (ECB) response to the market turmoil drawing on the experience of the past year.

2. The Separation Between Monetary Policy Formulation and its Implementation

Central bankers have, naturally, eyed the developments of the past year of financial turmoil — and, particularly, their recent intensification — with great concern, as they have the potential to adversely influence the ability of central banks to steer monetary policy rates, affect the transmission mechanism of monetary policy, and, more generally, may pose a threat to financial stability.

Once the credit concerns that had built up in the sub-prime mortgage market segment started to affect interest rates and traded volumes in the euro area money market, the ECB responded to these highly unusual market events by timely and forcefully adjusting its liquidity policy. I will not deal with the specifics of the ECB's liquidity management over the past year — this will be done by the ECB staff in tomorrow's session on "The Experience with Crisis Management" — but I would like to stress one fundamental principle underlying our response to the turmoil — "the separation principle". This principle relates to the dichotomy between the ECB's monetary policy and its liquidity policy or, in other words, between the formulation and implementation of monetary policy.

During the turmoil, the separation principle proved to be very effective. Supported by the flexibility of its operational framework, the ECB was able to react in a flexible and quick manner to a changing market environment, and it allowed the steering of interest rates close to the policy rate by means of temporary quantity adjustments, albeit without increasing the aggregate supply of euro liquidity to the banking sector.

The main objective of the ECB's immediate and lasting responses to tensions in the money market was to keep under control the very short-term interest rates as the first step in the transmission of monetary policy. Broadly speaking, the ECB's liquidity policy response consisted of three elements. First, it changed the timing of the liquidity provision within the maintenance period (the so-called "front-loading policy"), and thereby allowed banks to build up temporary liquidity buffers. Second, it lengthened the average maturity of its tender operations — before the turmoil, the bulk of liquidity was supplied through one-week operations, and only about 30% was auctioned for three months. As the turmoil unfolded, the ECB gradually increased the share of the three-month operations and moreover introduced a six-month maturity operation. Finally, it participated in the joint coordination effort of an increasing number of central banks around the world within the context of the Term Auction Facility.

More specifically, in collaboration with the Federal Reserve, the ECB offered U.S. dollar liquidity to European banks at various maturities in order to satisfy the exceptional demand for those funds. I believe that all of these actions proved to be effective in easing the tensions at the short-term end of the global money markets and in maintaining control of short-term interest rates in the euro area. I am sure that global money and funding markets will continue to benefit from our very close cooperation in the times to come. Still, term interest rates in the money market continue to be strongly influenced by credit concerns and, not surprisingly, have proved to be only marginally sensitive to changes in liquidity policy.

As a result, the transmission of monetary policy for the economy at large is affected by the ongoing turmoil. I will now turn to this very question.

3. The Impact of the Turmoil on the Monetary Transmission Mechanism

During the current turmoil, the role of banks in the transmission mechanism of monetary policy has been brought to the forefront. In Europe, as you know, universal banks continue to be important players in the financial landscape. This is why they also play a crucial role for the transmission of monetary policy, as upheld by several theories, notably the bank lending channel and supportive empirical findings.[2] According to this theory, the pass-through of changes in monetary policy interest rates to the real sector of the economy is influenced by banks' ability to provide credit to firms. This applies, in particular, to banks with less liquid balance sheets, often the smaller banks.[3] With a bank lending channel, the effects of monetary tightening on the supply of credit become more pronounced.

The European banking sector has undergone a phase of some structural changes over the past years. In particular, as in other parts of the world, the European market for structured financial products, such as asset-backed securities or collateralized debt obligations, has grown rapidly over the last decade. For instance, the quarterly issuance of euro-denominated asset-backed securities increased from just under €20 billion at the beginning of the present decade to above €150 billion in the second quarter of this year.[4] These developments potentially influence banks' ability to grant credit.[5]

Such changes are important for the conduct of monetary policy because, first, they affect monetary analysis (one of the pillars of the ECB's monetary policy strategy), and second, because they are likely to affect the monetary transmission mechanism. On one hand, increased securitization is expected to weaken the effects of the bank lending channel by dampening the effect of monetary tightening on the *supply* of credit.

---

[2] See Bernanke, B. and M. Gertler (1995). Inside the black box: the credit channel of monetary policy transmission. *Journal of Economic Perspectives*, 9, 27–48. For the euro area, see contributions collected in Angeloni, I., A. Kashyap and B. Mojon (eds.), 2003: *Monetary Policy Transmission in the Euro Area*, Cambridge University Press.

[3] Kashyap, A. and J. Stein (2000). What do a million observations on banks say about the transmission of monetary policy? *American Economic Review*, 90(3), 407–428.

[4] European Securitisation Forum (2008). ESF securitisation data report — Q2:2008.

[5] European Central Bank (2008). The role of banks in the monetary transmission mechanism. *ECB Monthly Bulletin*, August 2008, 85–98.

Indeed, some evidence points to the fact that the supply of loans is positively affected by securitization.[6] On the other hand, a more developed and efficient financial system can contribute to a more effective and smooth transmission of monetary policy.[7]

At the root of the problems that led to the current financial turmoil is precisely this growing segment of the financial industry. As valuations of asset-backed securities and other assets declined rapidly, and, in fact, the whole securitization model was shaken, the outstanding amount of structured products decreased significantly. Obviously, this affects bank credit: according to the latest bank lending survey conducted in the euro area, more than 80% of banks judged that difficulties in raising funds via securitization have had a negative impact on bank lending.[8]

Overall, the financial turmoil may have affected the efficient working of the banking sector and might have an impact on the supply of credit to the non-financial sector. In light of the fact that bank lending remains strong (the annual rate of growth of loans to non-financial corporations in August 2008 was still a robust 12.6 percent), it is too early to quantify the extent to which the turmoil may influence the provision of loans. Needless to say, the Eurosystem, and undoubtedly other central banks, will continue to closely monitor the situation.

4. The Role of Uncertainty

One of the most relevant features of the current turmoil has been the high degree of asymmetric information and the enormous increase in general uncertainty in the financial sector. I would like to distinguish between the two in the following way.[9]

Uncertainty owes mainly to imperfect information in relation to credit valuations. Uncertainty generally increased during the summer

---

[6] See, for instance, Altunbas, Y., L. Gambacorta, and D. Marqués (2007). Securitisation and the bank lending channel. ECB Working Paper No. 838.

[7] See, for instance, Gropp, R., C. Kok Sørensen, and J. Lichtenberger (2007). The dynamics of bank spreads and financial structure. ECB Working Paper No. 714.

[8] European Central Bank (2008). The euro area bank lending survey. January 2008.

[9] On this subject, see Cassola, N., M. Drehmann, P. Hartmann, M. lo Duca, and M. Scheicher (2008). A Research perspective on the propagation of the credit market turmoil. ECB Research Bulletin No. 7, June 2008.

of 2007, because market participants realised that the current practices used for valuations — often based almost solely on ratings — were no longer valid. With this type of uncertainty, market participants have difficulty in modelling the expected occurrence of defaults. Credit spreads can widen, also at the short end.[10] Another typical effect is the flight-to-quality phenomenon — as in previous episodes of high uncertainty, during the turmoil savers have shunned equity and credit risk products in favour of government bonds and commodities as well as cash and bank deposits. As a result, bank deposits increased significantly.

The term asymmetric information, on the other hand, applies to an adverse selection problem, notably in the interbank market, where market players can no longer distinguish solvent from insolvent borrowers. Such a "lemon's problem" induces banks to demand high risk premiums of their creditors and leads to a general increase in interbank market rates. Moreover, it can lead to the rationing of credit provision. Indeed, during the turmoil, a general tightening of credit standards has occurred and has been intense and widespread. Counterparty credit risk and uncertainty about the development of entire segments of the financial market — notably of more complex instruments such as collateralized debt obligations and other related products — were important elements in the development of the turmoil.

Central banks have to deal with this increase in uncertainty on several accounts. First, monetary policy needs to take into account the heightened uncertainty — central banks need to refine their monetary and financial analysis, and monitor extremely closely the developments in the financial system and their impact on the pass-through of policy rates to the economy.

Second, and to return to the beginning of my remarks, liquidity management has become more active. Counterparty credit risk as well as uncertainty about the development of their own liquidity needs have led banks to hoard liquidity and impaired the normal functioning of money markets. As a consequence, the liquidity provided to the market does not circulate as smoothly as it does in normal times. Moreover, the nervousness of market players sometimes implies stronger than anticipated interest rate reactions.

---

[10] This has been modelled formally by Duffie and Lando (2001). Term structure of credit spreads with incomplete accounting information. *Econometrica*, 69, 633–664.

5. Conclusion

I would like to conclude by saying that monetary policy implementation has certainly become a more challenging task as a result of the current financial turmoil. At the same time, the flexibility of the ECB's operational framework has very much helped us in coping with the turmoil. The ECB has been able to maintain control over the short end of the money market, though not surprisingly our influence on longer maturities, where prices are driven mainly by credit concerns, remained limited.

At the ECB, we believe that the separation principle (i.e., the separation of liquidity policy measures from any considerations about the monetary policy stance) has served us well. Indeed, the liquidity policy aided the transmission of monetary policy even in the turbulent times experienced over the past year, while monetary policy was left free to focus on its overriding objective of ensuring price stability. I strongly believe that especially at times of high uncertainty and rising inflationary pressures like the present, a stable and predictable central bank policy and the firm anchoring of inflationary expectations are of particular importance.

There is no doubt that these are very challenging times for our economies. Some scientists argue that wildfires can be in the long run beneficial to wildlife as over time barren burned areas are covered by healthier new growth. Without pushing too far the analogy, let's hope that the equivalent applies to the weakest segments of our financial systems. This will very much depend on the ability of all concerned parties — both public and private — to draw the right lessons and thoroughly implement them.

Bearing this in mind, I look forward to the second day of this conference, during which the regulatory implications of the ongoing events shall be discussed.

The Implications of the Credit Crisis for Public Policy

Charles H. Dallara*
Institute of International Finance

It is a pleasure to be here tonight. I'm not sure who in the Chicago Fed or at the European Central Bank (ECB) was so prescient to frame the focus of this discussion some time ago, but it is indeed one of the best timed conferences I have ever witnessed.

I thought I would spend much of my time this evening sharing a few thoughts on the public policy implications of this credit crisis and this credit turmoil, while also talking about the obligations of the financial institutions themselves.

Some of you may have seen the final report of the Institute of International Finance's (IIF) Committee on Market Best Practices (CMBP).[1] It is quite a remarkable document. And it represents, and I'm going to start on this point, if I may, because I think we're all so captured, rightly so, in the immediacy of the stress and the crisis in financial markets that it is easy to lose sight of some of the fundamental reforms that need to take place, both within the industry and in regulatory and global financial structures.

I understand you've already had some discussions yesterday and today about the changes that may be needed in the regulatory and global financial organizational environment, and I will share my own thoughts with you which are very much my own thoughts, not necessarily those of the institutions I represent. You know when you represent 395 financial

---

* Charles H. Dallara has served as managing director of the Institute of International Finance (IIF) since July 1993.

[1] Final report of the IIF Committee on Market Best Practices: Principles of Conduct and Best Practice Recommendations. Financial Services Industry Response to the Market Turmoil of 2007–08. Institute of International Finance, available at www.IIF.com.

institutions you obviously represent a very diverse spectrum of financial organizations and inherently a very diverse set of viewpoints.

Fortunately, on a lot of issues of concern and priority to the industry, we are able to work through a board structure and a committee structure to frame coherent views on a range of issues. While that is sometimes difficult to do, we work on it, because it is important that the banking community and the financial community, more generally, try to come together behind a particular perspective as to how to most effectively address an issue. And I might add, by the way, and I think probably some of you know this, that we're proud of the fact that the institute — that we're not just an organization representing the leading banks of the Group of Ten (G10) countries. Those 395 institutions include scores of institutions headquartered in emerging markets.

14 banks in China, 10 in Korea, a dozen in Turkey, over 60 headquartered in the Middle East, a half-dozen from Brazil, and I can go on. So we genuinely try to represent the broad views of a wide range of financial institutions. Of course, the center of our membership base and the center of our activity are the leading financial institutions of the U.S., Europe, Canada, and Japan, but as you can see from what I just mentioned, this has evolved and changed a good bit over the years.

When we saw the scale of the crisis emerging in the summer of 2007, the IIF board of directors realized that things would change fundamentally in terms of how markets operated and how the regulatory environment interacted with financial institutions. They focused appropriately so, in my view, on what the industry could do itself to clean up its own act. Collectively, the financial industry at the forefront, and the regulatory and official sector in the back drop, let down the people of this country and the people of Europe in a dramatic way. We have failed to supervise effectively the risks that were created. And this is, perhaps, the first period in the last century, if not even going further back, where it could be argued that we are on the verge of a recession caused by financial mismanagement by the private financial community. That's a rather sobering burden to contemplate, but I think it's a reasonably fair one.

So the industry has a huge responsibility in my view to restore its credibility and to address the mistakes that it made. I don't suggest for a moment that every financial institution was guilty of all of the excesses that we have seen. And I don't suggest for a moment that any financial institution can be held responsible for the system in which it operates. The system we have today is a result of many different forces that have created global capital markets and global financial and banking systems that I think it would be unfair and unreasonable to hold any individual financial institutions, or for that matter, the banking community in general, responsible for the structural deficiencies in the system.

But you can, and we should, hold the banking community responsible for the failures of risk management which have taken place inside individual institutions, for the failures of transparency and disclosure, for the failures of understanding that compensation systems can adversely affect your ability to manage your institution within a medium-term horizon.

We put together a committee of leading banks and leading bankers from around the world that worked for nine months to create the principles and the recommendations that you will see embedded in the final report of the Committee on Market Best Practices. And we chose that title because we wanted to see, if in the mist all of the turbulence and chaos, we could actually step back and identify what are the best practices that we should be following as risk managers, as executives, as liquidity risk experts, as transparency and disclosure experts, in our own industry. How can we identify those practices and how can we promulgate them throughout the industry? This was the mission of this group. And it also looked at regulatory changes that the industry felt need to be made.

Some of you may think that's a bit audacious, and questionable, that the industry should give advice to the regulatory community today. And yet it is our responsibility to share our thoughts with the regulatory and central banking community on how changes should be made, while recognizing that the primary responsibility lies with the banking community to deal with its own weaknesses.

When we presented this report to Chairman Bernanke some weeks ago, he not only received it with considerable endorsement, but he also asked a question. He said, "Well, what do you think of the approach we are taking to deal with the regulatory weakness in our system?"

And so we had to sit down and go through with him what some of our thoughts were, and I'll share those with you in a few moments. But, first of all, let me just stress a few of the key findings in our report on areas where the banking community itself needs to act.

First of all, risk management. Obviously, there are so many different components of risk management, but the essence of what went wrong here, in my view, has more to do with the lack of solid well-centered, corporate governance structures for risk management than, it has to do with the technical deficiencies of stress testing. Obviously, there are technical weaknesses in the risk-management systems of our financial institutions that contributed to today's situation. However, over the last few years, I think many of us saw the steady marginalization of the role of risk management in financial institutions where the deal flow, the volume of liquidity, the earnings, the compensation, drove firms increasingly to treat risk management as a source of information, not as an integral part of business decision-making. And gradually the risk officers and their teams in many of the leading financial institutions, even some of the best, were marginalized. Decisions were taken on risk positions without the debate that needed to happen. Some call this a matter of risk culture, and to a degree, it is. But it also has to do with governance structures inside organizations.

We need to see a re-empowerment of risk officers in financial institutions if we are to get through the next decade without the same disaster that has befallen us this time. There are many other aspects of risk management that we address in our report.

Liquidity risk is an area that we have concentrated on a good bit at the institute,[2] because for many months — many years really — during the first part of this decade, funding liquidity risk management was not really a serious matter of priority for many financial institutions. It was almost taken as a given. We addressed critical issues of liquidity risk management in a special report in March 2007, and we returned to this subject in the CMBP's final report. Today, this is a major topic because we now have extraordinarily dysfunctional interbank funding markets. Many of you professionals that are in the room know first-hand the scale of the stress that is now being seen. In fact, strains have been very evident for the last 13 months in the interbank funding markets. Until we're able to find the keys to unlock the key elements of stress, we will continue in my view to have an extraordinary amount of fragility in the financial system.

One other matter that I mentioned earlier, which has become a big topic in Washington this last week, is compensation in the financial system. When we initially formed the CMBP, one of the risk officers in a member firm said, "Are we going to look at compensation issues?"

---

[2] *Principles of Liquidity Risk Management — report of* the IIF's Special Committee on Liquidity Risk, March, 2007, available at www.IIF.com

And the immediate reaction among other risk officers was that this was above their pay grade. So we decided to take this to the Board. And we asked the Board for its support and authority and encouragement to look at what needs to be done to reform compensation practices.

Well, three hours later, after a very heated debate, finally the Board concluded that we could not avoid this issue. Today, it is clear that the industry needs to be held accountable for the extent to which its incentive compensation practices exacerbated poor risk management and contributed to the current situation.

We articulated six principles in the CMBP report that we feel should guide compensation practices. Fundamentally, it's all about aligning compensation with long-term shareholder interests and risk-adjusted return for the way in which capital is deployed in a financial institution.

And I've been asked this week, by many people in Congress, well, you know, what should we do on this matter? And I have said, it's pretty simple as far as I'm concerned. Just ask and expect, and demand, that firms develop their own particular plans to implement these principles. I don't think compensation can be micromanaged through legislation, but it's very clear that the American people will not accept a $700 billion dollar asset purchase program without some sense that Wall Street individuals will not unduly benefit from this.

There are many other areas where the industry needs to clean up its act. And we're determined at the institute with our 395 members to do what we can to encourage implementation.

I'll be leaving tomorrow to go to Amsterdam where I'll be joining some of our senior bankers to meet with the leadership of the Financial Stability Forum, which as many of you know, is a group of senior regulators created a decade ago. Not just regulators, but finance officials and central bankers as well, to provide a framework for looking at systemic stability. We shall be talking there about our plans for implementing this report, because putting recommendations down on paper is one thing, insuring that they are actually implemented is another thing.

I'm quite encouraged that many banks have already developed plans to analyze how well their current practices match up against the practices, the best practices articulated in this report, and that they also have plans for implementing steps to close that gap. And we will continue to push this hard as we go forward. Irrespective of what happens with legislation and with regulatory reform, the industry has its own responsibility to its shareholders and to the broader citizens of this country as well as the world at large.

Where does that leave us with regard for the need for policy changes? Let me divide my comments on this into two broad camps.

The first has to do with immediate policy actions and then, secondly, I'll turn to a few topics beyond the absolutely immediate situation. I think it goes without saying, and I doubt that I would find anyone in this room who would disagree with the need for urgent action by our Congress, in the hours and days ahead, to provide a framework to stabilize what, right now, is the most fragile, unstable financial system that I think any of us have ever witnessed. It's also my view that we need to look for comparable or similar action in Europe. Now this is not something that will be readily embraced by European governments. But I must say that I am a little perplexed that many European governments have been sitting and watching what's going on in Washington and have not yet recognized that this global problem requires a global solution. Now, this is not to say that we expect that similar legislation is going to be passed in every country around the world. Nor, necessarily, does similar legislation need to be passed in each of the European capitals that have been seriously affected. But, should they explore the need for some similar effects to support their own banks? In my view, absolutely.

Without this, I am afraid we will have not only political asymmetry but financial asymmetry, and already you are seeing a scramble by European financial institutions to be qualified to put their assets into the new pool that will be, presumably, acquired by the U.S. Treasury and the U.S. government.

Another aspect of immediate action is the continuance, and if need be, strengthening and reinforcement of the central bank liquidity facilities that have been put on stream over the course of the last 10 months. Whatever one thinks about the moves in the monetary policy arena, and whatever one thinks about the increasing concerns about moral hazard, I think we have to recognize the tremendous job the central banks of the world have done in creating increasingly flexible liquidity facilities to, in effect, insure that there is some continued flow of funding to support for the ongoing activities of the banks of the U.S. and Europe.

It may be necessary to make them more flexible and extend these facilities even more in the days ahead. Although, hopefully, the passage of legislation by the U.S. and similar action in Europe, might re-inject a degree of confidence into the system that banks can begin to trust one another again, and begin to renew term lending to one and another. This is such a fundamental foundation of our global banking system today, that it is hard for me to imagine that there are not going to be major mishaps going forward unless we can get the interbank funding markets working again.

Looking beyond these immediate areas of action, let me address some of the other issues that you've been talking about over the last day or two about reform in the regulatory structure, in policy prescriptions, and in the global financial architecture. You know, every crisis presents a challenge to manage it, but it also presents that rare opportunity to fundamentally change the way we do business in the global financial world. It has been paradoxical and unfortunate that even though financial markets have been increasingly globalized over the last two decades and that financial firms have been increasingly globalized in this period, the extent of globalization and standardization of regulatory policies and regulatory structures has been modest and in some ways begrudging.

That is not to say that those in the regulatory community should not be proud of what has been constructed around Basel II. But it has been frustrating, I must say, from the private sector side to have engaged in long standing discussions about the need for taking on simple matters, such as the definition of wholesale and retail clients. We've gone to regulators year in and year out and said, let's take a handful of manageable propositions and establish a global standard — a globally consistent set of rules and criteria — and it just doesn't happen.

Today, I think we need to step back and realize the absolute and essential necessity of developing a more globalized approach toward regulatory standards and regulatory policies. Of course, you will argue that it needs to be built on more coherent structures within individual countries. Let us hope that one thing that comes out of this crisis will be a unified coherent and effective regulatory structure in this country for the financial sector.

All of us have our ideas about what that would look like. In my own world, it's the Fed-centered regulatory, supervisory, structure that needs to oversee the largest 50 to 75 financial institutions of whatever shape, size, or form, or license. In my view such authority should be under the Fed umbrella and just for purposes of systemic stress, but also for day-to-day supervision as well. Whether or not you need a separate regulator for small community banks is another question. But, I think, it is way overdue that we have a unified structure to regulate and supervise our financial services industry.

When I was at JPMorgan in 1992, I had a couple of experiences that stayed with me. One of them goes back to this risk-management issue of risk officers not understanding or not having the authority within firms to really be part of the decision-making, and another one goes to this issue of semi-unregulated financial institutions getting into high risk businesses.

I was approached about a major, complex, financial transaction that was to be put on the balance sheet of AIG, and it was an attractive deal from the perspective of JPMorgan and we were maneuvering with a third party client to transfer a substantial portfolio with complex risks to AIG. And I remember, naively, asking the question as to whether AIG could handle those risks? And I was promptly told that they built up a very strong financial product group, and that, yes, they probably knew something about managing the risk involved. But there was no one supervising AIG's capacity to manage their risks; just as there has been no one performing this role in some of the other major financial institutions that have come under stress.

We absolutely need a capable, sophisticated supervisory structure that can supervise the risk of complex, large, global financial institutions irrespective of the type of license they may have hanging on their wall.

But let's go global for a minute and think about what we need in the global architecture. Again, I think we all have different ideas and different visions. I understand that Henry Kaufman shared some of his views with you earlier today, and he's certainly one of the most astute thinkers on this that I have heard.

My own thoughts are that it is well past time to create something along the lines of a global regulatory coordinating council that would have two tiers. The first would be for the Group of Seven (G7) or G10 countries where you would have some degree of authority transferred. Obviously, it could not be ultimate authority, because we're not going to be in a world where supervisory authority is transferred lock, stock, and barrel to a global entity. But you absolutely need something with more authority than you have today to frame globally consistent, coherent, regulatory and supervisory standards. You need a body that can sit atop the actual supervision of the world's largest 50 to 75 financial institutions — certainly those operating or headquartered in the G10 countries, plus Switzerland.

A second tier would bring into that structure the key regulators of the other top 20 countries in the world, whose economies and whose financial systems have become increasingly important to today's global marketplace. Without some codification and development of the architecture and global regulatory structures, I am afraid we could find ourselves paradoxically retreating to our own national capital markets, our own national banking systems, and our own idiosyncratic ways of doing business. In some sense, it does make one feel more secure, but it's the key to inefficiency and backward movement in the global financial system. I do regret it when I go to London and I hear someone say to me, well, you know whatever the Basel Committee does or whatever happens in Brussels, we're going to have our own liquidity rules. And then I go to Berlin, or I go to Zurich, and I hear that whatever happens on Basel II, we're going to have our own leverage rules. And then I go to other capitals and other regulatory centers and I hear each one for good reason, in their own political context, taking about, to a degree, going their own way.

This is not the way forward. We must insist upon global coordination and standardization of regulatory practices and policies even if it requires home country regulators or host country regulators, I should say, ceding a bit of their local control and authority which is a small price, in my view to pay, for global, financial stability.

What else do we need to do in the global architectural arena? Permit me to mention three other things quite briefly.

First, accounting issues. There are different views of the extent to which mark-to-market and fair value accounting have contributed to the current crisis — I think that they have significantly exacerbated the crisis. I believe it is compelling that we urgently organize a high level, globally endorsed, four-way dialogue involving the two important accounting standard setting organization, the Independence Standards Board (ISB) and Financial Accounting Standards Board (FASB), the Basel Committee representing the global regulators, a Bank for International Settlements (BIS) group representing the central banks, and the bankers themselves to try to find some reasonable countercyclical approaches to the way in which accounting standards can be applied, while remaining as faithful as possible to sensible, transparent, consistent accounting. We should recognize that going all the way down the road of market-to-market accounting in the absence of a market, simply doesn't lead you anywhere but to a dead end.

As Paul Volcker recently said at a conference that I attended, "that's a recipe for ensuring that we can find a price for everything and a value for nothing", I firmly share his view in that regard.

Secondly, on the global systemic front, how do we better anticipate global systemic stress? We have in this final report launched an idea which we're going to put into effect in the coming months. We're going to create a global, private sector Market Monitoring Group. What is the basic notion and what's the purpose? It is to bring together some of the best talent in the private banking community to detect risks that may have possible systemic implications. Now, that's a tall order, and I have no doubt that we'll struggle to find the recipe to really make this work. But I also have little doubt as the chairman of our board of directors, Dr. Josef Ackerman said recently, "That if once, just every four or five years, we're able to detect a potentially growing dimension of systemic stress and head it off at the pass, then this exercise will have been well worth the effort."

We believe that this group should probably join hands with an official sector group under the umbrella of the Financial Stability Forum, and we are talking with Federal Reserve Board officials today about that possibility. Because even though the private and the public sectors have their own different responsibilities in promoting global financial stability, it seems increasingly clear to me that we have kept these groups somewhat too separate as we have struggled to cope with the problems around us.

Finally, on the global architectural front, I would suggest that this is a profound and unique opportunity to step back and ask what we really want to do with some of our large multilateral organizations — they are full of talent, full of expertise, but ill-positioned to step into the breach in today's crisis.

I had lunch earlier in the week with my counterpart at the International Monetary Fund (IMF), and he said something to me which resonated, and I think we both agreed that it was an unfortunate reality that, as he noted, "This is not an IMF crisis." Well, it is not a traditional IMF crisis, but we do have to ask ourselves in the throes of such financial stress the fundamental question, what can we do and what should we do to take an organization as financially strong and as talent strong as the IMF is and restructure it so that it can be a useful and timely device to cope with the financial strains of the 21st century?

Should it be able to extend credit into the private financial community?

Should it be restructured in ways that it can take equity into its balance sheet?

These are extraordinary questions to be asking, but they are necessary because unfortunately the IMF, and to a lesser degree other organizations, have seen their effectiveness marginalized in recent years by the growth of global capital markets and the increasing tendency of both G7 and emerging market countries to reduce and marginalize the attention they pay to the IMF.

This has been a problem, of course, for the last 25 years with the G7 countries, who sometimes listen to the IMF and sometimes pay lip service. When I was the U.S. executive director at the IMF in the 1980s, we had serious disagreements, as you might imagine, over fiscal policy. This was during the Reagan Administration years. And the disagreements were professional, but they were serious. And after one such round of Article IV consultations, I went to my boss at the Treasury, who at that time was Jim Baker, and said Mr. Secretary, you know, I know that you're not going to agree with the IMF's advice, but I think it deserves a hearing. And he said, have them come on over. Instead, I suggested that we should not just have the traditional format of the IMF senior team briefing the Treasury Secretary and the Federal Reserve Chairman, but we should have a cabinet briefing instead. A cabinet meeting — Dallara, what in the world are you talking about? I insisted upon it and we actually presented the results of the Article IV consultation to the Cabinet of the United States.

I am not sure that a whole lot came out of this, but it was just one attempt to underscore the importance of stronger IMF engagement with its membership base. In recent years, emerging market economies, which need to benefit from the IMF advice even if they don't have a dire need for IMF funding, have largely ignored the fund. And in my view, they have ignored it at their peril.

I suspect we are entering another period when countries in emerging markets, especially those who have left themselves somewhat vulnerable because of huge current account or fiscal deficits because of failure to reform institutions and because of failure to structurally liberalize their economies, will be going to the IMF and asking for help. Unfortunately, they will probably do it a bit late in the game.

As this process is unfolding, it is crucial to realize that significant shareholding in the Fund extend beyond the G7. The G7 is perhaps the most anarchistic group that one can imagine today — it is a sad commentary on the inability of organizations and groupings to adapt to the rapid changing times. The G7 still consists of four European countries, Canada, the U.S., and Japan. This is not the composition that should be in place of the most important global economies.

Now, I think we have to be politically realistic enough to know that they're not all going to walk out the door and turn their seats over to the

Chinese and Indians and the Brazilians overnight, but they surely should be smart enough to invite them to join them at the table, so the G7 becomes a G11.

Whatever the group that tries to steer global financial architectural discussions, I would certainly encourage a fundamental re-look at the instruments of the IMF. It would probably require a change in the IMF's articles, but there is, I suspect, large uncommitted capital sitting in the IMF today — perhaps $120 billion to $140 billion — sitting on the sidelines watching this crisis unfold, and because of the way in which it is structured, it is unable to play any meaningful role.

I would say, however, that there is one crucial role that the IMF can play, even with its current constraints. As we come through this financial mess, the IMF should, in my view, organize a special ad hoc consultation with the G7, plus four — the major emerging market economies — and not just a special ad hoc consultation with China, which is what is in the cards. This consultation could help to frame a sensible set of macroeconomic policies in these countries to enable the world economy to avoid the recession that may be around the corner. I think many of us would say that today, we're sitting on the knife's edge in terms of whether or not the global economy will fall into a recession.

Frankly, I don't think it's there yet, and I don't think it has to happen. If this crisis is better managed by the official and private sector going forward than it has been over the last few years, then it seems to me that we have a chance of coming out of this with G7 growth next year and the 1 percent to 1.5 percent range in global growth, and the 3 percent to 4 percent range; and that's not a bad thing given where we are now.

But the IMF will have to step in and frame a mutually consistent set of macroeconomic policies and objectives and put it on the table with the G7 plus 4. I hope they can do that. I'm sure they are up to it, both analytically and team wise, but I don't know whether the politics will allow it.

It is a pleasure to be with you, and I'll be glad to take a few questions if you'd like. Thank you.

Where Are Our Leaders?

Kenneth W. Dam*
University of Chicago

Before I talk about the current crisis, I want to recount some experiences I have had observing the U.S. reaction to all kinds of crises. You will note from my biography that I have considerable experience as a government bridesmaid but never as a bride. But even bridesmaids often observe more than they really should.

And for a quick peek at my conclusion, it is that when crises break out, our U.S. leaders are often absent — sometimes physically and more often intellectually.

Let me take some examples from the national security realm. In October 1973, I was serving as the White House coordinator for economic policy, reporting not to the President but directly to the U.S. Secretary of the Treasury, George P. Shultz, who was named by President Nixon as a super-secretary for economic policy. Shultz and I had attended the IMF–World Bank fall meetings in Nairobi and were returning to Washington via Moscow. In Moscow we had economic discussions with ranking Soviet officials, including a two-hour meeting with the formidable Andrei Gromyko.

On the military plane back to Washington, the communications panel began to become more and more active. It was only well into the flight that I learned that Egypt and Syria had just launched coordinated surprise attacks on Israel. Of course, there was not too much that a Treasury

---

* Kenneth W. Dam is the Max Pam Professor Emeritus of American and Foreign Law and a Senior Lecturer at the University of Chicago, Law School. He served as deputy secretary (the second-ranking official) in the Department of Treasury (2001–2003) and in the Department of State (1982–1985). In 1973 he was executive director of the Council on Economic Policy, a White House office responsible for coordinating U.S. domestic and international economic policy. From 1971 to 1973 he served as assistant director for national security and international policy of the Office of Management and Budget.

secretary would have to say about how the U.S. should react. But as we crossed the Atlantic in the middle of that Saturday night, the U.S. National Security Advisor, Henry Kissinger, was sound asleep in a New York hotel, having given a speech earlier in the evening at the Metropolitan Museum of Art.

This Egypt–Syria attack was no simple border clash; it was carefully planned and was in effect Israel's Pearl Harbor. All ended well for Israel (at least in the short run, forgetting about the aftermath that continues even today), but Israel saved itself, no thanks to the United States. Let's just say that the U.S. was "asleep at the switch".

Let me jump ahead to 1983, again an October night, I was working in the State Department, for George Shultz, and again it was a Saturday evening in Washington. At 2:45 am, Secretary Shultz, the National Security Advisor Bud McFarlane, and President Ronald Reagan were awakened in their cottages at Augusta National Golf Club, where they were spending a golfing weekend. The news: more than 200 U.S. marines had been blown up in a terrorist truck bomb attack by unknown assailants. We now know that this was one of the earliest attacks by a group called Hezbollah. Again it is hard to see what these three leaders could have done just then, but again, they were asleep at the switch. Of course, the cause may have been a failure of intelligence, but the deeper cause of this and the 1973 Israeli case was a foreign policy quagmire.

Let me take a slightly different case, where again I happened to be a close observer of the Executive Branch. The date is one known to all of you: September 11, 2001, or 9/11. I was then serving in the U.S. Treasury as Deputy to Secretary Paul O'Neill. This time it was not the middle of the night, but rather morning. I was in my Treasury office preparing to go to the CNBC studios to offer some reassuring platitudes about the economy, when a Treasury press official burst unannounced into my office with the preemptory command, "Turn on your TV". A plane had hit the World Trade Towers in New York and, while I tried to figure out what was going on, I saw on the TV a second plane crashing into the Towers. Now again, where were my leaders?

President Bush was, as I am sure you recall, teaching kindergarten in Florida. Since an attack had just been made on the Wall Street complex, closing the NYSE, flooding some crucial commercial bank computer systems, and causing the New York Fed to be evacuated, it was not comforting that Fed Chairman Alan Greenspan was in Switzerland and Treasury Secretary O'Neill was in Tokyo. Even the CEO of Goldman

Sachs, a man named Hank Paulson, was in Asia. (I know because I had to arrange for his plane to enter U.S. airspace in order to get back to his Wall Street post — the U.S. airspace having earlier been closed to all planes and was still not open to private planes without special permission.)

These leaders were not necessarily asleep, but they certainly weren't at their economic battle stations. Again it is hard to see what they could have done had they been present, and again the prime cause may have been a failure of intelligence. But what I saw was that much of the U.S. government at the highest level was out of the loop.

Thus far, 1 have been talking about the oddity that my government betters were physically absent at a time of high national security crisis. But more relevant for us present here today at the Chicago Fed, I believe, is the question whether our leaders have not also been somewhat absent, if only psychologically and mentally, when economic policy crises are shaping up. After all, just an hour on Google will, I believe, convince any of you that the present crisis was foreseeable, and was in fact widely foreseen, well before credit markets began to freeze up in the summer of 2007.

The New York Times carried an interesting op-ed yesterday by Ron Suskind called "The Crisis Last Time". It is about a meeting in 2002 in the Treasury of the President's Working Group. This Group included Treasury Secretary Paul O'Neill, the Fed Chairman Alan Greenspan, CEA Chairman Glenn Hubbard, White House Economic coordinator Larry Lindsey, SEC Chairman Harvey Pitt, and others. I can testify to the accurateness of this story because I was there, and also because O'Neill is cited by Suskind as his source for the story, so Suskind clearly did not make it up.

The meeting on February 22, 2002, took place in the wake of Enron and other corporate financial scandals. On the Hill, the bill that became Sarbanes-Oxley was gaining traction and in fact became law shortly thereafter. The hostile reaction of most other participants to Greenspan's criticism of corporate financial reporting and to O'Neill's plea for far reaching statutory changes to hold corporate executives accountable showed me the following: the general Administration view, and particularly the White House view expressed by Hubbard and Lindsay, was that the Congress was the problem and not corporate financial fudging and outright malfeasance. And in a typical example of the kind of bureaucratic infighting that defeats most good ideas within any Administration, SEC Chairman Harvey Pitt seemed most concerned that legislative reforms might undermine the SEC's prerogatives.

So I commend the Suskind op-ed to you for insight into a likely reason why until the past week, the Administration failed to recognize that the financial crisis was not just inconvenient but actually life-threatening to the broader economy.

Now let me address a few international aspects of the subprime crisis, which has speedily morphed into a much broader economic crisis. The European view, judging by the European media, is that the subprime crisis was a virus produced in America that now threatens the European economy. But let me ask you this question? Why did the European banks buy all those subprime securities? And it was not just European banks. The Bank of China also loaded up on them. To me, the reason in Europe is the same as in the United States. The usually healthy balance between greed and fear gradually became overweighted on the greed side. This is particularly the case in Germany, where I spent much of this past year. It is striking that the biggest buyers of the subprime securities were publicly owned banks—the Landesbanken. And just like the selling American banks, the buying Landesbanken used SIV's and conduits, off-balance sheet entities, to be able to buy the securities without worrying about Basel capital adequacy regulation. Example: the Sachsen Landesbank, located in Dresden deep within the boundaries of the old East Germany, opened a unit in Dublin, Ireland, of all places, to engage in these kinds of supposedly high yielding transactions.

Question: why don't the Americans and the Europeans get together and try to solve the crisis jointly? Here we run into institutional problems. It is true that both continents are working hard in Basel through the Financial Stability Forum to make sure that better regulations about off-balance sheet entities, better Basel II rules, and so forth are adopted. But that will not deal with the present crisis. The idea is to have them ready to prevent the next crisis, not to fix this one.

Europe is, of course, divided between the Eurozone and the other EU countries, particularly the United Kingdom. But within the Eurozone, the European Central Bank does not have any authority to engage in normal bank regulation: it is concerned with macro monetary policy. Bank regulation is still the province of each member state's bank regulatory agency.

Even the effort by the farsighted man who was until recently Italian finance minister, Tomasso Padoa-Schioppa, to work for a common European "rule book" was almost unanimously rejected. To be sure, the

EU Commission seems to recognize the problem, but it has to work through a consensus building system, the laborious Lamfallusy process, to make any progress at all in unifying bank regulatory rules.

So Europe cannot speak with one or even two voices. Efforts have nonetheless been made to help iron out differences in regulatory requirements. We have of course the Basel Committee on Banking Supervision to work out changes to Basel II and thereby, hopefully, to avoid future crises. (I would caution that increasingly complex rules are as likely to cause unanticipated problems as to prevent them, based on experience with the present crisis.) But in any event the Basel Committee process will not help us to deal with the current crisis.

We also have something called the informal US-EU Financial Market Regulatory Dialogue. This dialogue, now about half a dozen years old, has helped on minor issues like smoothing out differences in securities legislation. And at German Chancellor Angela Merkel's urging, we now have a TEC, a Transatlantic Economic Council, but it is just a series of meetings, mostly high level meetings, not a working system for coordination in crisis conditions.

Nor is there any present hope of being able to resolve these problems at the international organization level. The IMF might seem to be a candidate, but thus far it is better at issuing reports than it is in coordinating action. This is not for lack of talent in the IMF staff. I find the semi-annual IMF Financial Stability Reports of high quality and, by the way, required reading if one wants to understand the international aspects of any given financial problem, including the present crisis. But the IMF is simply absent from the action on the present crisis. The IMF is not a player in developed country coordination on developed country crises, in contrast to their work on developing country crises.

The IMF is now trying to deal with this weakness through a new Committee on IMF Governance. This Committee was created to deal with the problem that the governance arrangements, particularly the inefficient Executive Board arrangements that the Americans foisted on the British in forcing aside the 1945 Keynes plan in favor of the Americans' own cumbersome White plan. This new Governance Committee held its first meeting earlier this week, and clearly has some momentum behind it coming from Managing Director Dominique Strauss-Kahn and the IMF Independent Evaluation Board. One reason for hope is that the Governance Committee seems to have the support of the United States

Treasury. Nonetheless, the IMF is simply not a player in the present crisis.

My conclusion is that the U.S. and Europe have very far to go in learning to work together. Let's hope that our leaders will figure out how to handle financial globalization and become better able to work together to deal with future crises.

Trust and Financial Markets

Paola Sapienza*
Northwestern University

It is a pleasure and an honor to be here. We are in the middle of a financial crisis and many commentators are suggesting that one key issue in dealing with this crisis is to restore trust. I will disappoint those of you who expect, based on the title of my speech, that I will be able to explain how to do that. Rather, I will give you an overview of the current research on trust and financial markets. This is very much a work in progress for several economists who have been thinking hard about the relationship between trust and economics in general. It provides us with some interesting insights, but I do not think it gives us recipes on how to modify trust and restore confidence in financial markets just yet.

I am not going to deny that there are many implications of this research for current events, but I will argue that the mechanisms how trust is formed, maintained, and destroyed are not yet fully understood. We are still at the beginning, but during this process, we have learned very interesting facts. For example, one understudied area is the relationship between trust and regulation, which I will speak about at the very end of my talk. The relationship between trust and regulation is very important for policymakers.

There are still a lot of unanswered questions in this literature and perhaps additional interesting research in this area will be spurred by the fact that right now every single newspaper is talking about confidence in the stock market.

---

* Paola Sapienza is at the Kellogg School of Management of Northwestern University. This speech was the keynote address at the Eleventh Annual International Banking Conference on "Credit Market Turmoil of 2007–08: Implications for Public Policy," held in Chicago on September 25 and 26, 2008.

1. Trust and Finance

Economists and other social scientists have actually believed that trust is very important. Ken Arrow (1972) said that "virtually every commercial transaction has an element of trust, so that lack of trust is what drives us backward in essence". More recently, Antonio Damasio (2005), influential neuroscientist, said "Given the polarities of reward and punishment that pervade biology at various levels, trust is essential for the normal operation of human societies. Remove trust and you compromise love, friendship, trade, and leadership".

Since financial contracts are trust-intensive contracts, different levels of trust may have important consequences for the functioning and development of financial markets. Financing is nothing but the exchange of a sum of money today for a promise to return more money in the future. Whether such an exchange can take place depends not only on the legal enforceability of contracts, but also on the extent to which the financier trusts the financee.

The finance literature completely ignores trust in modeling financial decisions. For example, one of the most important puzzles in finance is the lack of participation in the stock market even at high levels of wealth. The way academics have tried to understand this phenomenon was to use some standard models of preferences and obtain an indirect measure of stock market participation consistent with the data (Vissing-Jorgensen, 2002).

In my work, "Trusting the Stock Market" (Guiso *et al.*, 2008a) with Luigi Guiso and Luigi Zingales, we conjectured that one reason for a lack of participation could be a lack of trust. We thought that investors making the decision whether to invest in the stock market or not will heavily rely on their belief that there is a probability that the money will not be returned to them, not because the stock market does not perform as expected, but because either the broker run away with the money or the manager will not maximize shareholders' interest. We will call the subjective belief that the investor has regarding this probability "the investor's mistrust in the stock market".

We developed a simple testable model in which the decision to buy stocks depends not only on the objective expected return, but also on the subjective priors of the investor regarding the probability of being cheated. Less trusting individuals are less likely to buy stock and, conditional on buying stock, they buy less. The calibration of the model

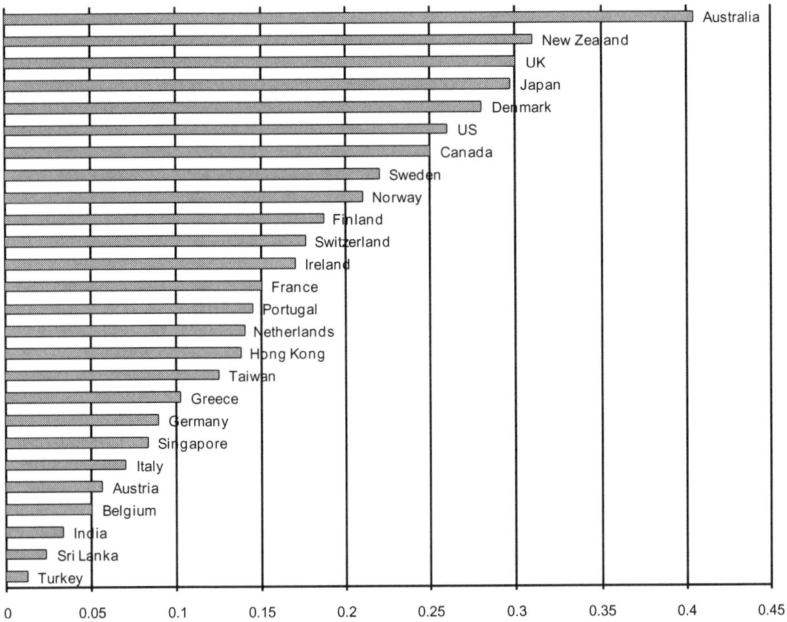

Figure 1. Stock Market Participation Across Countries.
The figure shows the fraction of individuals that invest directly in stocks across countries. The data come from Giannetti and Koskinen (2005).

indicates that mistrust is sufficiently severe to account for the lack of participation of some of the wealthiest investors in the United States as well as for differences in the rate of participation across countries.

One way to test this hypothesis is using international data. Interestingly, world data on stock market participation show very interesting cross-country differences. Figure 1 presents data on direct stock market participation around the world. Some countries have much more direct stock market participation than others (similar results, for a restricted set of countries, can be shown for direct and indirect measures of stock market participation). Many reasons (including legal characteristics and corporate governance) account for these differences. To measure trust, social scientists use data of representative households in various countries, "Generally speaking, do you think other people be trusted, or you should always be careful?" Figure 2 shows the fraction of people in each country answer "yes".

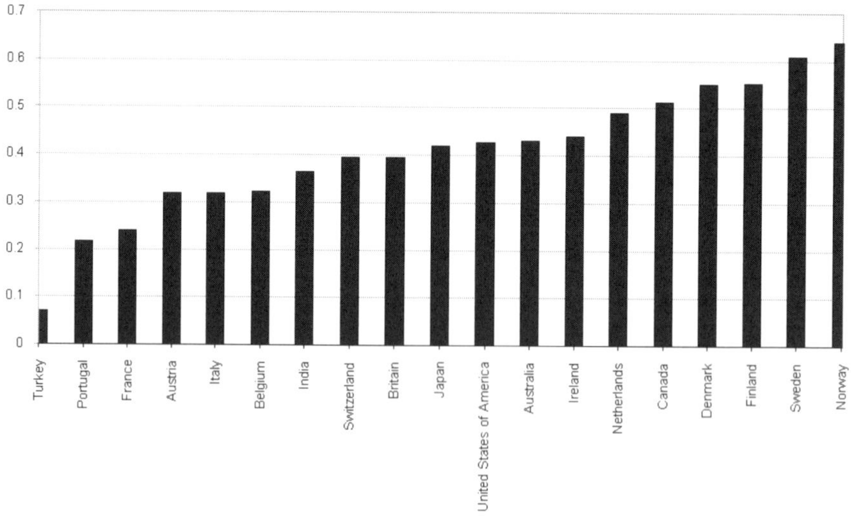

Figure 2. Generalized Trust in a Selected Number of Countries. The figure shows the percentage of people in each country that answer yes to the question "Generally speaking do you think that others can be trusted?" Data are from the World Values Survey, for a selected number of countries during the period 1980–1995.

The initial question we asked was whether the patterns shown in Figures 1 and 2 may be related. In order to address this question in a more scientific manner, we collected data within countries. We picked two countries: the Netherlands and Italy.

The reason we restrict our analysis to households within the same country is that differences across countries could be driven by institutional differences (again, corporate governance and legal enforcement), but as the institutions are the same within a country, we can avoid this problem. Therefore, comparing the behavior of different households in the Netherlands (one with a high level of trust and one with a low level of trust) could be more informative than comparing the average behavior of households in the Netherlands and the UK.

For households in the Netherlands, we collected data on their portfolio, wealth, and demographic. In addition, we asked some questions to measure their generalized trust, their risk aversion, and their subjective expectations on stock market performance. By analyzing these data, we actually found confirmation that trust mattered much more than risk aversion in explaining stock market participation.

We find that trusting individuals are significantly more likely to buy stocks and risky assets and, conditional on investing in stock, they invest a larger share of their wealth in it. This effect is economically significant — trusting others increases the probability of buying stock by 50 percent of the average sample probability and raises the share invested in stock by 3.4 percentage points (15.5 percent of the sample mean). These results are robust to controlling for differences in risk aversion and ambiguity aversion.

Stock market participation can be discouraged not only by generalized mistrust, but also by mistrust in the institutions that should facilitate participation (brokerage houses, etc.). To assess the role of specific trust, we use a customer survey conducted by a large Italian bank where people were asked about their confidence in the bank as a broker. We again find that trust has a positive and large effect on stock market participation as well as on the share invested in stocks.

This work extends beyond stock market participation. At the aggregate level if trust is important, it may affect the use and availability of financial contracts. In order to study this question, Luigi Guiso, Luigi Zingales and I, in the paper "The role of social capital in financial development," (Guiso *et al.*, 2004), investigate how social norms (trust among them) affect financial development. The concept of social capital is widely used in social sciences outside of economics and it is broadly defined as "features of social life — networks, norms, trust, that enable participants of a given community to act together to pursue shared objectives" (Putnam, 1993). As such, the level of social capital of a community may affect economic efficiency by enhancing the prevailing level of trust among economic agents belonging to the group, where trust is defined as "a particular level of the subjective probability with which an agent assesses that another agent or group of agents will perform a particular action" (Gambetta, 1988).

In relational contracts what matters is personalized trust, the mutual trust people develop through repeated interactions (Greif, 1994). However, for the development of anonymous markets, what matters is generalized trust, the trust people have in a random member of an identifiable group (for example, McEvily *et al.*, 2002). Sociological research shows that areas where social capital is greater have higher generalized trust and, thus, are more likely to develop financial relations.

We study this empirical prediction on a variety of households' financial choices: portfolio allocations, use of checks, availability of loans, and reliance on informal lending. Consistent with social capital being important, we find that in areas characterized by high levels of social capital, households invest a smaller proportion of their financial wealth in cash and a bigger proportion in stock. This result holds true even after we control for a large set of households' characteristics and environmental variables, such as quality of legal enforcement, the average level of education, and the per capita Gross Domestic Product (GDP). In social-capital-intensive areas, households are also more likely to use personal checks and to obtain credit when they seek it.

Our results also indicate that the effect of social capital is stronger when legal enforcement is weaker and that the effect of social capital is more pronounced among less-educated people, who need to rely more on trust because of their limited understanding of contracting mechanisms. These results have strong implications for developing countries because social capital seems to matter most when education levels are low and law enforcement is weak.

2. Does It Matter Who You Trust?

In separate research, we looked at whether bilateral trust — trust between citizens of different countries — affects investment decisions and portfolio allocation. Table 1 presents a simple example how to think about this problem. The data in this table were collected by a consulting firm that surveyed 500 managers in five European countries who were asked to score fellow managers of different countries on the basis of their trustworthiness. The table reports the ranking (where 1 is the best and 5 the worst). There is a main diagonal effect or a "home-country bias": managers trust their fellow countrymen more than managers from other countries. For instance, Italian managers rank themselves fourth in trustworthiness, while they are ranked fifth (last) by every other group.

The other thing that these data show is that there are some match-specific attitudes. French managers rate British managers much lower than any others except the Italians, which seems at odds with the ranking chosen by every other group. However, the British managers reciprocate this attitude. This attitude probably is probably related to the history of

Table 1. Trust from World Values Surveys (1980–1995).

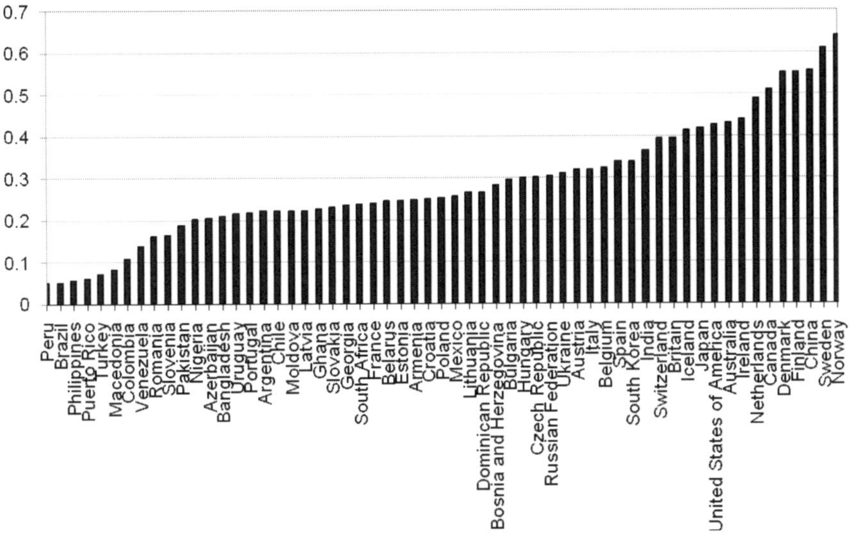

conflict between these countries. Indeed, the Duke of Wellington famously said, "We've always been, we are, and I hope will be detested in France."

In "Cultural Biases in Economic Exchange" (Guiso *et al.*, 2008b), we use a rich dataset that contains the trust European citizens have for citizens of other countries and find that lower relative levels of trust toward citizens of another country lead to less trade with that country, less portfolio investment, and less direct investment in that country, even after controlling for the country's objective characteristics.

3. What Determines Trust?

If trust is so important for financial markets, it is crucial to understand its determinants. However, this is probably the most difficult issue to address — many people in different fields have been working on a complete understanding of the determinants, but progress is coming slowly.

Alesina and La Ferrara (2002) have studied the microeconomic correlates of trust. They found that in more homogenous societies (by income and ethnicity) people tend to trust each other more. We confirmed these results by looking at bilateral trust data. Relative trust is affected not only by objective characteristics of a country's citizens (country-fixed effects), but also by cultural aspects such as religion, a history of conflicts, and genetic similarities between the pair of countries. Individual characteristics play a role too. The impact of both wars and religion on relative trust is reduced by half for people with a college degree. That the effect of cultural variables fades with education is consistent with the hypothesis that cultural stereotypes become less important in shaping people's priors when individuals are more educated.

In "Does Culture Affect Economic Outcomes?" (with Guiso and Zingales, 2006), we grouped U.S. individuals by ancestors' origin to better identify the effect of culture on trust. The average trust of these groups correlates with the level of trust of people living in the country of ancestry. In Figure 3, I plot the estimated impact of having ancestors from different areas of the world — measured vis-à-vis having British ancestors — against the difference between the level of trust that prevails today in those areas minus the average level of trust in Great Britain per the World Values Survey. There is a strong positive correlation (0.6) between the two. This finding is consistent with the idea that priors have a cultural component, which is transported to the new world and continues to impact individual beliefs even in the new environment and even several generations later.

The literature on the determinants of trust has used very different approaches and many of them provide very interesting insights into this question. For example, Kosfeld *et al.* (2005) studied the biological basis of trust among humans. They administered oxytocin, a neuropeptide that plays a key role in social attachment and affiliation in non-human mammals, to some subjects and compared their behavior to the behavior of a control group who received a placebo. They found that oxytocin causes a substantial increase in trust among humans, thereby greatly increasing the benefits from social interactions. New studies in neuroeconomics are trying to uncover the foundation of trust and social behavior.

4. Trust and Regulation

An interesting question is whether trust and regulation are correlated and what is the direction of causality? It has been argued that after the Enron

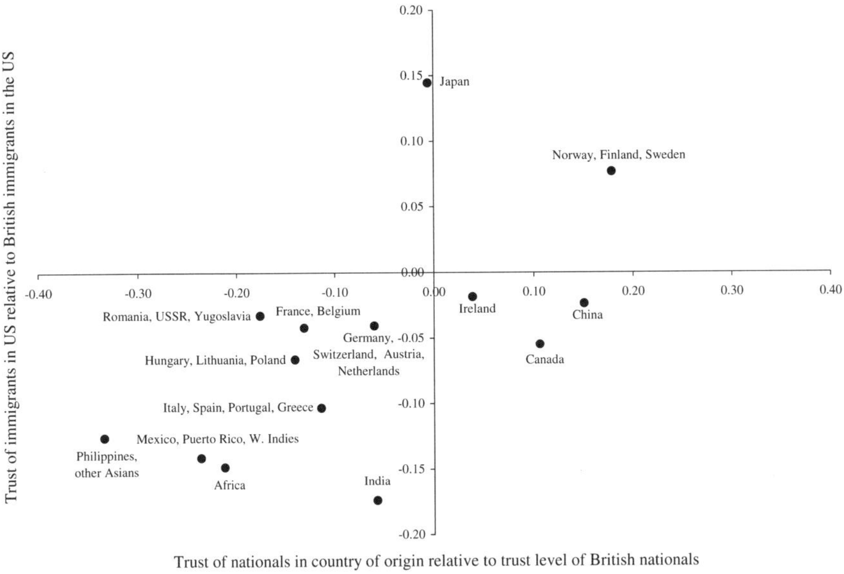

Figure 3. Correlation between Trust of Country of Origin and Trust of Immigrants relative to Great Britain.
Source: World Values Survey, General Social Survey.
Note: On the horizontal axis we report the difference between the average trust of each group of countries and the average trust of Great Britain, computed using data from the World Value Survey. On the vertical axis we report the estimated coefficient ethnic group.

crisis, it was easier to pass increased regulation, on the premise that lower trust in the stock market could have long-term consequences and that to restore trust, tighter regulation was needed. But, some commentators have argued that Congress overreacted to the Enron crisis and overregulated.

Aghion, *et al.* (2008) looked at some data across countries and found a negative correlation between trust and regulation: in countries where there is little trust, there is more regulation. In their model, less trusting societies will demand more government regulation and more government regulation will crowd out cooperation and trust. Thus, more regulation will induce less interpersonal trust. Less interpersonal trust in turn implies more regulation. This interesting first step for understanding the connection between trust and government intervention warns us not only about the importance of prompt action to restore market confidence, but also about the potential risks of excessive or chaotic government intervention in financial markets. Thank you.

References

Aghion, P., Y. Algan, P. Cahuc, and A. Shleifer (2008). Regulation and Distrust. Harvard University Working Paper.

Alesina, A. and E. L. Ferrara (2002). Who trusts others? *Journal of Public Economics*, 85, 207–234.

Arrow, K. (1972). Gifts and exchanges. *Philosophy and Public Affairs*, 1, 343–362.

Damasio, Antonio (2005). Human behaviour: Brain trust. *Nature*, 435, 571–572.

Gambetta, D. (1988). Can we trust trust? In Gambetta, D. (ed), *Trust, Making and Breaking Cooperative Relations*. Basil Blackwell, Oxford.

Giannetti, Mariassunta and Yrjö Koskinen (2005). *Investor Protection and Demand for Equity*. Stockholm School of Economics working paper.

Greif, A. (1994). Cultural beliefs and the organization of society: a historical and theoretical reflection on collectivist and individualist societies. *Journal of Political Economy*, 102(5), 912–50.

Guiso, L., P. Sapienza, and L. Zingales (2004). The role of social capital in financial development. *The American Economic Review*, 94(3), 526–556.

Guiso, L., P. Sapienza, and L. Zingales (2006). Does culture affect economic outcomes? *Journal of Economic Perspectives*, 20, 23–48.

Guiso, L., P. Sapienza, and L. Zingales (2008a). Trusting the stock market. *Journal of Finance*, 63(6), 2557–2600.

Guiso, L., P. Sapienza, and L. Zingales (2008b). Cultural biases in economic exchange? *Quarterly Journal of Economics*, forthcoming.

Kosfeld, M., M. Heinrichs, P. J. Zak, U. Fischbacher, and E. Fehr (2005). Oxytocin increases trust in humans. *Nature*, 435(2), 673–676.

McEvily, B., R. Weber, C. Bicchieri, and V. Ho (2002). Can Groups Be Trusted? An Experimental Study of Collective Trust. Carnegie Mellon.

Putnam, R. (1993). *Making Democracy Work*, Princeton University Press, Princeton, NJ.

Vissing-Jorgensen, A. (2002). Towards an explanation of household portfolio choice heterogeneity: nonfinancial income and participation cost Structures. National Bureau of Economic Research, Working Paper, No. W8884.

II. WHAT HAPPENED, WHERE?

A View of the U.S. Subprime Crisis

Robert DiClemente*
Citigroup

Kermit Schoenholtz
New York University

1. Introduction

The financial crisis that began in the summer of 2007 has become the deepest, broadest and one of the longest crisis since the Great Depression. More than one third of the financial institutions in the global Morgan Stanley Composite Index have seen their stock prices plummet by more than one third. Bank failures or "near-bank near-failures" have triggered unprecedented public rescues in several countries in the face of obvious systemic risks.

Here in the United States, financial institutions have reported $252 billion worth of losses and have felt compelled to raise roughly $191 billion to replenish their depleted capital.[1] Their equity market capitalization (using the S&P 500 financial sector) has plummeted by approximately $1,250 billion — about five times the gross losses and twenty times the net losses after recapitalization — since peaking in May 2007. The five largest U.S. investment houses have failed, lost their independence, or become commercial banks under the supervision of the Federal Reserve System (the Fed).

On the policy side, the Fed acted *in extremis* to forestall disorderly workouts of the liabilities of non-bank financial institutions (NBFI) — including a broker–dealer and the world's largest insurance company — and opened

---

* Robert DiClemente is managing director and head of U.S. economic and market analysis for Citigroup, based in New York City. Kim Schoenholtz is an adjunct professor at the Stern School of Business, New York University.

[1] Calculated from Bloomberg page WDCI (a writedown measurement tool) on September 24, 2008.

the discount window to other NBFIs. It has shifted more than half of its balance sheet away from plain vanilla Treasuries into assets with credit risk in order to boost liquidity, as well as arranged to accept extraordinary Treasury deposits so as to expand its balance sheet without altering the policy rate.

This month, the U.S. government placed into conservatorship the two massive Government-Sponsored Enterprises (GSEs) in the residential mortgage arena and promised to acquire mortgage securities in the open market. It has also proposed a $700 billion fund to acquire mortgage securities to clean up financial institutions' balance sheets, and has moved to implement federal insurance for money funds. However, the authorities also allowed a major broker–dealer to fail with potentially systemic repercussions. In addition, it is unclear whether the new fund would address the financial system's capital shortage, which threatens to exacerbate and sustain the credit crunch (Kashyap and Stein, 2008).

Finally, even after 15 months of unprecedented policy actions, financial conditions are extremely depressed, while liquidity in key capital markets remains all but nonexistent.

Today, I have been asked to describe what happened in the United States. How and why did we get here? How has the policy responded? How has it worked? Where are we headed to? Because the crisis now has lasted so long, most of these issues have already received widespread attention, from U.S. and international authorities, distinguished scholars, legislators, and of course, financial analysts and the media. In the next 20 minutes, I can hardly hope to summarize this rich material.

Instead, I will proceed with a brief synopsis of the setting in which the subprime shock revealed systemic vulnerabilities, focusing on the etiology and ongoing symptoms of the illness. Much of this material is already well known. I will then quickly summarize the policy response, highlighting the persistent conflict between efforts to exit this crisis and concerns about inducing future crises. Only future historians will be able to judge whether the moral hazard costs of rescuing Bear Stearns, or the cost of limiting moral hazard amid a crisis in the case of Lehman, has been acceptable, let alone optimal.

A central theme of my analysis will focus on the role of financial conditions in setting monetary policy. To preview that theme, I will argue that a more consistent focus on financial conditions as an indicator of the policy stance would have helped the Fed to achieve its implicit inflation goals *and* contributed to financial stability, but I make no claim that it would have prevented this crisis, which has deeper origins, as crises usually do.

Finally, I will speculate a bit about where we go from here with regard to monetary policy, the economy, the financial system, and the long-term prospects for regulation. The future will decide whether the economy's resilience thus far in the crisis is only a matter of delayed impact, or whether the relationship between finance and real activity has evolved in ways that are still unfathomed. My goal today is to help kick off a lively debate, rather than to settle any of these complex and troubling issues.

2. The Setting

Ultimately, our description of the financial crisis posits at least three related ingredients: large asset mispricing, rampant "agency" failures that fostered complacency, and the rise of systemic vulnerabilities to individual failures.

The initial conditions for the crisis of 2007–08 may be viewed as rather typical in the pantheon of financial crises. A variety of favorable fundamental factors had boosted asset prices — in this case, housing — to repeated highs over an extended period of time.[2] Market and financial innovators then extrapolated this good news beyond what fundamentals could justify, until a specific shock prompted a broad reevaluation that led to a price collapse and a loss of liquidity in the related financial instruments.

The resulting hit to bank capitalization turned the asset price and liquidity shock into a persistent financial crisis in which the location of the underlying risk exposures remains uncertain even now.

What were the favorable fundamentals for housing that provided the initial basis for rising prices, prior to the surge of recent years? We see three key factors. First, two decades of the "Great Moderation" had lowered economic and inflation volatility and fostered a genuine sense of reduced risk for long-term assets. Second, as a result, the risk premia on long-term assets declined over an extended period of time, beginning in the 1980s.[3] Third, in the aftermath of the Asian financial crisis of the late 1990s, declining investment and a dramatic shift to excess savings in the emerging world (and later in oil-producing countries) helped depress the

---

[2] For a description of the financial market disruption that focuses on the housing bubble and its origins, see Shiller (2008).

[3] See, for example, Lettau, Ludvigson, and Wachter (2006).

real cost of long-term funds both in absolute terms and relative to short-term funds (see Bernanke, 2005).

Over this same 20-year period, the U.S. (and to a lesser extent, the global) financial system was evolving away from commercial banks and savings and loans and toward a capital market intensive system, in which nondepositories (and the off-balance-sheet arms of depositories) took advantage of capital market liquidity and financial innovations to outcompete and displace traditional lenders and liquidity providers. Markets and intermediaries developed new means of shifting risk. Their success contributed to financial efficiency — helping to reinforce the Great Moderation — but depended on a broad variety of new "delegated monitors" to ensure the quality of new assets.[4] In the case of residential mortgage instruments, these necessary monitors included mortgage originators, securitization specialists, rating agencies, and the ultimate security buyers.

Other key trends added over time to systemic risks. For example, the extraordinary expansion of the U.S. GSEs had probably placed these institutions in the category of "too big to fail" more than a decade ago. Since that time, their share of residential mortgages, held or guaranteed, rose substantially further, exceeding 40 percent of outstandings or more than the entire volume of marketable federal debt. Separately, the meteoric expansion in this decade of some instruments of risk transfer — particularly over-the-counter derivatives — linked the largest global financial intermediaries in a convoy-like fashion, making the entire system vulnerable to a single failure. Finally, a larger portion of bank liabilities has become vulnerable to a systemic shock: the share of deposits of U.S. commercial banks and savings and loans that are insured declined from 74 percent in 1994 to 52 percent recently. Over the same period, the ratio of insured deposits to total assets in depository institutions fell from 53 percent to 33 percent.

As is typical of earlier crises, the breakdown of this evolving system arose after complacency had led financial innovators — especially the creative and profitable ones in the United States — to expand rapidly a set of relatively new and untested instruments for intermediating between potential users and sources of funds (in this case, for residential mortgages). Innovators extrapolated the good fundamentals. The credit

---

[4] For evidence that financial innovation helped to reduce economic volatility, see Dynan, Elmendorf, and Sichel (2005).

expansion fostered liquidity, lowered financial volatility, and amplified the usual procyclical character of financial institution risk management (partly related to value-at-risk modeling and capital management), thereby boosting risk tolerance, leverage and intermediation.

In the run-up to the crisis, complacency depressed credit quality so far that only a sustained rise of housing prices from record levels would have prevented losses on many mortgages for which the borrowers had no jobs and no documented income or wealth and the lenders had no recourse. For several years, financial institutions and markets had seriously underpriced credit and liquidity risk, and had sharply overestimated the resilience of the financial system itself, partly encouraged by banks' relatively high reported capital ratios. These ratios did *not* reflect the cyclical and systemic threats from the loss of liquidity that ultimately compelled many firms to bring off-balance-sheet exposures (ranging from structured investment vehicles, SIVs, to incomplete securitizations to loan commitments) on to their balance sheets. Ultimately, the risk management of key intermediaries simply failed to keep pace with the financial innovation that they themselves promoted.[5] More broadly, the financial infrastructure failed to keep pace with the changing institutions and instruments of finance, inadvertently adding to systemic risks (Bernanke, 2008d).

The disincentives driving this credit expansion were multiple and mutually reinforcing: Securitization allowed originators to sell such low-quality loans in such quantities that they had little reason to do otherwise (Keys *et al.*, 2008). Brokers created securities that were so complex and opaque that they would prove difficult to evaluate — and therefore illiquid — in a pinch. Rating agencies assessed these instruments on the basis of brief data histories that included no period of falling housing prices nationwide. Intermediaries used low-cost liquidity provisions to foster business. Finally, buyers around the world trying to sustain profitability in a world of narrow risk premia failed to monitor all these monitors until it was too late to avoid a large shock.

Variations of these "risk mispricing" and "agency failure" themes have been emphasized by several authors. For example, Gorton (2008) highlights the importance of the unusual sensitivity of subprime mortgage securities to the underlying asset price, the opaqueness introduced by the

---

[5] Differences across major banks in the effectiveness of risk management are highlighted in the Senior Supervisors Group report (2008). Interestingly, the reported losses have been concentrated in regulated, rather than unregulated, intermediaries.

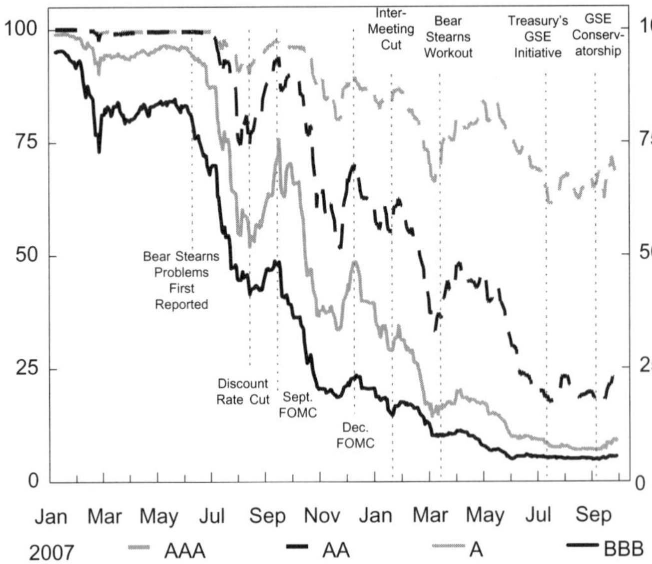

Figure 1. Prices of Subprime RMBS (ABX 06-02), 2007–September 23, 2008.
Source: Bloomberg and Citi.

complexity of subprime-related derivatives, and the lack of aggregated market information about the evolving housing-related risks until the advent of the Asset-Backed Securities index (ABX) market, which created an efficient means to short mortgage securities (see Figure 1). Calomiris (2008a) emphasizes the incentives of investment firms to expand their asset positions even as the attractiveness of new investments declined. Like others, he also criticizes the ratings agencies for their assumptions about the underlying risks of the securitized assets, but views the resulting grade inflation as a development favored by regulated institutional investors. Case (2008) highlights the lack of a synchronized nationwide housing price decline in the historical data upon which widely used mortgage models were based. Gerardi *et al.* (2008) emphasize the failure in anticipating the housing price decline, rather than the deterioration in lending quality.

With regard to U.S. housing, some would argue that the real price had already sharply exceeded sustainable levels years before the crisis. Our own view is different. Even as late as 2004, the combination of lower

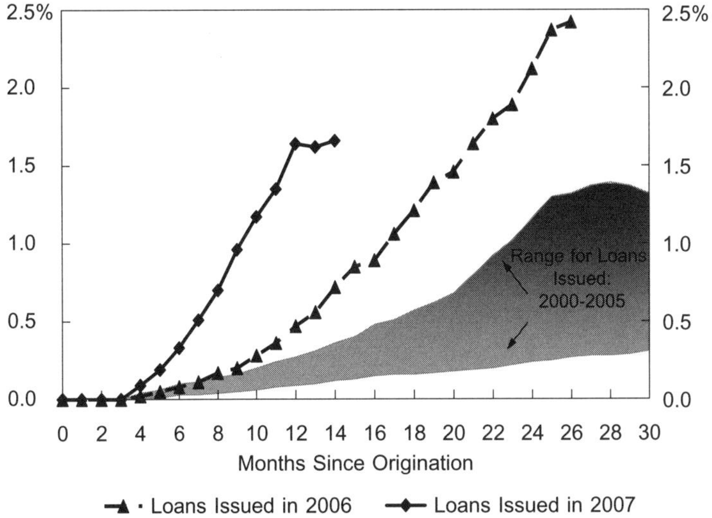

Figure 2. Cumulative Delinquencies for Jumbo Adjustable Rate Mortgages by Vintage and Year of Origination (Percent), June 2008.
Source: First American Loan.
Note: Delinquencies are more than 60 days.

long-term yields, rising incomes, and reduced economic volatility made U.S. housing reasonably affordable at then-record prices. The critical excesses appear to be more recent. Indeed, a chart of mortgage delinquencies by loan vintage shows the extraordinary deterioration that began in 2005 and continued until the subprime market closed in early 2007. The pattern of prior vintages remains unremarkable (see Figure 2).[6]

The link between credit laxity and the scale of the housing price bust appears close even at a geographically disaggregated level. In our own work, we find that the greater the prevalence of subprime and alt-A loans in a state or in a metropolitan statistical area, the larger the peak-to-current drop of house prices (even using price measures that *exclude* houses with nonconforming mortgages; see Figure 3). Just as Bernanke and Lown (1991) used regional data to identify the credit supply curve in the

[6] In a similar vein, Case (2008) highlights the enormous and "disastrous 2005 and 2006 books" of loans and the increased leverage of the housing sector in 2006–07, when $2 trillion in debt was added without an increase of collateral.

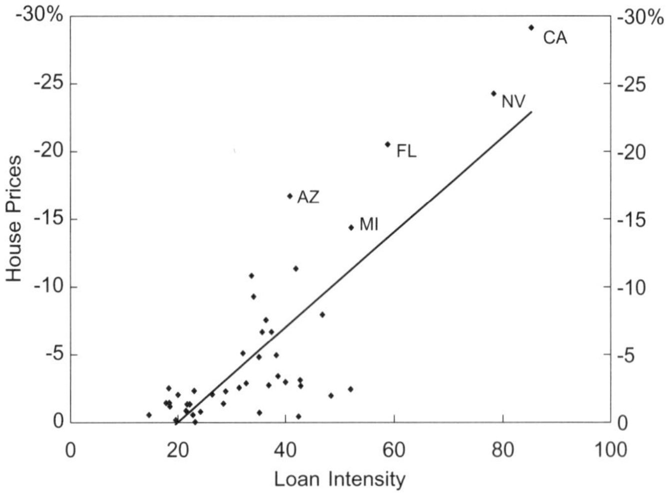

Figure 3. State-by-State Intensity of Nonconforming Loans versus Percent Change of House Prices from Peak to Latest, 2008Q2.
Source: Office of Housing Enterprise Oversight and Federal Reserve Bank of New York.
Note: Loan intensity measures the number of subprime and alt-A loans per thousand houses as of April 2008, and the latest house price measure was the OFHEO purchase-only index of 2008Q2.

early 1990s crunch, regional patterns appear to highlight the key role of supply in the current episode.

However, the common view that links mortgage default risk with interest rate resets appears to lack solid empirical foundation. Rather, defaults appear more closely linked with high loan-to-value ratios after adjustment for house price declines. In all likelihood, falling house prices both reflect and intensify the residential credit crunch (Foote *et al.*, 2008), even if history suggests that most houses with negative equity will *not* end in foreclosure (Foote, Gerardi, and Willen, 2008).[7]

Why did the subprime shock cause such a vicious circle, even as it hit? After all, outstandings in the subprime mortgage market never

[7] Foote *et al.* (2008a, b) also argue that forbearance programs will be more successful than loan modifications at limiting foreclosures, because defaults arise primarily in households with both negative equity *and* cash-flow problems.

exceeded $1.5 trillion, which is only a fraction of the roughly $11 trillion *plunge* of U.S. equity market capitalization at the start of this decade. The key answer — as was the case in Japan in the 1990s but not in the U.S. equity collapse of 2000–01 — is that the subprime losses directly affected the capitalization of major financial intermediaries. Moreover, the loss of market liquidity compelled an involuntary balance-sheet expansion, intensifying the capital shortage.

One natural response of intermediaries — to sell assets — amplified the shock, helping to depress asset prices, boost financial volatility, and lower risk tolerance and liquidity further. Once the "Great Deleveraging" had begun, it also expanded well beyond those institutions whose capital had been damaged. The so-called shadow banking system had to shrink, too.[8] Ultimately, the cycle went so far as to raise doubts about the solvency of major intermediaries, as reflected in the massive decline of their equity values.

At the same time, as Calomiris (2008a) has emphasized, this financial crisis stands out in part because of the extraordinary volume of capital raising that has taken place. According to Bloomberg, announced losses by global intermediaries of $522 billion have been partly offset by $380 billion of new capital as of this writing. In contrast, capital raising was not a key feature of the U.S. credit cycles of the early 1980s and early 1990s. In our view, this capital raising has played a key role in limiting the economic fallout from the financial crisis. Consequently, the inability of some institutions to raise new capital also has profound economic implications.

Symptoms of financial stress have been evident throughout the crisis. The most persistent and oft-cited example is the elevated charge that banks pose each other for short-term liquidity. The LIBOR–OIS (London Interbank Offered Rate–Overnight Indexed Swaps) spread has remained in a heightened range for more than a year, with various studies attributing some portion of this premium to counterparty risk. The loss of liquidity extended over time to other funding markets, boosting typical haircuts relatively early (see Figure 4). As the crisis progressed, rising doubts about solvency have boosted financial institutions' cost of funding, eventually surpassing the funding cost of nonfinancials for the first time since the

[8] Greenlaw *et al.* (2008) emphasize the role of leverage in amplifying the boom and bust. Brunnermeier (2008) highlights several channels of amplification that were operative as intermediaries transformed short-term liabilities into longer-term, less liquid assets: balance-sheet deterioration, funding uncertainty, runs on institutions, and network risk (in which liquidity hoarding arises from concerns about others' potential failure to pay).

	Mar 07	Mar 08
AA corp bond	0–3	8–12
BB lev loan	15–20	25–35
BB HY bond	10–15	25–40
Equities	15	20
IG CDS/derivs	1	5

Figure 4. Typical Haircuts by Asset Class (Percent, Approximate Estimates). March 2007 and March 2008.
Source: Citi.

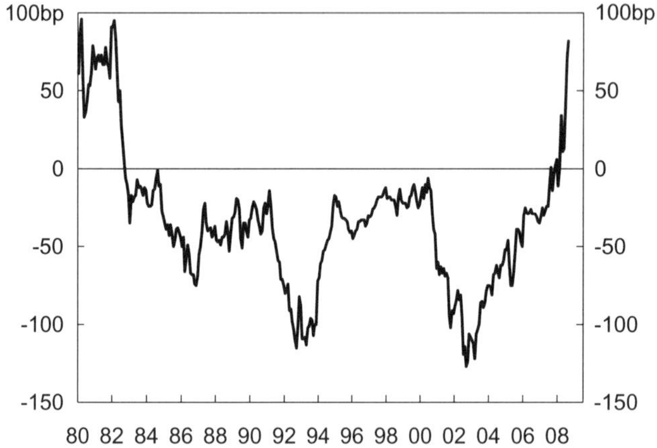

Figure 5. Spread Between Financial and Industrial Corporate Bond Yields (Basis Points), 1980–August 2008.
Source: Citi.

early 1980s (see Figure 5). Finally, deleveraging has triggered a sharp tightening of lending conditions, a delayed slowing of credit (which had been sustained in 2007 by involuntary balance-sheet expansion), wider credit spreads, and in some cases, like nonconforming mortgages, a near-shutoff of supply. Liquidity losses have also contributed to the weakening of price discovery in key securities markets.[9]

[9] Blundell-Wignall (2008) argues that market price methods of estimating mortgage losses are exaggerated by the loss of liquidity: "To get anything like recent mark-to-market losses would require a zero recovery rate — which seems extreme even for the most bearish".

3. The Policy Response

The breadth and depth of this crisis have prompted a series of unprecedented policy responses. Indeed, there can be few examples of a more active policy response to a U.S. financial crisis. At the same time, concerns about moral hazard recently prompted policymakers to acquiesce in the failure of a major broker–dealer with potentially systemic repercussions.

Since the crisis began, the U.S. central bank has endeavored to sharply distinguish between two aspects of its policy: the provision of crisis liquidity and the setting of the fed funds rate. More so than in previous crises, it has assigned the former set of instruments to restoring financial stability and market functionality, while reserving the setting of policy rates for the usual purpose of economic stabilization.

Innovations in Fed liquidity supply have occurred more rapidly and in a greater degree than at any time since the Great Depression. For the first time since the 1930s, the Fed felt compelled to exercise its emergency powers under the Federal Reserve Act in order to lend directly to nonbank intermediaries: first in March, in the case of Bear Stearns and other large investment banks, again in July, in the case of the GSEs, and, most recently in the case of AIG.

Prior to the Bear Stearns episode, brokers (such as Drexel Burnham Lambert in 1990) had been allowed to fail even in a weak economy and without dire consequences. However, the March run on Bear posed a threat that the Fed viewed as systemic. Conversely, the recent decision *not* to use public resources to forestall a Lehman bankruptcy apparently reflected two considerations: 1) concerns about the moral hazard effects of repeated creditor bailouts; and 2) a judgment that a Lehman bankruptcy could be absorbed by markets without serious disruption. Authorities cited the time that investors and counterparties had to "take precautionary measures" against a Lehman failure (Bernanke, 2008e). Reports also referred to the balance-sheet assessment of Fed supervisors who had gained access to the investment banks following the Bear episode.

However, the Fed's Lehman view appears to have been too sanguine: the failure helped trigger a run on money market funds and boosted risk aversion sharply, resulting in a further severe tightening of financial conditions. Even the decision to support the world's largest insurer one day after Lehman's failure did not forestall the panic on Wednesday, 17 September. This panic drove three-month Treasury bill rates to zero for the first time since World War II, pushed the equity market capitalization of the financial sector to crisis lows, and brought a swift end to the investment banking era.

The scope of the Fed's policy changes over the past year is reflected in the range of accepted collateral and of counterparties. There has been some debate over the collective efficacy of the myriad new credit facilities. Recent analysis suggests that Term Auction Facility (TAF) announcements helped to narrow the liquidity portion of the LIBOR–OIS spread (see McAndrews, Sarkar, and Wang, 2008). Because the Term Securities Lending Facility (TSLF) developed around the time of the Bear Stearns episode, it is difficult to determine the precise source of the observed narrowing of collateral spreads. The Primary Dealer Credit Facility (PDCF) almost certainly helped to lower — temporarily — the perceived risk of default by nonbank primary dealers.

Further liquidity innovation has already surfaced with Treasury's supplemental financing, which is providing the Fed with a means to expand its balance sheet without lowering the policy interest rate.

Treasury's Troubled Asset Relief Program (TARP) proposal anticipates a much larger direct intervention to remove troubled assets from the balance sheets of the financial sector, in order to revive credit creation. Debate about the proposal focuses on its efficacy, not its urgency. It is plausible that illiquidity has driven prices of troubled assets well below the present discounted value of the expected future stream of returns (Blundell-Wignall, 2008). Figure 6 shows estimates of the present value of expected cash flows for a variety of subprime mortgage backed securities under alternative assumptions about additional declines in U.S. housing prices. The prices of higher-rated tranches — the value of which likely dependents on the recovery of principal appear to be below the present value of expected cash flows, even under severe house price assumptions. While these estimates are based on the work of our colleagues in mortgage research at Citi, other analysts, using different techniques, come to essentially the same conclusion.[10]

If so, it will be possible for Treasury to acquire assets at a price that allows taxpayers to earn a positive return over time. However, the financial sector appears to be short of the capital needed to expand aggregate credit, while access to private capital has been severely diminished following the

[10] See Fender and Scheicher (2008); and Bank of England (2008), chapter 1.

	Market Price		Present Value of Expected Cash Flows under Alternative Assumption for Further House Price Declines — Additional Price Decline (%)			
	17-Sep	22-Sep	-50%	-30%	-20%	-10%
Super Senior	50.6	56.6	68.7	88.3	94.1	98.4
AAA	45.1	51.9	64.3	84.7	91.2	99.9
AA	10.5	11.5	6.5	7.8	8.6	21.2
A	8.0	8.4	5.3	5.8	5.8	6.4
BBB	5.5	5.8	3.9	4.1	4.1	4.3
BBB-	5.3	5.7	3.1	3.3	3.3	3.4

Figure 6. Market Prices and Present Value of Expected Cash Flows for Tranches of Subprime Mortgage Pools (ABX 07-2, Percent of Face).
Source: Citi.
Notes: House prices are based on the Case-Shiller national index. Cash flows are discounted using LIBOR.

plunge of financial sector market capitalization. Treasury's plan to purchase assets will boost aggregate capitalization only if the purchase price exceeds the balance-sheet marks that intermediaries have placed on the assets, *or* if removing the downside risk posed by these assets restores access to private capital markets. If neither condition is satisfied, then efforts to limit a credit crunch likely would depend on direct public injections of capital into the banking system. Such injections have been used in previous financial crises in other countries (including Japan and Sweden), but this approach also carries a political challenge associated with "picking winners".

The decision by the Fed and the Treasury *not* to backstop the debt of Lehman Brothers — in contrast to the Bear Stearns episode — fueled a one-week revolution in the U.S. financial system, as the three remaining large investment banks lost their independence or converted into commercial banks. It also left open the possibility of systemic repercussions. Undoubtedly, concerns about moral hazard played a key role in the policy process. However, policymakers probably did not anticipate the panic that subsequently emerged — even after the bailout of AIG creditors. Treasury moves to insure money market funds (initially through the Exchange Stabilization Fund and eventually through a new legislative mandate) represent another ad hoc response to a long cycle of deterioration that policymakers have failed to arrest. The renewed hit to the prices of risky assets probably further undermined the aggregate capital of the financial system, adding to overall fragility and to the need for a large-scale bailout. In short, attempting to impose market discipline against moral hazard in the midst of a crisis is both risky and expensive.

4. The Role of Financial Conditions

The persistent erosion of financial conditions in the face of aggressive monetary policy stabilization efforts has been an especially important feature of the current crisis. As gauged by the Citi Financial Conditions Index (FCI), the combination of reduced liquidity, tightening credit, and falling equity values, among other factors is now at an extreme negative reading, which surpasses those that prevailed at the depths of the credit crunch period of the early 1990s (see Figure 7).

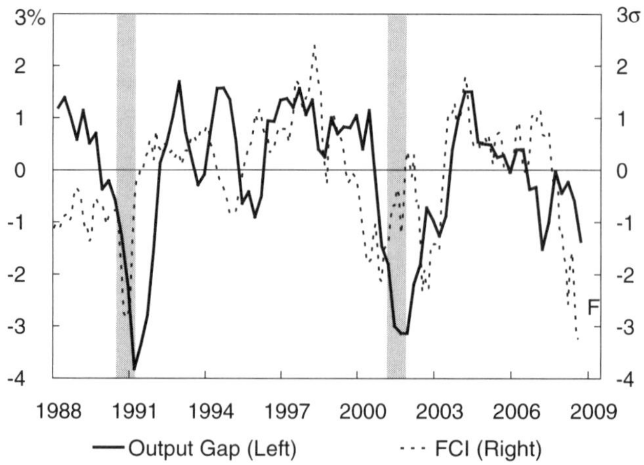

Figure 7. Citi Financial Conditions Index (Standard Deviations) and Output Gap, 1988–2008Q2.
Source: Bureau of Economic Analysis, Congressional Budget Office and Citi.
Note: Final FCI observation is Aug 08. Shaded regions denote recessions.

More generally, a focus on financial conditions also underscores the limits of separating and assigning the Fed's liquidity and interest rate tools to different policy goals. Neither policy rates nor aids to market functioning alone determine financial conditions. More specifically, liquidity and credit developments may either support or undo the usual mechanism through which policy affects the economy. The current circumstance exemplifies this disconnect.

Accordingly, the construction and use of financial conditions measures have become increasingly popular in part because of the growing complexities of financial markets and their recognized role in affecting economic behavior.[11] While monetary policy effects have always been analyzed through changes in risk-free interest rates and their impact on the cost of capital, the ultimate transmission of policy actions may be misestimated if we do not account for changes in the cost and availability of credit as well. Of course, it remains an empirical question whether a single index is sufficient over a long period of time to summarize the financial conditions relevant for the economic outlook.

The Citi index is a weighted average of six variables, including option-adjusted corporate credit spreads, equity values, the money stock, the trade-weighted dollar, mortgage rates, and energy prices. It is stated in terms of standard deviations from a mean value. A reading of plus one sigma, for example, would suggest financial conditions are imparting a strong tailwind to aggregate demand that could promote inflationary imbalances and therefore may be a signal that monetary policy is overly accommodative. A reading of minus one sigma is suggestive of financial drag on the outlook that may point to undesirable slowing and rising unemployment.

As of August, the Citi FCI stood at minus 3.2 sigma, rare by definition but especially troubling in light of the fact that the Fed has at least notionally adopted an accommodative stance. Looking back over two decades of major easing cycles, the FCI has typically improved promptly and substantially with the beginning of policy rate cuts (see Figure 8). Even in those cycles when conditions began from a highly restrictive setting, the index on average was back to neutral readings roughly within a year.

Tight credit is an especially important source of the deterioration in the index since rate cuts began. Investment-grade corporate credit spreads

---

[11] See, for example, Swiston (2008).

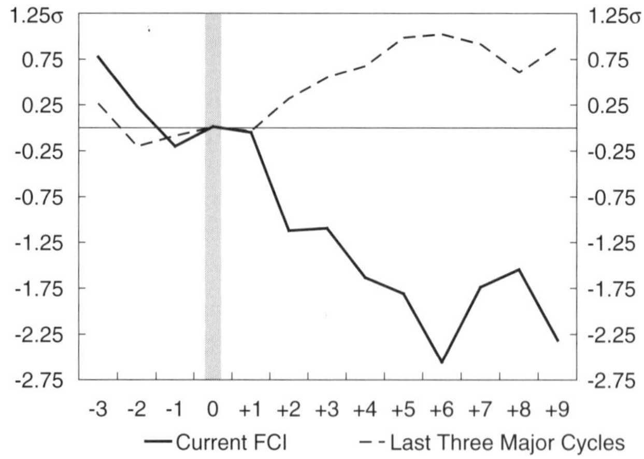

Figure 8. Cumulative Quarterly Change of Citi FCI (Standard Deviations) from Start of Policy Easing, 1989–2008.
Source: Citi.
Note: Shaded area depicts start of policy easing.

account for 29 percent of the index and have contributed nearly three-quarters of the decline in the overall FCI over the past 15 months. When the crisis began, the index was at a neutral (or zero) reading and with the worsening of the crisis in September, it is probably nearing a minus 5 sigma reading, strongly suggesting that the prospects for a sustained recovery in demand are limited.

The relative lack of responsiveness of financial conditions to policy efforts during the bust might have been anticipated by the mirror opposite insensitivity to Fed tightening in the boom years (see Figure 9). Recall then Fed Chairman Greenspan's "conundrum" in which after a year of steady rate hikes and promises of more, long-term interest rates had actually fallen by 80 basis points. The FCI during that period lent support to the view that despite notionally less accommodating policy, financial conditions remained relatively buoyant throughout. Debate at the time featured some concern that low bond yields were a warning that Fed action might be *overdone*, but a more thorough review of financial conditions as suggested by the FCI at the time indicated that policy's stance never became effectively restraining in that period. While we make no claim that the Fed's accommodative stance in 2004–05 triggered the financial excesses of the period, a policy more attuned to financial conditions might have plausibly diminished their scale.

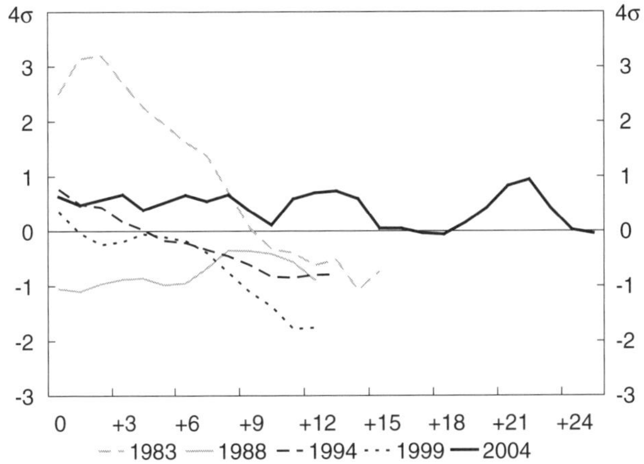

Figure 9. Cumulative Monthly Change of Citi FCI (Standard Deviations) Following Start of Policy Tightening, 1989–2008.
Source: Citi.
Note: Shaded area depicts start of policy easing.

The key issue for us in forecasting the course of the current slowdown is to what extent our FCI captures the financial circumstances most relevant to the outlook and also, insofar as restrained credit *supply* is a potentially critical drag, is this drag over and above the deterioration reflected in the index. In our judgment, the Citi FCI probably incorporates most of the financial headwinds that will affect the outlook (see DiClemente, 2008).

In the current episode, the credit supply constraint seems larger and is hinted at by the sharp slowing in bank credit in recent months. This slowing was delayed by pre-crisis lending commitments and the involuntary shift of off-balance-sheet entities into the banks as funding sources dried up.

The housing correction plays a central role in the increasing restraint on the supply of credit, and in turn on the broader economic outlook. The large overhang of unsold homes remains a weight on home prices. Yet, mortgage rates are as high or even noticeably higher now in the case of jumbo rates than at the start of the crisis. Without easing in credit, the burden of restoring housing affordability to levels necessary to restore balance falls disproportionately on existing homeowners' equity, generating negative wealth effects and further exacerbating the risk of foreclosures.

The Citi FCI does *not* incorporate direct proxies for the supply of credit. Nonetheless, both theory and history suggest that it does capture financial developments most relevant to the outlook even when credit availability is strained. The falling share prices of financial firms have been a dominant feature of the bear market and it seems almost certain that some part of this decline reflects the impact of reduced lending capacity on profit expectations. Similarly, wider credit spreads should reflect in part the perceived risk of default if investors decline to rollover debt. Finally, the rise of jumbo mortgage spreads proxies for the shutdown of nonconforming mortgage supply.

On balance, we believe the FCI sheds important light on the likely economic impact of financial developments. At its present reading, it reinforces the judgment that the ongoing crisis still presents serious downside risks to the outlook.

5. Where Do We Go from Here?

Let us turn now to the most speculative element of my remarks: prospects for monetary policy, for the evolution of the financial crisis, and (over the long term) for regulatory and systemic change.

Throughout the crisis, Fed officials have been forced to counterbalance concerns about a potentially severe downturn against the threat that rising commodity prices could boost long-term inflation expectations. Nonetheless, it is very unlikely that the Fed's actions have undermined their long-term price stability goals. Although the policy is notionally accommodative, policymakers increasingly draw attention to the fact, as Eric Rosengren has pointed out, that "while the Federal Funds rate is low ... one cannot capture the stance of monetary policy by only looking at this one rate, particularly during a period when the transmission of monetary policy has been impeded by problems with securitization, financial institutions, and GSEs (Rosengren, 2008)".

In this context, the Citi FCI challenges the notion that rate cuts have offset credit restraint and other negative signals. In our view, financial turmoil is not likely to recede before the prospective decline of housing prices is circumscribed in a way that reduces fears of major insolvencies and the end of the Great Deleveraging comes into view. The mix of stubbornly high borrowing costs, tight credit, and substantial wealth loss points to significant overriding policy headwinds. This pattern is consistent not only with subpar economic growth but also very likely with diminishing price pressures, signs of which have been evident in housing-related commodities but now may be poised to spread to other goods and services. Against this background, the renewed surge of liquidity and deleveraging pressures on asset prices has revived prospects for a lower funds rate.

Apart from Fed policy, Treasury actions have aimed at checking systemic tail risks in the near term, but have not arrested the vicious cycle of asset price declines and erosion of capital in the financial system. It remains to be seen whether the TARP proposal will plug the downside risks in the financial sector sufficiently to re-attract private capital investment.[12]

To what extent has the housing debacle altered the "best practice" response of policy to asset price bubbles and busts? For more than a decade, the conventional wisdom of the Federal Reserve has been that policy should not attempt to prick a bubble, and that policy rates should respond only insofar as asset price changes alter prospects for aggregate demand (see Mishkin, 2008). Widespread concerns about U.S. housing prices after 2004, combined with the acknowledged deterioration of lending standards, cast doubt on the view that bubbles cannot be reliably identified in advance. The fallout from the bubble — including record foreclosures and the increasing probability of a prolonged recession — makes clear that rapid Fed rate cuts have been insufficient to prevent substantial damage to the economy, or even to forestall a dramatic tightening of financial conditions. The impaired financial system is impeding the normal transmission of monetary policy.

Yet, it probably remains infeasible for central banks to prick a bubble by hiking policy rates without triggering a recession. Consequently, the hurdles for such action will likely remain high. However, policymakers will probably be less reluctant in the future to dramatize the risks for investors of extraordinarily low risk premia. They may also be more inclined to favor countercyclical regulatory actions when lending standards weaken. In his recent speech at Jackson Hole, Chairman Bernanke articulated a case for such macroprudential oversight (Bernanke, 2008d).

[12] There has been no shortage of proposals for aggressive Treasury action. For example, Feldstein (2008) advocated federally subsidized "mortgage replacement loans" to help limit the downward spiral of housing prices. Spaventa (2008) proposed the issuance of Brady-like public debt that would be exchanged for illiquid assets on bank balance sheets. Calomiris has proposed "Government injections of preferred stocks into banks" to restore aggregate capital (2008b).

Finally, in the most extreme cases, such as Japan's land and equity bubbles in the 1980s, policymakers may need to consider whether the failure of first-best policy approaches (such as effective prudential regulation) to limit systemic risks also threatens the central bank's goal of medium-term price stability.

In the current episode, an extended period of recuperation will almost certainly be needed to restore health to the U.S. financial system and the housing market to which it remains highly sensitive. Treasury actions may reduce the risks that housing prices will plummet sharply below some equilibrium level, but it remains to be seen how aggressively Treasury will act to push mortgage yields lower to support housing. If the initial TARP approach fails to boost aggregate capital in the financial system, further actions will likely be needed. And the longer the vicious cycle of falling asset prices and financial capital persists, the larger the intervention that will be needed to support economic expansion.

For now, credit default swap prices indicate that investors still lack confidence about the solvency of major financial institutions, implying that serious downside risks persist. Lack of visibility with regard to housing prices makes such confidence elusive. The July equity market plunge of major financial institutions already warned that the window for private capital raising — which previously had been a major contributor to stability in this episode — had narrowed or closed for some firms. Observers ought not be surprised by a long period of gradual balance sheet repair during which institutional risk tolerance will remain low.

The longer-term outlook seems certain to include an intensification of financial regulation with potentially profound implications for the economy. The broadening of regulation to investment banks has already been effected by these firms' new choice of structure (either by attachment to a bank or by converting to a bank holding company). However, the Fed's decision to support AIG highlights how firms *outside* the banking and broking world can threaten costly disruptions. Consequently, a key issue will be to determine the range of institutions that will be subject to bank-like oversight (Geithner, 2008a). Ultimately, we suspect that authorities will wish to oversee and extend central bank liquidity access to *any* intermediary of systemic importance. Policymakers will have to be concerned about the incentives for regulatory arbitrage that could be fostered by an excessively rigid definition of this class.

The feasibility of such regulation is also a first-order concern: Without broad international cooperation, it may not be possible to implement a credible oversight regime for systemically significant firms (if any) that are currently outside the regulatory net. For example, local efforts to regulate may prompt the largest hedge funds to relocate without reducing the threat to financial stability.

One factor distinguishing bank-like supervision from earlier broker oversight is the level of capital requirements. What might a large change in capital requirements imply for the financial system and asset prices? For purposes of illustration, imagine in the extreme that the leverage of all brokers and hedge funds that existed in 2007 were to be halved. The initial effect — before any changes of capital in the system — would be to lower intermediation in the United States by an estimated $2.7 trillion, or about 12 percent of leveraged financial sector assets (see Figure 10). The direction of the impact on risky asset prices would be unambiguously negative. In persuading others to hold the outstanding stock of such assets, their prices must decline. The price at which this absorption occurs also must reflect the loss of "risk-pooling" and "monitoring" services from intermediaries. And it must restore equilibrium between the supply and the demand for *new* credit.

Policymakers will also have to dampen the cyclical effects from raising and broadening the application of capital requirements. Financial firms alter leverage procyclically in response to their capitalization and to changes in value at risk. These, in turn, depend on market prices, volatility, credit ratings, and liquidity conditions. The resulting "financial accelerator"

	Assets ($bn)	Leverage
Commercial banks	$11194	9.8
Savings Inst	1815	8.7
Credit Unions	759	8.7
Finance Companies	1911	10
Brokers/hedge funds	5597	27.1
GSEs	1669	23.5
Leveraged Sector	**22945**	**12.0**

Figure 10. Assets and Leverage of Selected U.S. Financial Institutions.
Source: Exhibit 4.5 from Greenlaw *et al.* "Leveraged Losses: Lessons from the Mortgage Market Meltdown", *Proceedings of the U.S. Monetary Policy Forum 2008.*

is likely to be even more powerful in a world of broader capital requirements. One recent proposal to limit the overall costs, disincentives and cyclical distortions of higher capital requirements is the introduction of "catastrophe insurance" as an option for meeting rainy day needs of financial institutions (Kashyap *et al.*, 2008).

Policymakers have also highlighted the need to make the system less vulnerable to individual failures (Geithner, 2008b). Timely, incentive-compatible workout regimes are necessary for all systemically important firms, not just depositories. Similarly, transactions need to be shifted where possible to transparent markets where institutions have the means and incentive to manage collective counterparty risks (Alexander and Schoenholtz, 2008b). Recent moves to develop a centralized clearing party for over-the-counter credit derivatives fit this definition. More broadly, updating and upgrading the financial infrastructure can help limit systemic fragility (Bernanke, 2008d).

Regulators are also likely to focus on the failures of liquidity management and the incentive problems in securitization that drove and intensified the current crisis (Financial Stability Forum, 2008; and Basel Committee on Banking Supervision, 2008). While market forces are likely to promote stricter discipline going forward, supervisors will probably look askance at any new buildup in the course of securitization of opaque instruments on the balance sheets of major intermediaries.

International supervisors have also admonished the rating agencies to distinguish their ratings of opaque, illiquid instruments from those for plain-vanilla debt and to improve on their asset models. More broadly, proposals for new compositional and overall leverage requirements to contain systemic risks are gaining regulatory attention, especially following the run on Bear Stearns (see Morris and Shin, 2008; and Kohn, 2008).

While many changes are already in train — especially for the former investment banks — the full timetable for regulatory evolution is likely to be a matter of years. The combination of a complex U.S. supervisory structure — involving multiple federal and state regulators with overlapping jurisdictions — and a major election cycle suggests that proposed reforms (U.S. Treasury, 2008) will still be a subject of U.S. legislative debate for some time to come. The international aspects of the crisis and of systemic vulnerabilities only add to the complexity of prospective regulatory change.

But it is not too early to consider the likely impact of long-term regulatory developments. In a future equilibrium, we expect that reduced leverage and intermediation will be associated with higher risk premia (say, compared to the average of the past decade) to induce final investors to hold some of the assets that financial institutions no longer acquire. From the perspective of users of capital, average costs may be higher (especially for debt).[13]

We also expect that the equilibrium level of policy rates will be somewhat lower than before. In a world of reduced leverage and intermediation, financial conditions would probably be relatively restrictive at the policy rate that had been viewed as neutral in the earlier high-leverage equilibrium. At that rate, final investors would have insufficient incentive to substitute completely for the loss of intermediation.

The long-run effects on economic volatility are more difficult to foresee. Reduced leverage and policy efforts to counter the procyclical character of existing capital requirements would tend to dampen the financial accelerator but higher funding costs may reduce the degree to which households and firms use debt to smooth spending across income fluctuations, contributing to volatility. Ultimately, the mix and scale of these effects will depend on how policymakers meet the new regulatory challenges, but that topic awaits a future conference.

References

Alexander, L. and K. Schoenholtz (2008a). Prospects for the financial markets: crisis begets change, May 15.

Alexander, L. and K. Schoenholtz (2008b). Old thinking to manage new risk. *Financial Times*, June 4.

Bank of England (2008). *Financial Stability Report*, Chapter 1, April.

Basel Committee on Banking Supervision (2008a). Principles for sound liquidity risk management and supervision, June 2008a. Basel Committee on Banking Supervision (2008b). Proposed revisions to the Basel II market risk framework, July.

Bernanke, B. (2008a). Addressing weaknesses in the global financial markets: the report of the President's working group on financial markets. *Speech at the World Affairs Council of Greater Richmond*, April 10.

[13] Don Kohn recently presented a similar view: "In the steady state, lenders will get greater returns for taking risk than they did two years ago, intermediaries will be less leveraged and better capitalized, and the financial system will be more robust and resilient to shocks (see Kohn, 2008)".

Bernanke, B. (2008b). Financial regulation and financial stability. *Speech at the FDIC Forum on Mortgage Lending*, July 8.

Bernanke, B. (2008c). Liquidity provision by the federal reserve. *Speech to FRB Atlanta Financial Markets Conference*, May 13.

Bernanke, B. (2008d). Reducing systemic risk. *Federal Reserve Bank of Kansas City Jackson Hole Symposium*, August 22.

Bernanke, B. (2008e). U.S. financial market. *Testimony before the U.S. Senate Committee on Banking, Housing and Urban Affairs*, September 23.

Bernanke, B. (2005). The global savings glut and the U.S. current account deficit. *Sandridge Lecture, Richmond*, March 10.

Bernanke, B. S. and C. S. Lown (1991). The credit crunch. *Brookings Papers on Economic Activity*, 2.

Blundell-Wignall, A. (2008). The subprime crisis: size, deleveraging and some policy options. *OECD Financial Market Trends.*

Brunnermeier, M. K. (forthcoming). Deciphering the 2007–08 liquidity and credit crunch. *Journal of Economic Perspectives*, May 19, 2008 draft.

Calomiris, C. (2008a). The subprime turmoil: what's old, what's new, and what's next. *Federal Reserve Bank of Kansas City Jackson Hole Symposium*, August.

Calomiris, C. (2008b). A matched preferred stock plan for government assistance. *Financial Times* website, http://blogs.ft.com/wolfforum/2008/09/a-matched-preferred-stock-plan-for-government-assistance/), September 19.

Case, K. E. (2008). The central role of house prices in the current financial crisis: how will the market clear? *Brookings Panel on Economic Activity*, September.

Counterparty Risk Management Group III (2008). Containing systemic risk: the road to reform. August 6.

DiClemente, R. (2008). The benign dollar. *Comments on Credit*, Citi, August 21.

Dynan, K. E., D. W. Elmendorf, and D. E. Sichel (2005). Can financial innovation help to explain the reduced volatility of economic activity? *FEDS Working Paper No. 200554*, November.

Feldstein, M. (2008). How to shore up America's crumbling housing market. *Financial Times*, August 26.

Fender, I. and M. Scheicher (2008). The ABX: how do markets price subprime mortgage risk? *BIS Quarterly Review*, September.

Financial Stability Forum (2008). *Report on Enhancing Market and Institutional Resilience*, April.

Foote, C. L., K. Gerardi, L. Goette, and P. S. Willen (2008). Subprime facts: what (we think) we know about the subprime crisis and what we don't. *Federal Reserve Bank of Boston Public Policy Discussion Paper No. 08–2*, May 30.

Foote, C. L., K. Gerardi, and P. S. Willen (2008). Negative equity and foreclosure: theory and evidence. *Federal Reserve Bank of Boston Public Policy Discussion Paper No. 08–3*, June 5.

Geithner, T. F. (2008a). Reducing systemic risk in a dynamic financial system. *Remarks at the Economic Club of New York*, June 9.

Geithner, T. F. (2008b). Systemic risk and financial markets. *Testimony Before the Committee on Financial Services, U.S. House of Representatives*, July 24.

Gerardi, K., A. Lehnert, S. M. Sherlund, and P. Willen (2008). Making sense of the subprime crisis. *Brookings Panel on Economic Activity*, September.

Gorton, G. B. (2008). The panic of 2007. *Federal Reserve Bank of Kansas City Jackson Hole Symposium*, August.

Greenlaw, D., J. Hatzius, A. K. Kashyap, and S. S. Hyun (2008). Leveraged losses: lessons from the mortgage market meltdown. *Proceedings of the U.S. Monetary Policy Forum.*

IMF (2008a). *Global Financial Stability Report: Containing Systemic Risks and Restoring Fiscal Soundness*, April.

IMF (2008b). *Global Financial Stability Report: GFSR Market Update*, July.

Kashyap, A. K., R. G. Rajan, and J. C. Stein (2008). Rethinking capital regulation. *Federal Reserve Bank of Kansas City Jackson Hole Symposium*, August.

Kashyap, A. K. and J. C. Stein (2008). The $700 billion question. *The New York Times*, September 22.

Keys, B. J., T. Mukherjee, A. Seru, and V. Vig (2008). Did securitization lead to lax screening? Evidence from subprime loans, April.

Kohn, D. (2008). Comments at the Brooking Panel on economic activity, September 11.

Lettau, M., S. C. Ludvigson, and J. A. Wachter (2006). The declining equity premium: what role does macroeconomic risk play? *Review of Financial Studies* (published July 2008), August 2006 draft.

McAndrews, J., A. Sarkar, and Z. Wang (2008). The effect of the term auction facility on the London inter-bank offered rate. *Federal Reserve Bank of New York Staff Reports No. 335*, July.

Mishkin, F. S. (2008). How should we respond to asset price bubbles? *Speech at the Wharton Financial Institutions Center Annual Financial Risk Roundtable*, May 15.

Morris, S. and S. S. Hyun (2008). Financial regulation in a system context. *Brookings Panel on Economic Activity*, September.

Rosengren, E. (2008). Implications of a credit crunch. *Speech to the Business and Industry Association of New Hampshire*, September 3.

Senior Supervisors Group (2008). *Leading-Practice Disclosures for Selected Exposures*, April. *Senior Supervisors Group (2008). Observations on Risk Management Practices during the Recent Market Turbulence*, March.

Schoenholtz, K. (2008). Credit supply and the U.S. economic outlook. *International Market Roundup*, Citi, February 1.

Shiller, R. J. (2008). *The Subprime Solution*, Princeton University Press.

Spaventa, L. (2008). Avoiding disorderly deleveraging. *Centre for Economic Policy Research Policy Insight No. 22*, May.

Swiston, A. (2008). A U.S. financial conditions index: putting credit where credit is due. *IMF Working Paper 08–161*, June.

The President's Working Group on Financial Markets (2008). *Policy Statement on Financial Market Developments*, March.

Taylor, J. B. and J. C. Williams (2008a). A black swan in the money market, April 2.

Taylor, J. B. and J. C. Williams (2008b). Further results on a black swan in the money market, May 23.

U.S. Treasury (2008). *Blueprint for a Modernized Financial Regulatory Structure*, March.

U.S. Treasury (2008b). *Fact Sheet: Proposed Treasury Authority to Purchase Troubled Assets*, September, 2008.

What Has Happened in Europe? Monetary Policy, Lending Cycles, Banking Competition, Risk-Taking, and Regulation

Jesús Saurina*
Banco de España

1. Introduction

The objective of this paper is to analyze what has happened in Europe since the financial turmoil started in August 2007.[1] An excellent and very detailed analysis of the financial crisis in Europe is in the *Financial Stability Review* of the European Central Bank/Eurosystem (ECB, 2008). Moreover, a useful analysis of individual country financial systems can be found in the *Financial Stability Reports* of many European central banks. I review the impact of financial turmoil on banks, in particular, using information of equity markets. I also point to the banks that have suffered episodes of crisis or specific difficulties. Finally, I focus on the developments in securitization markets in Europe (both covered bonds and asset-backed securities), raising some questions about potential

---

* Jesús Saurina is Director of the Financial Stability Department at the Banco de España and member of the European Central Bank's Banking Supervision Committee. The views expressed here are the author's and not necessarily those of the Banco de España or the Eurosystem. The author thanks A. Almazán, John Fell, the discussants at the conference, and V. Salas for providing insightful comments, as well as María Martínez-Alvarez for outstanding research assistance. All the remaining errors are the author's sole responsibility.

[1] Importantly, the period covered in the paper ends in early September 2008. Since then, European banks have encountered many more problems, including deeper declines in equity prices, prompting government interventions (rescue packages, liquidity provision, guarantees, injection of capital, and partial or total nationalization of some banks). However, despite all these important changes, the thrust of the analysis remains, in particular, regarding competition and risk-taking and the need to enforce proper banking regulation across countries and financial intermediaries.

mispricing in some of these markets due to a significant retrenchment of investors.

In order to understand what has happened, I explore several issues. First, the intensity of banking competition across European markets: using empirical evidence of the relationship between the degree of competition and bank risk-taking, I signal a potential incentive problem for those bank managers who face steep competition from other banks and/or financial institutions. Second, I also study the role that monetary policy plays in bank risk-taking; and third, how lending standards evolve with the business cycle. As an extension, I explore the role that prudential regulation may play in smoothing lending cycles and contribute to the growing debate on whether there is a need to counterbalance the (excessive) procyclicality of the financial system. Finally, I draw some preliminary lessons for bank supervisors.

2. What Has Happened in Europe?

Since 8 August 2007, the day before central banks started to pump liquidity into interbank markets, there have been very significant declines in bank stock prices. In contrast with credit markets (e.g. money markets, securitization markets, and interbank markets), equity markets in Europe, in the U.S., and in most countries around the globe, have been working properly for the last 13 months: that is, with significant liquidity.

These declines have not been homogeneous across banks but quite the opposite — they follow a clear pattern depending on the banks' business models rather than on the country where their headquarters are located (Figure 1). In general, investment banking activities have been significantly penalized, either if they were carried out by investment banks or by universal banks with significant investment banking business lines. Meanwhile, strong retail franchises and geographic diversification have shown lower declines in market capitalization. These patterns are similar in Europe and in the U.S. The former raises doubts on the ability to measure, manage, and control risks by some large banks.

Some European banks have also faced significant difficulties. In general, these were small banks, some of them public, focused on specialized business. In the UK, Northern Rock suffered a depositor run on 14 September 2007. It was the first run on a British bank in more than a century, and eventually it was nationalized on 17 February 2008.

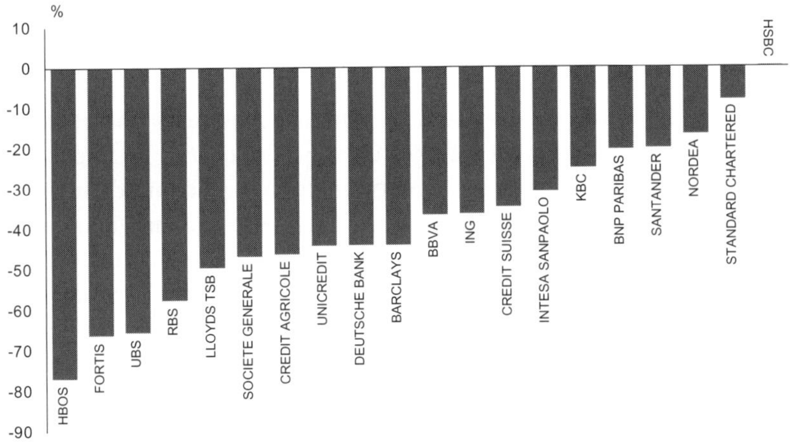

Figure 1. Changes in Equity Prices, 20 Largest European Banks, 8/8/07 to 09/19/08 (percent).
Source: Datastream.

Northern Rock, with a market value of around €5 billion at the beginning of August 2007. It was the fifth mortgage lender in the UK (18 percent market share), had no U.S. subprime exposures, and small Non-Performing Loan (NPL) ratios. Its business model was increasingly based on wholesale markets for funding: retail deposits were only 23 percent of total liabilities, 70 percent of funds were obtained through wholesale markets, and RMBS (Residential Mortgage-Backed Securities) were more than 60 percent of the mortgage portfolio. Therefore, Northern Rock was dependent on funding markets that contracted sharply in August 2007.[2]

Some small German banks have also experienced difficulties. Sachsen LB (the smallest German Landesbank, which are regional public banks) and IKB, whose largest shareholder (38 percent) was a public bank (KfW Bankengruppe), both had large conduits off-balance-sheet which invested in structured complex products linked to the U.S. subprime market, funded using short-term Asset-Backed Commercial Paper (ABCP). They lacked the experience and understanding of the risks

[2] Other quoted British mortgage lenders have also suffered significant declines in market value (since August 8, 2007, until the end of June 2008, Alliance and Lester and Bradford and Bingley fell by 73 percent and 85 percent, respectively).

involved and put up disproportionately large vehicles. Both seem to have followed a search for yield strategy, with a huge off-balance-sheet leverage. Sachsen LB was bought by Landesbank Baden-Württemberg while IKB was rescued by a consortium of banks and its main shareholder as well as through government funds. Recently, Lone Star, a U.S. investor in distressed financial assets, is reported to have acquired more than 90 percent of IKB. Finally, Duesseldorfer Hypothekenbank, a very small and family controlled bank and issuer of Pfandbriefe, the German covered bonds, experienced difficulties as a result of market turmoil, and there was a transfer of property to the deposit guarantee fund of the German banking association, apparently to avoid any negative impact on the Pfandbriefe market.[3]

In addition to crisis episodes at a few European banks, there have been significant losses related to U.S. subprime products, including complex Collateralized Debt Obligations (CDO) products which had embedded subprime exposures. Those losses have hit some of the largest and most internationally active banks in Europe (Figure 2). According to the International Institute of Finance (IIF, 2008), those losses were approximately US$233 billion, until September 2008, while in the U.S. they were about US$255 billion. They estimate that 15 percent are credit losses and 85 percent mark to market losses.

Other banking systems in Europe have suffered almost no loss as a result of their lack of significant exposures to the U.S. subprime market (Italy, Spain, Portugal, and Greece and the Nordic and Eastern European countries). Therefore, the business model, as well as risk management and control, are two key elements in understanding what has happened to European banks since the crisis started in summer 2007.

Securitization markets have been hit hard in Europe by the financial crisis. There has been a significant increase in risk premiums and a deep contraction in the issuance. Both covered bonds and Asset-Backed Securities (ABS) have been in difficulty. Before August 2007, there were many analysts, particularly at central banks, who pointed toward an

---

[3] In Europe, since August 2007 there has also been a risk-control episode at Societé Générale, a French bank, although unrelated to the subprime crisis. It looks like a classic risk-control problem of a trader who had quite exceeded his limits to operate in equity derivatives going unnoticed. The episode is significant because of the sheer size of the loss (€4.9 billion), the timing of the discovery (in the middle of the turmoil), and the impact on the markets when closing the position.

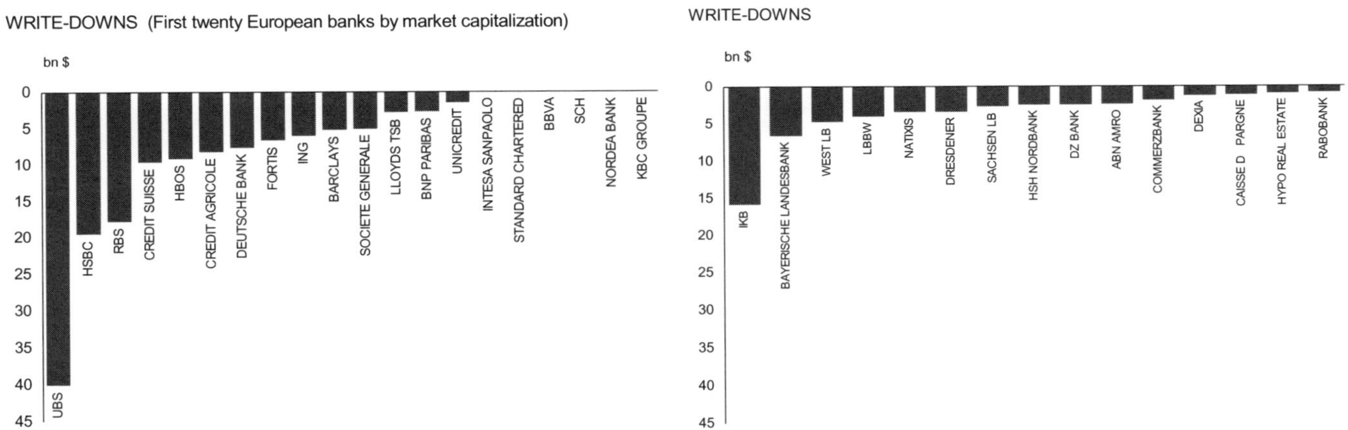

Figure 2. Market Capitalization, 20 Largest European Banks, Millions of €.

Source: Lehman Brothers.

underpricing of risks in international financial markets. The abundance of liquidity together with the search for yield were the driving forces. Given the significant differences between actual (i.e. mark to market) and model-implied-prices (i.e. cash-flow-based estimates) for the most senior securitization tranches,[4] it could be argued that it might now be the opposite: that is, there may be an overshooting in risk premium, and what I see is an overpricing of risk, particularly, in securitization tranches of the highest quality.

Conduits and Structured Investment Vehicles (SIVs) used to be very important operators in the securitization markets, buying medium and long term securitized products and funding them with ABCP. The difficulties in renewing the ABCP funding and their absorption in banks' balance sheets, together with the increase in capital requirements for banks, put considerable pressure on these investors and had a direct impact on their willingness/capacity to buy more securitized assets. Moreover, those more leveraged or with less capital buffers became sellers in the market. The huge decline in liquidity in the secondary markets helps to explain a significant part of the increase in the spreads of securitized assets.

One could argue that another case for overshooting in risk premiums and, therefore, in spreads, are the Spanish covered bonds. Covered bonds have been widely used in continental Europe for a long time. The German Pfandbriefe, initially based on loans to the public sector but more recently based also on mortgages, is the classical covered bond. Spanish covered bonds are called *cédulas hipotecarias*.

A *cédula hipotecaria* is a secured funding instrument for banks. They have, first of all, the guarantee of the issuing bank. On top of that, they are secured by the whole mortgage portfolio of the bank. Thus, in case of insolvency, the holder of the *cédula hipotecaria* has a preferential claim on the whole mortgage portfolio. Moreover, cash flow from mortgage loans is segregated and dedicated to service the *cédula hipotecaria*.

There is a significant degree of overcollateralization in *cédulas*. First, there is an eligible mortgage portfolio. Currently, the eligible portfolio consists of residential mortgages with a loan to value below 80 percent and/or commercial mortgages with a loan to value below

---

[4] See the Bank of England (2008).

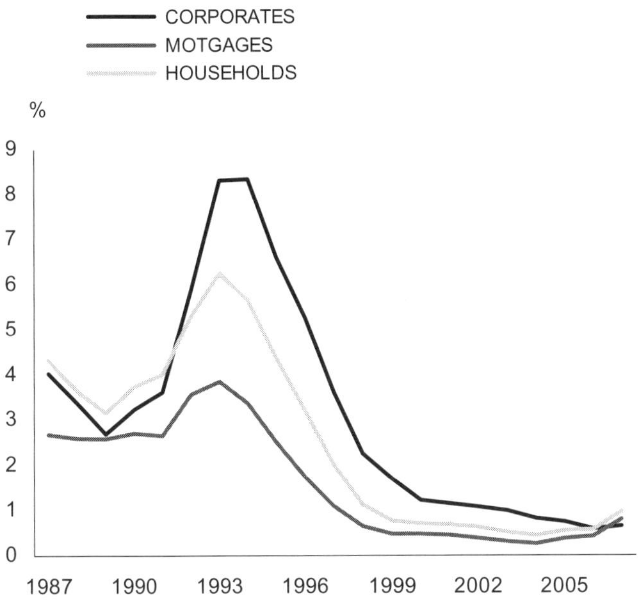

Figure 3. Non-Performing Loan Ratio, Deposit Institutions in Spain.
Source: Bank of Spain.

60 percent. Over this eligible mortgage portfolio, there is a limit of issuance of 80 percent, which means a minimum overcollateralization of 25 percent.

It is important to note that mortgages have been the lowest credit risk portfolio in Spain, as is the case in many other countries. Historically, consumer loans and loans to firms have been far riskier than mortgages (Figure 3). They are the lowest risk products because the probabilities of default have been low and, on top of that, the recovery rate has been close to one (i.e. loss given default in the last recession was close to zero percent, after house prices recovered). Finally, the issuance of *cédulas hipotecarias* requires approval and supervision by the market supervisor, Comisión Nacional del Mercado de Valores (CMNV). All the issuers are banks regulated and supervised by Banco de España.

All in all, the double guarantee (the bank itself plus the whole eligible mortgage portfolio), the overcollateralization, and the historical performance of the underlying collateral seem incompatible with the current level of spreads observed in the Spanish covered bond secondary market.[5]

Therefore, there seems to be an overshooting in risk premiums which points toward a lack of liquidity in the market. Investors have disappeared because they have become totally risk averse or because they themselves do not have the liquidity to buy those products. However, many investors are forced to mark these assets to market. But, if there is almost no market (i.e. there is no investor buying assets), or no liquidity in the market, what do those market prices mean? If markets collapse, are the prices based on a small number of transactions and/or on a small trade volume meaningful? However, these prices can force investors that mark to market to dump these securities, putting even more downward pressure on the prices.[6]

We need to think carefully about accounting rules and financial stability. Fair value is the right model. However, it has shown significant limitations in both good and bad times. The International Financial Reporting Standards (IFRS) contain a significant degree of procyclicality. A way to deal with this problem may be through transparent valuation reserves (or transparent valuation adjustments). Those reserves should be a function of the uncertainty about model valuations, those that have to be used when markets are closed and the prices observed in them are not informative. We need to learn from the current crisis and understand that there are some points in time when markets might collapse and fair value is a difficult concept to grasp. The idea of valuation reserves encompasses forward-looking loan loss provisions, which I analyze below.

3. Why Has It Happened? Some Potential Explanations

3.1 *Competition and risk-taking*

Figure 4 shows German banks' Return On Equity (ROE) by type of bank. The profitability of German banks was low at the beginning of the current

[5] The spreads of Spanish RMBS are much higher, even for AAA bonds. In the average RMBS, the AAA tranche is around 93 percent of the total securitization. Thus, for that tranche to be hit by losses, it would need, for example, a PD of 14 percent and a loss given default (LGD) of 50 percent, which are more than three times larger than those observed in residential mortgages at the worst point in the last recession (around 1993).

[6] Plantin, Sapra and Shin (2008) point out the limitations of fair value, in particular, for long-term, illiquid and senior financial assets, that is, for most of the bank assets. They argue that fair value creates endogenous or artificial volatility.

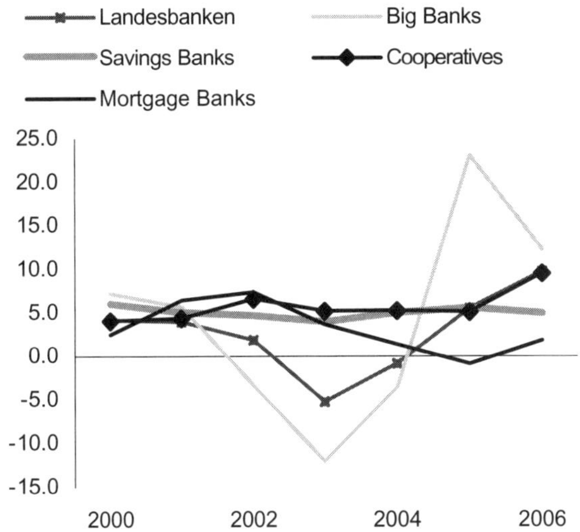

Figure 4. Return on Equity (ROE) of Different Types of German Banks.
Source: Bundesbank, Lehman Brothers research.

decade, when a significant slowdown hit the German economy as well as other core European economies. With domestic demand for credit almost flat, German banks explored other investment opportunities to obtain the profits they were not able to produce in the domestic market. Thus, they started to invest in subprime-related products which, at that time, had a high rating and offered attractive returns given the rating assigned.

The ratio of Return On Assets (ROA) over Return On Equity (ROE) is a rough measure of leverage (equity over total assets). Figure 5 shows how, on average, the profitability of the Spanish and the British banking system was very similar, although the latter obtained it through a much higher leverage, closer to the German banks at the end of the period.

Focusing on the large European banks, there is a significant degree of dispersion across them in terms of leverage (Figure 6). Equity over total assets dropped very low at some banks. A bank with one percent equity over total assets that has, say, 10 percent of its assets marked to model (level 2 and level 3 assets in the U.S. accounting terminology) and that suffers a loss of 10 percent in those assets, is literally bankrupt. This back-of-the-envelope calculation seems to explain the significant correlation

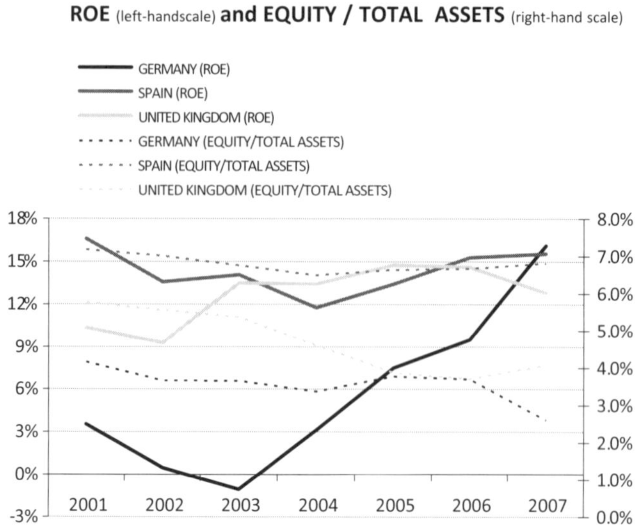

Figure 5. Return on Equity and Leverage Ratio (Equity over Total Assets).
Source: BankScope.

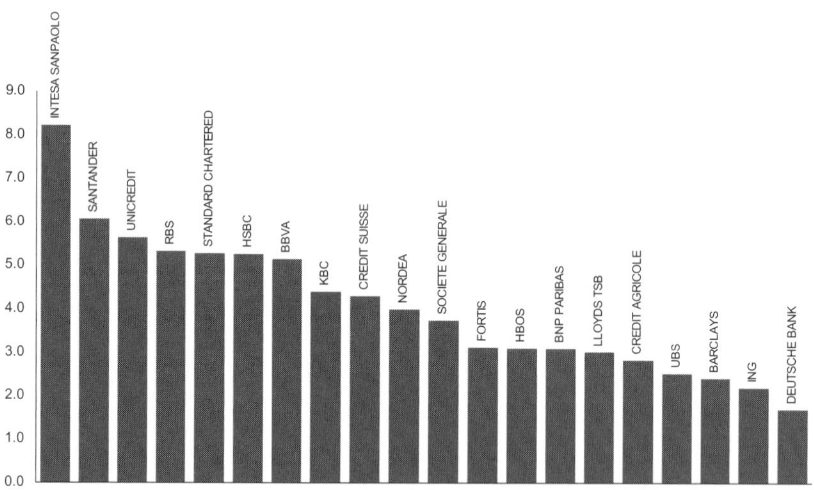

Figure 6. Leverage Ratio (Equity Over Total Assets), 20 Largest Cap European Banks, June 2008 (percent).
Source: Datastream and Bank of Spain.

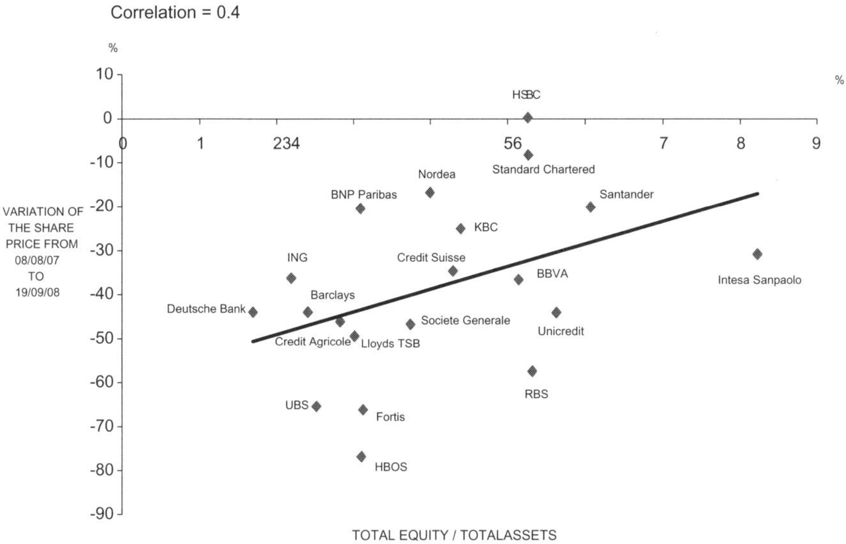

Figure 7. Leverage Ratio (Equity Over Total Assets) and Equity Price Decline, 20 Largest Bank Cap European Banks.
Source: Entities, Datastream and Bank of Spain.

between the ratio of equity over total assets and the cumulative decline in market capitalization since August 2007 for the largest European banks (Figure 7).

There are significant differences in competition intensity across European countries. Figure 8 ranks the countries according to a mixed index of market power proxies. In effect, a combination of concentration measures such as the Herfindahl-Hirschman Index (HHI), the market share of the five largest banks in each country (C5), the Panzar-Rose H-statistic, and the λ index of Bresnahan-Lau, both a summary measure of the degree of market power in a banking market, shows that the German banking system is the one where there is most competition across entities. It is important to point out that Germany has many small banks (both savings banks and credit cooperatives) with significant combined market shares. On the other hand, it is the country in Europe where the large commercial banks have the lowest market share.

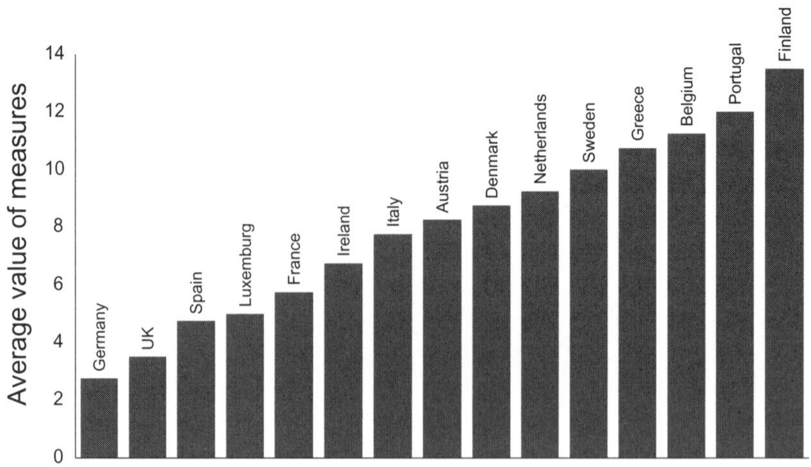

Figure 8. Banking Competition Index by Countries. Ranking Based on Concentration Indexes (HHI and C5) and Summary Indexes of Market Power (Panzar-Rose H-statistic and λ index of Bresnahan-Lau).
Source: Bank of Spain.

The conventional wisdom is that more competition in a banking market means more incentives to risk-taking.[7] As the franchise value of a bank deteriorates (less current and future expected profits) with increasing competition, bank managers have more incentives to take greater risk in order to reach past profitability figures or/and fewer incentives to protect solvency levels. Given the fact that the German banking system is one of the most fragmented in Europe, with far less concentration and many more small banks (including savings banks, credit cooperatives, and regional banks), the incentives of some German banks' managers may have shifted in the past years toward more risk-taking. Thus, we need a careful balance between bank competition

[7] Jiménez, López, and Saurina (2007) test the relationship between competition and bank risk-taking. They focus on the Spanish banking market to take advantage of a detailed database that allows a calculation of a precise Lerner index (market power measure), while using non-performing loan ratios and their volatility as bank risk measures. Results show that increases in Lerner indexes bring about declines in non-performing loans and their volatility. Thus, for Spain, a mature banking market, their results suggest that more competition means more incentives to risk-taking.

(efficiency, financial innovation) and financial stability (risk-taking) through a better regulatory framework.[8]

3.2 *Monetary policy and risk-taking*

The turmoil is seen as the long-run consequence of the easy global money and credit conditions that prevailed over the last five years. Some observers have attributed the roots of the problem to the so-called great stability of steady growth and inflation and in particular to the period between 2001 and 2006 of persistently low nominal interest rates which led to overconfidence, underpricing of risks, and bad lending at the top of the cycle.[9]

What is the relationship between monetary policy and risk-taking? Do persistently low interest rates encourage banks' risk-taking? Is there a difference in interest rate changes in terms of outstanding and new loans granted? Jiménez *et al.* (2008) contains evidence of such a trade-off for Spain using very detailed information on credit risk.

That paper uses loan by loan data (defaults and other loan characteristics) from the Spanish Credit Register. This database is comprehensive as it includes all loans to firms above €6,000 granted by all banks operating in Spain. Monetary policy in Spain is treated exogenously, given that, between 1988 and 1998, Spain had a policy that aimed at a fixed exchange rate with the Deutsche Mark, and from 1999 onward Spain is a Eurosystem member (with a relative weight around 10 percent). They use, first the German, then the euro overnight interbank rates as the measure of monetary policy. Using duration models, controlling for bank, firm, loan, and macroeconomic characteristics, they investigate how short-term interest rates prior to loan origination, and during the life of the loan, affect the loan hazard rate.

Jiménez *et al.* (2008) find that banks soften their lending standards during periods of low interest rates. Banks lend more to borrowers with

[8] Recent developments since mid-September confirm the importance of competition and risk-taking analysis. In fact, a reduction in competition (i.e. capacity consolidation, entry barriers, sponsored takeovers, partial or total nationalization) seems to be, probably unintentionally, part of the answer to the current crisis.

[9] See, for instance, Gieve (2008) and Hannoun (2008).

a bad credit history and with higher uncertainty when monetary policy is loose. That paper shows robust evidence of the duality of interest rates: credit risk increases with lower interest rates at loan origination but also increases as a result of higher rates during the life of the loan (i.e. conditional on the loan being granted, lower rates reduce the credit risk of outstanding loans). Therefore, low rates encourage risk-taking, which reduces credit risk in the short term but worsens it in the medium term. That paper finds a trade-off between origination and current interest rates that connects monetary policy and financial stability policy discussions. Such a trade-off, which of course may be different depending on the country and/or the period analyzed, shows that a small decline in interest rates has a limited impact on incentives to risk-taking while significantly improving the prospects of the outstanding loan portfolio.

3.3 *Lending standards*

Supervisors' experience is that banks' lending mistakes are more prevalent during upturns when borrowers and lenders are overconfident about investment projects (i.e. they are financing negative net present value projects). Banks' over optimism implies lower credit policy standards. On the contrary, during recessions, banks suddenly turn very conservative and tighten credit standards (well beyond positive net present value). Lending cycles have an impact on the real economy.

The literature has put forward arguments to rationalize fluctuations in credit policies based on information imperfections: 1) disaster myopia, Guttentag and Herring (1986); 2) herd behavior, Rajan (1994); 3) agency problems, Williamson (1963); and 4) the institutional memory hypothesis, Berger and Udell (2004). As argued above, increasing bank competition as well as a monetary policy too lax for an excessively long period contributes, through risk-taking incentives by banks, to amplify lending cycles (search for yield, Rajan, 2006). Collateral may also play a role in credit cycles, since loan booms are intertwined with asset booms.

Jiménez and Saurina (2006) show that there is evidence of a direct, although lagged, relationship between credit growth and credit risk (a lag between three and four years). A rapid increase in loan portfolios is positively associated with an increase in nonperforming loan ratios later on.

Moreover, loans granted during boom periods have a higher Probability of Default (PD) than those granted during slow credit growth periods. Finally, in boom periods collateral requirements are relaxed while the opposite happens during recessions.

Therefore, we have evidence of looser credit standards during expansions. Given that banking supervisors' concerns are well rooted both in theoretical and empirical grounds, do we need a prudential tool to cope with the potential problems due to too rapid credit growth?

4. What Can Be Done? Countercyclical Regulation

Financial market turmoil and its impact on banks and other financial companies has spurred a growing interest in the role regulation might play in lending cycles and, in particular, whether regulation is procyclical or not (i.e. it enhances, is neutral or restrains the behavior of agents along the business cycle).[10]

The IFRS are very procyclical, in particular, regarding loan loss provisions. The IFRS loan loss provisions are set aside to cover incurred losses both identified individually on a specific loan and incurred losses not yet individually identified. Both incurred losses evolve procyclically. Basel II, the new framework for capital requirements at banks, is probably going to be more procyclical: partly by construction (capital will be more proportional to risk, and risk is procyclical), and partly because the point in time (PIT) probabilities of default are very procyclical. All in all, credit cycles might become more volatile and that might hurt the real economy.

If procyclicality of the regulation (both accounting and capital rules) is an issue, there are ways to control them through (minor) changes in

---

[10] The Financial Stability Forum (2008) has made public its concerns on this issue: "II.7. Supervisors will assess the cyclicality of the Basel II framework and take additional measures as appropriate." Market analysts seem to share those concerns and quite clearly advocate countercyclical regulatory devices: "Capital requirements should rise during booms and fall in busts," *The Economist*, March 29–April 4, 2008; "If regulation is to be effective, it must cover all relevant institutions and the entire balance sheet, in all significant countries; it must focus on capital, liquidity and, transparency; and, not least, it must make finance less procyclical," Martin Wolf, *Financial Times*, April 16, 2008.

those regulations. The idea is not to change the current rules. It is possible to amend them slightly in order to incorporate macroprudential concerns and to enhance financial stability.

If IFRS were more flexible, it could be possible to address directly rapid credit growth, which is one of the underlying causes of the current difficulties. The LLP could be based on the credit cycle position of the bank: the higher the credit growth of the bank, the more it has to provision; the lower the credit growth, the more provisions can be liberated from the previously built-up reserve. During boom periods, the LLP would be positive; during recessions, negative. Overall, the underlying idea is quite simple: the more rapid the credit growth, following our empirical results, the higher the credit risk the bank is assuming and, therefore, the higher the LLP required.[11]

To operationalize the proposal, Jiménez and Saurina (2006) propose:

$$LLP_{total} = specif + g\Delta C + \alpha(\Delta C - \delta C_{t-1}),$$

where δ is the average loan growth rate for the total lending institutions during a credit cycle, C_{t-1} the stock of loans the previous period, ΔC the absolute increase in loans, and g the latent risk.

The mechanism is quite simple. While loan growth rates are above the average loan growth rate (δ), the countercyclical provision is positive and the amount charged in the profit and loss is accrued in a fund. When loan growth is starting to fall below the average, the countercyclical provision is negative, and it is accrued in the profit and loss account from the cyclical fund previously built up. Finally, the cyclical provision resumes a positive value when a new expansionary credit cycle starts again. Different values of the parameter α imply different countercyclical intensity in the loan loss provisions. In order to improve transparency, banks should publish the total loan loss provisions as well as their components and the level of the loan loss reserves.

The former mechanism can also be adapted to capital requirements; for instance, through pillar 2 in the new Basel II framework. In any case, it is far from clear that Basel II is going to be much more

[11] In fact, since mid-2000, Banco de España has been effectively applying a countercyclical loan loss provision. An assessment of its impact can be seen in Banco de España (2005). The provision is fully transparent so that banks communicate to the market the amount of the loan loss provision incurred each quarter.

procyclical; in particular, if through the cycle (TTC) probabilities of default were to be used for computing capital requirements (Saurina and Trucharte, 2007).[12]

More broadly, countercyclical regulation can be discussed on a more general framework. Following Goodhart (2005), if two policy objectives require two policy instruments, interest rates should be used for monetary stability while regulatory devices, such as countercyclical loan loss provisions or capital should be used for financial stability. In the short term, and in the absence of the regulatory device, interest rates can also help to foster financial stability.[13]

5. Lessons for Bank Regulation/Supervision

One of the unexpected lessons of the current financial crisis has been that what we thought were best practices in risk management and control, were not that good. Similarly, bank supervisors need to think carefully about some of their practices. Conduits and SIVs were, in fact, parallel banks without capital. They proliferated in several jurisdictions, despite the fact that IFRS made it compulsory for them to be consolidated with the parent company (i.e. the sponsoring bank in most cases).

The "originate to distribute" model was flawed. A significant part of the originators were regulated much less tightly than commercial banks. There were no incentives to screen and monitor properly the borrowers, precisely because the credit risk was being transferred to other investors who, apparently, were willing to buy it.[14] Moreover, it seems that there was a lack of understanding of the risks involved in complex securitizations. Investors did not look into the complexities of the securitized assets

---

[12] Arguments for and against increased procyclicality of Basel II can be found in Persaud (2008) and Saurina (2008), respectively. A more detailed discussion is in Gordy and Howells (2006). Repullo and Suárez (2008) find that Basel II capital buffers are going to be countercyclical but not enough to avoid higher credit rationing than under Basel I during recessions.

[13] Borio (2003) argues in favor of macroprudential tools.

[14] This is not necessarily the case in all securitizations. For instance, in Spain, banks provided a significant credit enhancement to the securitization vehicle, thus, absorbing a certain percentage of the first losses (around 2 percent). Preliminary work by Almazán, Martín-Oliver, and Saurina (2008) shows that the main objective of Spanish ABS was funding, not risk transfer or capital arbitrage.

they were buying, partly because they had blind confidence in rating agencies.

Fair value has proved much more difficult to apply than expected. When markets collapse, prices coming from a few transactions do not seem to reflect properly the value of the financial instrument, in particular, if those prices are used for the whole portfolios of those instruments. Therefore, we need to think carefully about how to carry out value adjustments for financial instruments that are traded in markets that are not deep enough.

Another issue that needs calm discussion is the optimal structure of bank supervision. As it is well known, during the 1990s there was a significant shift in European countries in terms of who was carrying out banking supervision. The integrated model (i.e. a central bank that has supervisory responsibilities) was abandoned in many countries for a separated model where the central bank was stripped of banking supervision tasks and responsibilities (the UK, Germany, Switzerland, the Nordic countries, and the Central and Eastern European countries are examples). Another unexpected finding of the current developments is that, up until now, banks with more difficulties, both in terms of crisis or in terms of losses and negative impact on profits and market capitalization (as discussed in section 2) pertain to countries where central banks are not responsible for banking supervision. This does not imply that separation is bad; it implies that a central bank with banking supervision tasks is not an inferior institutional arrangement. The first time that reality has tested the separation model, the results are somewhat challenging.

6. Conclusion

Monetary policy has an impact on bank risk-taking and on outstanding loans. Thus, monetary and financial stability impact each other. There is a trade-off between current and future interest rates. Therefore, there is a need to incorporate banks (i.e. credit risk and incentives) into macro models.

It seems that if banking competition increases significantly, bank managers may have incentives to take much more risk. Thus, banking competition has to go hand in hand with a strict regulatory framework that closely monitors bank risk-taking.

We cannot relinquish the ability to control credit cycle excesses by using smart regulation. Banking regulation may be a "second instrument" to pursue financial stability, the first instrument being interest rates for monetary stability, provided that: 1) all regulators share the objective and aim for it; 2) there is no room for complacent supervision in any jurisdiction; 3) supervisors coordinate and cooperate very closely; 4) the (potentially different) supervisory frameworks work properly; and 5) there is a close monitoring of financial innovation without stifling it.

Regulatory tools to rein in credit cycle excesses might be forward looking loan loss provisions and/or countercyclical mechanisms for capital requirements. Procyclicality of regulation is an important issue. This paper contains some proposals to deal with it, which aim to be a departure point for discussion.

References

Almazán, A., A. Martin-Oliver, and J. Saurina (2008). Securitization. A corporate finance approach. *Mimeograph.*

Banco de España (2005). *Financial Stability Report*, May.

Bank of England (2008). *Financial Stability Report*, April.

Berger, A. and G. Udell (2004). The institutional memory hypothesis and the procyclicality of bank lending behavior. *Journal of Financial Intermediation*, 13(4), 458–495.

Borio, C. (2003). Towards a macroprudential framework for financial supervision and regulation? *BIS Working Papers*, 128, February.

European Central Bank (2008). *Financial Stability Review*, June.

Financial Stability Forum (2008). *Report of the Financial Stability Forum on Enhancing Market and Institutional Resilience*, April.

Gieve, J. (2008). The return of the credit cycle: old lessons in new markets. *Speech at the Euromoney Bond Investors Congress*, February.

Goodhart, C. A. E. (2005). Financial regulation, credit risk and financial stability. *National Institute Economic Review*, 192, April, pp. 118–127.

Gordy, M. B. and B. Howells (2006). Procyclicality in Basel II: can we treat the disease without killing the patient? *Journal of Financial Intermediation*, 15, 395–417.

Guttentag, J. M. and R. J. Herring (1986). Disaster myopia in international banking. *Princeton University Essays in International Finance*, 164, September.

Hannoun, H. (2008). Policy lessons from the recent financial market turmoil. *Speech at the XLV Meeting of Central Bank Governors of the American Continent*, May.

International Institute of Finance (2008). *Capital Markets Monitor.*

Jiménez, G., J. A. López, and J. Saurina (2007). How does competition increase bank risk-taking? *Federal Reserve Bank of San Francisco, Working Paper 0723.*

Jiménez, G., S. Ongena, J. L. Peydró, and J. Saurina (2008). Hazardous times for monetary policy: what do twenty-three million bank loans say about the effects of monetary policy on credit risk? *Working Paper 0833 Banco de España.*

Jiménez, G. and J. Saurina (2006). Credit cycles, credit risk, and prudential regulation. *International Journal of Central Banking*, 2(2), June, 65–98.

Persaud, A. (2008). Will Basel II help prevent crises or worsen them? Sending the herd over the cliff. Again. *Finance and Development*, June, 32–33.

Plantin, G., H. Sapra, and H. S. Shin (2008). Mark-to-market accounting: panacea or pandora's box. *Journal of Accounting Research.*

Rajan, R. (1994). Why bank credit policies fluctuate: a theory and some evidence. *Quarterly Journal of Economics*, 109, 399–441.

Rajan, R. (2006). Has finance made the world riskier? *European Financial Management*, 12, 499–533.

Repullo, R. and J. Suárez (2008). The procyclical effects of Basel II. CEMFI. Mimeo.

Saurina, J. (2008). Will Basel II help prevent crises or worsen them? Banking on the right path. *Finance and Development*, June, 30–31.

Saurina, J. and C. Trucharte (2007). An assessment of Basel II procyclicality in mortgage portfolios. *Journal of Financial Services Research*, 32(1–2), October, 81–101.

Williamson, O. (1963). Managerial discretion and business behavior. *American Economic Review*, 53, December, 1032–1057.

The Subprime Crisis Effects in the Rest of the World

Laura E. Kodres*
International Monetary Fund

Thank you for inviting me today and asking me to speak about how the credit market turmoil has affected the "rest of the world." Before I begin, the usual disclaimer applies: my views are my own and do not represent those of the International Monetary Fund's (IMF) executive board or those of other IMF staff.

Last spring, when I was asked to speak, I thought that this would be a short and easy presentation to give — after all, until recently, countries outside the United States and Europe had remained relatively unscathed by the subprime crisis. Over the last several weeks, however, this is no longer true.

Let me briefly outline my remarks before digging into the topic.

1. Before and Now

Prices in a number of financial markets across the globe reacted to the events of the last several weeks and most precipitously in the last week, when systemic risks intensified in the United States. Most of what I will talk about are the so-called "emerging markets" where the knock-on effects have been most evident.

Let's start with equity markets (Figure 1). Unlike in most advanced markets that reached their peaks in late fall last year, the peaks in nearly all emerging market regions were reached in late spring or early summer. Emerging market equity prices, taken together, had outperformed

---

*Laura E. Kodres is division chief of the Global Financial Stability Division at the International Monetary Fund.

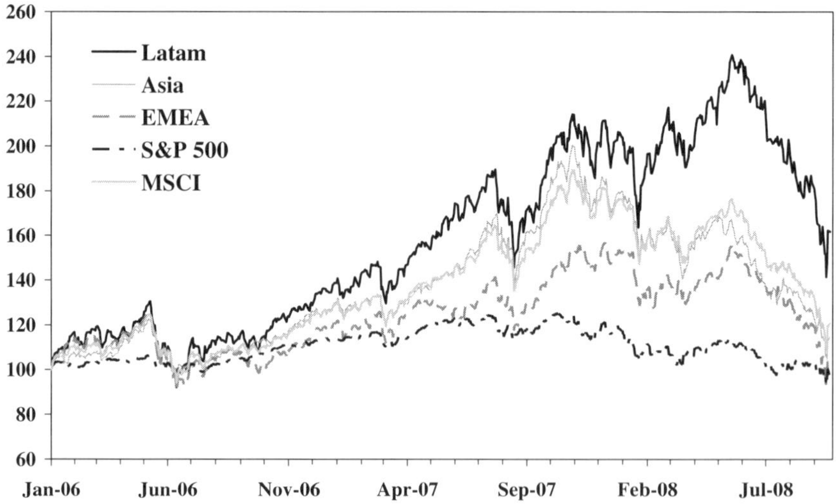

Figure 1. Equity Market Performance (January 2006 = 100, in U.S. Dollar Terms).
Source: Bloomberg L.P.

advanced countries markets since the beginning of the crisis in July 2007. That is, equity price rises were further to the peak and have fallen less — at least until recently. This notion, however, hides a great deal of diversity.

Some countries, such as Russia and Brazil, have had such dramatic run-ups that their declines still leave them well ahead of other emerging market countries (Figure 2). Other countries did not see such large advances. Note that in the advanced economies, the run-ups have been less evident, and their declines have been more muted as well. The scales on the two charts are quite different with the advanced country increases of, at most 200 percent, whereas Brazil has seen an 800 percent rise, trough to peak.

Equity prices have taken declined precipitously over the last week or so, not quite fully recovering somewhat following the announcements of the U.S. government at the end of the week (Figure 3). This week has not been so favorable as the new proposals are being worked out in Washington.

While there is differentiation across countries with some being hurt less, the notion that emerging markets equities could be immune from external events would be naïve. Some of my colleagues have just completed

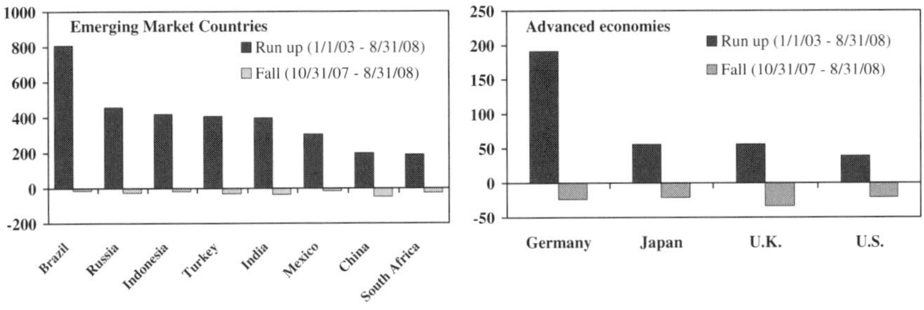

Figure 2. Stock Price Change (In Percent).
Source: Bloomberg L.P.

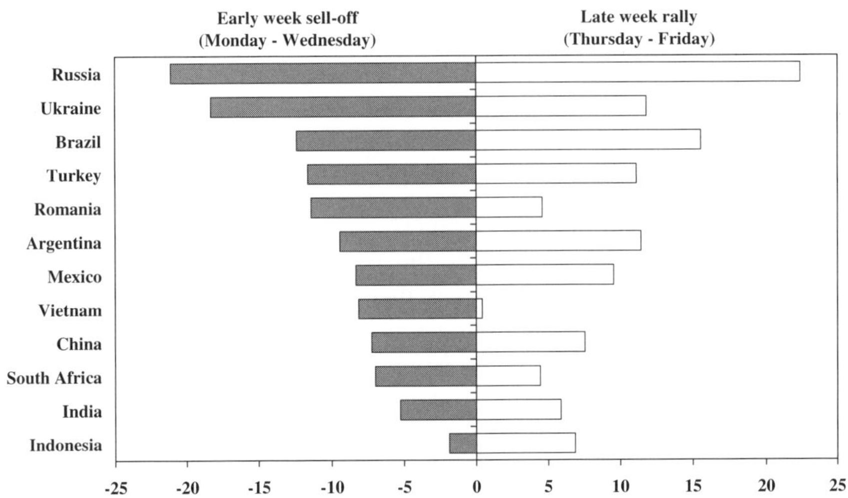

Figure 3. Emerging Market Equity Moves Last Week (In Percent).
Source: Bloomberg L.P.

some research that will be appearing in our forthcoming *Global Financial Stability Report*, looking at the determinants of emerging market equity prices. They have shown that external factors, such as global liquidity, credit risks, and market risks, help to drive prices. Domestic economic factors are also important, but globalization increasingly is determining what happens locally. Thus, we should not be surprised to see more reactions both as external factors deteriorate and local factors also start to worsen.

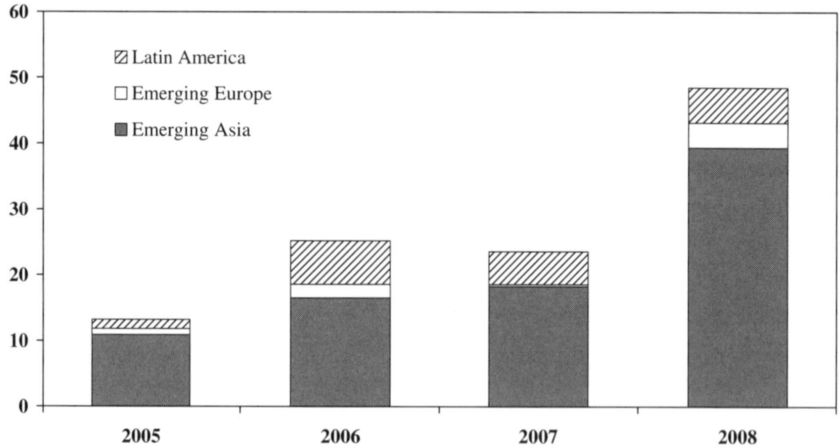

Figure 4. Local Corporate Bond Issuance (In Billions of U.S. Dollors).
Source: Bloomberg L.P.
Note: 2008 data are as of September 15.

Looking at bond markets in emerging market economies, the local domestic corporate bonds is where the action has been recently as these markets have grown steadily over the last several years (Figure 4). These markets are still small compared to all corporate bonds outstanding in the international markets. Nonetheless, the turbulence has been leading to a shift from external to domestic issuance in most regions, as demand for domestic corporate debt, denominated in local currency, has grown.

Though harder to track the prices and spreads of these bonds, there are some indices (Figure 5). They had shown a relatively gradual increase since the start of the crisis in 2007, but really exploded last week. Most of the rise is in emerging European countries where much of this debt is issued by banks — that is, this not nonfinancial corporate debt, but all corporate debt. Note the larger increases relative to Emerging Bond Index Global (EMBIG) — the index covering sovereign external debt.

Turning to sovereign bond spreads in emerging market economies, they too have been increasing steadily since the crisis began, but also shot up last week alongside the significant events in the United States (Figure 6). Again we should not paint all countries with the same brush.

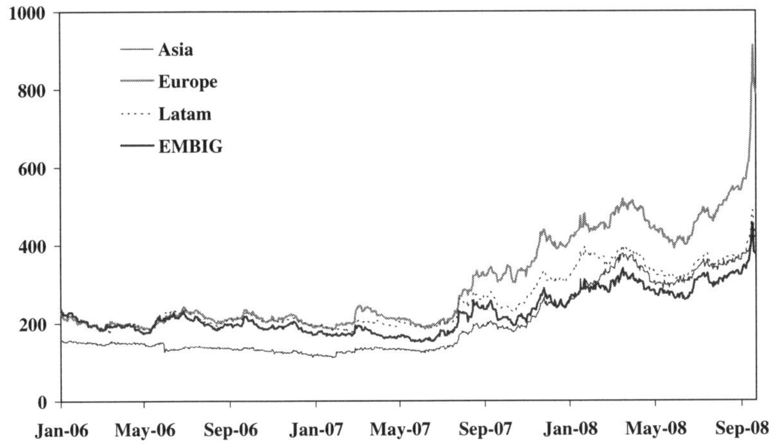

Figure 5. EM — Corporate Bond Spreads (In Basis Points).
Source: Bloomberg L.P.

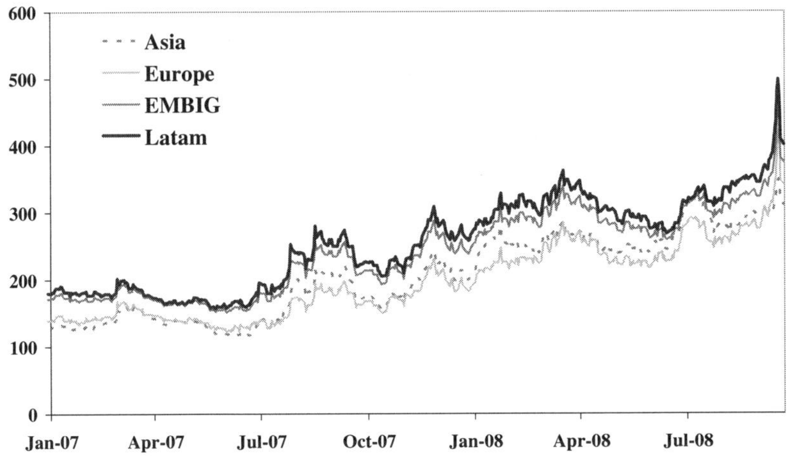

Figure 6. EM — External Debt Market Spreads (In Basis Points).
Source: Bloomberg L.P.

Some countries' spreads have moved relatively little, while others have reached levels in excess of previous crises.

During most of this crisis, emerging market currencies have not been at the center of attention. We normally worry about devastating depreciations

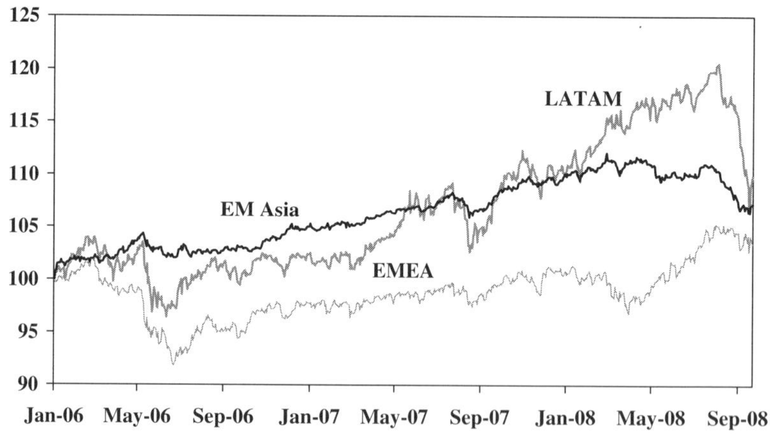

Figure 7. Currencies (January 2006 = 100; versus U.S. Dollors).
Source: Bloomberg L.P.

in countries suffering crisis or contagion effects. For most of the duration of the crisis, currency appreciations (in nominal) terms have been more prevalent (Figure 7). It has only been in the last week or so that we have seen significant changes in currency values vis-à-vis the dollar, with countries in Latin American suffering the most.

Again, there has been a fair amount of differentiation across countries, with implied currency volatility increasing for some currencies much more than others (Figure 8).

2. Why?

So why have the effects on the rest of the world been so delayed and how did most emerging market countries manage, at least until now, to avoid most of the subprime crisis?

Looking most directly at what went wrong in advanced economies — the issuance of a lot of subprime mortgages and the packaging of mortgages into all sorts of structured credit products — the reason that emerging market economies were less affected seems self evident. Most did not develop the types of mortgages sold in the United States, and most were only just beginning to adopt the securitization methods of the United States, if at all. In short, there were hardly any indigenous subprime

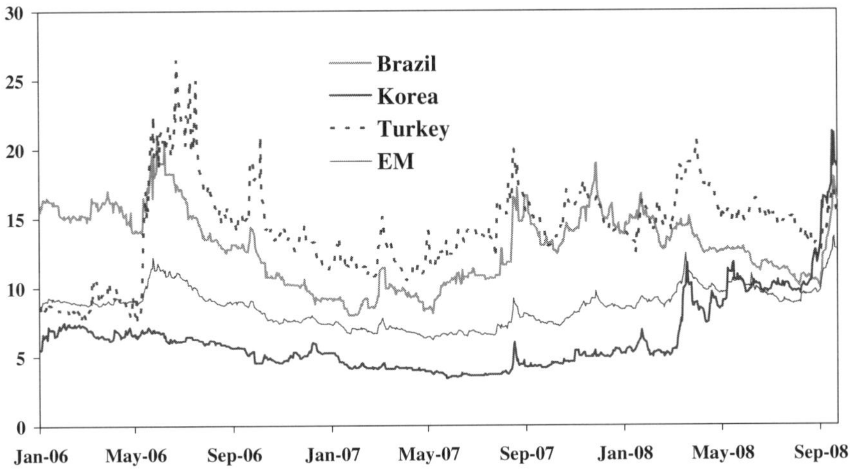

Figure 8. Implied Currency Volatility (In %, 3-Months).
Source: Bloomberg L.P.

mortgages or structured products based on mortgages in most other countries.

Moreover, most of the securities produced in the United States were not purchased by investors in emerging market economies. Our reckoning is that a few were purchased by Asian countries, but hardly any (Figure 9). Our loss estimates suggest that the vast majority of the U.S.-structured credit and loan losses will be borne by the United States and western Europe.

If we look more deeply at the reasons for the subprime issuance and the growth of structured credit products, we can see why the rest of the world is less immune to the crisis. The underpinnings of the U.S. phenomenon were global. That is, global liquidity, low nominal yields, and hence the ability and desire to take risks were nearly everywhere. It is just that these underlying factors manifested themselves differently depending on the available investments. For instance, in emerging Europe, the low yields and abundant liquidity allowed local banks and subsidiaries of larger western European banks to extend credit to less creditworthy borrowers than before. In some countries, the money went into real estate and some others into equity markets. Thus, while it may have looked like the subprime crisis might pass by emerging market countries because they

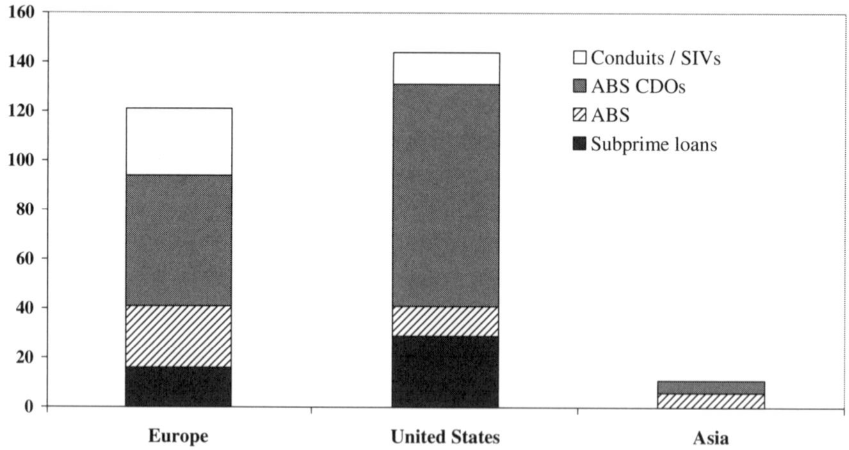

Figure 9. Expected Bank Losses as of March 2008 (In Billions of U.S. Dollors).
Sources: Goldman Sachs; UBS; and IMF staff estimates.
Note: Losses aggregted over a five year period. ABS = asset-backed securities; CDPs = collateralized debt obligations; SIVs = structured investment vehicles.

were "behind the curve" in terms of constructing complex structured credit products, there were still common factors that were making many emerging market countries vulnerable to changes in external conditions.

So why did the effects on emerging markets take so long to manifest themselves and only now are we seeing the more serious effects? One reason is that flows into these markets from foreigner investors were still quite robust following the onset of the crisis. Total bond, equity, and loans did fall in the fourth quarter of 2007 as the crisis became evident, but picked up in early 2008 as some felt emerging markets may provide a safe haven and diversification from the turmoil (Figure 10). Flows of most types have fallen, but were still positive, going into the second quarter of 2008. It is also useful to recognize that the economies of most of the rest of world have helped as well — economic growth has remained high — almost twice as high as the 1980–2000 average. And thus, domestic interest in financial markets — equities specifically — has been robust.

Now, however, we are seeing a more substantial pull-back from risky assets of all types. With such dramatic events in advanced countries coming to the fore, so-called risk aversion is rising rapidly (Figure 11).

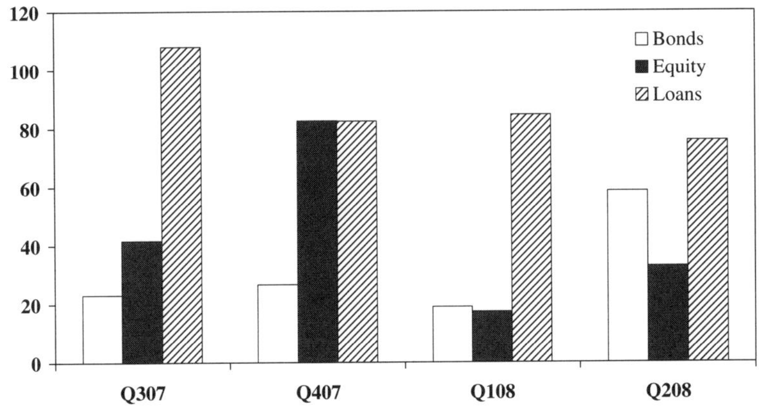

Figure 10. EM — Bond, Equity, and Loan Issuance (In Billions of U.S. Dollors).
Source: Data provided by the Bond, Equity and Loan database of the International Monetary Fund sourced from Dealogic.

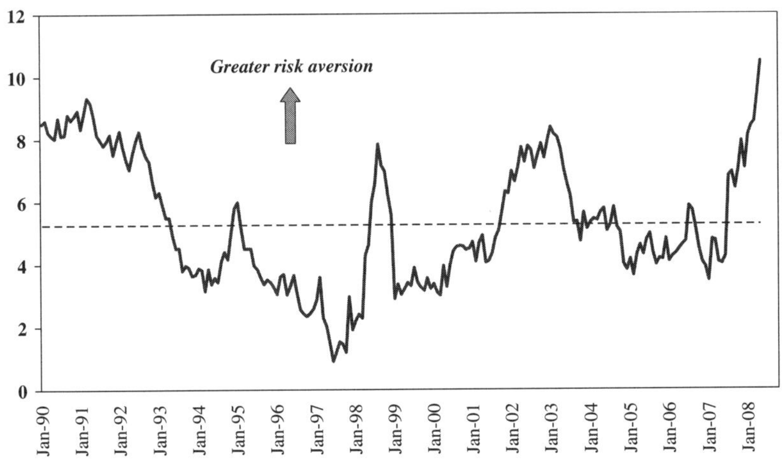

Figure 11. Goldman Sachs Risk Aversion Index.
Source: Goldman Sachs.

More concretely, the ability of foreign investors to finance positions is now seriously impaired. Money markets rates, and the related repo financing rates, have risen precipitously. Those depending on any sort of collateralized or uncollateralized financing — such as hedge funds and

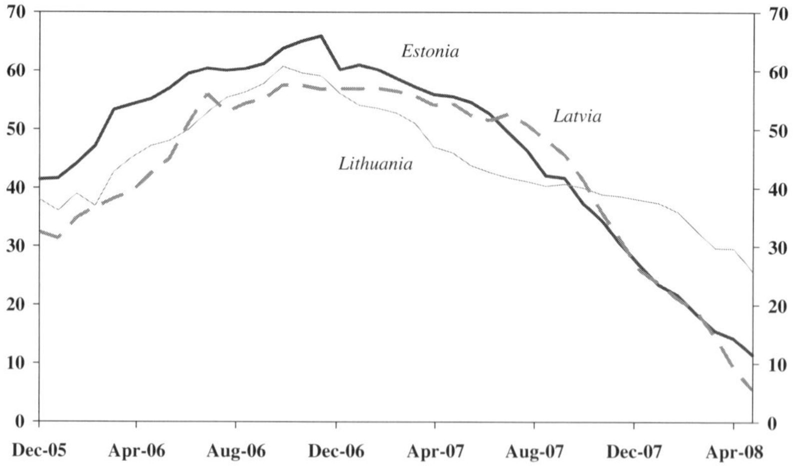

Figure 12. Baltic States: Bank Loan Growth to Nonfinancial Private Sector (In Percent Real Terms, Year-On-Year Change).
Sources: Bloomberg L.P.; European Central Bank; and IMF staff estimates.

other asset managers — are finding it far more difficult to find money to invest on a leveraged basis.

As liquidity tightens, so do credit markets and the ability to lend. This in turn affects housing markets through availability of mortgages. These sorts of effects are currently most acute in countries that had large run-ups in house prices — places such as the Baltics, where now growth of non-financial private credit has declined precipitously and GDP growth has been negative for Latvia and Estonia for the last two quarter (Figure 12).

3. Who? Linkages Known and Unknown

The question of the day seems to be "who is next?". Of course, this question is applied mainly to institutions, and mainly to those in the United States. But it is also being asked more broadly "which countries are likely to be most affected." Answering either of these questions is very difficult without a lot of information and thorough analysis, but let me simply point to some linkages that we know about and some that we are just discovering.

First, we are all aware that, broadly speaking, equity markets around the world are more integrated and that information about the largest companies

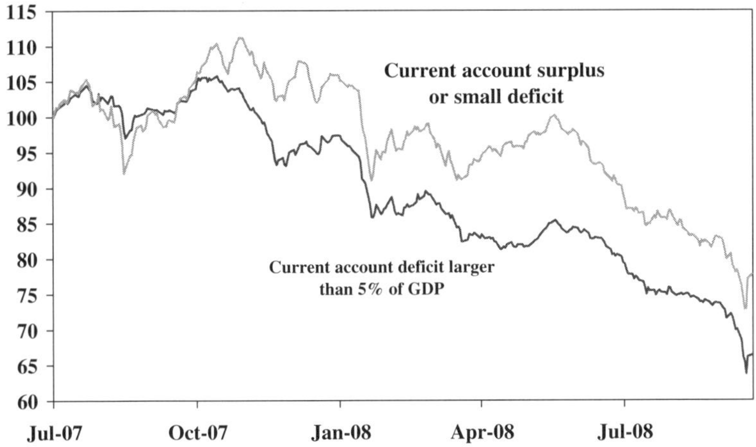

Figure 13. EM — Equity Prices (Index 7/1/2007 = 100).
Source: IMF, World Economic Outlook database.

in each market travels fast. We can expect these linkages to be active. Still, investors are differentiating across countries more than they were before. For instance, if one separates those countries that have current account deficits greater than 5 percent of GDP, we find that their equity prices have underperformed, or have been lower, than those with current account deficits less than 5 percent of GDP since the start of the crisis (Figure 13). A similar story exists for sovereign Credit Default Swap (CDS) spreads.

Second, sovereign bond markets are highly dependent on global factors — particularly monetary policy changes in the United States and so-called global risk aversion, a variable that shows up with a great deal of force in many models of price determination — as well as domestic factors. We can expect these markets to be affected and the differentials will depend on how well the domestic factors — such as amount of official reserves, current account to GDP ratios, sovereign external debt levels and government deficits, the credibility of policies, and so on — hold up following their improvement in recent years.

In the area of sovereign bond markets, let me just highlight a couple of points. While we broadly believe emerging markets are in better shape than in the past, one should be a bit careful about such generalizations. One is the fact that overall, emerging markets are running current account surpluses, but this fact is based on the current account surpluses of 5 emerging market countries — China, Russia, Algeria, Venezuela, and Malaysia. Taking some 44 other emerging market countries, the current account deficits have increased to $337 billion in 2008 from $160 billion in 2007 and only $80 billion in 2006. The dependence on oil is a big part of the discrepancy, as oil exporters are still seeing some improvement in their external balances even with falling oil prices, while at the same time oil importers are seeing further degradation.

Third, it is the linkage based on support to the banking system from flows from other countries. Many countries in emerging Europe and Latin America depend on parent banks in other jurisdictions. In fact, despite the attention placed on emerging Europe, Bank for International Settlements statistics about exposures of industrial countries to various emerging market countries show that the exposure to Asian emerging market countries amounts to about $900 billion whereas the exposure of emerging Europe is nearly the same. The exposure of industrial country banks to Latin America is about half that at slightly below $450 billion. This indirect credit channel whereby industrial country banks to fund their subsidiaries or lend directly to EM countries is also a very important connection.

These linkages are now the ones that are very active, but in perhaps a different way and not just between advanced and emerging market countries. In this latest bout of liquidity strains, we are seeing that banks in many countries are pulling out of interbank markets — both in a cross-border sense, but also domestically. Denmark for instance has had difficulties lately with its central bank attempting to supply liquidity. Countries and regions in the Far East, Hong Kong specifically, are also suffering their own counterparty credit concerns as even just a few banks are rumored to buckle. Thus, even if there are "regular" so-called healthy failures in a banking system, the effects of the crisis and its failure to be resolved at the epicenter is now affecting the confidence in other money markets and these markets are starting to seize up.

The linkages we are learning more about are those related to Over-The-Counter (OTC) derivative holdings. Both traditional OTC derivatives, such as interest rate swaps, and the ones that have been initiated in recent years, such as credit default swaps, are relevant. The most critical is the credit default swap market amounting to some $54.4 trillion as of the first half of 2008. There are CDS contracts on emerging market sovereigns, on large emerging market corporates, and on emerging market banks. Who holds these contracts is becoming more evident as various offsets are applied following the bankruptcy of Lehman and the distress at the AIG insurance company.

Looking forward, there will likely be other linkages across banking institutions that may not be very visible now as many banks attempt diversify their funding sources. For instance, sourcing retail deposits abroad has become more popular in recent months, setting up linkages that may make work-outs of various types of bank failures more difficult to execute. For instance, Icelandic banks are attempting to gain foreign retail deposit accounts to help fund their banks.

4. What's Next?

An even harder question is "what's next" for the fallout of the subprime crisis. So far, the United States is still the epicenter, but the shock waves are getting larger and are affecting more countries, institutions, and people. As regards emerging market countries, it is at least somewhat comforting that they are, over all, in better shape to withstand the shock waves than before.

Many countries have built up substantial reserves; a few are running current account surpluses and many of those are due to still-elevated commodities prices — of these, many have put away their export earnings into sovereign wealth funds. Many countries have genuinely improved their fiscal position, but how durable these improvements are will become clearer if conditions deteriorate. Policymaking institutions, overall, are better equipped and those governments run by centrists are likely to get a more positive reception in international markets than by leftists; central bankers had brought down inflation, but are having difficulty in trying to keep their hard-won gains as inflation rises.

Thus, even if the shock waves continue, as they are likely to do, for the most part, the "rest of the world" is better able to withstand the waves better than in previous periods.

5. What Can Anyone Do about It?

Lastly, let me address a final question: "What can anyone do about it?" For those on the receiving end of the crisis, it is hard to influence the direct response that needs to be taken at the heart of the crisis.

In the short-run, then the answer is to prepare for the shock waves. Crisis planning — fixing the weak spots in the infrastructure (such as payment systems and clearing houses). Make sure those that may need liquidity in times of need can receive it easily, without having to set up accounts at the central bank or elsewhere. Coordinating with other authorities — both from the countries where the shocks may originate and among those that might be recipients. Being forthright about what is being done will help remove uncertainties that bring panic.

In the longer-run, clearly the job of those at the forefront of the crisis and those that are not, is to put in place a better means of managing leverage and risk-taking, and removing a reward structure that ends in self-fulfilling crises. This job is not just for policymakers and governmental authorities (although supervision and regulation was weak and will need to be made stronger), but also for the private sector. Thank you for your time.

III. HOW SERIOUS IS THE DAMAGE?

Bank Failures: The Limitations of Risk Modeling

Patrick Honohan*

Trinity College and Center for Economic Policy Research

1. Introduction and Summary

Overconfidence on the part of bankers and regulators in mechanical risk-management models has been the distinct driver of bank failures in the current crisis. As the inadequacy of these models became evident, exposing the vulnerability of all market participants, a revulsion to risk set in. This dynamic impacted different institutions in somewhat different ways. Some large banks were sufficiently diversified to survive heavy losses; in contrast, some smaller banks were grossly overcommitted to risky strategies, and were ruined by their gambles; a third group comprised institutions too opaque to survive in the market when risk aversion and risk perceptions increased. Falling house prices increasingly drove failures of overleveraged mortgage lenders.

Drawing on case studies from the first 16 large banks that failed, as well as on the experiences of one large bank that survived this part of the crisis thanks to its size and diversification, this paper illustrates how the risk-management dynamic translated into the failure of individual financial firms. The key implication of the cases is the need for a return to a more holistic and less mechanical approach to risk management and prudential regulation.

Events and decisions at banks and other financial intermediaries are at the heart of all banking crises. Each crisis triggers a learning process

* Patrick Honohan is a professor of international financial economics and development in the Department of Economics and Institute for International Integration Studies at Trinity College Dublin and a research fellow at the Center for Economic Policy Research (CEPR). E-mail: phonohan@tcd.ie. The author thanks Chris Kent for a helpful discussion.

and corrective measures are designed to prevent a repetition. But, like viruses, banking crises display small but crucial mutations on each return. It is these mutations which mean that even experienced and well-trained risk managers who believe they have insulated their systems against the causes of crisis can be caught out by its emergence in a slightly different guise.

The really distinctive feature this time was the overreliance by bankers and regulators on a new generation of mechanical models of risk. Lulled into a fall sense of security by exaggerated beliefs about the efficacy of these models, banks proceeded to operate huge volumes of business with wafer-thin margins of both capital and liquidity.[1]

Some other features of the crisis may seem new, but are not fundamentally so (Caprio *et al.*, 2005; Honohan, 1997). For example, the originate-to-distribute model for mortgages is certainly a key and damaging aspect of what we have recently seen — and has been damaging to the borrower in a way that may appear new. But the underlying problem with the originate-to-distribute model is essentially the same as that of the skewed incentive packages offered to many traders now and to loan officers in the not-so-distant past. Much as the mortgage originators do not hold the mortgages on their books, so the loan officer was often not around to see his poorly underwritten loan book come unstuck. And how different is the distress of the evicted borrower who has been oversold a mortgage from that of the developing country sovereign on whom petrodollar loans were pressed in the 1970s?

Some observers have dubbed this the "structured finance crisis", and this is not a bad description. Indeed, the financial engineering revolution which enabled the use of complex instruments to pool and hedge risks has been a key driving force setting the scene for subsequent failures. It drove growth in financial intermediation as it offered low-cost automation of risk-management functions thereby allowing new markets, especially retail markets, to be reached. But surely those who foresee only a moderation and improvement — not an abandonment — of structured finance are correct.

Instead, it has been the overreliance on what has proved to be unrealistically simple mechanical risk-management models that has turned

---

[1] Calomiris (2008) suggests that risk models were being used to provide "plausible deniability" for conflicted agents and intermediaries rather than being truly believed as risk-management tools.

structured finance into the lethal weapon it has become. It was only because (at some level) risk-takers believed that the models were good enough that the structures became so complex and opaque (Honohan, 2008).

Banking is a volume business, and the 20th century saw a historic rise in leverage, however measured. But the explosion of gross positions and gross transactions that has been seen in the past two decades took the risk pyramid into new territory, placing risk models under severe strain. Slight errors in the models are amplified by the volume of transactions. The cliff-edge type consequences of model error in some structured transactions only make this worse (cf. Joint Forum, 2008). Likewise, basis risk can assume an enormous institution-engulfing scale. This is what we see in the case studies. In principle, those risks could be rewarded sufficiently well to justify the capital cushion that would be needed to truly give adequate assurance of solvency. But, in practice, the negotiated margins have too often been slender indeed, the risks scarcely noticed let alone adequately assessed, and capital assigned zero or negligible.

For smaller participants, much of the reliance on models was indirect: by relying on rating agencies, they were trusting the models used by the raters. They were also trusting the raters. Calomiris (2008) has stressed the agency problems involved here, as did many *ex ante* (cf. Honohan, 2001). Agency was not the only problem; market participants were dazzled by the new technology and believed it would work far better than it was ever going to be possible.

Unwarranted confidence in risk models also had a systemic effect on market participants' expectations regarding the likely availability of funding liquidity. If everyone's risk models were so good, one could ignore the negligible chance of a contagious loss of market confidence leading to a drying-up of funding liquidity to a solvent bank. Hence the overleveraging occurred in liquidity as well as on the other side of the balance sheet.

There are policy implications. For all that rules may trump discretion in monetary policy, the opposite seems true for banking risk and bank regulation. The rules of Basel II are no better than those being applied by market participants. Quite apart from the procyclical and herding effects which rules-based regulation may induce (as has been argued for example by Dewatripont and Tirole, 1994; Goodhart and Persaud, 2008; Greenlaw *et al.*, 2008), the rules simply do not represent a sufficiently precise tool for risk management. The Basel Committee's working groups are currently revising and adapting the rules to acknowledge some of the most glaring omissions — a Sisyphean task. The limitations of the rules need to be recognized and a greater discretionary and judgmental element restored to risk management.[2] That will often mean requiring more capital than the rules calculate and that, in turn, raises numerous complexities about level playing fields, the political pressure on and even corruption of regulators (a point stressed by Barth, Caprio, and Levine, 2005). This will all make different and, in some respects, greater intellectual demands on risk managers, both regulators and regulated.

2. Four Failure Categories

Before the introduction in many countries of general bank recapitalization and support schemes made it hard to distinguish between failure and voluntary capital strengthening, 16 medium or large European and U.S. banks and a large insurance company had failed.[3] There is much to be learned from these and other case studies.

I begin with the important category of banks that make and report huge losses but survived — at least until the introduction of blanket assistance schemes in October 2008 — without government assistance. These *diversified survivors* managed to avoid failure because they were sufficiently large and diversified to have been able to raise additional capital to replace those eroded by credit losses. My main example here is UBS (Union Bank of Switzerland); numerous other cases exist from Citibank ("Citi") down.

Every crisis sweeps away some incompetent, reckless, or corrupt bankers and their banks. This is the second category: the *ruined gamblers*. The main case here is Sachsen LB, and I mention some other which fall into the same kind of area, notably IndyMac and IKB Deutsche Industriebank.

---

[2] Note that models that are good enough for private sector decisions may not be good enough for public regulation. The risk–return trade-off that each is conducting is complementary to, not the same as, the other. For example, beyond the total probability of insolvency, the probability density for payoffs in the insolvency zone may be of no interest to the owner of a financial intermediary.

[3] Total assets in excess of US$10 billion or prospective deficiency in excess of US$2 billion. Failure here is defined broadly to include receipt of exceptional case-specific financial assistance, including takeovers brokered by the deposit insurer.

Then there is the important category of firms that proved *too opaque to survive* in the market and ran out of liquidity. My main example of this type is the simplest one: Northern Rock — indeed one of its misfortunes was to face liquidity problems before this became widespread. Much more complex and opaque cases were the investment banks Bear Stearns (rescued) and Lehman (not rescued). Probably Fortis, Dexia, and Hypo, which received sizable government rescue injections in late September 2008, are also in this category. Mention is also made of AIG — not a bank, but caught up in the crisis through insuring banks (notably with credit default swaps) and falling likely into the "too opaque" category.

The final category, and one which seems likely to grow, is mortgage lenders whose main problem was to be too leveraged in a weak property market. I discuss the two largest U.S. government-sponsored financial agencies Fannie Mae and Freddie Mac. Other cases which could be mentioned under this heading are Washington Mutual, which became the biggest regulated bank to fail in U.S. history in September 2008, and Bradford and Bingley, intervened by the U.K. government at the end of that month. With the continuing decline in property prices in many countries and the deepening recession, the prospect of more banks falling into this category was increasingly evident.

With the introduction of blanket capital injection, guarantee, and lending schemes by the U.S. and most European Union (EU) governments in October 2008, a blurring of the boundaries occurred. In order to restore improved functioning of the interbank market and relieve the credit crunch, assistance under these schemes was extended to banks which were not failing. This makes it difficult to identify subsequent bank failures in that a failing bank receiving assistance under such schemes could masquerade as healthy.

2.1 *Case A: "Diversified survivor" — UBS*

Unlike the other main cases examined, UBS had not failed before the general government capitalization and support schemes began to be introduced in October 2008, at which time it did avail itself of the Swiss government's offer of a capital injection. Its survival through the early stages of the crisis was in spite of reporting by early 2008 losses in excess of US$40 billion — much larger than any of the others. The reason is not only that UBS is a much larger entity, indeed it is one of the world's largest banks (being ranked second in the world at end-2006 by total assets and 20th in the world by equity capital in *Euromoney*'s mid-2007 listing and one of about 15 groups classified by the Bank of England as large and complex financial intermediaries, LCFIs), but also because it has been subject both to the standard international regime of capital adequacy (Basel I and now Basel II) and to the market discipline that demands even more capital from banks that wish to source uninsured funding in the market. Nevertheless, it has been a fairly close-run thing. Thus, at mid-2007, before the crisis broke, UBS had CHF (Swiss francs) 51 billion (US$42 billion) of capital. By end-March 2008, this had eroded to CHF 16 billion (US$16 billion) before capital raising efforts to offset losses incurred brought the total back up to CHF 44 billion (US$44 billion) by mid-2008.

The experience of UBS, large losses related to acquisition of mainly U.S.-based mortgage-backed securities (MBS), is clearly similar in several respects to the large losses made by other LCFIs. It has been better documented so far and therefore serves as a useful exemplar of a half a dozen other cases of large losses by large banks.

Even though the losses could be and were absorbed by the shareholders, they represented a severe blow for a bank which prided itself on — and was widely admired for — its risk management.[4] And they occurred and were reported early in the crisis and cannot be blamed on a generalized downturn. In fact, as is revealed by a report to the shareholders following an independent consultant's *post mortem* (UBS, 2008), the failure must clearly be laid at the door of the risk-management system itself. It was not sufficiently elaborate to capture the full dimensionality of the risks being undertaken by this complex institution: Short cuts were taken in the interest of having prompt information available, but these short cuts could be and were systematically gamed by ambitious operations staff who took very large risks but seem to have structured them in such a way that they did not show up at all in the calculation of risk and therefore triggered neither the capital charge nor the kinds of trading limits that would have been warranted.

Many of the MBS which contributed so much to UBS' losses were being warehoused for sale to other entities. Evidently, the mark-to-market value of these assets fell sharply during 2007. In broad terms, what

[4] For example, winning *Euromoney* magazine's "Global Best Risk Management House" award for excellence in 2005.

appears to have happened — in respect of at least some of the losses — is that insurance and derivatives were bought to hedge only the amount of variation (known to the traders) to which the portfolio was being stress-tested.[5] Market fluctuations larger than envisaged in the stress test were not hedged (otherwise the profit potential of the positions being taken would have been eliminated). In other words, the profits being booked (in the relevant parts of the business) arose primarily because of — and were the reward for — the assumption of catastrophic risk outside that envisaged in the stress test. Senior management understood that certain units were taking large positions, but they assumed that the risk models were good enough to protect against serious loss. Perhaps they would have been good enough if not gamed, but they were not perfect, and that they were gamed was perhaps inevitable.

Indeed, already in 2006–07 the bank's senior management had coped with an explicit attempt by a significant segment of its capital markets staff to escape from the constraints of the bank's austere risk-management structures. Hughes, Larsen, and Simonian (2008) recount the establishment of a hedge-fund subsidiary whose activities would not be scrutinized by the bank's risk-management systems in a detailed way, but only as an equity investment. The mispriced risks soon undertaken by the newly liberated subsidiary quickly proved to be large. The bank realized its strategic error, reported significant losses, and folded the capital markets unit back into the normal risk-management system.

Huge gross volumes of business built on wafer-thin capital by an entity with access to the world's best financial engineering and mathematical risk models: This makes UBS a prime exhibit for our argument that too much unthinking reliance has been placed in the precision of mechanical models leading to extraordinary losses when the models prove inadequate.

2.2 *Case B: "Ruined gambler" — Sachsen Landesbank*

Established in 1992 after German reunification, Leipzig-based Sachsen was the smallest and newest of the German state banks. Because of legislation

[5] The bank states that "this level of hedging was based on statistical analyses of historical price movements that indicated that such protection was sufficient to protect UBS from any losses on the position", (UBS, 2008, p. 14). The level of hedging also seems to have been designed to meet internal risk-management rules (Hughes, Larsen, and Simonian, 2008).

intended to level the EU playing field, these banks lost the competitive advantage of a state guarantee of deposits at the beginning of July 2005. Media reports suggesting a less than stellar top management and board-room skills combined with a desperate need for a new source of profits to allow the bank to survive as a profitable entry likely point to other important characteristics. This back story helps to explain why large and growing profits from an offshore affiliate (based in Dublin's International Financial Services Centre) seem to have been uncritically welcomed by the bank's top decisionmakers.

The affiliate's business plan resembled what many other banks were doing; only its scale differed, relative to the scale of the sponsoring bank. It had established off-balance-sheet "conduits" to hold mainly U.S. mortgage-backed securities in a volume equivalent to about one-third of the parent bank's balance sheet. These highly rated securities were financed by short-term borrowing in the market at rates very slightly finer than the securities were yielding. The Dublin operation contributed 90 percent of the group's total profit in 2006. The catch, from Sachsen's point of view, was that the conduits had also been given in effect a back-up loan facility from the parent bank Sachsen itself. Failure to rollover its borrowings would lead to the conduit calling on Sachsen to provide the refinancing. The scale of the commitment was huge: the eventual rescue involved a liquidity injection approaching 25 percent of the total balance sheet of the parent bank.

A reading of Sachsen's 2007 *Annual Report* (p. 81) suggests that the risk-management systems of the bank did not consider this as credit or liquidity risk, but merely as an operational risk, on the argument that only some operational failure could lead to the loan facility being drawn down. As such, it was assigned a very low risk weight requiring little or no capital.

Press reports indicate that the German banking regulator Bundesanstalt für Finanzdienstleistungsaufsicht (BaFin) was not altogether happy with the risks surrounding the activities of the Dublin affiliate of Sachsen. The BaFin had commissioned a special onsite study by external consultants KPMG as far back as August 2004; who are reported to have made some very critical comments, but who may also have been unlucky in their sampling of the funds and conduits, so that they did not see the worst of the portfolio (Balzli, Schießl, and Winters, 2008).

With repeated downgrades of mortgage-backed securities and the seizing-up of European money markets in the late summer of 2007, the scale and costs of the Dublin commitments became evident to all.

Conduits could not be refinanced and Sachsen could not itself borrow enough in the market.

The prospect of Sachsen failing, and official fears that this would result in a systemically damaging market reassessment of the credit risk of German financial institutions, prompted a pool of banks to step in (August 17, 2007) with a temporary credit line for the conduits, at a penalty rate.[6]

After several months of negotiation, Sachsen was sold to another German state bank, the much larger Stuttgart-based LBBW, which has continued Sachsen's regional small and medium enterprises and other business under its old name in its existing regional market, which complements that of the purchaser.

Costs and losses: The transactions surrounding the sale of Sachsen and write-downs and losses over the past year are quite complex but in broad terms it appears that the owners have lost about €1.5 billion from Sachsen's MBS adventure, a rather small sum, compared with some of the other banks (and compared with the scale of the liquidity bailout) but enough to wipe-out the end-2006 book value of Sachsen's capital. There is still a contingent liability from a new "super-structured investment vehicle (SIV)" created to hold some of the worst-performing parts of mortgage-backed portfolio, totaling €17.3 billion. This structure benefits from a first-loss guarantee of €2.75 billion from the State Government of Saxony (which was in effect a controlling shareholder of Sachsen Bank before the sale). That guarantee is 2.5 times LBBW's worst case stress-test estimate of the negative value of the super-SIV.

The crucial error at the heart of Sachsen's business model was not so much its reliance on underpriced guarantees from the parent to its off-balance-sheet vehicles, but the scale on which these guarantees were made in relation to capital. They "bet the bank" on the validity of the ratings and lost.[7]

---

[6] At least 50 basis points of penalty (European Commission 2008); this penalty was equivalent to 5 percent per annum on the end-2006 capital of the bank.

[7] From this point of view, the case of the other small German bank IKB is somewhat contrasting. They also acquired MBS both on- and off-balance-sheet and their crisis was also triggered by a failure (at end-July 2007) to rollover short-term financing for an off-balance-sheet vehicle to which they had guaranteed a line of credit which they were unable to deliver. But IKB had taken much lower-rated tranches: for example only 73 percent of their sizable on-balance-sheet MBS were rated AAA or AA. A rescue led by the large development bank KfW (owned by the German federal government) was organized. Eventually the sale of IKB to a venture capital fund was announced in August 2008; KfW stated that its losses from the IKB rescue would be about €8 billion.

2.3 *Case C: "Too opaque to survive in the market" — Northern Rock*

Northern Rock (NR), a moderate-sized mortgage bank based in the North of England and which saw exceptionally rapid growth in the past decade, generated the most spectacular events of the early weeks of the crisis when, on September 14, 2007, retail depositors flocked to queue at all of its branches to withdraw their funds. The run was triggered when the announcement of a liquidity support package by the authorities failed to include any clear assurance to depositors that their money was safe.[8] At the time, the U.K. deposit insurance scheme fully guaranteed only the first £2,000, plus 90 percent of the next £33,000 of the depositor's funds — and the scheme had no track record of prompt payment.

Like Sachsen, NR's immediate difficulties arose from its inability to rollover short-term wholesale funding on which it relied very heavily as part of their overall lending-driven growth strategy. The growth had been vigorous: total assets under management grew from just over £20 billion at end-1999 to over £100 billion at end-2006. All but £11 billion of this growth was funded through wholesale resources: retail deposits equaled only 22 percent of the total by end-2006. Indeed, so good was NR thought to be at this end of its business that it received the *International Financing Review*'s prestigious "Financial Institution Group Borrower of the Year" award for 2006. And its internal risk procedures were highly considered by its regulator, the U.K. Financial Services Authority (FSA): earlier in 2007, it was granted the Basel II "waiver" allowing it to lower its capital requirement by calculating it on the basis of internal ratings.

Although its operations did involve securitizations funded through special purpose vehicles, constructed for the purpose of generating and separately financing highly rated tranches of MBS, the underlying assets being financed were in the main originated by NR itself (rather than being part of the U.S. subprime market).[9] NR was popular with its borrowers,

[8] The tripartite statement by the Bank of England, the Treasury, and the Financial Services Authority (FSA, the regulator) could have been read as indicating that the liquidity support was conditional on Northern Rock having sufficient "appropriate" collateral, and that the FSA's opinion that Northern Rock was solvent was not shared by the other two authorities. The statement is at http://www.bankofengland.co.uk/publications/news/2007/090.htm

[9] Note that the accounts of the special purpose entities created to hold the securitized mortgages were consolidated line-by-line into NR's accounts, a practice that was not followed at Sachsen.

and there has been little suggestion of the kinds of abuses involving pressure sales, fraudulent valuations, documentation, and the like associated with the U.S. subprime market. But with market sentiment moving against MBS and spreads rising, NR was particularly badly hit by funding difficulties. Even if they could roll over the funding at prevailing rates in the market, the higher spreads were on such volumes of business that the whole bank would become severely loss-making. Besides, the market was aware of NR's liberal lending (which included lending combinations amounting to 125 percent loan-to-value ratio) and inferred that NR's loan loss ratios would be above industry average as the market turned down.

The market's refusal to roll over the funds sent NR to the Bank of England. The latter was at first reluctant to accommodate because NR was unable to provide collateral to the Bank's normal standards. Eventually, after a conspicuous delay and public statements which accelerated NR's funding difficulties, the Bank acceded to the largest liquidity loan provided by any central bank up to that time.[10] NR depositors' funds were unconditionally guaranteed by the U.K. Treasury (which also embarked on an overhaul of the deposit insurance scheme, eliminating the deductible and increasing coverage).

Continued high funding costs, continued falls in house prices in the North of England, and rising delinquencies made sourcing new equity for NR difficult. Eventually it was taken into "temporary" public ownership (shareholders are to be compensated on the basis of an independent valuation), and some £3 billion of the Bank of England's loan was converted into equity provided by the U.K. Treasury.

Underestimating the volatility in the cost and availability of wholesale funding was a serious error, which led NR to leave itself very exposed. Given its rollover needs, even the £5.9 billion it had in cash in early September 2008 counted for little. It could be said that part of the NR's woes were attributable to the self-fulfilling fears of wholesale funders; by withholding their funding, they made NR's business model unsustainable. But at a deeper level, the model itself was highly vulnerable, with no fall-back position. Even a small deterioration in its funding costs was always on the cards. Once again a mechanical model — this time of liquidity

---

[10] By end-2007, NR's indebtedness to the Bank of England stood at £28.5 billion = US$56.9 billion (€38.6 billion).

availability rather than market or credit risks — had been exploited beyond its range of reliability. Not only did the bank build a very large business on fragile funding, but the business it built embodied very evident credit risks (growth, loan-to-value) that inevitably fed back on the margin of confidence of its wholesale funders.

The NR's capital cushion was also low, and was being pared down as much as possible: indeed, the bank's 2006 *Annual Report* (published in March 2007) noted with satisfaction that the soon-to-be implemented regime of Basel II would allow NR to cut capital even further (a fact which should give pause to enthusiasts of Basel II and those who feel that small modifications to the Basel II capital adequacy mechanics are all that is needed).

It remains to be seen just how well NR's mortgage book performs through the coming years. Could the firm have survived if it had been able to secure funding on a continuing basis at average market rates? This is not yet clear.

Other banks also suffered runs[11]:

Bear Stearns became the biggest early victim of the crisis despite its huge pool of liquidity totaling US$18 billion just days before it ran out of cash (like other investment banks, its liabilities were very short-term in nature). Its creditors were wholesale institutions. When Bear Stearns had lost its credit[12] with them, the whole structure imploded, as its franchise (common with that of the other investment banks) was based on its credit and its teams of skilled wholesale financiers: the former was gone, the latter both mobile and ineffective without access to funds (Burrough, 2008; Kelly, 2008). This failure prompted official intervention, not least because of Bear Stearns' central role as a market maker in the credit default swap market. Interestingly, Bear Stearns subsequently published a balance sheet as of February 29, 2008 — just over two weeks before it failed — showing shareholders equity at a satisfactory US$12 billion. If this is correct

[11] Two other cases where runs led to failure in early October 2008, Belgium's Dexia and Germany's Hypo RE, were both wholesale concerns whose reliance on short-term funding became a fatal weakness as money markets seized up.

[12] Aa with the GSEs, there has been the suggestion that speculators, having taken a short position, spread rumors about the insolvency of Bear Stearns with the intention of driving down the share price. However, restrictions subsequently imposed on short-selling of certain firms' shares have not resulted in outperfomance of those shares since (Brunnermeier, 2008).

(and that will not become clear for some time), it implies that Bear Stearns was a classic Bagehot-type case, unusual enough in the crises of recent years: a solvent bank that became illiquid because of loss of market confidence.

Lehman Brothers and AIG insurance group are two other complex financial institutions which foundered because the market lost confidence in their solvency. Lehman became unable to secure the continued wholesale financing on which its business model, like that of Bear Stearns, relied. Despite its size and the elaborate structure of customer links in its business, the federal authorities decided it was neither too big nor too connected to preclude allowing failure and it filed for bankruptcy on September 15, 2008, at the start of what was to become a week of exceptional market turbulence.[13,14] Later that week, the even larger insurance group AIG saw its credit ratings downgraded, triggering significant margin calls which gave rise to an immediate requirement for emergency access to liquidity. In this case, bankruptcy was averted by the establishment of a special revolving loan facility of up to US$85 billion at the extraordinarily high interest rate of LIBOR (London interbank offered rate) plus 8.5 percent. (The Fed was also to receive warrants for almost 80 percent of AIG's equity). This facility (subsequently augmented) exceeded the previous record for an emergency loan by a central bank established by Northern Rock. The interest premium will partly compensate the Fed for credit risk, and also provide a strong incentive for AIG to liquidate assets and downsize. In the market conditions of mid-September, it was impossible to say whether AIG or Lehman were solvent in underlying asset value terms. Both proved to be too opaque to survive in the market. The decision to rescue one and not the other was likely based more on the relative disruptive consequences.

---

[13] Several money market mutual funds held Lehman debt at the time of the bankruptcy. One of the largest, Reserve Primary saw its net asset value fall consequentially below par value — not a failure event *per se*, but quite exceptional for such funds. This led within days to the introduction by the authorities of an insurance facility for money market funds, as well as other measures to support the high quality asset-backed commercial paper market through direct official purchases and non-recourse lending to banks collateralized by ABCP acquired effectively at cost from money market funds.

[14] The proposed purchase of Merrill Lynch by Bank of America, and of Britain's HBOS by Lloyd's Bank were the largest other institutional ownership restructurings announced that week.

Fortis, which was rescued by a government[15] injection of equity funds at end-September 2008 was struggling to digest its purchase of parts of ABN-AMRO; the market lost confidence in its ability to come through the turbulent market conditions. Digestion problems with acquisitions also clouded the prospects of Wachovia bank, which received open-bank assistance in the form of guarantees on its asset portfolio from the Federal Deposit Insurance Corporation (FDIC) to enable it to be taken over by Citi on September 29, 2008. So this too was a too opaque-to-value case — though in the following weeks another large bank, Wells Fargo, outbid Citi to acquire Wachovia without an FDIC guarantee.

California's IndyMac (which has been criticized for many loan origination abuses in the subprime market) also saw runs when an influential politician indicated (correctly) that its survival was in doubt. Once again the institution lasted only days. In this case, however, it was not a case of a self-fulfilling panic; the institution was already deeply insolvent when the run began. Interestingly, many of the customers who ran the bank — at evident personal inconvenience — were fully insured by the FDIC whose record in ensuring prompt access to insured funds of failed institutions is exemplary. It is not easy to explain this apparently irrational behavior but it does reinforce the idea that limited deposit insurance is not a foolproof tool for avoiding runs, but instead serves at best to provide political acceptability for bank closures. Fundamentally, though, IndyMac's weakness was more conventional: poor — if not abusive — underwriting and increasing difficulties in on selling mortgages originated. As such, IndyMac arguably belongs more to the previous category of failure, the "ruined gambler".

2.4 *Case D: "Overleveraged mortgage lender" — The GSEs*

Because of their curious hybrid character, seemingly in the private sector, but established under special statute, separately regulated from the rest of

[15] In this case, it was a coordinated intervention by the governments of Belgium (which was the home regulator), the Netherlands, and Luxembourg. In the case of Dexia, rescued the following day, coordination of public sector stakeholders in France, Belgium, and Luxembourg was required. Surprisingly, the fiscal coordination was effective, possibly because decisionmakers felt that the banks' equities were undervalued in then current market conditions and that they would therefore stand to make a profit on the intervention.

the banking system, and with their debt benefiting from various regulatory privileges, the systemic risks potentially presented by the two largest U.S. government-sponsored financial enterprises (GSEs), FNMA and FHLMC (known as Fannie Mae and Freddie Mac), had already been extensively discussed in the literature before the crisis broke (cf. Jaffee, 2003; Eisenbeis, Frame, and Wall, 2007; Poole, 2007). In fact, by mid-2008, the focus on these two entities had shifted to the scale and nature of the likely U.S. government bailout of creditors, and in particular what the prospects were for the private shareholders.

In terms of the total value of mortgage-related securities owned or guaranteed, Fannie and Freddie are at the other end of the scale from Sachsen, with about US$5 trillion, an amount equivalent to over one-third of U.S. gross domestic product (GDP) in 2007. More than two-thirds of this relates to guarantees mainly on securitized mortgages packaged by the GSEs out of "conforming" (moderately sized and *not* subprime) mortgages offered to it by other market participants; the remainder relates to an on-balance-sheet portfolio of mortgage-backed assets which can and does include nonconforming loans.[16]

The on-balance-sheet MBS are subject to the risk that the underlying fixed rate mortgages will be prepaid, whether because interest rates have fallen or for other reasons. This risk is hedged by the GSEs' treasury function through the funding instruments and derivatives, but perfect hedging is not practicable, leaving the agencies with appreciable non-credit risk as well as the credit risk of the underlying mortgages. Indeed, the non-credit risk has long been thought the dominant one (Jaffee, 2003; Eisenbeis, Frame, and Wall, 2007), hence the regulatory capital requirement (leverage)[17] for the on-balance-sheet risks was set much higher

[16] About 15 percent of the agencies' total mortgage book of business relates to subprime or Alt-A mortgages (U.S. CBO, 2008).

[17] The GSEs are subject both to the higher of the leverage requirements as specified in the text and a risk-based capital which is based on a stress-test and in practice has been lower. (Following accounting irregularities uncovered in 2003–04, the GSE regulator OFHEO imposed a temporary surcharge onto these requirements; the surcharge was lowered in February 2008). However, independent modeling by Posner and Brown (2005) of Morgan Stanley generated much higher *economic* capital requirements (of between 4.5 and 7 percent) to meet a standalone AA rating. They took account of such modeling uncertainties as the likelihood of prepayment depending on turnover in the housing market as well as the costs of hedging prepayment risk (convexity). The gap between the regulatory and economic capital measures understates the subsidy value of the implicit government guarantee

(2.5 percent) than that on the guarantees (0.45 percent). Still, the result is that the GSEs reported stockholder's equity totaling only US$68 billion at end-2006 supporting that US$5 trillion. By mid-2008 the total reported equity had fallen to US$54 billion — supporting an even larger total mortgage book.[18]

Sure enough, with the recent turbulence — including volatility and unexpected cross-instrument correlation patterns — in short-term money markets, there was the potential for surprises and losses in the hedging function.[19] But that does not in practice seem to have been the main problem causing the deteriorating financial position of the GSEs in 2007–08. Of course, while there is no evidence yet that the complex non-credit risks will generate losses in excess of the capital allowed for them, it is too early to say that this will remain true. However, according to the accounts up to the first half-year of 2008, it seems that credit-related losses both realized and unrealized, were by far the most damaging. Between them, the agencies acknowledge credit-related losses of US$16.3 billion in the 18 months to mid-2008. So it seems that plain vanilla credit losses on a portfolio of largely conforming or prime mortgages have been sufficient to wipe out almost all of the capital assigned to credit risk, if we assume that the figure of 0.45 percent applied across the board.

But they also note additional net mark-to-market losses on their mortgage book totaling US$35.2 billion which they have not realized in their income account (because they believe these reflect liquidity conditions which are temporary and do not imply a probability of default). Since the

---

in that the agencies funding costs have been much lower than that applying to AA firms. Thus at August 2008 Standard and Poors gave Fannie Mae a "Risk to the Government" rating of just A+, while it was still rating the agency's long-term debt at AAA.

[18] And that is according to the GAAP conventions. At fair value, Freddie Mac's liabilities actually exceeded its assets by early 2008, and at fair value the two agencies' aggregate assets exceeded liabilities by only US$7 billion (U.S. CBO, 2008). The agencies also placed considerable value on deferred tax write-offs to which they were entitled, but whose realization would require them to make sizable profits. Their valuation procedures for delinquent loans were also relaxed in 2007–08, again flattering their accounts.

[19] The agencies' accounts make no attempt to estimate the net effect. Fannie Mae lost over $4 billion on its derivatives portfolio in 2007 but it is not stated how much of this merely offset interest rate-related gains in the remainder of its portfolio.

reporting date of end-July, the agencies acknowledged a further worsening in the risk of credit losses. Adding the realized and unrealized losses we get a total in excess of US$50 billion lost in 18 months — only 1 percent of the mortgage book, but well over three-quarters of the shareholders' funds at end-2006!

This was apparently not the result of unknowingly acquiring a more toxic part of a structure than expected. The models employed seem to have simply understated the plausible range of loan loss rates on a portfolio of mortgages. All of the elaborate models constructed to hedge the prepayment and other structure-related risks have proved an irrelevancy relative to the simple move of mortgage defaults outside the historic range. It is not clear how a mechanical model could have improved over a historically informed sense of the potential for risks to arise in unexpected places.

The overall range of plausible losses that will ultimately be borne by the two GSEs remains wide. On July 22, 2008 the U.S. Congressional Budget Office (2008) released its calculations of the possible draws that might be made on U.S. government funds to insulate creditors of the GSEs from loss and thereby ensure systemic financial stability. Their estimate was in a range from zero to US$100 billion, with an expected value of US$25 billion.

Legislation to enable the U.S. Treasury to commit such funds was enacted at that time, and on September 7, 2008, action was initiated to inject funds. On that day, the two firms were taken into the conservatorship of their new regulator the Federal Housing Finance Agency (FHFA); dividend payments were suspended and the chief executive officers (CEOs) replaced. At the same time the Treasury (1) injected US$1 billion and received senior preferred shares carrying a 10 percent coupon and warrants for 80 percent of the two firms' common stock with a nominal exercise price; (2) undertook to make good any future capital shortfall as determined by FHFA in accordance with U.S. generally accepted accounting principles (GAAP) (i.e. ensuring compliance with a zero capital adequacy requirement); and (3) started a program of acquiring agency-backed MBS in the market. In addition, the two firms were given access to a new liquidity facility at the Fed.

Given the drastic perceived consequences by a wide range of authoritative commentators of a default on agency paper, in terms of market turbulence, political fallout (given the large foreign official holdings of

GSEs), and the functioning of the mortgage market,[20] the U.S. government's action to step in was all but inevitable. The technique used minimized formal disruptions: thus, the government did not formally take over all of the firms' debt, nor were the firms closed and liquidated. Shareholders were diluted by 80 percent and dividends frozen; although their share prices had already fallen more than 90 percent from their peak, they suffered a further sharp fall immediately after the announcement to about 1 percent of their peak value. The inevitability of the intervention and the open-ended nature of the government's liability in this condition confirms that the regulatory model used allowed these firms to operate on far too thin a cushion of capital. It remained unclear why tighter regulation had not been imposed earlier: Close supervision of the agencies' complex activities and limitations on their assumption of additional risk would be the conventional regulatory guidance for such entities. But because of their perceived role in sustaining mortgage availability, the GSEs actually saw a relaxation in capital adequacy requirements and risk-taking in early 2008, and they had responded by increasing their portfolio of mortgage-backed securities since this relaxation.

If the GSEs had a rationale in the new century, it was that mortgage banking remained fragmented and the main participants did not have the scale or geographical range to diversify credit risks and to lay-off prepayment and other risks. These risks could be laid-off using financial engineering, but a large share of this engineering was captured by just two intermediaries thanks to the implicit government guarantee which they enjoyed. Inadequate modeling of the underlying housing market risks allowed regulators to tolerate capital levels so low that they have now triggered what is likely to become a sizable call on that implicit guarantee.

---

[20] Whether the U.S. mortgage market really needed the agencies has long been debated. Estimates in the literature suggest it has probably helped lower the cost of conforming mortgages by up to 25 basis points (Eisenbeis, Frame, and Wall, 2007). But there is little evidence that increases in their purchases of non-conforming assets affect mortgage rates or spreads (Lehnert, Passmore, and Sherlund, 2005). Other industrial countries rely on other forms of subsidy to support home ownership and none has closely imitated the U.S. model.

3. Conclusion

Fifteen years ago, Robert Merton (1994) cautioned; "The mathematics of [hedging] models are precise, but the models are not, being only approximations to the complex, real world. Their accuracy as a useful approximation to that world varies considerably across time and place. The practitioner should therefore apply the models only tentatively, assessing their limitations carefully in each application". As Merton (1995) also points out whereas equity capital is a wonderful all-purpose risk absorber, it is costly; on the other hand, hedging (for example through the use of derivatives) is targeted and relatively inexpensive.

Each of the banks studied failed — or at least got a bad fright — because their models of the risks to which they were subject proved to be too sanguine. Some of the banks with the biggest reported losses did not fail because their businesses were diversified and included profit streams and capital reserves from other lines that were not affected by the mortgage-related problems.

Risk-management textbooks are replete with advice on the need for holistic assessments avoiding silos and involving a fundamental look-through approach.[21] But it is clear from the pattern revealed by these failures that the implications for discretion as opposed to rules, for overall judgment as an override on mechanical models, has not been fully taken on board whether by intermediary managements or by prudential regulators.

References

Balzli, B., M. Schießl, and S. Winters (2008). Casino provincial — Das Milliardendesaster der Sächsischen Landesbank. *Der Spiegel*, 28, 80–86 (7 July 2008).

Barth, J. R., G. Caprio, and R. Levine (2005). *Till Angels Govern*, Cambridge University Press.

[21] Recent reports by Senior Supervisors Group (2008) and IIF (2008) reiterate these familiar but widely ignored counsels. See also Honohan and Stiglitz (2001).

Brunnermeier, M. K. (2008). Deciphering the 2007–08 Liquidity and Credit Crunch. NBER Working Paper 14612.

Burrough, B. (2008). Bringing down Bear Stearns. *Vanity Fair*, August.

Calomiris, C. W. (2008). The subprime turmoil: what's old, what's new, and what's next. *Vox*, 22 August. http://www.voxeu.org/index.php?q=node/1561

Caprio, G., D. Klingebiel, L. Laeven, and G. Noguera (2005). Banking crisis database. In Honohan, P. and L. Laeven (eds.), *Systemic Financial Crises*, Cambridge University Press.

Dewatripont, M. and J. Tirole (1994). *The Prudential Regulation of Banks*. Cambridge, MA: The MIT Press.

Eisenbeis, R. A., W. S. Frame, and L. D. Wall (2007). An analysis of the systemic risks posed by Fannie Mae and Freddie Mac and an evaluation of the policy options for reducing those risks. *Journal of Financial Services Research*, 31(2–3).

European Commission (2008). *State aid C 9/2008 — Germany Sachsen LB*.

Goodhart, C. (2004). Bank regulation and macroeconomic fluctuations. *Oxford Review of Economic Policy*, 20(4), 591–615.

Goodhart, C. and A. Persaud (2008). How to avoid the next crash. *Financial Times*, January 30.

Greenlaw, D., J. Hatzius, A. K. Kashyap, and S. S. Hyun (2008). Leveraged losses: lessons from the mortgage market meltdown. *U.S. Monetary Policy Forum Conference*, http://www.chicagogsb.edu/usmpf/2008forum.aspx

Honohan, P. (1997). Banking system failures in developing and transition countries: diagnosis and prediction. *BIS Working Paper 39*. Basel, Bank for International Settlements, http://www.bis.org/publ/work39.htm

Honohan, P. (2001). Perverse effects of an external ratings-related capital adequacy system. *Economic Notes*, 30(3), 359–372.

Honohan, P. (2008). Risk management and the costs of the banking crisis. *National Institute Economic Review*, 205, 15–24.

Honohan, P. and J. E. Stiglitz (2001). Robust financial restraint. In Caprio, G., P. Honohan, and J. E. Stiglitz (eds.), *Financial Liberalization: How Far, How Fast?* Cambridge University Press.

Hughes, C., P. T. Larsen, and H. Simonian (2008). Corroded to the core: how a staid Swiss bank let ambitions lead it into folly. *Financial Times*, April 20.

Institute of International Finance (2008). Principles of conduct and best practice recommendations financial services industry response to the market turmoil of 2007–2008. (Final Report of the IIF Committee on Market Best Practices.)

Jaffee, D. M. (2003). The interest rate risk of Fannie Mae and Freddie Mac. *Journal of Financial Services Research*, 24(1), 5–29.

Joint Forum. Basel Committee on Banking Supervision, International Organization of Securities Commissions, International Association of Insurance Supervisors (2008). Credit risk transfer: developments from 2005 to 2007, http://www.bis.org/publ/joint18.pdf

Jorion, P. (2002). Fallacies about the effects of market risk-management systems. *Bank of England Financial Stability Review*, 13, 115–127.

Kelly, K. (2008). The Fall of Bear Stearns. *Wall Street Journal*, May 27, 28, 29.

Lehnert, A., W. Passmore, and S. M. Sherlund (2008). GSEs, mortgage rates, and secondary market activities. *Journal of Real Estate, Finance and Economics*, 36(3), 343–363.

Merton, R. C. (1994). Influence of mathematical models in finance on practice: past, present and future. *Philosophical Transactions (Royal Society)*, 347(1684), 451–462.

Merton, R. C. (1995). The role of capital in financial institutions." *Journal of Banking & Finance* 19(3–4), 461–481.

Poole, W. (2007). *The GSEs: where do we stand?* Federal Reserve Bank of St. Louis. http://www.stlouisfed.org/news/speeches/2007/01_17_07.html

Posner, K. and D. Brown (2005). Fannie Mae, Freddie Mac, the road to redemption. *Morgan Stanley Equity Research.*

Senior Supervisors Group (2008). Observations on risk management practices during the recent market turbulence. *Financial Stability Forum*, March, http://www.newyorkfed.org/newsevents/news/banking/2008/SSG_Risk_Mgt_doc_final.pdf

UBS (2008). *Shareholder Report on UBS's Write-Downs*, April 20.

U.S. Congressional Budget Office (2008). CBO's estimate of cost of the administration's proposal to authorize Federal financial assistance for the government-sponsored enterprises for housing. U.S. Congress.

Comments: How Serious is the Damage?

Christopher Kent*
Reserve Bank of Australia

1. Overview — Lessons from Australia's History of Financial Turmoil

I'd like to thank Philipp Hartmann and the other organisers from the ECB and the Chicago Fed for the opportunity to come to this conference and to this great city for the first time.

One thing that Australia doesn't share with North America or Europe is large inland cities. Our geography and climate are such that we tend to concentrate ourselves close to the coastline. However, we have many other things in common, including an obsession with property. We've also had our fair share of financial turmoil — built mostly on the back of periods of rising credit and speculative excesses in property markets.

Philipp asked me to comment on three papers and to do so through the lens of Australia's experience with credit cycles. Let's start with a quick tour of four episodes of credit market turmoil in Australia.[1] Two occurred during depressions — in the 1890s and 1930s — one during the mid 1970s, and one during the early 1990s recession. All were associated with boom-bust cycles in credit and property prices. Cycles in property prices — much more so than cycles in many other asset prices — were, and still are important since property is a key source of collateral. Rising collateral prices generate the backing for additional loans, reinforcing a boom in

* Christopher Kent is Head of the Economic Research Department, Reserve Bank of Australia. He thanks Adam Cagliarini and Jarkko Jaaskela for helpful discussions related to these comments. The views here are the author's and are not necessarily those of the Reserve Bank of Australia.

[1] For a more detailed analysis of these episodes see D'Arcy and Kent (2000), Fisher and Kent (2009), Kent and Lowe (1998) and the references therein.

credit. If this turns out to be unsustainable, falling collateral prices can cause large losses for financial institutions and weaken the balance sheets of borrowers, with adverse consequences for economic activity and the potential for further rounds of losses.

The severity of financial system problems was quite varied across these four episodes. Problems were mild in the 1970s, moderate during the 1930s (despite the severity of the depression), relatively severe during the 1990s, and acute during the 1890s. This is evident in the behaviour of credit, the failures of banks and non-bank financial institutions, and the losses incurred by banks.

Figures 1 and 2 and Table 1 below summarize these credit cycle episodes along these lines. The most costly in terms of economic activity were the two depressions, but the 1890s was the Great Depression from Australia's perspective. The run-up in credit up to the 1890s was astonishing even from today's perspective.[2] The fall was more spectacular

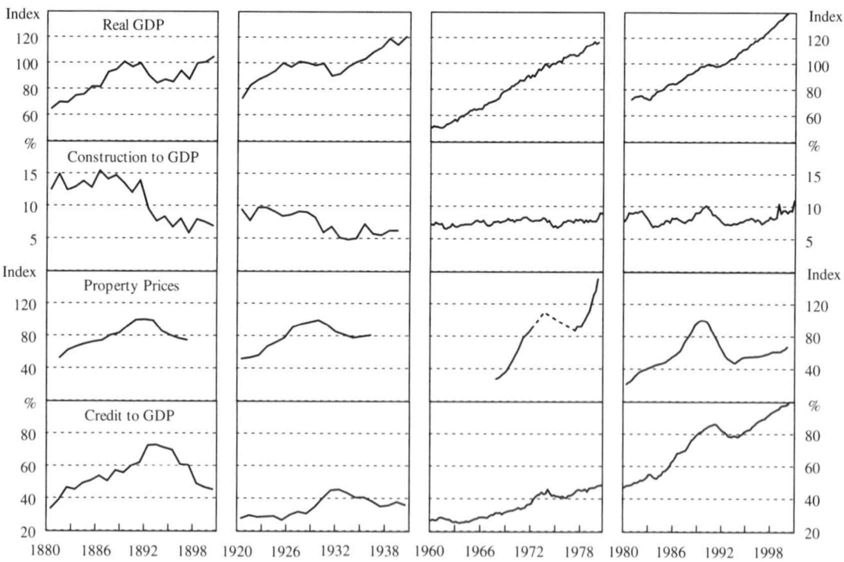

Figure 1. Four Australian Cycles in Credit.
Source: see D'Arcy and Kent (2000).

[2] The rise is even more striking given that these early data exclude non-bank financial institutions which were at the forefront of the boom in credit for property speculation.

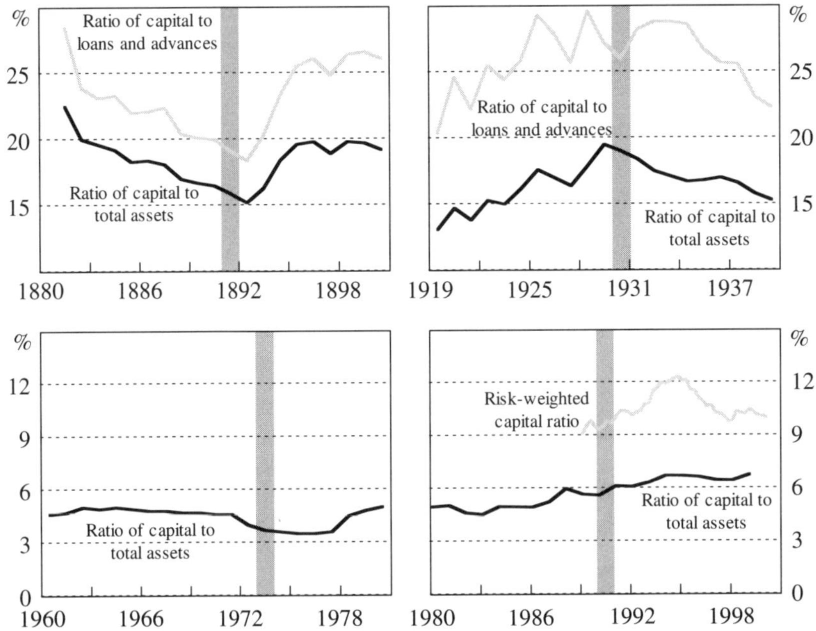

Figure 2. Capital Ratios Through Four Australian Credit Cycles.
Source: see D'Arcy and Kent (2000).

still and associated with the failure of about half of the banking system and the bulk of the non-bank financial institutions. The banking sector also suffered sizeable losses in the 1990s, when there were some failures and a relatively protracted recession as financial headwinds slowed growth.

One especially interesting aspect of the 1890s episode is the contrast between the behaviour of surviving and failing banks. Older, more conservative banks warned of the dangers of excessive lending. Newer banks expanded rapidly, lowered their lending standards, and expanded their branch networks as a means of gaining market share — over the decade up to the crisis their branch networks had more than doubled, and while networks of older banks had also grown substantially, on average they added only half the number of branches and remained smaller than the failing banks. This expansion of networks contributed to a loss of central control and forced banks to hire relatively inexperienced managers. In part these events were triggered by a relaxation of

Table 1. Summary of the Severity of Financial System Problems.

		Episode			
		1890s	**1930s**	**1970s**	**1990s**
Fall in real GDP	Relative ranking[a]	1	2	4	3
Bank failures	Number of banks "failing"	13	3	1	2
Bank credit losses	Cumulative bad and doubtful debts (share of initial capital)	77%	n.a.	n.a.	82%
Performance of banks	Cumulative decline in profits (share of initial capital)[b]	108%	19%	0.4%	43%
Fall in ratio of credit to nominal GDP	Relative ranking[a]	1	2	4	3
Problems at non-bank financial institutions	Change in the number and assets of non-bank financial institutions (relative ranking)[a]	1	4	3	2

Source: see D'Arcy and Kent (2000).
Notes:
a. Ranking in declining order of severity from 1 (the most severe) to 4 (the least severe).
b. Cumulative difference between profit before tax relative to profit before tax in the year prior to the onset of financial system difficulties.

what limited banking regulations had existed and by rising competition from the non-bank financial institutions. Similarly, in the 1980s, competitive pressures increased at a time when banks were still in the process of developing the internal credit controls necessary in a newly deregulated environment.

In short, both the 1890s and 1990s stand out as episodes where prudential behaviour acted to amplify the business cycle and contributed to severe problems for financial institutions during the downturn in activity.

The bankers of the 1920s were relatively conservative, helping them to escape relatively unscathed despite the impact of the depression. This conservatism was borne largely out of the experience of the 1890s banking collapse, aided by the subsequent easing in competitive pressures (both from other banks and from non-bank financial institutions). In stark contrast to the lead up the 1890s, in the 1920s banks were building up a buffer of capital, which they were able to draw upon during the depression. In the 1990s, attempts by banks to build up their capital ratios during a period of financial instability appear to have contributed to the severity of the slowdown in economic activity.

The cycle in credit in the 1970s was driven largely by the non-bank financial institutions, with lending by the banks constrained by a range of mandated controls. Again, much of this was channelled into property speculation and investment — commercial property prices rose more than three-fold from 1968 to 1974. Despite a relatively sharp run up in property prices, the correction in real prices was achieved via only a moderate decline in nominal property prices given the relatively high rates of inflation overall.

The lessons that can be drawn from a comparison of these episodes are no doubt familiar to those well versed in the long history of financial crises from around the world. In general terms, it seems that crises are more likely and more costly if during the "expansionary" phase:

- **credit** growth has increased significantly relative to trend, possibly indicating excessive risk taking on both sides of the market;
- the prices of assets that form the basis of **collateral** have risen rapidly in tandem with credit, taking them well above their "fundamental" longer term levels;
- there has been excessive **concentration** of lending and investment in particular sectors/industries and/or extensive growth in innovative financial products/arrangements;
- **capital** has not been accumulated by financial institutions at the center of the credit creation process;
- **competitive** pressures have intensified, perhaps because of a liberalization of markets and/or the effects of financial innovations.

Rising competitive pressures — characterised by attempts to maintain market share and an intensification of shareholder demands for high returns — can be a catalyst for procyclical financial behaviour. While capital markets could in theory provide much needed discipline to help keep this in check, this market is susceptible to the same excess optimism that clouds the appreciation of system-wide risks.

This does not mean that rising credit and asset prices, financial innovations, economizing on capital, and competitive pressures are not to be valued. They are all important facets of a financial system that helps to efficiently link savers and investors and redistribute risk to those most able to bear it. Rather, the potential concern is that these changes can occur at such speed that they risk creating unnecessary system-wide risks. One problem is that it takes time to get accurate information about how new financial products and players that emerge during expansionary phases are likely to perform, particularly during a contractionary phase; learning by doing takes time.

Borio and Lowe (2002) present international evidence on the role of credit, asset prices, and a measure of the strength of investment as indicators of financial crises. They find that (using only *ex ante* information): a large deviation of credit (relative to GDP) above trend is a reliable indicator of a forthcoming financial crisis. Still more accurate predictions are obtained when using deviations of credit from trend over longer horizons (of up to three years) and when combined with deviations of real asset prices from trend.

Of course, developments during the onset of a contractionary phase will also play a role. An easing in monetary and fiscal policies can have a significant offsetting effect. On the other hand, pressures from regulators and/or overly pessimistic markets to rebuild capital rapidly could exacerbate problems by unnecessarily reducing leverage.

Let me now turn to each of the three excellent presentations in this session.

2. Patrick Honohan — Bank Failures: The Limitations of Risk Modelling

I found Patrick's paper to be a fascinating read. His central thesis is that recent bank failures have been driven in large part by overconfidence in mechanistic risk management models, which have been a key innovation underpinning much of the expansion in lending during the expansionary phase of the current episode. He illustrates this with some detailed case studies of failing financial institutions. He also presents some estimates of the direct costs associated with these failures in terms of write-downs and fiscal support. In terms of the policy implications, he argues for less rules based and more discretionary approaches to risk management. He also examines the policy responses to failing institutions, noting that in some cases responses have been too slow, and while equity holders have appropriately lost out, he's less convinced that the same can be said of senior management.

I've talked already about how risk appetites might be procyclical. I think that the mechanistic use of models may also impart a degree of procyclicality. The key problem is the way in which risks are perceived or assessed. Perceived risks could differ considerably from actual risks if perceptions are driven by relatively recent realizations of risk. A mechanical use of models may do reasonably well during 'normal' times, when empirical relationships seem stable and are well described by recent data. However, most models are not so adept at handling adverse events in the tail of the distribution. Long-Term Capital Management (LTCM) is an obvious example — things appeared to be fine until Russia defaulted. Who knew that could happen?

Why might perceptions of risk be so driven by recent experience? It may reflect the view that "this time things are different", in which case there would be little value in using data from earlier periods. Or perhaps the data do not exist (particularly likely with new products). In either case, during upturns perceptions of risk will tend to be low relative to actual. For example, non-performing loans are likely to be low and profits are high, with even the riskiest of borrowers or counterparties benefiting from buoyant economic conditions. However, actual risk may well be rising near the peak of the business cycle, though this is only recognized during the contractionary phase.

So what can be done? How do we bring in the sort of judgement that Patrick speaks of? If such models are to be used, they would need to be better stress tested. And such tests should be based on scenarios born out of a long experience with periods of financial instability, and not driven so much by technical specialists that design and operate the models, but by those with a broader, system-wide perspective.

I wonder if in addition to the concern about overconfidence in models, there is also a problem of over-reliance on very similar models (or modeling assumptions). It seems plausible that this would tend to lead to very one-sided markets, both on the way up and on the way down. Models are not likely to account for the fact that others using similar models will be following similar strategies, leading to a greater correlation of asset prices. This may be a further mechanism contributing to procyclicality of the financial system.

The case studies presented by Patrick were particularly interesting. A theme running through these was similar to the one I alluded to in my discussion of the earlier Australian experience. Some institutions expanded into new business too quickly, beyond their capacity to manage and learn about the risks. This appears to have been driven by concerns to maintain or build market share and confounded by problems in assessing true risks and a general sense of optimism. These issues were also discussed at length in Blundell-Wignall and Atkinson (2008), a paper presented at the Reserve Bank of Australia's recent conference on the financial turmoil. These authors highlight that as late as 2006 a prominent global bank adopted a strategy recommended by an external consulting company to close gaps with key market leaders in high-yield, mortgage-backed securities. As the drive for market share in this area gained traction within the bank, power shifted away from managers with a risk management focus towards those with a "sales" background; not surprisingly, there seemed to be little if any concern for adjusting higher expected returns for risk when evaluating the prospects for this line of business.

Once the dust has settled on the current crisis it will be interesting to examine strategies that enabled some institutions to do relatively well. What allowed "successful" institutions to ignore pressures to gain or at least maintain market share in areas that got failing institutions into trouble? It may be that many were truly prudent. Or perhaps they got involved in these newer business lines but more modestly, or with the benefit of greater skills and/or a degree of luck? A very early examination by the Senior Supervisors' Group (2008a) suggests that some institutions fared better for a number or reasons, including: better sharing of quantitative and qualitative risk assessments across the whole institution; a more disciplined assessment of the risks inherent in complex and potentially illiquid securities (and a scepticism of the value of external ratings); and a more flexible approach to adjusting assessments of risks according to different assumptions, such as asset correlations, used in value-at-risk models and stress testing exercises.

A final question that arose while reading this paper is why capital appears to be so expensive? One could argue that without sufficient capital, the cost of debt should be relatively high. Perhaps the problem then is with the discipline provided by capital markets. Maybe this stems from a lack of disclosure — but if this is the case, why don't capital markets punish those whose disclosure is thought to be poor? More likely, either creditors feel that they will not lose — perhaps because they feel that they'll be bailed out or can exit their positions quickly — or they suffer from the same problem of excess optimism during expansionary periods.

3. David Greenlaw — Costs for the Real Economy of Balance Sheet Problems

Drawing on an earlier paper (Greenlaw, Hatzius, Kashyap, and Shin, 2008), David presents estimates of the extent of losses by financial institutions (on their current stock of outstanding loans) over the past year or so and how these are likely to translate into a contraction in domestic lending. He then focuses on how this in turn might affect economic activity (the growth of GDP). To do this he needs to identify the effect of changes in domestic lending associated with contractions in supply. He uses a single equation estimate based on an instrumental variables approach. His results suggest that credit losses of about $200 billion imply a fall in domestic lending of about $1 trillion, which, if sustained for a year will (eventually) lead to lower GDP growth in the order of almost ½ a percentage point.

I think this approach has to be commended for its simplicity. At the same time, however, it is so simple that it might miss a number of important effects.

- The first is the role of the financial accelerator, whereby shocks that reduce creditworthiness adversely affect the macroeconomy, which further asset prices and the creditworthiness of lenders *and* borrowers. This may be missed by ignoring other features of the credit cycle, such as the behaviour of the prices of assets that form the basis of collateral, as well as by restricting the analysis to a relatively short horizon (of one year). Another issue of relevance here is the possibility of asymmetric effects, since the failure of lenders can severely limit access of their borrowers to capital markets (at least during the crisis). These considerations by themselves would imply that the economic slowdown could be worse than David's estimates suggest.

- A second omission is the role of policy in mitigating the adverse affects of the credit crisis. This could imply that David's estimates are too large if the policy responses have been especially vigorous compared with earlier episodes of slowing credit. David's assumption that policy is not such a relevant consideration is one that I would think should be put to the test.

Both of these general points could be addressed by estimating a system of equations and allowing a role for financial accelerator effects (for example by including variables such as the price of collateral, or other indicators of financial stress, such as foreclosure or loan default rates) and for policy. Of course, standard measures of the stance of monetary and fiscal policies may not be sufficient, given the importance of direct injections of public funds into failing institutions and greater provision of liquidity during the current episode.

4. S. "Vish" Viswanathan — Damage to Financial Markets

In Vish's illuminating presentation, he takes us through the many inefficient aspects of network markets that have been close to, if not at the center of the financial turmoil over the past year or so. These stand in stark contrast to consolidated markets, which maintain liquidity in difficult times, provide timely and accurate price discovery, trade relatively standarized products, benefit from a central clearing house, provide information on large positions, and allow for relatively straightforward resolutions following defaults. He then takes us through how a series of network markets have failed during the current episode, and contributed to amplification of shocks during both the upturn and the downturn. He provides a nice summary of how various aspects of these markets have caused these problems, including the role of collateral, margin calls, and mark-to-market accounting. One thing that I thought he might have said more about was the role of rating agencies in helping to convert low-grade securities into high-grade ones, in part by understating risks to end-investors of many products originating in these markets.

I'll reserve most of my comments though for a discussion of the relevant policy implications. Vish argues strongly for a range of regulatory changes to overcome inefficiencies in these markets. It is hard to fault efforts that would lead to greater standardization, more market makers, increased transparency, and provide a role for central clearing houses. I think that the key question is how to encourage these and the extent to which regulation should play a role. Vish points strongly to a role for regulators — the Federal Reserve and the Securities and Exchange Commission — in designing nascent markets, suggesting that more robust markets would allow for less reliance on capital regulations.

Perhaps the key point I would make in this regard is that simply forcing financial instruments to be traded on exchanges would not, on its own, make the instruments simpler. Rather, if instruments become simpler and more standardized in the future, this may increase the prospects for them to become exchange traded. We see some evidence of the evolution of some securities onto exchange-based markets. One example is interest rate derivatives, which have a longish history. OTC markets in these derivatives grew much more rapidly through the 1990s than the exchange-based markets, as interest-rate derivatives were still evolving reasonably quickly and there was considerable innovation (see Figure 3 below taken from Kearns and Lowe, 2008). But in more recent times — as the products have become more standardized — the two market types have seen similar growth rates.

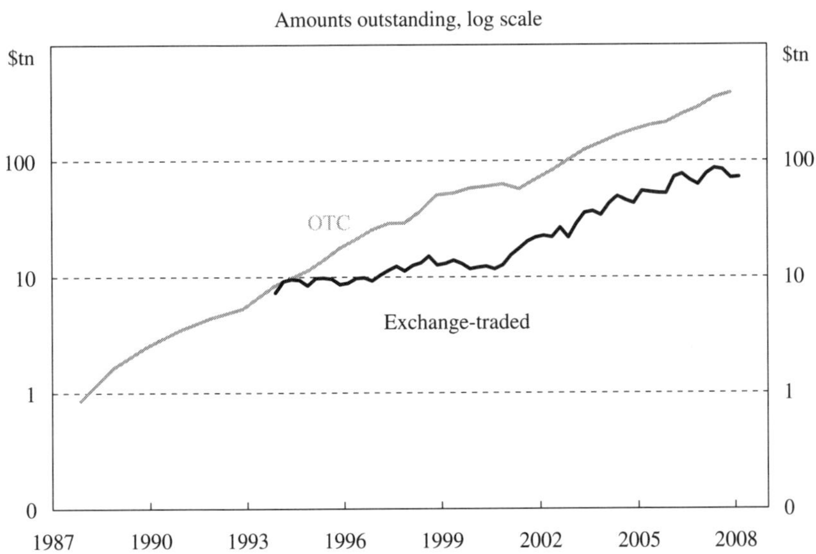

Figure 3. Interest Rate Derivatives.

Source: BIS; ISDA.

Would such a transformation be something we would expect to occur without much intervention? I suspect that there will need to be some involvement of regulators to promote better disclosure, transparency, and documentation, including with regard to the information on structured products provided by rating agencies. Also, I suspect that there may be scope for at least some of this to occur without new initiatives, but rather by a more vigorous application of, and adherence to, existing disclosure requirements (see Senior Supervisors' Group 2008b for further discussion of this point). At the same time, however, one hopes that there will be a greater recognition by the markets of the difficulties and costs of monitoring highly complex products, which by itself will lead to more standard, simpler products.

Finally, it's not entirely clear to me that we can expect all asset types to migrate from OTC to exchange-traded markets, nor whether this is attractive given the characteristics of many assets which have been tailored to meet specific demands.

5. Concluding Remarks

The long history of financial crises suggests that the more momentum there has been in the growth of credit, collateral prices, and the intensification of competition and/or innovation, the more damage is done when the expansion comes to a halt. The question remains, however, how to take away some of this momentum before it is too late.

Clearly, much can be done on the regulatory front. Some of these reforms will likely reflect concerns raised by Patrick and Vish in this session. However, whether the types of reforms many people have in mind will directly address the problem of financial system procyclicality is unclear. No doubt, fear will stay with the market for quite a while. But eventually the pendulum will swing back to greater risk taking again — probably just as we've put to bed much of the analysis of the current crisis! So how will we respond to future periods of excess optimism, bubble-like conditions in key asset markets, and sharply rising leverage? I'm sure we'll be focusing over the coming months and years about the potential for cyclical regulatory policies. The practical difficulties here are many. One problem is that if done too vigorously, it may push financing activities outside of the regulatory net, just at a time when we would want them to be subject to greater oversight.

What about something with a broader effect on risk taking, across all financial institutions and markets, households, and businesses? It seems to me that there is a role for monetary policy to at least lean against possible excesses. No doubt these debates will be with us for years to come.

References

Blundell-Wignall, A. and P. Atkinson (2008). The sub-prime crisis: causal distortions and regulatory reform. In Kent, C. and P. Bloxham (eds.), *Lessons from the Financial Turmoil of 2007 and 2008*, Proceedings of a Conference, Reserve Bank of Australia, Sydney, 55–102.

Borio, C. and P. Lowe (2002). Asset prices, financial and monetary stability: exploring the nexus. BIS Working Papers No. 114.

D'Arcy, Patrick and Christopher Kent (2000). Cyclical prudence — credit cycles in Australia. Paper presented at BIS Conference of Economists, *Marrying the Micro- and Macro-prudential Dimensions of Financial Stability*, 9–10 October, Basel, Switzerland.

Greenlaw, D., J. Hatzius, A. Kashyap and H. S. Shin (2008). Leveraged losses: Lessons from the mortgage market meltdown. US Monetary Policy Forum Report No. 2.

Kent, C. (2000). Two depressions, one banking collapse Revised version (available on request) of Reserve Bank of Australia Research Discussion Paper No. 1999-06.

Kearns, J. and P. Lowe (2008). Promoting liquidity: why and how? In Kent, C. and P. Bloxham (eds.), *Lessons from the Financial Turmoil of 2007 and 2008*, Proceedings of a Conference, Reserve Bank of Australia, Sydney, 139–173.

Kent, C. and P. Lowe (1998). Property-price cycles and monetary policy. In *The Role of Asset prices in the Formulation of Monetary Policy*, BIS Conference Papers Vol. 5, 239–2630.

Senior Supervisors' Group (2008a). *Observations on Risk Management Practices During the Recent Market Turbulence*, 6 March. Available at http://www.newyorkfed.org/newsevents/news/banking/2008/SSG_Risk_Mgt_Doc_Final.pdf.

Senior Supervisors' Group (2008b). Leading-practice disclosures for selected exposures, 11 April. Available at http://www.newyorkfed.org/newsevents/news/banking/2008/SSG_Leading_Practice_Disclosures.pdf.

IV. WHY DID IT GO UNDETECTED/ UNDERESTIMATED FOR SO LONG?

Cliff Risk and the Credit Crisis

Joseph R. Mason*
Louisiana State University

1. Introduction

Many recent financial institution failures have taken investors and the public by surprise. In recent years, investors and regulators have witnessed steady — even high-flying — firm performance that seems to suddenly fall off a cliff. Throughout economics and finance, however, discrete outcomes such as those recently witnessed do not just come out of nowhere. Indeed, the proper way to think about discrete dependent variable econometrics is as a handy tool to merely make up for the lack of adequate data on an underlying unobservable — or merely unobserved — continuous process. Seemingly discrete outcomes, therefore, necessitate the search for proper underlying continuous processes that can explain the outcome. Investigation of the sudden cliff-like failures we have witnessed in the credit crisis reveals continuous processes stemming from shortcomings in firm rights and responsibilities in securitizations that can explain recent firm failures and help better understand firm performance and guide regulation in the new world of off-balance-sheet finance.

---

* Joseph Mason is the Moyse/Louisiana Bankers Association Professor of Finance, Ourso School of Business, Louisiana State University, Senior Fellow at the Wharton School, and Financial Industry Consultant, Empiris, LLC. Contact information: joseph.r.mason@gmail.com; (202) 683-8909 office. The author thanks Douglas Evanoff, George Kaufman, and participants at the October 2008 Federal Reserve Bank of Chicago and European Central Bank International Banking Conference for helpful comments and assistance. Any remaining errors are solely the author's own.

It is useful to teach securitization using the notion of a pool of assets segregated from the seller[1] and funded by tranches of bonds and residual equity. The standard approach is to emphasize the intent to segregate the assets from the seller in a bankruptcy remote subsidiary to achieve lower-cost financing in a sort of "super-collateralized" loan arrangement. Securities representing claims against the collateral pool are then structured and sold as asset-backed or mortgage-backed securities.

Of course, that simplified paradigm — while useful to teach the first lessons about securitization — does not come close to accurately reflecting real-world practice. In the real world, the ability to skew earnings is a powerful temptation to increase securitization period after period to maintain growth in accounting (non-cash) earnings.

One way to increase securitization from period to period is to "sell" the loans for accounting purposes without really selling them in any true economic sense. No true economic sale takes place because asset-backed and residential mortgage-backed securities are tranched, so that the bottom securities in the structure absorb losses first. When the majority of risk is concentrated into those bottom securities the resulting "senior-subordinate" structure dictates that the proper paradigm is not a "distribution" of risk, but a "distillation" of risk. Because of the high risk, the bottom (most risky) securities cannot typically be sold to outside investors, so they are kept on-balance-sheet. Hence, the risk does not really leave the seller/servicer (or bank) at all.

Realizing that risk resides in the lower tranches, bank regulators in 2001 approved policy to deal effectively with the situation, requiring regulated commercial banks to hold 100 percent risk-weighted capital against those riskiest bottom securities held on-balance sheet. FASB approached variations on the theme (most famously promulgated in response to Enron) in 2003.

But, as loan underwriting and securitization moved outside the banking sector in response to closing the 2001 loophole, "representations and warranties" replaced holding the riskiest bottom securities as the chief credit enhancement mechanism for investors, subsidizing pool

---

[1] I will use the term seller throughout to refer to the originator of the loans or the originator of the pool of loans. Sometimes the term sponsor is used interchangeably with seller, though I will find it useful to use seller later on when discussing loan servicing performed by the seller, in which case the seller is a seller/servicer. Such circumstances are important because the most egregious problems have occurred with seller-servicers.

performance so that no asset- or mortgage-backed security investor ever experienced losses. Indeed, therefore, ratings agencies are correct in maintaining that "even a cow could structure" a highly rated securitization and the ratings would hold — that is, until the seller/servicer, itself, fails and is no longer able to honor the representations and warranties to support the pool.

Despite repeated demonstrations of the dynamic over the past several decades, regulators, policymakers, and seller/servicers time and again feign surprise at interconnected relationships upon the failure of a securitizing firm, calling for bailouts on the basis of purported "systemic risk," despite their own lack of attention. Those regulators, misunderstanding (or refusing to see) the continuous process of securitization distress, misguidedly claim that incentives of sellers and investors, as well as borrowers, can be aligned by having sellers retain some risk in their securitizations. The reality is that sellers have always retained risk, and that retained risk is precisely what has created the seeming cliff.

2. How to Post Record Profits with Negative Cash Flows

Understanding the dynamic outlined above begins with a lesson in gain-on-sale accounting. Probably the most widely-acknowledged scourge of securitization over the years, gain-on-sale accounting usually draws yawns from those who think it is too complex and arcane to fathom.

The idea is actually very simple: the firm follows three easy steps.[2] First, the firm estimates the value of the thing they want to sell with a financial model; then, the firm receives a promise of some money and other items to be received in the future in the actual sale of that thing; the firm finally gets to record the difference between their own valuation of the thing that they sold and the net present value of the cash and other items received over time in the (often less than arms-length) sale as cash profit "gained" on the sale. Gain-on-sale accounting therefore creates problems when artificially low asset valuations are transformed into artificially high sale price valuations.

[2] Financial Accounting Standards Board (2005) explains gain-on-sale accounting most succinctly and clearly.

According to Moody's (2002):

> In the late 1990s, several subprime home equity and auto lenders encountered financial difficulty arising in part from explosive growth patterns, in part from using securitization as a source of funds, and in part from overly aggressive use of gain on sale accounting. Such accounting methodology made these companies look much stronger financially on paper than they actually were. Companies that used gain on sale accounting included, among subprime mortgage issuers, Contifinancial Corp., Southern Pacific Funding Corp., Cityscape, and United Companies Financial Corp. … Once the effect of gain on sale accounting was removed from financial statements, leverage ratios were often high. These companies also had weak capital positions compared to more diversified finance companies. (p. 14)

After the crisis of the late 1990s, surviving firms sought to become more conservative about the valuation inputs they used in their gain-on-sale accounting and, in some cases, even forego gain-on-sale accounting altogether. Rather than revise the approach, however, the SEC threatened that earnings manipulation charges would be levied against firms that attempted to consciously adopt a more conservative approach.

Similar to the late 1990s, therefore, many recently-failed mortgage companies have never been cash-flow positive in their entire corporate lives. But instead of being restricted, the paradigm underlying gain-on-sale has been extended through a broader implementation of market-value accounting, more generally.

3. How to "Sell" Without Transferring Responsibility

The temptation to increase profits without actually having to earn cash creates an irresistible incentive to come up with ways to grow securitization quarter after quarter. One way to grow securitization is to make sure investors never lose. If the seller/servicer, therefore, does not really transfer the risk of loss to investors, investors will continue to buy asset- and mortgage-backed securities period after period and the seller/servicer gets to book the accounting profits — at least until the seller/servicer, itself, goes bankrupt.

The strategy is again very simple. Modern securitization is about creating a senior subordinate security structure where subordinate securities absorb risks before seniors, making those senior securities safer (and therefore higher-rated). As a result, essentially all the risk is distilled into the relatively small proportion of subordinate bonds.

Let's look at this from the perspective of risk transfer. Suppose we sell a pool with a 2 percent expected loss rate, meaning we fully expect 2 percent of the pool value to be lost to foreclosures after recovery. Certainly, if losses are less than 2 percent, the "first-loss" piece can be valuable. But if losses climb to more than 2 percent, the piece is worthless. Nonetheless, since the 2 percent loss rate is that which is *fully expected*, all other things equal no investor will buy an interest in that nearly-guaranteed 2 percent first-loss piece. Hence, the seller has to retain that 2 percent first-loss stake on their own balance sheet.

In the past, the seller (if it is a commercial bank) would hold the standard 8 percent Basel capital requirement against the 2 percent first-loss piece retained on the balance sheet. Economically, however, the average dollar value of risk level by the seller is the same whether the pool is securitized or not: 2 percent of the pool value. The distillation process therefore results in virtually no risk being removed from the bank balance sheet while capital is reduced.

The market has been aware of the limitations of securitizing while retaining the economic risk for quite some time. In September 1997, Moody's published a straightforward special report on sensible financial ratio adjustments for financial statements of securitizing firms. At the heart of the adjustments was the practice of putting securitizations back "on"-balanced sheet to adjust earnings and leverage ratios for the idea that while the notional value of the loans had been taken off-balance-sheet, the economic (or dollar-value) risk exposure to that notional principal often had not.

In September 1997, Moody's Investors Service wrote directly, that:

> … the simple act of securitizing assets can affect the appearance of the income statement and balance sheet in a profound manner without, in many cases, significantly altering the underlying economics of the [seller]. Under gain on sale accounting, income statements reflect the present-value of lifetime earnings from assets in a single quarter, predicated on numerous assumptions and calculations. Reported earnings may give a false sense of the long term ability of the company to repay debt. Reported balance sheet leverage declines as securitized assets are treated as "sold" for accounting purposes, although there may be little, if any, risk transference. (p. 2)

With respect to earnings, Moody's adjusted the standard ratio used to express the ability of companies to pay, or "cover," interest expense from operating earnings, EBITDA coverage, which is the ratio of earnings before interest, taxes, depreciation, and amortization to interest expense. According to Moody's this ratio may give a false sense of security when calculated for sellers. In particular, Moody's (1997) maintains, "... the inclusion of gain on sale in the numerator of this ratio is inappropriate as [those] gains cannot be used to pay interest expense. To adjust for this, [Moody's] simply deduct[s] any gain on sale from earnings when calculating EBITDA coverage. The result is adjusted EBITDA coverage". (p. 9)

To adjust leverage for securitizations, Moody's (1997) adds the securitizations back onto on-balance-sheet debt. Then Moody's adjusted common equity by reversing gains from securitizations (gains-on-sale) and adding back excess spread as income to common equity. Adjustments are also made for the different accounting methods firms would be subject to if they did not account for securitizations as sales.

Such adjustments help address industry dynamics that had been identified at least a decade earlier. Moody's (1987) points out that while "... the practices developed by the accounting and regulatory world are useful starting points for the credit analyst, ... these guidelines often do not fully capture the true economic risks of a securitized asset sale to the originator's credit quality". Hence, Moody's maintained even then that their focus was not on whether a sale of assets is arbitrarily put on or kept off the balance sheet, but rather on "... assessing the fundamental residual credit risks left with the originator from the asset sale and the amount of the firm's equity base that should be allocated to support the transaction". (p. 3)[3]

Hence, seller/servicers have long "sold" loans into securitizations while retaining the lion's share of economic risk in the transaction. Indeed, recognizing those economics, in 2001 bank regulators required banks to hold 100 percent capital against the 2 percent first-loss piece. (Calomiris and Mason, 2005) So in fact now *requiring* seller/servicers to

---

[3] Moody's prior analyses seem prescient in light of Structured Investment Vehicles and Auction Rate Securities taken back on to bank balance sheets following the abject failures of those structures in 2007 and 2008, respectively (See, for instance, Mason, 2008, on SIVs, ARS, and CPDOs). Of course, prior to the recent difficulties the industry was small and Moody's was still able to maintain an aggressive stance on clarity and accuracy.

retain that piece under the aegis of having "skin in the game" will change nothing.

4. Without Risk Transfer There Can be No True Sale

The retained interests that Moody's wrote about and bank regulators addressed are the focus the "variable interest entity" approach that is the foundation of recently proposed FASB revisions. FASB's approach, however, harkens back to a simpler time that is no longer relevant. Prior to financial engineering, ownership (and therefore on-balance sheet treatment) was dictated by voting interest: if a firm owned more than 50 percent of voting equity shares, they clearly owned the firm.

With financial engineering (as demonstrated by Enron), all that changed. The first attempt to establish ownership in a financially-engineered construct was attempted in FASB140, which stipulated that if somebody else did not own at least 3 percent of the funding liabilities and equity, the selling firm had to carry it on its own books. Of course, Enron found this requirement very easy to obviate by lending someone else money to buy the 3 percent and then selling the rest with Enron guarantees of the securities' performance, thus retaining a substantial first-loss stake in the arrangement.

Under FIN46, created to revise the rules that were used to construct the failed Enron securitizations, the 3 percent rule became the 10 percent rule. The entities used by Enron were labeled "Variable Interest Entities" (VIEs) and others "Qualified Special Purpose Entities" (QSPEs), which were excluded from the 10 percent rule because they are thought to be what FASB termed "passive securitizations".

The key problem with us today, therefore, is that the purportedly "passive" credit card, mortgage, home equity, auto loan and other qualified SPEs (QSPEs) are not passive at all. The FASB/bank regulatory approach ignores the fact that seller/servicers have always been able to affect pool performance through servicing, *regardless* of whether they hold a portion of the subordinate bonds, themselves. Hence — importantly for understanding today's crisis — when seller/servicers could no longer perfect the regulatory arbitrage by holding the first-loss piece, they increasingly relied upon "representations and warranties" to provide the desired credit enhancement for investors — that is, to make sure investors did not lose so that they would be sure to buy the *next* securitization.

Seller/servicers' relationship with the loans they have sold can never be passive as long as they offer substantially unlimited representations and warranties on loan performance. To form a view of the objective "truly passive" sale, suppose I sell you my car. I give you the car and receive cash in return. You drive away. If the engine falls out two weeks later you are out of luck. Classical caveat emptor applies. That is a true sale. From an accounting perspective, we can clearly take the car off the balance sheet and replace it with the cash at the time of the sale.

Now, suppose I give you a warranty at the time of sale: for six months, if anything happens I will give you your money back. I should probably keep some cash on hand to satisfy the obligation should you run into trouble. From an accounting perspective, it would make sense that I should not close the sale until the six months have passed. That is, I should hold reserves against the possibility that the car will break down. The entire car is still "on-balance-sheet" (as a contingent liability) but so is the cash so we have no effect until the warranty expires.

Now, adding complexity, suppose that I give you a warranty that states I will fix the car — not give you your money back — if anything goes wrong. Perhaps I don't have to reserve against the entire price of the car now, but only the cost of repairs. That could make sense, but the maximum cost of repairs is still the total value of the car. Even if I could estimate the probable cost of repairs, I may still want to remain aware of the total possible liability involved in honoring the warranty.

Back in the early development of securitization, and indeed still today with most Real Estate Mortgage Investment Conduits (REMICS), the underlying situation is that of the first example of the true sale above. A pool of loans is purchased from the seller and financed through RMBS. The pool is passive in the sense that the seller is legally restricted from swapping loans into and out of the pool to satisfy "representations and warranties".

But as different securitization structures and paradigms developed, seller/servicers saw the capacity for greater arbitrage through manipulating pools, rendering the passive view of many securitizations revealed in even FASB's view toward its FIN46 post-Enron reforms obsolete. In 1989, early credit card securitizations showed the path forward. Because credit card accounts are, on average, outstanding less than a year it is necessary to structure a "revolving" period so that the pool of loans can be funded by bonds of longer maturity than the loans.

During the revolving period, old credit card loans that have been paid off are replaced with new loans so that the pool balance remains constant. Since the early 1990s, there were concerns with "cherry picking" the new accounts to be added so as to increase the credit quality of the pool. While such practice has never been officially confirmed or denied, it has appeared as if regulators allowed such practices to encourage stable funding for the industry.

By 1997, industry concern rose to substantial levels after several sizeable pools had been supported. Already, substantial-sized issuers such as First Union, Prudential, and Green Tree Financial had supported securitizations to keep the deals from unraveling and coming back on-balance sheet. The transactions that are the focus of concern are outlined in Table 1. In January 1997, Moody's summarized the tradeoff:

> By supporting a transaction, an originator presumably expects the action to benefit the company. If it is correct, the action will result in a "win-win" situation — both the ABS investors and the company's investors will benefit. However, at the time of the action, there generally is no guarantee that the company's analysis of the situation is correct. As a result, pouring more — or higher-quality — resources into a transaction, or re-acquiring lower-quality assets from a transaction, might actually leave a company's creditors in a worse net position, notwithstanding the more optimistic expectations held by the company's management. (p. 2)

But the idea of selling the loans while not really passing along the full risk of performance was too attractive for the rest of the world to pass up. Hence, Enron embarked on a similar endeavor, "selling" something for accounting purposes while retaining the economic risk. Of course, the risk was truly borne by Enron until the firm failed, resulting in a spectacular disentangling of myriad funding conduits and instruments implemented in the process and sold throughout the world.

While FASB's FIN46 revised accounting rules to preclude another Enron, it specifically exempted consumer credit securitizations from its rulemaking. Having had their future demonstrated so clearly by Enron, however, non-bank financial firms like New Century, investment banks like Bear Stearns, and even some commercial banks and thrifts pursed the same strategy. Those firms sold pools of mortgages that bore little resemblance to the early REMIC structures. In the private-label RMBS, loans that didn't perform well were repurchased in a ready and fluid

Table l. Notable Instances of Voluntary Originator Support Before 1997.

Originator	Transaction or Master Trust Name	Date	Action
Chrysler Financial Corporation	CFC-2 Grantor Trust	5/89	Increased letter of credit by 2% of invested amount
Sears Roebuck & Co.	Sears Credit Account Trust 1990-C	11/91	Added higher-quality accounts
Household Finance Corp.	Household Credit Card Trust 1990-1	2/93	Boosted "linance charge" collections by purchasing the SPC's residual interest in the CCA in installments; the 9 installments were counted as "finance charge" collections
Tandy Credit Corp.	Tandy Master Trust Series A	8/93	Increased credit protection for investors by 7% of invested amount, by increasing and purchasing additional Class B (subordinated) certificates and subordinating part of seller interest
Household Bank N.A.	Household Private Label Credit Card Master Trust II	11/95	Increased discount on new and existing receivables
Mercantile Bank of Illinois N.A.	Mercantile Credit Card Master Trust	2/96	Increased discount on new receivables; supplemented resources allocated to servicing of securitized receivables

(*Continued*)

Table l. (*Continued*)

Originator	Transaction or Master Trust Name	Date	Action
Chrysler Financial Corporation	Premier Auto Trust 1991-4, 1995-1, 1995-2, 1995-3, 1995-4	3/96	Waived rights to funds scheduled to be released from reserve fund to increase enhancement for investors
First Union National Bank of Georgia	First Union Master Credit Card Trust	5/96	Removed lower-quality accounts
Prudential Bank and Trust Co.	PB&T Master Credit Card Trust II	5/96	Began discounting new receivables
1-CC National Bank	First Chicago Master Trust II	7/96	Added higher-quality accounts
AT&T Universal Card Services Corp.	AT&l Universal Card Master Trust	8/96	Added higher-quality accounts
Prudential Bank and Trust Co.	PB&T Master Credit Card Trust II	10/96	Added subordinated loan to increase enhancement
Green Tree Financial Corp.	Green Tree SNIMC 1994-B, 1995-A	10/96	Tiansferrecl portion of servicing fees on underlying transactions to enhance cashflows to investors
First Union National Bank of Georgia	First Union Master Credit Card Trust	11/96	Waived rights to portion of servicing fee to enhance cashflows to investors

fashion, unlike the sort of "passive" true sale securitization envisioned by FASB.

While sellers have voluntarily provided additional support to preserve the performance and bond ratings of their structured transactions, still, it would be egregious to maintain that securitization transfers no risk at all. After all, in the event of catastrophic asset quality problems, the seller may choose NOT to support a troubled deal, notwithstanding any legal or moral responsibility to do so. In such a case, the asset-backed bond investors and any third-party credit enhancers, such as a bond insurer, would absorb the residual losses. By contrast, a portfolio lender would have to absorb all losses.

Incentives along the path toward default, however, create the illusion of cliff risk. Trouble begins with the non-passive "representations and warranties" paradigm when loan performance sours beyond the ability of the seller to support pool performance out of regular operating earnings.

When performance deteriorates significantly, the seller has to either increase earnings or stem losses. Since the seller's cash earnings primarily arise through *making new loans to generate underwriting fees*, the seller counter-intuitively accelerates underwriting. Since better-qualified borrowers will most likely obtain cheaper loans from financially sound lenders, the seller targets down-market consumers — subprime borrowers — for the new business.

Of course, less creditworthy borrowers mean *more* losses. So the deterioration in loan performance that prompted the decline is met with more deterioration in loan performance. As the firm tumults down the death spiral, they attempt to modify loans using repayment and forbearance plans, while aggressively reaging[4] loans to classify as much of the portfolio as "performing" as possible. Some lenders, upon realizing that they were unable to generate enough repayment and forbearance plans to feed

[4] Reaging refers to the criteria for classifying a previously delinquent loan "current" again. Conservative reagers (including commercial banks, by FFIEC rulemaking, as per *Notices*, 65 Federal Register 113, Jun. 12, 2000 at 36905-6.) require an account to post three consecutive on-time payments to be classified as current again. Aggressive reagers (non-bank finance companies) can choose to reage on the mere promise of a payment. Aggressive reaging has been found to have played a role in many of the mortgage firm failures in the crisis (See, for instance, *Notices*, 70 Federal Register 249, Dec. 29, 2005 at 77257 for evidence of ongoing concern about reaging.).

the reaging process, resort to "amnesty" programs, wherein they merely write off the past due balance and call the loan current once again — sometimes without the delinquent borrower even knowing their loan has been awarded such "amnesty".[5]

Loan swapping under "representations and warranties" therefore, together with loan modifications carried out through ongoing servicing allow the seller to readily absorb the loan risk that was purportedly sold. Hence, Nomura (2004) notes that, "... without audits or third-party oversight, a ... servicer in financial distress may manipulate amortization triggers, divert deal cash flows, or otherwise misappropriate assets". (p. 41)

The financial prospects for a seller/servicer that is unable to muster the resources to voluntarily support a securitization are grim. Such a seller/servicer would likely no longer receive any excess spread from the securitization trusts and might have difficulty raising external cash due to uncertainty over the asset quality of its serviced portfolio. Such a seller/servicer would surely not be able to issue again in markets any time soon. Hence, the seller/servicer can be reasonably expected to fail outright in the near term. (Higgins and Mason, 2005)

Securitization investor rights in such circumstances are vastly irrelevant. Investors often have a legal right to replace the primary servicer with a backup servicer, since the performance of securitized assets can be impaired by actions taken by a servicer in financial distress. But they usually need to do so before bankruptcy, since the bankruptcy court may not allow replacement of the servicer since servicer rights may be viewed as property of the debtor's estate!

But servicers do not routinely and systematically report roll rates, advance rates (the money the servicer has to pay to investors "as if" it had been received from loans in delinquency) or modifications and related costs to either RMBS or mortgage bank investors, nor to regulators. Worse yet, as the crisis has deepened servicers who do produce such

---

[5] Similarly, there still do not exist regulatory and accounting rules for reaging modified loans. Do modified loans have to post three consecutive on-time payments to be considered current again, like other delinquent loans made by commercial banks? Should the standard be tougher, since the modified borrower can be considered worse off than a historically typical borrower that cures their delinquency without assistance? Will such a definition be applied outside commercial banks? Without answers to these questions investors in RMBS and mortgage banks have no ability to distinguish whether modification is mere accounting "window dressing" or truly valuable.

reports for their own use have become more reluctant to share their internally-generated reports with outside parties. Hence, investors and regulators alike have almost no means of judging whether servicing quality is maintained and whether modification programs are beneficial to borrowers or lenders. Investors are therefore reluctant to buy new RMBS and have little ability to judge the impact of servicer performance on the value of existing RMBS, while mortgage bank investors and regulators similarly have little means of judging bank safety and soundness and bank performance.[6]

Investors thus may have no choice but to continue with the original seller/servicer even if the quality of its servicing is poor. By the time the seller/servicer is willing to give up servicing rights, those can often be difficult to transfer because they are tainted by the servicer's malfeasance, and are therefore often of too little value for a follow-up servicer to maintain on any reasonably profitable basis. (Moody's, 2002, p. 4; Nomura, 2004, p. 41)

Servicing rights also create difficulties for a bankruptcy trustee — including the Federal Deposit Insurance Corporation (FDIC) — who seeks to liquidate the assets of a failed seller/servicer. Firms like IndyMac are difficult to liquidate because no other servicer is willing to service the portfolio without substantial remuneration to insulate them from the losses and legal ramifications of unwinding the potential fraud and malfeasance left over from the previous distressed servicer. That's why the FDIC was left servicing the NextBank credit card portfolio, and that is most likely the case at IndyMac as well (and some of that is probably behind Bank of America's purchase of Countrywide at a very favorable price at the behest of the FDIC).

The loan servicing rights are often the final remaining asset in the firm and the substantial potential for servicer malfeasance as the seller/servicer approaches bankruptcy can deteriorate their value significantly.

[6] But the situation is worse than that. Monitoring servicer performance requires — at the least — defining what a modification is and the procedural means by which it is to be administered. The first hurdle faced by Hope Now and the Office of the Comptroller of the Currency (OCC) reporting on modifications was the mere definition of a modification, and that hurdle has still not been overcome. Recall that lenders have already accommodated many borrowers through "repayment programs". Some observers say that repayment programs are not modifications, while others maintain they are. We still don't have an answer to that most basic question, nor do we have systematic reporting to track modification activity and subsequent performance.

Since there is so little to recover from a failed seller/servicer, the FDIC has maintained that it may disallow "true sale" status if it desires to seize those "truly sold" assets to recover deposit insurance outlays. Indeed, the legal status of securitizations remains unsettled. One of the most intriguing cases in the history of structured finance, In re LTV Steel Corporation, tested the fundamental tenet that assets can be isolated from the bankruptcy of their seller through a "true sale".

In December 2000, LTV Corporation (LTV), an integrated steel maker, and its operating subsidiaries filed for protection under Chapter 11. According to Moody's (2002), "LTV entered bankruptcy court without a DIP loan in place. Instead, LTV requested and the court granted permission to use the cash generated from two of LTV's securitizations in order to stay in business — despite the previous sale of these assets to two SPVs".

Even the court failed to see the logic in the securitization and was inclined toward allowing the estate to seize the securitized pools, maintaining, in a Memorandum Opinion, that, "[T]here seems to be an element of sophistry to suggest that Debtor does not retain at least an equitable interest in the property. ... To suggest that Debtor lacks some ownership interest in products that it creates with its own labor, as well as the proceeds to be derived from that labor, is difficult to accept". (Memorandum Opinion, 2001, cited in Moody's, 2002, p. 26) The case, however, was never ruled upon, therefore the issue of true sale — itself the keystone of securitization — remains contentious.

In summary, "true sale" as it has been practiced does not make sense. To get at any meaningful regulatory reforms, we need to go back to the basic tenet of a true sale. I sold you the car. Caveat emptor. Retaining servicing rights are like maintaining the car after the sale. Loan swap agreements are simple warranties. But even in this simple analogy, the recent credit crisis can be thought of as a systematic production line failure that is posing producers with massive recall warranty obligations.

In order to improve transparency, therefore, limits have to be placed on the amount of money that can be spent on maintenance, that is, loan servicing, after the sale. While the Financial Accounting Standards Board (FASB) has maintained that acting under representations and warranties is not optional, they are interpreting that optionality only in the strict legal sense. There is always the "real" option of simply refusing to support the pool representations and warranties. While that may result in some lawsuits, in reality those can be beaten back for several years giving the firm a chance to restore performance and eventually meet their contractual obligations. Hence, accounting policy also needs to financially value the option in the warranty.

5. Summary and Conclusion: Everything Old is New Again

The problem is a tragic collision of economics, finance, and accounting, where economic risk is placed where it is difficult to value financially and even the most complex accounting rules do not apply. While none of this augurs for prohibiting any of the above arrangements in the long term, it does provide a rationale for constraining financial product developments so that they do not grow systemically large before finance and accounting can properly characterize their risks and returns. Hence, there may be reason to curb the over-reliance on financial innovations — certainly within the realm of financial institutions that receive Federal and State safety net protection — and require public reporting of such exposures and values to better align incentives for innovation with the need for financial stability.

The interesting aspect, however, will be investor reactions moving forward. Developments like Countrywide's $8.4 billion settlement with eleven state Attorneys General, in which Countrywide (Bank of America in its stead) agreed to massive loan modifications seek to put modification losses to investors through the final "true sale" put, but ostensibly violating the "representations and warranties" in the securitization. Such a strategy is potentially viable since Countrywide, *per se*, will never seek to securitize again, so investor threats that they will no longer support Countrywide's gain-on-sale profits fall on deaf (dead) ears. But the issue may get even more interesting when, if losses become large enough, investors themselves seek to void true sale and reach back through to the seller/servicer bankruptcy estate for relief.

Rating agencies' characterizations of past crises eerily presage the present situation. In 2002, well prior to the current crisis, Moody's wrote, "The seller's capital structure, its diversity of funding sources, types of assets, and the business factors motivating its securitizations are all important considerations. The examples of deals gone 'bad' [such as those detailed in Table 2 from Nomura (2004)] reveal that an over-reliance on securitization as a funding source is an important risk factor. The overuse of securitization coupled with aggressive gain-on-sale accounting was a particularly lethal combination. ... new or unusual asset classes pose

Table 2. Problems and Lessons from Previous Securitization Failures.

Problems/Challenges Presented in Various Troubled ABS Deals						
	LTV Steel	DVI	Heilig-Meyers	NextCard	Spiegel/First Consumers	NCFE
Servicing fee too low to attract successor servicer				✓	✓	
Intervention by regulator to raise servicing fee					✓	
Creditors challenge "true sale" of assets	✓					
Asset performance linked to idiosyncratic servicing and collection practices		✓	✓			
Declining pool in early amortization (account closures)			✓	✓	✓	
Early amortization delayed by regulator				✓		
Early amortization delayed by issuer		✓			✓	
"Fraud losses" reclassified as "credit losses" by regulators				✓	✓	
Manipulation of triggers					✓	
Servicer misappropriates collections		✓			✓	✓
Fraud regarding the existence or character of the assets						✓
Securities fraud in sale of ABS					✓	✓
Triple-A-rated ABS downgraded		✓	✓	✓	✓	✓
Triple-A-rated ABS default (incl. forced exchange)	✓		✓			

(*Continued*)

Table 2. (*Continued*)

Lessons from Various Troubled ABS Deals	LTV Steel	DVI	Heilig-Meyers	NextCard	Spiegel/First Consumers	NCFE
Idiosyncratic servicing and collection practices can strongly affect the performance of securitized receivables		✓	✓			
Contractual early amortization triggers may not work		✓		✓	✓	
The "declining pool" scenario can really happen			✓	✓	✓	
Without audits or third-party oversight, an ABS servicer in financial distress may manipulate amortization triggers, divert deal cash flows, or otherwise misappropriate assets		✓			✓	✓
The performance of securitized assets can be impaired by actions taken by a servicer in financial distress	✓	✓	✓	✓	✓	
A deal's servicing fee must be large enough to attract a successor servicer			✓	✓	✓	
Regulator can increase the servicing fee in an ABS deal					✓	
Fraud risk is real and investors should demand protective features in the deals that they buy					✓	✓
No transaction is "bankruptcy proof"	✓	✓	✓	✓	✓	✓

particular risks as well". (p. 1) The current crisis merely wrapped all the most egregious influences into one and applied them to nearly all collateral types in the market.

In conclusion, while policymakers continue to try to pigeonhole securitization accounting into simple on- and off-balance-sheet classifications, the issue is far more complicated due to legacy accounting treatments surrounding the entire securitization process, as well as securitization's unsettled legal status. We cannot expect securitization to become more transparent without removing other perverse incentives in gain-on-sale accounting and true sale status. Given the amount of asymmetric information endemic in poor securitization reporting, it is not at all surprising that a crisis occurred once securitization reached sufficient scale. It is past time, therefore, to clean up reporting for the structured finance marketplace that has proven so useful in deepening banking system capital to fund myriad consumer and commercial loan products.

References

Calomiris, C. and J. Mason (2004). Credit card securitization and regulatory arbitrage. *Journal of Financial Services Research*, 26(1), August 5–27 (lead article).

Financial Accounting Standards Board (2005). *Accounting for Transfers of Financial Assets, An Amendment of FASB Statement No. 140*, (Financial Accounting Series No. 1225-001, Revision of Exposure Draft Issued June 10, 2003), August 11.

Higgins, E. and J. Mason (2004). What is the value of recourse to asset backed securities? A study of credit card bank ABS Rescues. *Journal of Banking and Finance*, April, 28(4), 857–874.

Mason, J. R. (2008). Structuring for leverage: CPDOs, SIVs, and ARSs. In Robert Litan, R. Herring, and Y. Fuchita (eds.). *Prudent Lending Restored: Securitization after the 2007 Mortgage Securities Meltdown*, part of the Brookings-Wharton Series on Financial Intermediaries, Brookings Institution Press (forthcoming).

Memorandum Opinion (2001). U.S. Bankruptcy Court for the Northern District of Ohio, February 5.

Moody's Investors Service (1997). *Alternative Financial Ratios for the Effects of Securitization*, September.

Moody's Investors Service (1987). *Asset Securitization and Corporate Financial Health*, December.

Moody's Investors Service (2002). *Bullet Proof Structures Revisited: Bankruptcies and a Market Hangover Test Securitizations' Mettle*, August 30.
Moody's Investors Service (1997). *The Costs and Benefits of Supporting "Troubled" Asset-Backed Securities*, January.
Nomura (2004). *ABS Credit Migrations 2004*, December 7.
Notices (2000). 65 Federal Register 113, June 12 at 36905-6.
Notices (2005). 70 Federal Register 249, December 29 at 77257.

The Credit Crunch of 2007: What Went Wrong? Why? What Lessons Can be Learned?

John C. Hull*
University of Toronto, Canada

Abstract

This paper explains the products that were used to securitize mortgages during the period leading up to the credit crunch of 2007 and explains why many of these products have performed so badly. It also examines some of the lessons that can be learned from the crisis.

1. Introduction

The overexpansion of credit in the U.S. housing market has led to huge losses by financial institutions and an almost unprecedented tightening of credit throughout the world. How long it will take world financial markets to recover and which financial institutions will fail is still unclear. In retrospect, the actions of almost all large financial institutions during the period leading up to 2007 were imprudent. It is clearly important for the regulators of financial institutions, and for financial institutions themselves, to analyze what went wrong and why. Hopefully, this analysis will result in the surviving financial institutions becoming stronger and more stable entities.

This paper has three objectives. The first is to explain the products that were used to securitize mortgages during the period leading up to the

* John C. Hull is a Professor of derivatives and risk management, Joseph L. Rotman School of Management, University of Toronto. E-mail: hull@rotman.utoronto.ca. He is grateful to Richard Cantor and Roger Stein for useful comments on an earlier draft. All views expressed are the author's own.

credit crunch of 2007; the second is to provide some insights as to why those products have performed so badly; the third is to suggest some lessons that can be learned from the crisis.

2. The U.S. Housing Market

A natural starting point for any discussion of the credit crunch of 2007 is the U.S. housing market. Figure 1 shows the S&P/Case-Shiller composite-10 index for house prices between January 1987 and June 2008. In about the year 2000, house prices started to rise much faster than they had in the previous decade. The very low Fed Funds rate between 2002 and 2005 was an important contributory factor, but the bubble was largely fuelled by mortgage lending practices.

Mortgage lenders thought they were taking very little risk during the 2000 to 2007 period because the value of the collateral underlying their loans was rising very fast. Mian and Sufi (2008) produce results showing that there was a relaxation of the criteria used for mortgage lending. Their research defines "high denial zip codes" as zip codes for which a high proportion of mortgage applicants had been turned down in 1996, and shows that mortgage origination grew particularly fast for these zip codes from

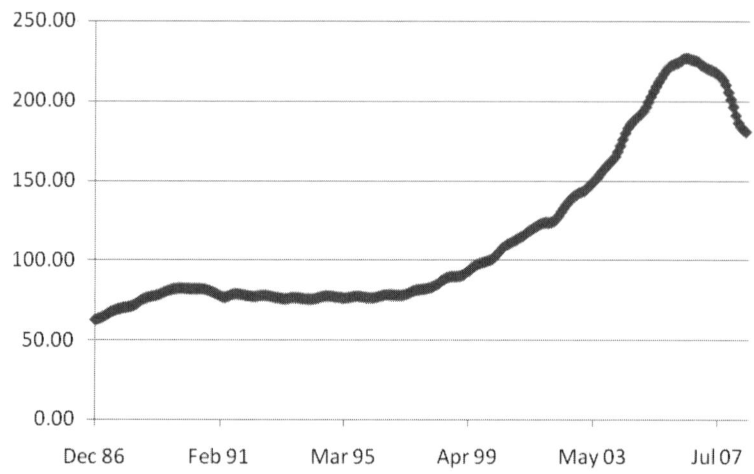

Figure 1. U.S. Real Estate Prices, 1987 to June 2008 S&P/Case-Shiller Composite-10 Index.

2000 to 2007. The new entrants to the real estate market created demand that was instrumental in pushing up prices.

Mortgages to less credit worthy borrowers are defined as "subprime". A rule of thumb is that a subprime mortgage is a home loan to someone with a credit (FICO) score of less than 620, but some lenders classify a mortgage as subprime when the borrower has a credit score as high as 680 if the down payment is less than 5 percent. Standard & Poor's has estimated that subprime mortgage origination in 2006 alone totalled $421 billion. AMP Capital Investors estimates that there was a total of $1.4 trillion of subprime mortgages outstanding in July 2007.

Mian and Sufi's results suggest that lending criteria were relaxed progressively through time rather than all at once, because originations in high denial zip codes are an increasing function of time during the 2000 to 2007 period. Zimmerman (2007) provides some confirmation of this. He shows that subsequent default experience indicates that mortgages made in 2006 were of a lower quality than those made in 2005 and these were in turn of lower quality than the mortgages made in 2004. Some market participants understood what was going on. Terms such as "Liar Loans" (referring to the fact that people could safely lie on their mortgage application because their statements would not be checked) and NINJA (referring to applicants who had No Income, No Job, and no Assets) have been used to describe the market. But the full extent of the risks and their potential impact on markets was not appreciated until well into 2007. Evidence for this is that the ABX BBB index was above 70 in February 2007. (By September 2008, it had fallen to about 5.)

As pointed out by Zimmerman (2007), once the housing bubble had started, mortgage lenders wanted to keep it going by attracting new entrants to the market. Because house prices were going up, they had to become creative in finding ways to make houses appear affordable. One approach was to offer an initial period of two or three years where rates were below market. In a 2/28 Adjustable Rate Mortgage (ARM) the rate might be fixed at 8 percent (or lower) for two years and then set equal to six-month LIBOR plus 6 percent for the remaining 28 years. To quote from Krinsman (2007), "In 2005 and 2006 lenders made it easier for borrowers to obtain subprime loans. For example, the typical subprime borrower with a credit score between 450 and 680 could obtain a loan with little or no down payment, provide little or no documented proof of income or assets, obtain a loan with a low initial 'teaser' interest rate that reset to a new, higher rate after two or three years".

As Figure 1 illustrates, the bubble burst in 2007. Many mortgage holders found they could no longer afford mortgages when teaser rates ended. Foreclosures increased. House prices declined. This resulted in other mortgage holders, who had borrowed 100 percent, or close to 100 percent, of the cost of a house having negative equity. Some exercised their implicit put options and "walked away" from their houses and their mortgage obligations. This reinforced the downward trend in house prices.

3. Securitization

Financial institutions frequently did not retain the mortgages they originated on their books. Subprime mortgages were securitized and sold to investors using Asset-Backed Securities (ABSs).[1] Securitization has been an important and useful tool in financial markets for many years, but it played a part in the creation of the housing bubble. For example, as I will describe later, Keys et al. (2008) show that there was a link between securitization and the lax screening of mortgages.

The basic structure of an ABS is shown in Figure 2. A portfolio of subprime mortgages (Asset 1 to Asset n) is created and the credit risks are "tranched out". The mechanism for doing this is known as a "waterfall". In the example shown, Tranche 3 is the senior tranche. Its principal is 75 percent of the total principal of the underlying mortgage portfolio. Tranche 2 is the mezzanine tranche. Its principal is 20 percent of the total. Tranche 1, with a principal of 5 percent, is the equity tranche.[2]

There are complicated rules defining what happens to the cash flows from the mortgages. Rules that are indicative of the design of an ABS are the following. Tranche 3 receives the cash flows until its promised return (6 percent in this example) is met. Any extra cash flows go to Tranche 2 until it has received its promised return. Only after Tranche 3 and Tranche 2 have received their promised returns does Tranche 1 receive anything. As an approximation, the structure can also be characterized in terms of who

---

[1] It has been estimated that 54 percent of subprime mortgages were securitized in 2001 and this rose to 75 percent in 2006.

[2] Figure 1 is somewhat simplified. There are usually more than three tranches, and subprime mortgages were sometimes mixed in with other financial instruments such as credit card receivables in the portfolio.

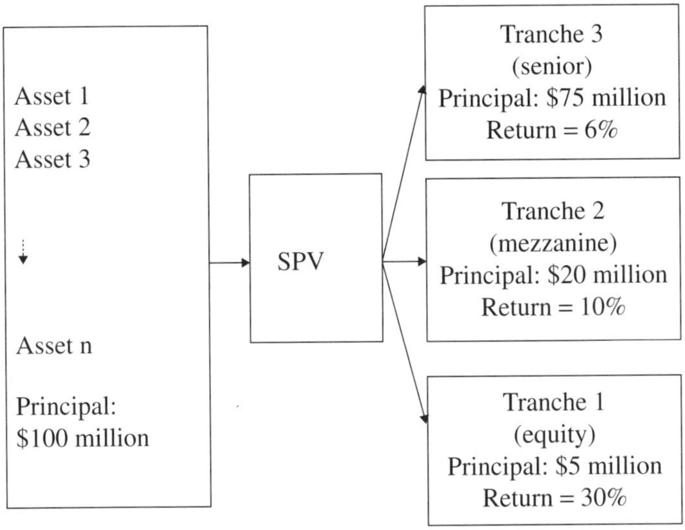

Figure 2. An Asset Backed Security (Simplified).

bears the losses on the underlying portfolio. Tranche 1 has 5 percent of the principal and bears the first 5 percent of the losses. As compensation for this, its return at any given time is 30 percent on the part of its principal that has not been eroded by losses. Tranche 1 is wiped out when losses exceed 5 percent. Tranche 2 bears losses between 5 percent and 25 percent on the portfolio. In return for doing this it earns 10 percent of its outstanding principal. Losses in excess of 25 percent are borne by the senior tranche, Tranche 3. (This characterization of the structure will be used for some "back-of-envelope" calculations later.)

The arranger of the ABS ensures that it is structured so that Tranche 3 is rated AAA. There is a huge unsatisfied demand for AAA-rated securities and so (at least until mid-2007) there was no difficulty in finding investors to buy Tranche 3. Tranche 1 was typically either retained by the originator or sold to a hedge fund. Finding a market for Tranche 2 proved to be more difficult. This is where financial engineers became creative (perhaps too creative). They designed a structure known as an ABS CDO or Mezz CDO. This tranches out the risks from a portfolio of mezzanine tranches in the same way that an ABS tranches out the risks from a portfolio of subprime mortgages when the original ABS is created. The structure is illustrated in Figure 3. The ABS CDO in Figure 3 is structured

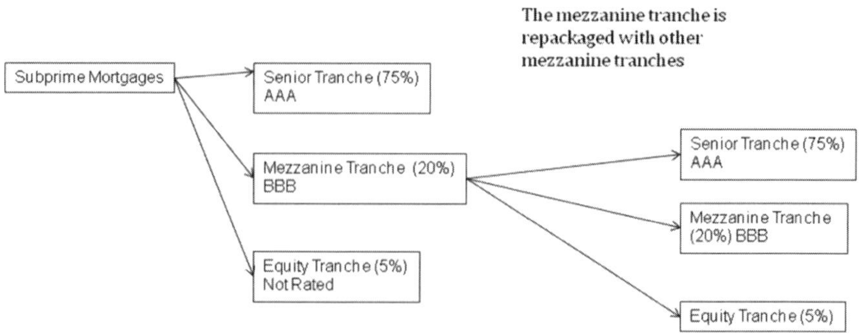

Figure 3. An ABS CDO (Simplified).

so that the senior tranche is rated AAA. This means that the total of the AAA-rated instruments created is 90 percent (75 percent plus 75 percent of 20 percent) of the principal of the underlying mortgage portfolio.[3]

In my example (admittedly simplified) the AAA-rated tranche of the ABS in Figure 2 would probably have been downgraded in the second half of 2007. However, it will receive the promised return if losses on the underlying mortgage portfolio are less than about 25 percent. The AAA-rated tranche of the ABS CDO in Figure 3 is not so lucky. It will get paid the promised return if losses on the underlying portfolios are less than about 10 percent. But, if they are 15 percent, 20 percent, and 25 percent, the losses on this tranche can be expected to be 33.3 percent, 66.7 percent, and 100 percent, respectively.[4] These results are shown in Table 1. The value of the tranches of an ABS is dependent on both the default rate and correlation. The ABS CDO incorporates a form of leverage and, as the example illustrates, the values of its tranches are very highly dependent on

[3] It is tempting to increase the 90 percent further by forming a new ABS CDO from the mezzanine tranches of other ABS CDOs. This did happen.

[4] To illustrate the calculations, consider the case where losses on the underlying mortgage portfolios are 20 percent. A total of 5 percent of the losses are borne by the equity tranche of an ABS and 15 percent by the mezzanine tranche. The mezzanine tranche has 20 percent of the principal, so that 15/20 or 75 percent of the principal of each ABS mezzanine tranche is lost. The ABS CDO therefore consists of a portfolio of instruments each bearing a 75 percent loss. Of the 75 percent loss on this portfolio, 5 percent is borne by the equity tranche of the ABS CDO, 20 percent by the mezzanine tranche of the ABS CDO, and 50 percent by the senior tranche. This means that the senior tranche loses 50/75 or 66.7 percent of its principal.

Table 1. Losses to AAA Tranches of ABS CDO in Example.

Losses to Subprime Portfolios (%)	Losses to Mezzanine Tranche of ABS (%)	Losses to Equity Tranche of ABS CDO (%)	Losses to Mezzanine Tranche of ABS CDO (%)	Losses to Senior Tranche of ABS CDO (%)
10	25	100	100	0
15	50	100	100	33.3
20	75	100	100	66.7
25	100	100	100	100

default rates and correlations.[5] The example helps explain why in July 2008 Merrill Lynch agreed to sell $30.6 billion of senior tranches of ABS CDOs that had previously been rated AAA to Lone Star Funds for as little as 22 cents on the dollar.[6]

4. Lessons

While acknowledging that it is easy to be wise after the event, this section will review some lessons that can be learned from the crisis.

4.1 *Agency costs: Originators and investors*

A key issue is the extent to which the behavior of mortgage originators was influenced by their knowledge that the majority of the loans would be securitized. Casual empiricism suggests that the interests of mortgage originators were not aligned with the interests of investors. Mortgage originators did not ask the natural question: "Is this a good lending opportunity? Will the borrower make payments as promised?" Instead the question was "Can I make a profit by selling this mortgage to someone else?"

[5] If the mezzanine tranches of ABS CDOs are themselves tranched out (see footnote 3), the dependence on default rates and correlations is even more extreme.

[6] Furthermore, Merrill Lynch agreed to finance 75 percent of the purchase price.

A key consideration in mortgage lending is the borrower's FICO score. For mortgages with little or no documentation a FICO score of 620 is a cut-off. Mortgages can be securitized relatively easily if the FICO score is above 620, but not if it is below 620. In their research Keys *et al.* (2008) compared low-documentation mortgages with FICO scores just below 620 to those with FICO scores just above 620 and found that the former were less likely to default. This suggests that originators were more careful about the loans they made when they knew that they might not be securitized and took soft data (i.e. data other than the FICO score) into account.

In an environment where securitization is common, it is clearly important that the interests of a loan originator are aligned with those of an investor in the loan. In making the decision on whether to lend, the originator should be motivated to look at the loan in the same way as an investor. Very often, after securitization, the originator becomes the administrator of a mortgage, deciding what to do when the borrower is behind with payments, when to foreclose, etc. The originator should be motivated to take these decisions in the best interests of investors.

In some cases, the mortgage originator keeps the equity tranche. This provides some alignment of interests. But when the equity tranche is worth zero (as it now is for most ABSs and ABS CDOs), the originator no longer has any financial interest in the portfolio.

If the securitization market is to have a rebirth, some changes are likely to be necessary to give investors confidence. One idea is that the originator should keep a certain percentage (say, 20 percent) of all tranches. Regardless of what happens, the interests of originators are then aligned with the interests of investors. Note that there is a big difference between (a) an originating institution securitizing 80 percent of its portfolio and (b) an originating institution securitizing 100 percent of its portfolio while keeping 20 percent of each tranche. In the first case there will always be a suspicion that the better loans have been retained by the originator and that screening was lax on the rest. Also, the originator has less incentive to be an effective administrator of the securitized portfolio in the first case. Rating agencies might reasonably assign a higher rating to tranches of a portfolio where a percentage of each tranche has been retained.

The results of Keys *et al.* suggest that this proposal might have reduced the market excesses during the period leading up to the credit crunch of 2007. However, it should be acknowledged that one of the ironies of the credit crunch is that securitization did not in many instances get the mortgages off the books of the originating banks. Often AAA-rated senior tranches were bought by other parts of the bank. Because banks were investors and originators, one might expect a reasonable alignment of the interests of investors and originators. But perhaps the part of the bank investing in the mortgages was far removed from the part of the bank originating the mortgages and there was little information flow from one to the other.

4.2 *Agency costs: Financial institutions and their employees*

It is clear from the current crisis that the interests of many employees of financial institutions are not aligned with the interests of the financial institutions and their shareholders. The huge bonuses paid by Wall Street are widely reported. For many employees, short-term cash bonuses are a large proportion of remuneration, more important than either the base salary or longer-term incentives such as employee stock options. Short-term bonuses are paid at a year end and relate to profits made during the year. If an employee generates huge profits one year and is responsible for severe losses the next year, the employee will receive a big bonus the first year and will not have to return it the following year. The employee might lose his or her job as a result of the second year losses, but even that is not a disaster. Financial institutions seem to be surprisingly willing to recruit individuals with losses on their resumes.

All this creates a situation where the employees of financial institutions have very short-term horizons. Many people saw the possibility, if not the inevitability, of a collapse in the U.S. housing market long before it happened (although few expected the consequences to be as severe as they have been.) Why did traders continue to expose the banks they worked for to this risk? Unfortunately, when trading and other decisions were being taken in 2006, many bank employees did not care what would happen in 2007. Their attention was focused on how large their bonuses would be in 2006.

The issue here is not the size of bonuses, but how they are calculated. It would be an improvement if annual bonuses reflected performance over a longer period (say, five years) with "clawback". One idea is the following. At the end of each year a financial institution awards a "bonus accrual" (positive or negative) to each employee reflecting the employee's contribution to the business. The actual cash bonus received by an employee at the end of a year would be the average bonus accrual over the previous five years or zero, whichever is higher. For the purpose of this calculation, bonus accruals would be set equal to zero for years prior to the employee joining the financial institution (unless another arrangement is negotiated) and bonuses would not be paid after an employee leaves it. Although not perfect, this type of plan would motivate employees to use a multi-year time horizon when making decisions.

4.3 *Transparency*

An ABS or ABS CDO is typically defined by a legal document several hundred pages long. It is safe to assume that most investors did not read the document when they bought AAA-rated tranches of the structures. They relied on the "AAA" label. Once the tranches were perceived as risky it became almost impossible to trade them.[7] This was because potential investors did not understand enough about the underlying portfolio and the algorithm used to determine the cash flows received by the various tranches.

ABSs (and particularly ABS CDOs) are arguably the most complex credit derivatives that are traded. Lawyers should move with the times and define these instruments using software rather than words. In addition to providing a data file with the attributes of the mortgages or other instruments underlying the instruments, lawyers should provide software enabling the cash flows realized by different tranches in different circumstances to be calculated.[8] The user's inputs to the software would define a possible outcome concerning interest and principal payments on the underlying instruments each year. The outputs would be the cash flows realized by each tranche holder each year.[9] Structures like ABS CDOs

---

[7] The rating measures credit quality not liquidity, but the two are sometimes confused.

[8] The software would be updated to reflect the performance of the underlying assets periodically.

[9] I understand that some investors did have access to waterfall software (from sources other than lawyers). My point here is that the more freely and easily available this software is to investors — and to independent researchers — the less the potential for transparency problems. Software is simply a more efficient and more transparent way of making the terms of a deal available to as wide a range of investors and researchers as possible. (This is particularly true when some components of a portfolio are tranches of other portfolios.)

where tranches are defined in terms of other tranches could be handled efficiently.

This would have a huge advantage. Investors and independent researchers would have no difficulties in running scenario analyses and forming their own opinions about the values of different tranches. The current illiquidity of the ABS and ABS CDO market might well have been avoided if ABSs and ABS CDOs had been defined in the way I have described. (Indeed with this type of software investors might have better understood the risks in the ABS CDO market in the first place.) A good case can be made for handling many derivatives (particularly the more complex ones) in this way so that confirms are replaced by subroutines.[10]

4.4 *The need for models*

Normally financial institutions do not trade instruments unless they have satisfactory models for valuing them. Typically there is a group within a financial institution that has the responsibility of vetting the model used for valuing a product and the product cannot be traded in any volume until the model has been approved. What is surprising about the subprime crisis is that financial institutions were prepared to trade senior tranches of an ABS or an ABS CDO without a model. Possibly it was thought that a model is unnecessary for valuing a AAA-rated instrument. But the lack of a model makes risk management almost impossible and causes problems when the instrument loses its rating.

The readiness of financial institutions to trade ABS CDOs is particularly surprising. An ABS CDO is a similar structure to what is called a CDO squared in the synthetic CDO market.[11] CDO squareds are recognized by traders in the synthetic CDO market as highly risky products that are difficult to price. The market for them almost disappeared largely for this reason a few years ago. A tranche of an ABS CDO is no less risky and no less difficult to price than a CDO squared, but was nevertheless considered by many financial institutions to be a good investment. Because

---

[10] In my work with financial institutions I have come across mistakes in confirms that were several years old, indicating that the parties did not really rely on the confirms for their understanding of how a deal worked.

[11] See for example Hull and White (2006) for a discussion of CDO squareds.

models were not developed, the key role of correlation in valuing ABSs and (particularly) ABS CDOs was not well understood.

4.5 *How models should be used*

Having the models to value ABSs and ABS CDOs would have helped, but it would not by itself have been enough to mitigate the subprime crisis. To understand how models might have helped we have to consider how they should have been used.

The risk measures used by regulators, and by financial institutions themselves, are largely based on historical experience. For example, value-at-risk measures for market risk are typically based on the movements in market variables seen over the last two to three years. Credit risk measures are based on default experience stretching back over 100 years. Stress testing often involves looking at the largest market moves experienced over the last 10, 20, or 30 years.

There can be no question that historical data provides a useful guide for risk managers. But historical data cannot be used in conjunction with models in a mechanistic way to determine if risks are acceptable.[12] In the risk management arena it is important that models be supplemented with human judgement. A risk management committee should meet regularly to consider the key risks facing a financial institution. Stress tests should be based on the scenarios generated by these managers in addition to those generated from historical data. The risk committee should be particularly sensitive to situations where the market appears to be showing bouts of "irrational exuberance".

One of the lessons from past financial crises is that correlations increase in stressed market conditions. Using standard value-at-risk techniques to estimate correlations from past data and assuming that those correlations will apply in stressed markets is not appropriate. One of the roles of the risk management committee should have been to recognize the bubble in house prices and insist that stress tests where default rates simultaneously rise in all parts of the country be carried. Of course

[12] There was in any case very little relevant historical data relating to subprime mortgages. This is because the subprime mortgages during the 2000 to 2007 period were different from subprime mortgages in previous years. The latter were primarily second mortgages.

it is also important that the senior management of a bank actually listen to their risk managers and other advisers during periods of irrational exuberance. There is some evidence that they did not,[13] but reducing the short-term nature of incentive plans as discussed earlier has the potential to help as far as this is concerned.

5. Conclusions

The underlying cause of the credit crunch was the high level of correlation between the default rates in different parts of the U.S. Investors in ABSs and ABS CDOs thought they were protected because the underlying mortgage portfolios were geographically diverse, but were proved to be wrong. Mezzanine tranches of virtually all ABSs suffered losses and as a result all the tranches of ABS CDOs suffered losses. The rough calculations given earlier for the simplified structures in Figures 2 and 3 illustrate how this happened.

Could the problems have reasonably been anticipated and the crisis made less severe? As already acknowledged, it is easy to be wise after the event. But it is difficult to avoid the conclusion that the period leading up to 2007 was one of irrational exuberance, where banks chose to ignore the housing bubble and its potential impact on some very complicated products they were trading. Agency problems in the banks' originate-to-distribute model and short-term employee incentives were contributing factors.

References

Hull, J. and A. White (2006). Valuing credit derivatives using an implied copula approach. *Journal of Derivatives*, 14, Winter, pp. 8–28.

Keys, B. J., T. Mukherjee, A. Seru, and V. Vig (2008). Did securitization lead to lax screening? Evidence from subprime loans, University of Michigan, working paper, April.

[13] Some bank employees, such as Keishi Hotsuki, co-head of risk management at Merrill Lynch, and David Rosenberg, chief North American economist at Merrill Lynch, did sound warning bells ahead of the credit crunch, but were ignored. Ed Clark, CEO at TD Bank, who had the foresight to close down the bank's structured products business ahead of the crisis, has indicated that this decision met with huge opposition within the bank.

Krinsman, A. N. (2007). Subprime mortgage meltdown: how did it happen and how will it end. *The Journal of Structured Finance*, Summer, pp. 13–19.

Mian, A. and A. Sufi, (2008). The consequences of mortgage credit expansion: evidence from the 2007 mortgage default crisis. Graduate School of Business, University of Chicago, working paper, May.

Zimmerman, T. (2007). The great subprime meltdown. *The Journal of Structured Finance*, Fall, pp. 7–20.

Overdependence on Credit Ratings was a Primary Cause of the Crisis

Frank Partnoy*
University of San Diego School of Law

1. Introduction

A primary cause of the recent credit market turmoil was overdependence on credit ratings and credit rating agencies. Without such overdependence, the complex financial instruments, particularly Collateralized Debt Obligations (CDOs) and Structured Investment Vehicles (SIVs), which were at the center of the crisis could not, and would not, have been created or sold. Long-term sustainable policy measures should take into account both regulatory and behavioral overdependence on ratings.

In the first part of the paper, I describe how over time credit rating agencies[1] ceased to play the role of information intermediaries. By the time market participants recently began to securitize large amounts of subprime mortgages, rating agencies were available, not to provide information about the risk associated with the securitized instruments, but to facilitate the use of "regulatory licenses"[2] by enabling those building the structures to create and maintain tranches of these instruments with unjustifiably high credit ratings. This role went well beyond the standard reputational model of the role of rating agencies.

---

* Frank Partnoy is the George E. Barrett Professor of Law and Finance at the University of San Diego.

[1] By credit rating agencies, I am referring to nationally recognized statistical rating organizations (NRSROs), as that term was defined during the early 2000s, and in particular to the two major NRSROs — Moody's Investor Service and Standard & Poor's Rating Services.

[2] By regulatory license, I mean the property rights associated with the ability of a private entity, rather than a regulator, to determine the substantive effect of legal rules. See Frank Partnoy, 1999, "The Siskel and Ebert of Financial Markets?: Two Thumbs Down for the Credit Rating Agencies," *Washington University Law Quarterly*, Vol. 77, p. 622.

In the second part of the paper, I suggest how future policy might minimize overdependence on credit ratings by removing regulatory licenses and by implementing "shock therapy" mechanisms to wean investors off ratings mnemonics. I also analyze how regulators and market participants can learn from the flaws in rating agency models, to avoid repeating similar mistakes. In particular, I focus on the misapplication of historical data with respect to estimates of expected default probability, recovery, and correlation. Finally, I assess how market measures of these estimates, based on actual prices of traded assets, might substitute for credit ratings for both regulatory and behavioral purposes.

2. Some Background and Theory: Reputation versus Regulatory Licenses

Historically, information intermediaries have arisen because of information asymmetry between buyers and sellers, particularly in markets where sellers have superior information but cannot costlessly convey this information to buyers.[3] If buyers are economically rational, prices in a market with information asymmetry will reflect the average quality of a product, and sellers with superior products will bear the cost of the information asymmetry. Consequently, sellers in such a market will have an incentive to disclose the superior nature of their product so that they can receive the highest price. In financial markets, to the extent that sellers cannot credibly make such disclosures, there are incentives for information intermediaries to play this role.

Information-gathering firms that certify asset quality typically must satisfy three criteria before their certification will be credible to outside investors. First, the certifying agent must have reputational capital at stake in the certification activity. In other words, the certifying agent credibly must be able to pledge that it will suffer a loss, related either to litigation or declining reputation, if its certification is systematically biased or false. Second, this expected loss must exceed the expected gain from false certification. Third, the agent's services must be costly and the cost must be related to the informational asymmetry between buyer and seller.

[3] Partnoy, op. cit., pp. 633–636.

In the early debt markets, credit rating agencies evolved to play an informational intermediary role, from the nineteenth century mercantile credit rating agencies through John Moody's application to bonds.[4] Moody's insight was that he could profit by selling to the public a synthesis of complex bond data into a single letter rating.

For the most part, credit rating agencies fit this reputational investor-pay model until the mid-1970s, when, not coincidentally, the Securities and Exchange Commission (SEC) began relying substantively on credit rating agencies for regulatory purposes and the agencies shifted to an issuer-pay model.[5] As the regulatory dependence on ratings increased, rating agencies became more profitable and also began providing ratings of transactions designed to achieve particular ratings. During the late 1980s and early 1990s, bankers and issuers created a range of highly rated asset-backed transactions and Collateralized Bond Obligations (CDO), as well as derivative product companies, financial guarantor transactions, and AAA-rated arbitrage vehicles. The first SIVs and asset-backed CDOs were created during this period.

As the credit rating agency model shifted from investor-pay to issuer-pay, the conditions necessary for the existence of a well-functioning information intermediary faltered. The rating agencies faced little or no risk of loss from inaccurate ratings, while the potential gains from inaccurate ratings increased. Ratings substantially lagged the revelation of public information about rated issuers and instruments, and rating agencies repeatedly were forced to revise ratings substantially downward. As rating agencies began rating substantially greater numbers of issuers and instruments, the resources expended per rating necessarily declined, and the cost of providing a rating became disconnected from the information gap between investors and issuers. Finally, the rating agencies' businesses became progressively more profitable, even as the informational value of their ratings declined.

---

[4] Partnoy, op. cit., pp. 637–638.

[5] More precisely, the regulatory dependence on credit ratings began in 1973, when the SEC proposed amending broker–dealer "haircut" requirements, which set forth the percentage of a financial asset's market value a broker–dealer was required to deduct for the purpose of calculating its net capital requirement. Rule 15c3-1, promulgated two years later, required a different "haircut" based on the credit ratings assigned by nationally recognized statistical rating organizations (NRSROs). See 17 C.F.R. 240.15c3-1. Since the mid-1970s, statutes and regulations increasingly have come to depend explicitly on NRSRO ratings. See Partnoy, op. cit., pp. 690–703.

During the 1990s, overdependence on credit ratings led many market participants to create highly rated fixed income instruments that carried attractive yields relative to comparable assets, but that also carried new risks typically not associated with highly rated bonds. The bond market crisis in 1994–95 was driven by structured notes and other derivatives transactions, including mortgage-backed transactions, which were designed to achieve high ratings, even though they carried other embedded risks. More recently, overdependence on credit ratings played a significant role in the collapse of Enron.[6]

With respect to mortgages, first-level securitizations were a response to the investment grade "cliff" noted by W. Braddock Hickman,[7] and later Michael Milken, who saw that portfolios of sub-investment grade rated bonds outperformed more highly rated bonds on a risk-adjusted basis. Market participants adapted this insight to mortgages of various types, which could be pooled into new highly rated fixed-income instruments. Surprisingly, this "cliff" persisted over time, in both corporate bond and mortgage markets; the large yield discontinuity between investment grade and below-investment grade ratings did not disappear even after large amounts of securities were issued. To the contrary, in the early 2000s, rating agency models, and assumptions about historical default, recovery, and correlation, suggested that extant mortgage-backed securities could be repackaged and resold in ways that would outperform, not only the mortgage-backed securities themselves, but other comparably rated securities.

3. The Growth of "Second-Level" Mortgage Securitization

As the credit derivatives market was experiencing record growth, fixed-income structurers and investors, with the assistance of credit rating

---

[6] The following assessment from Senator Joseph Lieberman, whose Senate committee held the first hearings on Enron, was typical: "The credit-rating agencies were dismally lax in their coverage of Enron. They didn't ask probing questions and generally accepted at face value whatever Enron's officials chose to tell them. And while they claim to rely primarily on public filings with the SEC, analysts from Standard and Poor's not only did not read Enron's proxy statement, they didn't even know what information it might contain". Senate Committee on Governmental Affairs, 2002, press release, "Financial oversight of Enron: The SEC and private-sector watchdogs", October 8.

[7] See W. Braddock Hickman, 1958, *Corporate Bond Quality and Investor Experience*, National Bureau of Economic Research.

agencies, searched for assets that could be securitized to create highly rated fixed-income instruments with attractive yields relative to comparable investments. For the first time, banks began seriously considering "second-level" securitizations of "first-level" mortgage-backed securities (which were securitizations of mortgages).

The fundamental economic rationale for second-level securitizations is not obvious. After all, the underlying mortgage assets have already been securitized. Indeed, the mortgage-backed securities market was already a deep market, driven by high demand from both originators and investors. Mortgage-backed securities were issued in a competitive environment in large numbers, and were already rated by the rating agencies. First-level securitization transactions were a response to gaps and inefficiencies in the underlying market for individual assets. To the extent mortgages were being allocated or bundled inefficiently, or not in ways investors desired, one might have expected that continuous first-level securitization would evolve to ameliorate these inefficiencies. Put another way, if there had been a more efficient way of pooling mortgages, or a pocket of unsatisfied demand for particular pool portfolios or structures, investors likely would have demanded it, and then banks would have created and supplied it.

Yet the proliferation of second-level mortgage-backed CDOs and SIVs suggested that billions of dollars of first-level mortgage-backed securities appeared to be mispriced. Market participants could pool those securities into new special purpose entities with tranched capital structures, and sell the slices of those structures for more than the value of the underlying mortgage-backed securities. These transactions, too, persisted over time, so much so that the appetite for second-level mortgage securitizations drove financial intermediaries both to originate new and increasingly risky mortgages, and to create synthetic exposure to mortgages, which then could be resecuritized through tranched special purpose entities, again at higher prices than the underlying mortgage-backed securities were trading in the market.

To obtain ratings for second-level mortgage securitizations, both the structurers and the rating agencies used models based on earlier corporate bond-backed transactions, which provided a methodology for labeling the risks associated with mortgage-securities-backed transactions. Bankers increasingly sought to combine the underlying securities and to stratify capital structures in ways that would create new investment grade-rated securities. In particular, CDOs and SIVs were designed to create large tranches of AAA-rated assets backed by lower-rated mortgage-backed securities.

Even after a mortgage-backed security had been resecuritized through cash-flow based CDOs, market participants suggested that there was no reason why investors could not take on exposure to a particular mortgage-backed security more than once. Arrangers created synthetic exposure based on side bets derived from the value of the underlying mortgage-backed securities so that investors could obtain exposure to the performance of a pool of mortgages without having an investment vehicle or special purpose entity actually buy the mortgage-backed securities. Synthetic CDOs and SIVs obtained exposure through derivatives transactions, most commonly credit default swaps.

4. Credit Ratings as Drivers of Second-Level Securitizations

The linchpin of a CDO or a SIV backed in whole or part by synthetic assets was the credit rating. Investors typically did not examine the underlying assets of a synthetic CDO or SIV in any detail or at all. One might criticize them for not doing so, except that the underlying assets were frequently not even specified when the deal was sold. Instead, investors relied on parameters set by the arrangers, bankers, and rating agencies to constrain the assets that could be purchased originally and held over time.

If the credit rating agencies, and their clients, had used reasonable and accurate models and assumptions, then in principle these transactions might not have been problematic. However, these parties faced financial incentives to use unreasonable and inaccurate assumptions and models to complete deals and thereby earn greater fees. These incentives were especially strong given the expected absence of any reputational consequence, particularly for individuals involved in transactions, who could essentially sell long-term options obligating their firms while pocketing shorter-term bonuses for themselves. The way to obtain sufficiently attractive ratings to pay the high transaction costs and fees for the various arranging parties, and still generate attractive yields for purchasers, was to use models and assumptions that did not reflect the actual risk of the underlying mortgages, including risks that already were impounded in the price of those securities in the market for mortgage-backed securities.[8]

The simplest way to generate unwarranted high ratings was to use outdated and inapplicable historical assumptions with respect to the underlying mortgage-backed securities. The inputs to the relevant models were straightforward: expected default rate, recovery rate upon default, and, for portfolios of assets, the correlation of expected defaults. The rating agencies created models, with the assistance of bankers and arrangers, that generated tranche credit ratings for second-level deals based on these inputs. Those models, in turn, typically depended on assumptions with respect to the expected statistical distribution that returns on the underlying collateral would follow.

Given these assumptions and models, arrangers were then free to find collateral that would generate the most attractive tranche yields, subject to ratings-based constraints. The restrictions on collateral typically were based on credit ratings; in other words, the second-level securitization methodology depended on previous first-level securitization ratings. As the prices of mortgage-backed securities rose, along with housing prices, it was difficult to generate second-level deals with highly rated tranches without using increasingly unreasonable assumptions. As collateral became more expensive and ratings of that collateral lagged increasing market prices, accurate and timely ratings would have appeared lower than would have been warranted. This lag provided a rationale for increasingly aggressive assumptions with respect to second-level deals.

Paradoxically, when housing prices began to fall but ratings on first-level securitizations did not, the historical ratings methodology made second-level securitizations increasingly attractive. If one could buy AAA-rated mortgage-backed securities that had fallen in price, but still use the same historical default, recovery, and correlation assumptions associated with AAA ratings in the relevant model, one could create a highly rated, high-yielding set of second-level transactions. As long as mortgage-backed securities ratings lagged market prices, as those prices

---

[8] Joseph R. Mason and Joshua Rosner, 2007, "Where did the risk go? How misapplied bond ratings cause mortgage backed securities and collateralized debt obligation market disruptions," SSRN, working paper, at http://ssrn.com/abstract=1027475, May 3.

declined, CDOs and SIVs backed by that collateral would appear increasingly attractive.

Rating agency assumptions and models did not accurately capture the risk associated with second-level securitizations.[9] Default rate assumptions were derived from historical information, including default data about other asset categories as well as asset price correlations, rather than default correlations. Moreover, assumptions for second-level deals were based on ratings of mortgage-backed securities, even when both the rating agencies and other participants in the resecuritization transactions were aware that both that the credit quality of the underlying mortgages had declined and that the expected default correlations associated with those mortgages had increased. Nevertheless, the simulations the agencies ran to calculate tranche ratings were based on stale and inaccurate assumptions.

Rating agency correlation assumptions were particularly important.[10] Inaccurate correlation assumptions based on incorrect statistical models enabled parties to structure deals with high ratings on senior tranches, given that the expected correlation of defaults of mortgage-backed securities was higher than the estimates used for the models.[11] The rating agencies have struggled to understand the importance of correlation assumptions for CDOs and SIVs, even as those assumptions supported a sharply increasing number of second-level securitizations. Moody's conducted an in-depth study of corporate bond correlation, which led to a new Monte Carlo simulation-based market tool in 2004 for measuring the

---

[9] The SEC investigation of the credit rating agencies found that they struggled to adapt to the complexity of mortgage-backed structured finance deals. See Securities and Exchange Commission, 2008, "Summary report of issues identified in the commission staff's examinations of select credit rating agencies," July, p. 12 ("One analyst expressed concern that her firm's model did not capture 'half' of the deal's risk, but that 'it could be structured by cows and we would rate it.'"). The SEC also found that "Rating agencies made 'out of model' adjustments and did not document the rationale for the adjustment," id., p. 14.

[10] See John Hull, and Alan White, 2006, "Valuing credit derivatives using an implied copula approach," *Journal of Derivatives*, Winter; Donald R. van Deventer, 2008, "CDOs and the credit crisis: Complexity and model risk in the collateralized debt obligation market are severe," *Bank Accounting and Finance*, June, p. 7 ("Management has often discovered that the working-level staff has been depending heavily on models, like the copula approach, that were known or should have been known to be wrong.").

[11] Moody's Investors Service, 2006, "Moody's modeling approach to rating structured finance cash flow CDO transactions," September, p. 10.

credit risk of synthetic transactions; it revised its methodology for structured finance asset correlations a year later.[12] S&P's inputs simply remained constant for years.[13] By 2006 and 2007 at the latest, it was apparent that the relevant mortgage asset correlations underlying CDOs and SIVs were significantly higher than the rating agencies had assumed. By February 2008, Moody's had downgraded at least one tranche of 94.2 percent of subprime residential mortgage-backed deals it had rated in 2006.[14]

In sum, the proliferation of second-level securitization transactions is consistent with substantial overdependence on credit ratings. If ratings had been accurate, or put another way if investors had relied on ratings only to the extent they were accurate, then there would have been little incentive for second-level securitizations. But because investors were willing to buy CDO and SIV tranches simply because of their high ratings and high yields, either because of regulatory reliance on ratings or because the mnemonic device of ratings came to play an overly important private role, CDO and SIV tranches had higher-than-justified ratings, even though they held collateral that already had been securitized. Without overreliance on ratings, investors would more likely have looked through the complexity of CDO and SIV transactions to the underlying mortgage-backed securities, and prices would have more accurately reflected market estimates of default probability, recovery, and correlation.

5. Regulatory versus Behavioral Overdependence

To what extent was overdependence on ratings driven by regulation? I have previously argued that rating agencies increasingly sell "regulatory licenses" rather than information, and that ratings are not "opinions", but instead are keys that unlock the financial markets for regulated entities.[15]

---

[12] See Moody's Investors Service, 2005, "Collateralized debt obligations: A Moody's primer," March, pp. 5–6; Moody's Investors Service, 2005, "Moody's revisits its assumptions regarding structured finance default (and asset) correlations for CDOs," June.

[13] See Frank Partnoy, 2006, "How and why credit rating agencies are not like other gatekeepers," in *Financial Gatekeepers: Can They Protect Investors?*, Yasuyuki Fuchita and Robert E. Litan (eds.).

[14] See Moody's Investors Service, 2008, "A short guide to subprime," March, p. 3.

[15] Partnoy, 1999.

Regulators recently have endorsed this explanation, and the SEC has proposed rules to eliminate certain aspects of regulatory dependence on ratings.[16]

In addition, it is apparent that, even putting aside regulatory influences, at least some market participants over rely independently on ratings. At its core, this overreliance likely derives from decades of regulatory dependence on ratings, but it has become a more widespread, behavioral phenomenon. Ratings are part of financial culture. Even after the massive dislocation associated with the recent crisis, and the abysmal performance of the rating agencies, market participants have continued to rely on letter ratings. One conclusion is that even if all explicit references to ratings were removed from regulation, some residual implicit overreliance would remain.

An interesting perspective on this behavioral point arises from the fact that the major banks selling second-level securitizations also misperceived the risks associated with the highest-rated tranches. Indeed, it appears that bank officers were so confident about the high ratings of super-senior CDO tranches that they concluded that such tranches posed virtually no risk. One reason, if not the primary reason, why they misperceived such risks was overreliance on credit rating agency assumptions and models. Some of this overreliance derived from bank regulations that depend on credit ratings; the rest was cultural.

Most strikingly, sanguine assessments of super-senior risk, and assumptions that senior tranches protected by AAA-rated junior tranches could not default, appeared to be so obviously correct that banks' exposure to these tranches remained apparently hidden from senior managers, investors, and regulators. No bank publicly disclosed risks associated with super-senior tranches before the crisis began. Bank directors and officers claimed, perhaps falsely, that they were unaware of risks associated with these tranches. Moreover, many regulators apparently were unaware of the exposure as well. The Bank of England, in its *Financial Stability Report*, noted that banks were net buyers of credit protection in 2006; that estimate apparently did not reflect the

[16] See Securities and Exchange Commission, 2008, "References to ratings of nationally recognized statistical rating organizations," Release Nos. IC-28327, IA-2751, File No. S7-19-08.

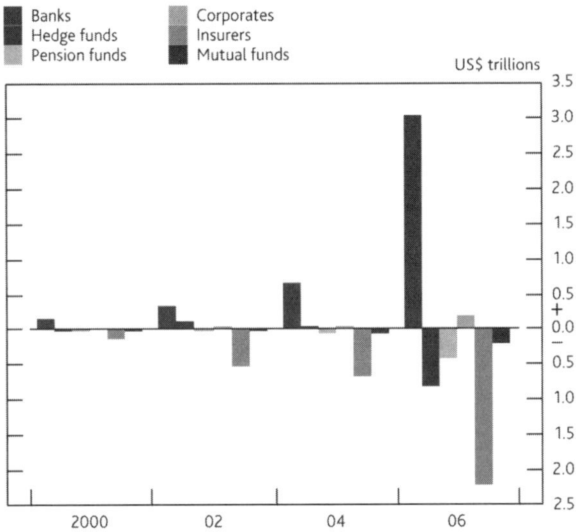

Figure 1. Outstanding Global Amounts of Credit Protection Bought by Institutions.
Source: BBA and Bank calculations.
Note: Amounts netted across long and short positions.

large amounts of notional credit protection sold by banks in super-senior transactions.[17] These estimates are set forth in Figure 1.

Much of the blame for overdependence on ratings can be placed on regulation, and I set forth below some measures designed to eliminate this overdependence. But market participants also independently over relied on ratings. High ratings replaced independent judgment, particularly when second-level transactions created the illusion of thick bands of highly rated protective tranches. The collapse of senior securities of both CDOs and SIVs illustrates that second-level securitizations require an analysis of something more than just tranche ratings. Because these instruments are so much more complex than the underlying first-level

[17] Bank of England, 2008, *Financial Stability Report*, April, Figure 2.17. The Bank for International Settlements had been warning about overreliance on ratings since early 2005. See Committee on the Global Financial System, Bank for International Settlements, 2005, "The role of ratings in structured finance: issues and implications," January.

securitizations, they generate a greater need for investigation, and are paradoxically more amenable to overreliance on ratings.

6. Some Policy Prescriptions

If the story about overreliance on credit ratings is even partially correct, what is to be done? There are two categories of policy responses, some of which already have been proposed. First, regulators should eliminate explicit reliance on credit ratings. To the extent regulators are concerned that such an approach would leave a substantive void, there are many substitutes for ratings, including market measures of risk, as described below. Second, regulators should implement some form of "shock therapy" to jar market participants from overreliance on ratings. The use of mnemonics is highly path dependent, and unless there are strong reasons for participants to switch, they will not.

With respect to the first point, the SEC has already proposed removing references to NRSROs in its own rules. For example, Rule 2a-7 of the Investment Company Act limits a money market fund's portfolio investments to securities that have received credit ratings from NRSROs in one of the two highest short-term rating categories.[18] The SEC recommended replacing this NRSRO "regulatory license" with a requirement that money market fund boards of directors determine "that each portfolio instrument presents minimal credit risks".[19] Likewise, other SEC proposals would replace several other rules that depend explicitly on NRSRO ratings.

Notwithstanding the intense lobbying effort against these proposals, the SEC should implement them as final. Moreover, other regulatory bodies should similarly excise references to credit ratings. In the United States, the most efficient mechanism for doing this would be for Congress formally to remove references from statutes, and then to hold hearings to encourage various agencies to remove any additional remaining references in both formal rules and informal policies.

Perhaps the most important regulatory references to ratings are in international banking regulations, particularly under the Basel II agreement

---

[18] See Investment Company Act, Rule 2a-7(a)(10), (21).

[19] See Securities and Exchange Commission, 2008, "References to ratings of nationally recognized statistical rating organizations," Release Nos. IC-28327, at 8.

of the Basel Committee on Banking Supervision. Basel II explicitly allows banking regulators to permit banks to use credit ratings from approved rating agencies in calculating their net capital reserve requirements. International regulators should remove this provision, and in place of letter ratings substitute market-based measures, such as credit spreads or credit default swap prices, and/or discretionary estimates of default probability, expected recovery, and correlation. The Bank for International Settlements has long been a leader in publicizing problems associated with the use of ratings in structured finance.[20] It now should explicitly disclaim the use of ratings in regulation generally.

Ratings and rating agencies have also been subsidized by other forms of regulation, and those subsidies should be removed as well. NRSROs are specifically exempt under U.S. securities law from Section 11 liability and Regulation FD; they should not be. Nor should rating agencies be exempt from liability for statutory and common law private claims based on any freedom of speech or journalistic privilege rationales. Historically, the rating agencies have interposed First Amendment objections in civil litigation, with some success.[21] As new cases based on second-level securitizations arise, judges should distinguish those prior cases, and make it clear that rating agencies are subject to civil liability and are not protected by any First Amendment privilege. Legislators also should consider clarifying the viability of private rights of action against rating agencies.

The rating agencies' position that ratings are merely "opinions", and therefore are entitled to the same protection as other "speakers", is specious in the context of complex securitization transactions. Ratings of second-level securitizations are not protected speech, and rating agencies are doing much more than merely speaking. They have a high level of initial and ongoing involvement in these deals, at early and later stages, and receive significantly higher fees for them. Rating agencies determine the capital cushions that are required for particular tranches; they provide capital matrix parameters that govern the operation of special purpose entity issuers; they are involved in the operation of the issuers on an ongoing basis; they instruct the asset manager regarding the kinds of assets the issuers can acquire, both initially and over time; and the deal documentation

---

[20] See Bank for International Settlements, 2005.

[21] See Partnoy, 2006.

for these transactions typically includes descriptions of the simulation models the rating agencies use to determine the relative proportions of an entity's capital structure, as well as the necessarily overcollateralization ratios and triggers, both initially and over time. Moreover, unlike corporate bond transactions, CDOs and SIVs require a much more in-depth analysis by the rating agencies, including the use of their mathematical models and assumptions. For these reasons, judges should reject the claim that ratings of second-level securitizations are merely "opinions".

With respect to second point regarding "shock therapy", regulators should encourage investors not to apply the same ratings and analysis to corporate bonds versus structured finance assets.[22] Ratings of these instruments are categorically different, and it was and is a mistake for anyone to use the same mnemonic for each category. A highly rated CDO does not pose the same risks as other highly rated securities, including the collateral underlying the CDO. To the extent regulators and investors continue to rely on ratings, which they should not, at minimum their rating-based rules should distinguish between the symbology of corporate bonds and structured finance instruments, if not other categories as well. Ideally, regulators and investors should find independent means of assessing the risks of different investments within different categories. Forcing investors to split ratings among categories should lead private actors to reassess their approach to risk.

Disclosure with respect to credit derivatives and credit rating-based transactions also must improve. Current disclosure of notional amounts and Value-At-Risk (VAR) does not enable investors to assess the risks associated with default, expected recovery, and correlation of fixed income exposure. One reason for the recent collapse of major financial institutions such as Bear Stearns, Lehman, Fannie Mae, Freddie Mac, and AIG was the lack of transparency with respect to second-level securitizations. When no one has enough information to evaluate the risk of portfolios held by financial institutions, the valuation of their issued securities becomes at best a guess. At minimum, bank regulators should require that financial institutions disclose to examiners not only VAR-related measures, but also more robust worst-case analyses and stress tests based on a wide range of assumptions about expected default, recovery,

[22] The SEC has proposed such a split. See Securities and Exchange Commission, 2008, "Proposed rules for nationally recognized statistical rating organizations", Release No. 34-57967, File No. S7-13-08, June.

and correlation. Requiring such disclosures also would encourage market participants to rely on these measures directly, instead of on letter ratings. It also would encourage dissemination of risk disclosure to bank officers and directors.

As regulators and investors seek substitutes for credit ratings, they should consider looking to market measures and prices. Notwithstanding recent market volatility and dislocations, market prices provided a far more accurate assessment of risk than credit ratings. Such prices and related market measures are available from true information intermediaries, which now play a modern version of the role John Moody originally envisioned in the early twentieth century: providing valuable information about credit risk. Most prominently, Markit Group Limited provides credit default swap pricing and other data that investors could use to assess the risk of their portfolios over time. It would vastly improve policy and market efficiency if regulators and investors relied on this kind of data instead of credit ratings.

An example based on data from Markit is set forth in Figure 2. The figure depicts the daily five-year Bear Stearns senior credit default swap closing spreads, along with 30-day and 90-day rolling averages of these spreads. Note that the credit ratings applicable to Bear Stearns's senior debt were constant at single-A throughout this period.

To the extent regulators or institutions are concerned about the volatility of market based measures, it would be straightforward to reference a rolling average like one of those depicted above. Reliance on market measures instead of credit ratings likely would have led institutions with exposure to Bear Stearns securities to assess their exposure more closely during the period leading up to that firm's collapse. Instead of regulating and making investment decisions based on a Bear Stearns' credit rating that remained unjustifiably high and unchanged during that bank's crisis and collapse, regulators and institutions instead could have looked to a rolling average of market measures. Credit default swap spreads provided an early warning to market participants regarding Bear Stearns.

Moreover, the use of market measures would have beneficial ex ante effects, particularly if regulators also adopt the heightened disclosure requirements outlined above. For example, if Bear Stearns' officials had known both that their firm would not be rescued and that investors would sell their securities in response to a rapid deterioration in prices, they would have been forced to be more proactive about disclosing risks in advance, particularly with respect to second-level securitizations, and

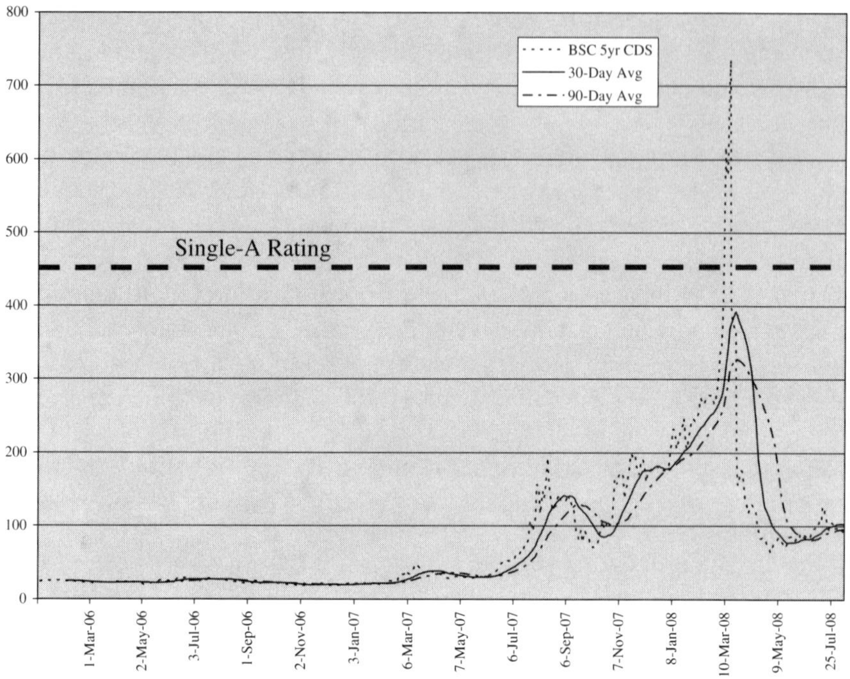

Figure 2. Bear Stearns' Five-Year CDS Market Spreads (bp).
Source: Markit.

perhaps as a result bank employees would not have taken on the key risks that led to the bank's collapse.

Not every regulator or market participant would need to rely on market measures as a substitute for ratings. Some could rely on professional judgment, as the SEC has suggested in its proposed Rule 2a-7 amendments. Others could rely on third-party information providers. Some might continue to rely on Moody's and S&P, although the overwhelming evidence suggest that such reliance would be misguided. In any event, a shift to permitting reliance on market-based measures would help discourage overreliance on letter ratings.

Switching to market-based measures is not a radical concept. Indeed, even the credit rating agencies themselves increasingly use market-based measures. Letter ratings essentially have become shorthand labels based on assumptions about key variables: probability of default, expected recovery in the event of default, and correlation. Internally, the rating agencies generate letter ratings based on estimates of these variables.[23] At minimum, regulators and market participants should switch to relying on actual estimates of these variables instead of letter ratings that amalgamate the variables in an opaque, outdated, and incomprehensible fashion.

7. Conclusion

Causation is a complex concept. It has both "but for" and "proximate" elements. As a matter of "but for" causation, there is a strong argument that credit ratings and credit rating agencies caused the crisis. Second-level mortgage-backed securitizations, particularly CDOs and SIVs, explicitly depended on rating agency letter ratings. Without those ratings, the transactions could not, and would not, have happened. Without the ability to obtain high ratings for CDO and SIV tranches, there would have been little appetite for overpriced lower-rated mortgage collateral. Without that appetite, there would have been little pressure leading to the proliferation of sub-prime mortgages, because those mortgages could not have been offloaded through second-level securitizations. Without the proliferation of low quality mortgages, there would not have been a dramatic housing market rise and fall, with the attendant ripple effects.

It is more difficult to say whether credit ratings were a "proximate" cause of the crisis, but there are strong arguments here as well. Overreliance on ratings led banks to hold super-senior exposure they otherwise would have assessed more carefully. Overreliance on ratings led regulators to misperceive the extent to which speculation on sub-prime mortgages had spread, or to where. Overreliance on ratings led institutional investors to take on hidden correlation bets, which their directors, officers, and shareholders did not understand.

Overreliance on ratings was a central component of the credit crisis. In responding to the crisis, and in planning and implementing reforms, regulators should not focus exclusively on proposals related to lending abuses, bank rescues, credit expansion, and macroeconomic or cyclical factors. They should not miss the crucial role of credit ratings.

[23] With respect to mortgage-backed securities, prepayment risk also is a relevant variable. Prepayment risk was an important factor during the 1994–95 interest rate crisis, but did not play a major role during the recent subprime crisis.

V. EXPERIENCE WITH CRISIS MANAGEMENT

Liquidity Management Under Market Turmoil: Experience of the European Central Bank in the First Year of the 2007–2008 Financial Market Crisis

Nuno Cassola*
European Central Bank

Cornelia Holthausen
European Central Bank

Flemming Würtz
European Central Bank

1. Introduction

This paper analyzes the crisis management tools and policies of the European Central Bank (ECB) during the first year of the 2007–2008 financial market turmoil. The turmoil exposed widespread market failures in various segments of the money and credit markets. By turning to the open market operations of the Eurosystem, many banks in the euro area avoided credit rationing, which prevented a sudden funding liquidity crisis from escalating into a generalized solvency problem and the emergence of

---

* Nuno Cassola is deputy head of the Financial Research Division in the Directorate General Research at the European Central Bank (ECB); Cornelia Holthausen is an advisor in the Financial Research Division of the ECB; and Flemming Würtz is head of the ECB's liquidity management section in the Market Operations Analysis Division. Corresponding author: Nuno Cassola, Financial Research Division, Directorate-General Research, European Central Bank, Kaiserstrasse 29, D-60311, Frankfurt am Main, Germany. E-mail: nuno.cassola@ecb.int. The views expressed in this paper are the exclusive responsibility of the authors and do not necessarily coincide with those of the European Central Bank.

a systemic financial crisis. Given the source of the disturbance — global retrenchment by investors from exposure to credit risk transfer and related instruments and institutions — individual targeted liquidity assistance was not feasible, at least in the early stages of the turmoil.

We argue that the prevention of a systemic crisis was supported by automatic adjustment mechanisms embedded in the operational framework of the Eurosystem, which were also supported by (and allowed) an active liquidity management and communications policy by the ECB. Until August 2008, it has not been necessary to make any significant changes to the operational framework of the Eurosystem in order to be able to respond to the market turmoil.

Four features of the operational framework of the Eurosystem seem to have been crucial in crisis management, having played a role as *automatic stabilizers*: 1) the (large) *number of counterparties* that have direct access to the Eurosystem's intraday credit, overnight standing facilities, and open market operations; 2) the characteristics of the *minimum reserve requirement* (sizable, remunerated, with averaging provision); 3) the *collateral framework* (acceptance of a broad range of collateral including nonmarketable securities); and 4) the availability of an automatic *lending facility* with no significant stigma attached to it.

Liquidity management policy played an additional important role in managing the crisis: the ECB used a flexible allotment policy in its main refinancing operations (MROs) and changed the maturity structure of its refinancing by increasing the relative weight of its regular longer-term refinancing operations (LTROs) and by adding other, special longer-term refinancing operations; fine-tuning operations were carried out more frequently and have been used to mop up liquidity provided in MROs and LTROs and fixed-rate tender procedures with full allotment have been used when markets conditions were severely strained. In addition, at the turn of the year 2007, the ECB joined the Bank of England, the U.S. Federal Reserve, and other central banks in an unprecedented international cooperation in the field of liquidity management.

The remainder of the paper is organized as follows. In Section 2 we present a simple model of the overnight interbank market in order to explain the ECB's liquidity management under calm market conditions and set the ground for the analysis of the turmoil period. Section 3 introduces the ECB's crisis management tools and policies covering automatic stabilizers (3.1), fixed rate tenders with full allotment (3.2), the separation principle and liquidity draining fine-tuning operations (3.3), frontloading (3.4), asymmetric narrow corridor (3.5) and other measures (3.6). Section 4 makes a preliminary assessment of the effectiveness of the crisis management by the ECB. Conclusions and open issues are presented at the end.[1]

2. ECB Liquidity Management Under Normal Market Conditions

As a rule, the Governing Council (GC) of the European Central Bank (ECB) decides the level of the key policy interest rates at its monthly policy meeting. The main policy rate is the minimum bid rate in the ECB's weekly Main Refinancing Operations (MROs). These are liquidity-providing repo operations conducted as variable rate tenders, subject to the minimum bid rate,[2] in which the ECB determines the total amount that is allotted to counterparties, while banks submit bid schedules expressing the price they are willing to pay for liquidity in these operations.

The other two policy rates apply to the standing facilities. Counterparties may at any time, and in unlimited amounts, either deposit funds overnight with the Eurosystem at the deposit facility, which are remunerated at i^d, or borrow funds overnight from the marginal lending facility at a rate i^l. Thus, banks can obtain central bank liquidity either in the open market operations or via the marginal lending facility, both against collateral.

The rates on the two standing facilities set a corridor around the minimum bid rate, which effectively bounds movements in the overnight interest rate therefore dampening its volatility. Since April 1999, the GC of the ECB has set the interest rate corridor in a symmetric manner, with a width of ±100 basis points around the minimum bid rate. The volatility of the overnight interest rate is proportional to the width of the corridor. Narrow corridors are preferable from the perspective of reducing interest rate volatility. However, a too narrow corridor may hamper market activity also in the unsecured segment of the overnight interbank market. The optimal

---

[1] For a comprehensive description of the events and policies see ECB (2007) and ECB (2008).

[2] The ECB also conducts longer-term refinancing operations of three-month maturity (LTROs), to which no minimum bid rate applies. For further information on the main features of the operational framework of the Eurosystem, see ECB (2006).

width should strike a balance between these considerations. Moreover, with unlimited access to the lending facility, the narrower the gap between the lending facility rate and the market rate, the higher the risk of inducing moral hazard behavior as it would offer as an ill-devised (for example, no penalty) permanent lender of last resort facility.

The choice, by the ECB, of the allotment amounts provided in the main refinancing operations follows a relatively simple rule (referred to as benchmark allotment).[3] We illustrate the main issues using a stylized two-day reserve maintenance period à la Poole (see Poole, 1968). For a more general formalization, taking into account the institutional features of the euro area the reader is referred to Gaspar, Pérez-Quirós, and Rodríguez-Mendizábal (2007), Pérez-Quirós and Rodríguez-Mendizábal (2006), and Välimäki (2003).

2.1 *Last day of the reserve maintenance period*

In this section, we formalize interest rate behavior in the overnight interbank market in a stylized model of a two-day reserve maintenance period (RMP). Assume that there are two days in the reserve maintenance period ($t = T-1$ and T). The maintenance period starts with an MRO whereby the ECB refinances the banking system with two-day maturity funds. On the last day, the ECB conducts a fine tuning operation with a maturity of one day (one-day maturity) to compensate for the forecast error of aggregate liquidity needs made on day $T-1$. Under normal market conditions, the interest rate in the overnight interbank market on the last day of the reserve maintenance period (day T), i_T, is determined, to a close approximation by the following equation:

$$i_T = p_T^{DF} i^d + p_T^{MLF} i^l, \tag{1}$$

where i^d and i^l refer to the rates of the standing facilities; and p_T^{DF} and p_T^{MLF} are, respectively, the probability of a liquidity surplus and of a deficit on the last day of the reserve maintenance period, in which case counterparties would need to make use of either the deposit facility (DF)

[3] For details on ECB's liquidity management and calculation of the benchmark allotment, see ECB (2002).

or the marginal lending facility (MLF), respectively. Equation 1 states that the overnight interest rate is a weighted average of the rates of the two standing facilities. Note that this equation is derived from the individual demand for reserves by banks and aggregation, considering a representative bank so that (1) holds for the market as such.

The reasoning behind this relationship is the following. Banks must fulfill their reserve requirements on average. The constraint imposed by the minimum reserve requirement becomes binding only at the end of the reserve maintenance period. On the last day, banks know that if they hold excess funds on their central bank account, these will be remunerated at i^d, while if they have a deficit, they will be charged the rate i^l. The ECB tries to adjust the liquidity supply to the banking sector so that the aggregate recourse to either facility is equally likely and therefore equal to one-half ($p_T^{DF} = p_T^{MLF} = 0.5$). In this case:

$$i_T = \frac{i^d + i^l}{2} = i_{mbr}, \tag{2}$$

where i_{mbr} denotes the minimum bid rate.[4] In order to achieve this outcome, the ECB usually supplies the amount of liquidity that allows banks to fulfill their reserve requirements smoothly over time. This defines the *benchmark allotment*. If the ECB's forecast errors of aggregate liquidity needs are unbiased, the overnight rate on the last day in the reserve maintenance period should be, to a close approximation, determined by equation 2. In what follows, we will assume that the ECB has credibly committed to ensuring equation 2 and, therefore, this condition also holds in (unconditional) expectation, $E(i_T) = i_{mbr}$. Figure 1 illustrates equilibrium in the overnight interbank market on day T; Figure 2 shows the empirical evidence.

2.2 *Before the last day of the reserve maintenance period*

On the first day of the two-day reserve maintenance period, the equilibrium in the overnight interbank market is slightly more complicated. The

---

[4] Even under ideal circumstances, this equation is only an approximation, as the interest rates in question have different characteristics. In particular, 1) the minimum bid rate refers to one-week operations, while the other rates refer to overnight transactions; and 2) the market rate referred to is usually an unsecured rate, while ECB loans are collateralized.

Figure 1 illustrates equilibrium in the overnight interbank market on the last day in the reserve maintenance period. D_T is the (inverse) aggregate demand for liquidity and S_T is the supply of liquidity. For simplicity the demand schedule is drawn with linear segments, which is correct only around the equilibrium point (R, i_T). The slope of the inverse demand schedule captures uncertainty about idiosyncratic (that is, bank specific) liquidity shocks. Higher uncertainty implies flatter (inverse) demand schedules. To simplify the presentation, the vertical portion of the aggregate supply schedule is set at the average daily reserve requirement level, therefore assuming that the other factors that generate liquidity demand (that is, banknotes) have mean zero. The underlying total outstanding allotment is 2R.

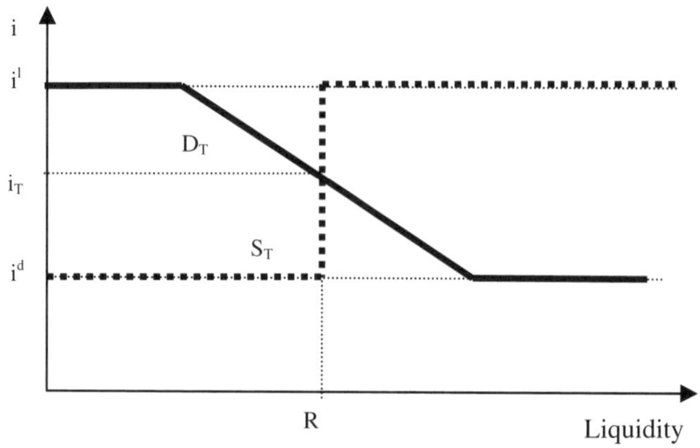

Figure 1. Money Market Equilibrium on the Last Day of the Maintenance Period.

reason is that, early in the maintenance period, banks can postpone the accumulation of reserves until the last day, which gives them an option for how much to hold in their account at the central bank. The only constraint that applies early in the reserve maintenance period is that overnight overdrafts are not allowed. Given that marginal lending from the central bank is costly, banks try to manage their current accounts at a level that keeps the likelihood of an overdraft close to zero. On the other hand, banks try to avoid an early fulfillment of the reserve requirement — avoid being *locked-in* — as any surplus will be remunerated at a penalty rate i^d. For example, by keeping daily current accounts close to their daily minimum reserve requirements, banks can simultaneously avoid overdrafts and keep the probability of being locked-in low until close to the end of the RMP.

Figure 2 plots the EONIA[5] spread over the MBR against the aggregate liquidity conditions on the last day of each reserve maintenance period (RMP) between March 2004 and July 2008. Aggregate liquidity conditions are measured by the net recourse to marginal lending (NSF). According to the estimated relation between the EONIA spread and the liquidity conditions, when the RMP ends perfectly balanced EONIA is set at about 5 basis points above the minimum bid rate. For each EUR 1 billion of liquidity shortage (NSF>0) the predicted spread is approximately 12 basis points (7 + 5).

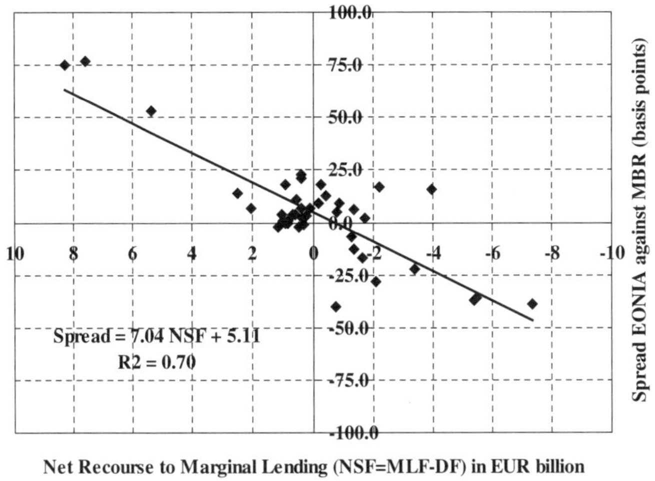

Figure 2. EONIA Spread and Liquidity Conditions on the Last Day of the RMP.
Notes: The scale in the *x*-axis is in reverse order. MLF is the recourse to the marginal lending facility; DF is the recourse to the deposit facility; NSF = MLF-DF is the net recourse to marginal lending. Benchmark allotment targets NSF = 0.

Under these assumptions, the equilibrium interest rate on the first day of a two-day reserve maintenance period is given by:

$$i_{T-1} = p_{T-1}^{DF} i^d + p_{T-1}^{MLF} i^l + \left[1 - p_{T-1}^{DF} - p_{T-1}^{MLF}\right] E(i_T). \tag{3}$$

[5] EONIA is an effective overnight rate computed as a weighted average of all overnight unsecured lending transactions in the interbank market, initiated, within the euro area, by a panel of banks.

Equation 3 states that the equilibrium overnight rate on day $T-1$ is a weighted average of the rates of the standing facilities and of the expected rate on the last day of the reserve maintenance period. To better understand equation 3 note that, under normal market conditions, p_{T-1}^{DF} and p_{T-1}^{MLF} are small given: 1) the large size of the reserve requirement in the euro area; 2) the benchmark allotment policy of the ECB; and 3) the smooth reserve requirement fulfillment path followed by banks.[6] Thus, to a close approximation, equation 3 simplifies to $i_{T-1} = E[i_T]$. The left hand side of this simplified equilibrium condition is the benefit for the representative bank of postponing by one day the accumulation of one unit of reserves (as the bank can lend the unit to other banks earning i_{T-1}); the right hand side is the expected cost of accumulating one unit of reserves tomorrow (for example, borrowing one unit from other banks). In equilibrium the marginal benefit equals the marginal cost of overnight funds, which is exactly what equation 3 describes.

Equation 3 also applies, as a good approximation, to maintenance periods that have longer durations, leading to the so-called *martingale hypothesis*. According to this hypothesis, interest rates throughout the reserve maintenance period should equal its expected value for the last day, that is, $i_t = E[i_T]$ for all $t<T$. This holds because, due to the reserve averaging provision of reserve requirements, banks are essentially indifferent between holding liquidity on different days in the reserve maintenance period, and therefore will not be willing to pay higher rates (or accept lower rates) in the interbank market than the expected one.[7]

Figure 3 illustrates equilibrium in the overnight interbank market on day T-1; Figure 4 shows the empirical evidence.

Summarizing, under normal market conditions, the overnight interest rate can be steered close to the minimum bid rate as long as it is firmly anchored on the last day of the reserve maintenance period via an appropriate liquidity supply policy. Note that an important hypothesis underlying the model illustrated in Figure 1 and expressed by equations 1 to 3 is the absence of market frictions (that is, market segmentation, asymmetric information, transaction costs, etc.) whereby any bank with a liquidity surplus will be willing to lend it to any other bank with a liquidity need. The interbank market perfectly redistributes liquidity across banks so that the

[6] On the reserve fulfillment path of euro area credit institutions see Cassola (2008).

[7] Since the March 2004 reform of the operational framework of the Eurosystem, key policy rate changes are implemented, as a rule, from the start of the reserve maintenance period. This has reduced significantly the impact of expectations of changes in policy rates on the demand for liquidity within the reserve maintenance period.

Figure 3 illustrates equilibrium in the overnight interbank market on the first day of a two-day reserve maintenance period. D_{T-1} refers to the (inverse) aggregate demand for liquidity and S_{T-1} refers to the supply of liquidity. For simplicity the demand schedule is drawn with linear segments. Also to simplify the presentation the vertical portion of the aggregate supply schedule is set at R, the daily average reserve requirement. The inverse demand schedule is flat at (R, $E(i_T)$) which implies that aggregate liquidity supply shocks (unless very large) do not have any impact on the overnight interest rate. This is the 'buffering function' resulting from the averaging possibility.

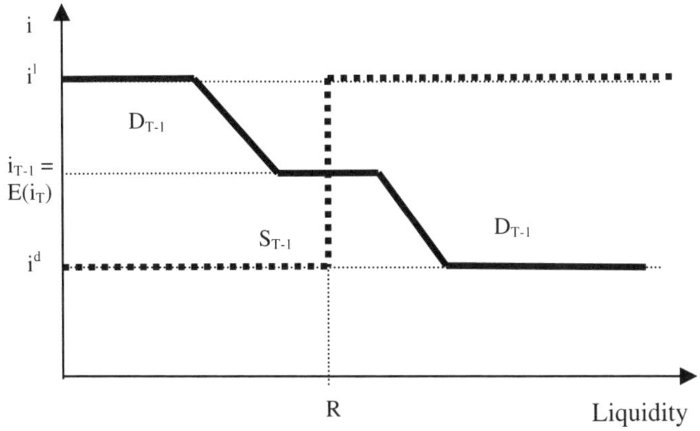

Figure 3. Money Market Model on the Penultimate Day of the Maintenance Period.

ECB can concentrate on ensuring balanced aggregate liquidity conditions and a smooth flow of refinancing to the banking system over time. The following sections will discuss why and how the ECB's liquidity policy had to be adjusted during the market turmoil. In what follows, however, we still abstract from asymmetric information effects on the overnight interbank market and the potential market breakdown that it may cause.

3. ECB Liquidity Management Under Turbulent Market Conditions

3.1 *Automatic stabilizers*

Four features of the operational framework of the Eurosystem can be considered as *automatic stabilizers* in the context of crisis management: 1) the (large) *number of counterparties* that have direct access to the Eurosystem's

Figure 4 plots the EONIA spread over the MBR against the aggregate liquidity conditions on all but the last two business days of each reserve maintenance period between March 2004 and July 2007. Aggregate liquidity conditions are measured by the daily reserve surplus. According to the estimated relation between the EONIA spread and the liquidity conditions, EONIA is set 7 basis points above the minimum bid rate, irrespective of the daily liquidity conditions.

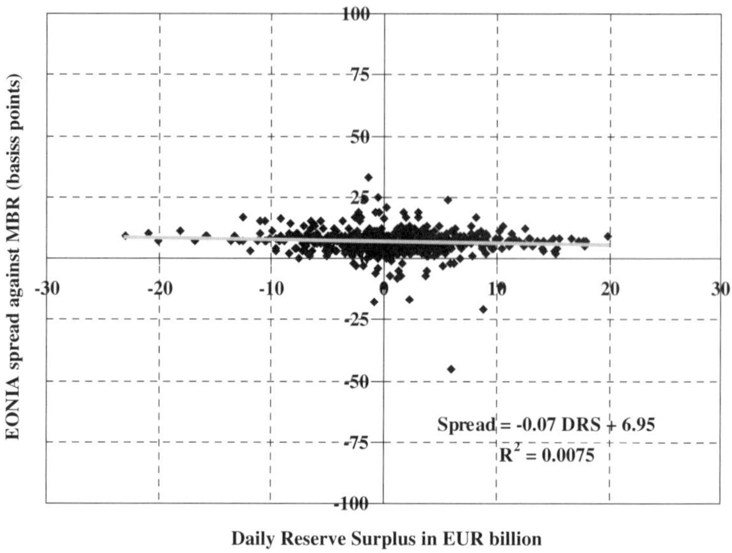

Figure 4. EONIA spread and liquidity conditions during the RMP.
Notes: Daily Reserve Surplus is defined as the difference between the daily current accounts of credit institutions with the Eurosystem and their daily average minimum reserve requirement.

intraday credit, overnight standing facilities, and *regular* open market operations; 2) the characteristics of the *minimum reserve requirement* (sizable, remunerated, with averaging provision); 3) the *collateral framework* (acceptance of a broad range of collateral including nonmarketable securities); and 4) the availability of an automatic *lending facility* with only limited stigma attached to it.

3.1.1 *Counterparties and size of operations*

A very large *number of credit institutions* interact directly with the Eurosystem. About 2,000 credit institutions registered in the euro area have access to the marginal lending facility of the Eurosystem, and just over 1,700 can participate in the regular refinancing operations of the ECB which are large in volume (making up to around 30 percent of Eurosystem's total assets); 130 are eligible to participate in fine-tuning operations. The fact that the main credit and refinancing facilities of the Eurosystem are accessible to such a large number of institutions supported confidence in the ability of the banking system to prevent a spiraling liquidity crisis, therefore contributing to avoiding bank runs and to limit contagion (due to either asymmetric information or overlapping claims).

3.1.2 *Reserve requirements*

The sizable *reserve requirement* that banks have to fulfill in the euro area coupled with the averaging provision, provide an immediate liquidity buffer for the banking system during the early stages of any market turmoil; moreover the sizable reserve requirement has allowed the implementation of a liquidity policy (frontloading, see Section 3.2.3) which, to some extent, has contributed to reducing the funding liquidity risk of banks.

The fact that reserve requirements are remunerated at the marginal rate of the main refinancing operations of the ECB, which is a result of banks' bidding behavior, makes current accounts with the Eurosystem (up to the minimum reserve level) a very attractive asset for banks to hold, in terms of risk-return characteristics, as it is a highly liquid, risk-free asset with a return higher than the return on the risk-free rate. The downside is that a sizable reserve requirement may put banks under additional pressure to get refinancing given the penalties attached to nonfulfillment.

3.1.3 *Eligible assets*

The *collateral framework* of the Eurosystem, with its broad range of eligible assets encompassing asset backed securities, credit claims, and nonmarketable assets, allows banks to get funding from the Eurosystem without undue constraints. This became even more relevant during the turmoil, also because the ECB did not enforce stricter risk control measures during the period under review.[8] The downside is that, over time, central bank refinancing may become increasingly collateralized with illiquid assets, which raises complex issues for risk management and market functioning.

The above mentioned four characteristics of the operational framework interacted in a virtuous manner enhancing financial stability: the sizable reserve requirement and volume of operations, the large number of counterparties and the broad range of collateral implied that financial assets that had suddenly become illiquid in private markets (*market liquidity risk*) could still be used as collateral with the Eurosystem, thereby significantly adding to market liquidity whilst at the same time reducing *funding liquidity* needs of, and risk for credit institutions.

3.1.4 *Marginal lending facility*

Under market turmoil the lending facility plays the role of an automatic lender of Last Resort Facility, which fulfills the *Bagehot principle*: unlimited lending to solvent, illiquid institutions, at a penalty rate and against collateral. However, the marginal lending facility of the Eurosystem was conceived to be used only sporadically and not to provide regular refinancing to the banking system or to replace National Central Banks, domestic supervisory entities and fiscal authorities in their tasks related to the Lender of Last Resort function.

When the market turmoil began, the *marginal lending facility* of the Eurosystem had *no stigma* attached to its use. In fact, credit institutions in the euro area have been accustomed to using the marginal lending facility since January 1999. Recourses to marginal lending during the maintenance period can usually be explained by imperfect monitoring of current accounts by individual credit institutions (customer order flows, payments and securities settlement systems problems, human errors, operational failures, etc.). These recourses have had a very low frequency and have been, in general, for small amounts. The most significant usage tends to

[8] Risk control measures have been refined in September 2008 in the context of the bi-annual review. However, implementation is scheduled for February 2009.

occur on the last day of the reserve maintenance period and, to a large extent, is related to the aggregate liquidity imbalance caused by the inevitable errors made by the Eurosystem in forecasting the daily aggregate liquidity needs of the banking system.

The Eurosystem publishes on a daily basis the recourses to the standing facilities, in the context of the release of other information about daily liquidity conditions (for example, consolidated balance sheet of the Eurosystem). However, the names of the credit institutions involved are not disclosed by the ECB or the Eurosystem. Still, it cannot be excluded that, under market turmoil, some stigma may emerge in case large and recurrent recourses to marginal lending occur namely because they could trigger market rumors about which institutions have been involved.

3.2 *Liquidity management*

Before the turmoil, the ECB provided the bulk of its refinancing to the banking system via its weekly MROs (70 percent; one-week maturity), which were complemented with a monthly LTRO (30 percent; three-month maturity). After February 2005, the ECB started conducting, on a frequent basis, a fine-tuning operation on the last day of the reserve maintenance period. Before the turmoil, the ECB's open market operations had a relatively low frequency and the stabilization of the overnight interest rate was mainly achieved through the averaging mechanism as explained in Section 2. In this section we review why and how the ECB's liquidity policy has changed after August 2007.

3.2.1 *Fixed rate tenders with full allotment*

Liquidity management policy has played an important role in crisis management: Fine-Tuning Operations were carried out more frequently and fixed rate tender procedures with full allotment were applied when market conditions were perceived as severely strained. This was clearly the case on August 9, 2007.

Figure 5 gives a graphical interpretation of the events that occurred on that day, in the euro interbank market for overnight funds. In our

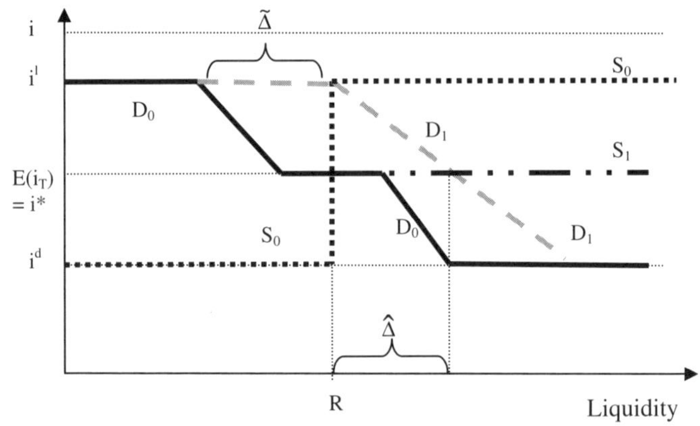

Figure 5. Fixed Rate Tender with Full Allotment on August 9, 2007.

simplified framework the shock occurred on the first day of the two-day reserve maintenance period. Ex ante demand for liquidity by banks (for example, before the turmoil) is represented by the bold step-wise function (D_0). As explained in Section 2.2, early in the maintenance period, under calm market conditions, the (inverse) demand function is highly interest-elastic (flat) at the expected future overnight rate (and around the daily reserve requirement level). The supply of funds by the ECB (S_0) was the benchmark amount — which, for simplicity, is set equal to the daily reserve requirement (R). The ex-ante equilibrium overnight interest rate was at the middle of the interest rate corridor.

Our interpretation of the August 9, 2007, events is that a *funding liquidity shock*[9] affected the demand for reserves by banks in two different ways: 1) a parallel rightward shift; and 2) a reduction in the elasticity of the (inverse) demand schedule (that is, a steeper curve without a flat segment). The former movement captures the idea that the sub-prime crisis was perceived by banks as implying an increase in the likelihood of a large (aggregate) liquidity draining shock. As a consequence banks set (stricter) targets for their daily current accounts, with the result that the

[9] The ultimate source of the funding liquidity shock was (arguably) asymmetric information and the fear of credit rationing and also anxiety about credit lines/support commitments towards special purpose vehicles and about the realization and/or rolling-over of securitization programs.

averaging mechanism weakened and "liquidity effects" emerged on the first day of the reserve maintenance period (the flat part of the demand curve vanished). Graphically, the shock is represented by the parallel shift in the demand curve from D_0 to D_1, where $\tilde{\Delta}$ is the (highly uncertain) increase in the demand for reserves.

On August 9, 2007, the ECB allotted liquidity through a fine-tuning operation with a fixed rate tender procedure with full allotment (FA). This is represented in Figure 5 by an infinitely elastic supply function, S_1. This procedure allowed the ECB to get an estimate of the additional liquidity demand by banks (a measure of the liquidity shock), represented by the bid amount $\hat{\Delta}$ as R was already in the market.

In the model, the immediate impact of the turmoil was an increase in banks' expected recourses to the marginal lending facility. From equation 3, it can be seen that an increase in the probability of taking recourse to the marginal lending facility on day $T-1$, $\tilde{p}_{T-1}^{MLF} > p_{T-1}^{MLF}$, immediately translates into: 1) higher market overnight rate on day $T-1$, and 2) weakening of the anchoring provided by the expected overnight rate $E(i_T)$, even if the liquidity shock is perceived as transitory. Equation 4 shows the equilibrium condition in the overnight interbank market before the fine-tuning operation:

$$i_{T-1} = \tilde{p}_{T-1}^{MLF}\, i^l + [1 - \tilde{p}_{T-1}^{MLF}].E(i_T) > i_{mbr}, \tag{4}$$

where, for simplicity, we have assumed that the unusual market conditions imply $p_{T-1}^{DF} = 0$.[10] The provision of temporary liquidity by the ECB can influence market rates by reducing banks' expected recourse to the marginal lending facility and thus bring down overnight rates by accommodating the perceived sudden increase in liquidity demand. The equilibrium in the interbank market after the fine-tuning operation will be discussed in the following section.

3.2.2 *The separation principle*

The fine-tuning operation conducted as fixed rate tender with full allotment left the banking sector with a large daily reserve surplus. The surplus had to be drained over the remaining days of the reserve maintenance period

[10] In the limit, $i_{T-1} = i^e$.

because otherwise the overnight rate would fall sharply towards the deposit facility rate level, compromising the signaling of the monetary policy stance. Given *the separation principle* between monetary policy stance and implementation, this could not be allowed unless the Governing Council of the ECB decided to change the policy stance, which was not the case.

According to the separation principle, the assessment of the monetary policy stance and related decision by the Governing Council of the ECB on the minimum bid rate and on the rates on standing facilities, are separated from the day-to-day liquidity management — a task whose responsibility is delegated to the executive board of the ECB.

Figure 6 gives a graphical interpretation of the problem using the two-day RMP model. It portrays the expected liquidity situation in the inter-bank market on the last day of the reserve maintenance period (day T) should the ECB not drain the surplus created by the fixed rate tender fine-tuning operation with full allotment. This would leave a liquidity surplus in the banking sector and, with high likelihood, would lead to an aggregate recourse to the deposit facility on the last day of the RMP, $\tilde{p}_T^{DF} > p_T^{DF}$. Demand for liquidity by banks on the last day of the reserve maintenance period is represented by the bold step-wise function (D_0). Given that only the reserve requirement (R) is remunerated (in the example at the policy rate in the mid-point of the interest rate corridor), any excess reserves in the central bank account $\hat{\Delta}$ would be remunerated at the deposit facility rate of the ECB (i^d). This would likely change day $T-1$ and day T money

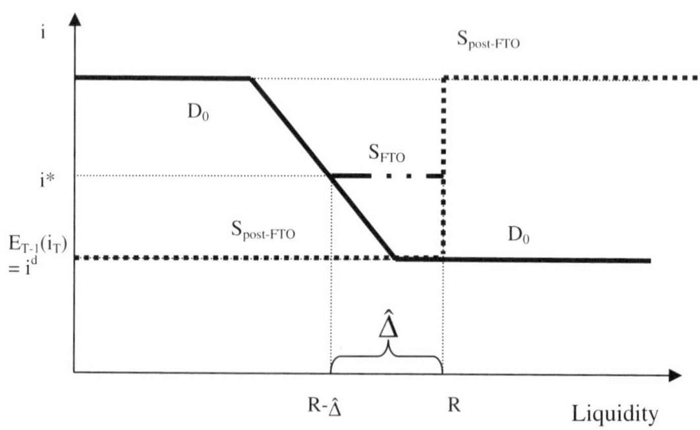

Figure 6. Liquidity Drain on Last Day of Reserve Maintenance Period.

market expectations about the overnight interest rate, which would then start falling towards the level of the deposit facility rate. Equation 5 and equation 6 are the equilibrium conditions in the overnight interbank market on day T–1, after the fine-tuning operation, if the additional liquidity is not drained on the last day:

$$i_{T-1} = \tilde{p}_{T-1}^{MLF} i^{l} + \tilde{p}_{T-1}^{DF} i^{d} + [1 - \tilde{p}_{T-1}^{MLF} - \tilde{p}_{T-1}^{DF}].E_{T-1}(i_{T}) \quad (5)$$

$$E_{T-1}(i_{T}) = E_{T-1}(\tilde{p}_{T}^{DF}) i^{d} \approx i^{d}, \quad (6)$$

where $E_{T-1}(i_T)$ denotes expectation of i_T conditional on information available at time T–1.

To avoid a significant drop in interest rates towards the deposit rate, the ECB had to drain the liquidity surplus from the market.[11] However, because a sudden drain (on day T–1) could create volatility in the money market, the ECB decided to stretch the adjustment of liquidity conditions over the remainder of the maintenance period. In the two-day model the liquidity surplus is drained on day T rather than on day T–1. Given that equilibrium in the overnight market with $i_T = i_{mbr}$ is achieved when total liquidity supply (L_t) is such that $R + \hat{\Delta} + R - FTO = 2R$, the fine-tuning operation must be calibrated to drain the surplus, $FTO_T = \hat{\Delta}$. It is worth noting that the size of the reserve requirement puts a limit to the feasibility of the policy with unchanged policy rates as $\hat{\Delta}$ cannot be so large as to imply negative current accounts with the central bank after the FTO. In that case the central bank would not be able to prevent a drop in the overnight interest rate.

3.2.3 *Frontloading*

Against the experience of one full reserve maintenance period with the market turmoil, in the following reserve maintenance periods the ECB initiated a frontloading liquidity management policy. The frontloading policy consists in allotting significantly above benchmark at the beginning of the reserve maintenance period, and gradually reducing the surplus until the end of the reserve maintenance period. On the last day of each period, a liquidity draining fine-tuning operation is carried out,

[11] The ECB also took care of communicating its intentions in all extraordinary allotments.

mopping-up the remaining surplus and therefore generating expectations of an overnight rate, on the last day, close to the minimum bid rate. It should be emphasized again that, frontloading aims at creating a temporary surplus in the market, not a permanent one. That is, on average, the supply of liquidity to the banking system is the same as before the turmoil — just enough for banks to fulfill their reserve requirements — only the timing of the provision is changed.

During turmoil times, the market interest rate is, in principle, still influenced by expected liquidity conditions on the last day of the maintenance period (as in equations 1 and 2). However, several changes should be introduced into the equations. First, credit rationing, market segmentation, and liquidity hoarding imply — throughout the maintenance period — a higher probability of recourses to the marginal lending facility. Second, in times of rapidly changing asset valuations, there is an increasing risk that access to the marginal lending facility might be restricted, either because of lack of sufficient collateral or because of a rating downgrade. The latter is captured by introducing an extra term in the overnight interbank market equilibrium conditions $p_T^{NOCOL} > 0$. Should these circumstances materialize, banks would be forced to resort to more expensive liquidity (at a higher rate i^h). Without a frontloading policy, short-term interest rates would then roughly obey the following equations:

$$i_{T-1} = \tilde{p}_{T-1}^{MLF} i^l + [1 - \tilde{p}_{T-1}^{MLF}]\, E_{T-1}(i_T) \tag{7}$$

$$E_{T-1}(i_T) = E_{T-1}(\tilde{p}_T^{MLF}) i^l + E_{T-1}\,(p_T^{NOCOL}) i^h > i_{mbr},$$

where $\tilde{p}_t^{MLF} > p_t^{MLF}$, for $t = T{-}1$, T and $p_T^{NOCOL} > 0$, $p_T^{DF} = 0$, and $i^h > i^l$. We assume, for simplicity, that the downgrade and/or the collateral shortage affects market rates only through expectations for day T (that is, we assume that banks know/reveal their current state early in the morning). Again, our analysis is based on the assumption that there is a representative bank. In this case, the two equations govern the aggregate demand of the banking sector.[12]

The frontloading policy of the ECB counteracts the upward pressure on the overnight interest rate in two ways: on the one hand, by allowing for some early accumulation of central bank reserves, it reduces the probability (and volumes) that banks may need to borrow in the unsecured

[12] In the limit, $i_{T-1} = i^l$.

market at a very high rate, should they run out of collateral or face a downgrade. On the other hand, frontloading increases the probability that banks fulfill their reserve requirements early in the maintenance period and, as a consequence, increase the probability of "locking-in," that is, that banks may have to deposit excess funds at the deposit facility at rate i^d. Both mechanisms contribute to reducing the short term interest rate via increasing $E_{T-1}(p_T^{DF})$ and by decreasing $E_{T-1}(p_T^{NOCOL})$. With the frontloading policy, short-term interest rates become determined by the following equations:

$$i_{T-1} = \tilde{p}_{T-1}^{MLF} i^l + \hat{p}_{T-1}^{DF} i^d [1 - \tilde{p}_{T-1}^{MLF} - \hat{p}_{T-1}^{DF}] \, E_{T-1}(i_T) \tag{8}$$

$$E_{T-1}(i_T) = E_{T-1}(\tilde{p}_T^{MLF}) i^l + E_{T-1}(\hat{p}_T^{DF}) i^d + E_{T-1}(p_T^{NOCOL}) i^h, \tag{9}$$

where $\hat{p}_{T-1}^{DF} > p_{T-1}^{DF}$ and we assumed that frontloading reduces but cannot eliminate completely the other term, $E_{T-1}(p_T^{NOCOL}) \neq 0$. The main challenge to the frontloading policy is to calibrate the allotment such that in equation 9:

$$E_{T-1}(i_T) = E_{T-1}(\tilde{p}_T^{MLF}) i^l + E_{T-1}(\hat{p}_T^{DF}) i^d + E_{T-1}(p_T^{NOCOL}) i^h = i_{mbr}. \tag{10}$$

This can be achieved (at least in the model) through the combination of an allotment on day T–1 above $2R$ (R each day) and a liquidity draining operation on day T. Note that with frontloading, the link between the current and the expected future overnight rates is weakened as in equation 8 the term between the squared brackets is smaller than 1. The martingale hypothesis no longer applies and daily liquidity shocks start having an impact on the overnight interest rate. Moreover, given that $\hat{p}_{T-1}^{DF} < \hat{p}_T^{DF}$, as the probability of being locked-in, which can be substantially different from zero with frontloading, generally increases in the course of a maintenance period, with frontloading the overnight rate is expected to decline over the course of the maintenance period which, in the two-day RMP model implies $i_{T-1} > E_{T-1}(i_T) = i_T = i_{mbr}$. This again shows that the martingale hypothesis is not valid under turmoil.

Figure 7 illustrates how the frontloading policy works. Demand for liquidity by banks is represented by the bold step-wise function (D_1). During the turmoil, the demand for reserves by banks, on day T–1, shifted rightwards and became less elastic (see Figure 1). Demand at the MRO is represented by the curve D_{MRO}. It is a downward sloping bid

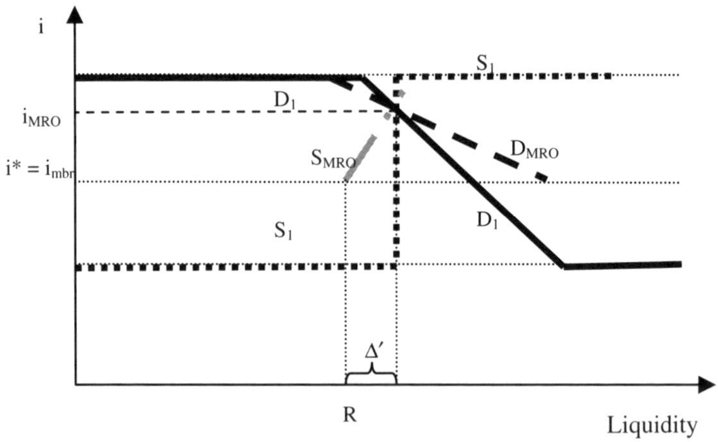

Figure 7. Frontloading.

curve rather than a pre-turmoil (almost) flat curve. After the turmoil, the allotment policy consists of providing liquidity above the benchmark $(R + \Delta')$. The supply at the tender is represented by S_{MRO}, demand at the tender is represented by D_{MRO} and the minimum bid rate by i_{mbr}. After the tender, supply in the overnight market is represented by S_1. On day T, the ECB conducts an FTO and drains the surplus $2\Delta'$ from the market. Note again that the size of the reserve requirement puts a limit to the feasibility (and effectiveness) of the frontloading policy as $2\Delta'$ cannot be so large as to imply negative current accounts with the central bank on day T.

From equations 8 and 9 and the above discussion, we may conclude that in the model MRO tender rates, under turmoil, become elevated through the expectation effect of a downgrade and the increased probability of marginal lending:

$$i_{MRO} = (½)(i_{T-1} + E_{T-1}(i_T)) > i_{mbr}.$$

Under market turmoil a positive spread emerged between the MRO tender rate and the policy rate. However, and contrary to the prediction of the two-day RMP model, the overnight interest rate during the turmoil has been consistently below tender rates throughout the reserve maintenance period. In this regard, two points are worth noting. First, the situation described in Figure 7 could not represent equilibrium in normal market conditions as banks would not bid up the MRO rate; and most probably would also not bid for an amount much larger than the reserve requirement. Second, the surplus allotted by the ECB does not fully accommodate the increased demand for reserves ($\Delta' < \widetilde{\Delta}$) and, as a consequence, the marginal price of liquidity rises, though by less than without the allotment above benchmark.

What kinds of banks are willing to bid up the MRO rate? What elements have implied a spread between the overnight inter-bank market and the marginal MRO rate?

To answer these questions it is useful to think of the inter-bank market as being populated by two types of banks, let's call them *ostracized* banks and *sound* banks. *Sound* banks are those with a large pool of liquid collateral (for example, government bonds), not dependent on wholesale funding (securitization), without committed back-up credit lines (to special investment vehicles, etc.), and without off-balance-sheet exposures. Sound banks have, say, AAA credit rating. Actually, these banks may not even need to participate in the MROs (or LTROs) and instead may rely on the private repo market and/or overnight borrowing to meet their reserve requirement needs. *Ostracized* banks are those with a small pool of liquid collateral, heavily dependent on wholesale funding (securitization), with committed back-up credit lines (to special investment vehicles, etc.), and/or large off-balance-sheet exposures. *Ostracized banks* must have at least A– credit rating to be eligible to ECB operations. The ostracized banks will be eager to participate in the MROs (and other operations) in order to buy insurance against credit default, downgrade, unexpected drawing from back-up lines or in order to prevent a "run" on the bank by investors and/or depositors. They typically will get funding from the ECB using rather illiquid collateral (that is, loans, asset-backed securities, residential-mortgage-backed securities). However, as *ostracized* banks receive more reserves from the central bank than they need to fulfill their reserve requirements they lend to the sound banks in the overnight interbank market. In fact, because the alternative for the ostracized banks is to use the deposit facility of the ECB at a penalty rate (100 basis points below the minimum bid rate), they will likely lend to the sound banks at a rate close to the (risk-free) policy rate. Moreover, ostracized banks would prefer to frontload while sound banks would be willing to backload their fulfillment of the reserve requirement waiting for softer rates as they do not face the risk of being downgraded.

This situation would represent a *separating equilibrium* with *market segmentation*: sound banks borrowing in the interbank market (or in the private repo market using high quality collateral), and ostracized banks borrowing in the MROs and LTROs. This works like an insurance mechanism whereby ostracized banks pay sound banks and the Eurosystem the difference between the MRO rate (which is the remuneration of R for all banks and is the cost of R only for ostracized banks) and the overnight rate (which is the cost of R only for sound banks). In the process, the Eurosystem applies risk mitigation measures (haircuts, among other measures). A more realistic and complex model of the overnight interbank market would be needed to fully incorporate liquidity provision by the central bank under asymmetric information and credit rationing. To our best knowledge, however, such a model does not exist.[13]

With some variation and adaptation, the frontloading model has been applied since the first maintenance period with financial turmoil. In spite of the success of the frontloading policy in aligning the overnight interest rate with the minimum bid rate in the first month of the turmoil, it became clear that liquidity policy alone could not solve the underlying asset-valuation uncertainties and credit-risk problems, which were the main causes underlying the funding crisis. In the maintenance periods ending in November and December, the ECB took forceful control of the overnight rate. This will be discussed in the next section.

3.2.4 *Narrow corridor with large surplus*

Toward the end of the year 2007, renewed money market tensions revealed that banks were struggling to ensure funding liquidity. Under such extreme circumstances, the frontloading policy was not likely to be strong enough to tie down the overnight interest rate close to the minimum bid rate. In terms of the two-day model in equation 9, the probability of having a shortage of funds, $E_{T-1}(p_T^{MLF}) + E_{T-1}(p_T^{NOCOL})$, was simply too high.

[13] In a different setup, Heider *et al.* (2008) provide a model of asymmetric information in the interbank market which explains the benefit of intermediation by the central bank.

The ECB managed liquidity in this period in an innovative way. First, the maturity of the MRO that covered the Christmas period was extended to two weeks, so that also the year-end was covered. Second, the ECB announced that all bids submitted at or above a certain rate (4.21 percent, the marginal rate of the previous MRO) would be served in full. Third, following this operation, the ECB offered to drain some of the liquidity provided by a series of liquidity-absorbing fine-tuning operations at the minimum bid rate.

Even if not stated explicitly, combining a fixed rate tender with full allotment (even if at a rate above the minimum bid rate) with (daily) liquidity draining fine-tuning operations is very similar to setting a (synthetic) narrow interest rate corridor. The "narrow corridor policy" differs from the pure frontloading policy. While frontloading affects the probabilities of having a liquidity surplus or shortage and thus affects the expected recourse to the standing facilities, a narrow corridor (or the mimicking of such a corridor) affects the overnight rate directly. In the two-day maintenance period model, a narrow corridor policy results in an overnight rate very close to the policy rate level:

$$i_{T-1} = i_{mbr} \tag{11}$$

$$E_{T-1}(i_T) = i_{mbr}. \tag{12}$$

This result is driven by banks' bidding at the fixed rate tenders with full allotment the amount that allows complete hedging of the funding liquidity risk associated with a potential downgrade in period T (provided that sufficient collateral is available). In fact, in our simplified two-period model, a very large bid with $\hat{\Delta} = R$ ensures (endogenously) that both on day T–1 and on day T, banks start the day with $2R$ on their current accounts (guaranteeing the fulfillment of the reserve requirement). In that case, banks will be willing to offer to the ECB, at the daily fine-tuning operation, an amount $\hat{\Delta} = R$. In equation 8 and in equation 9, the large allotment will lead to a very high usage of the synthesized deposit facility, $\hat{p}_{T-1}^{DF} = \hat{p}_T^{DF} = 1$. The downward pressure of the liquidity provision is counterbalanced by the liquidity drain at the policy rate i_{mbr}.

Note that when the martingale property is weakened, a narrow corridor has the advantage of influencing rates on each day directly, without relying solely on effects stemming from liquidity conditions on the last day of the maintenance period. Thus, the synthetic narrow corridor seems most adequate to steer overnight rates in times of extreme market conditions, albeit with the downside of some potential volatility in market conditions if the liquidity providing (draining) operations are overbid (underbid).

3.2.5 *Lengthening the maturity structure of refinancing and the term auction facility*

The Governing Council of the ECB decided to lengthen the overall maturity structure of refinancing by increasing the volumes of the regular LTROs and by introducing special LTROs with three- and six-month maturities. This was achieved by reducing the volume allotted at the weekly MROs such that the total refinancing remained unchanged. These measures were aimed at addressing the drying-up of money market activity at longer maturities. They were not designed to steer longer-term money market interest rates, even if they were expected to bring some relief to money market conditions. As a side-effect, the operational risk involved in rolling over, every week, most of the refinancing provided to the banking system was mitigated. The MRO volumes have been reduced to about 40 percent of total refinancing, from 70 percent, and therefore no longer provide the bulk of liquidity to the market.

On December 12, 2007, it was announced that the Bank of Canada, the Bank of England, the ECB, the Federal Reserve, and the Swiss National Bank would take exceptional measures designed to address elevated pressures in short-term funding markets. The Governing Council of the ECB decided to take joint action with the U.S. Federal Reserve by offering U.S. dollar funding to Eurosystem counterparties. Note that the U.S. dollar provision by the ECB to banks in the euro area does not have any direct impact on liquidity conditions in the euro money market. However, to the extent that some borrowing pressure in the MROs or in the euro overnight interbank market was related to frictions in the U.S. dollar money market and the foreign exchange swap market, direct provision of U.S. dollar to euro area banks might have contributed to easing funding pressure also in euro.

4. An Overall Assessment of the Liquidity Policy

In this section, we draw the main lessons that can be extracted from the ECB's experience during the first year of the financial turmoil and highlight some problem areas. The limits of liquidity policy for dealing with the underlying causes of the turmoil are discussed at the end of the section. Our conclusions are fully in line with the policy recommendations in CFGS (2008).

4.1 *Short-term interest rates before and during the turmoil*

Figure 8 shows the average EONIA spread on each day in the reserve maintenance period (0 is the last day). The scale of the chart corresponds to the ± 100 basis points interest rate corridor set by the standing facility rates around the policy rate. In the chart the daily average spread during the turmoil (August 2007 to June 2008) is compared to the daily average spread before the turmoil (March 2004 to July 2007).

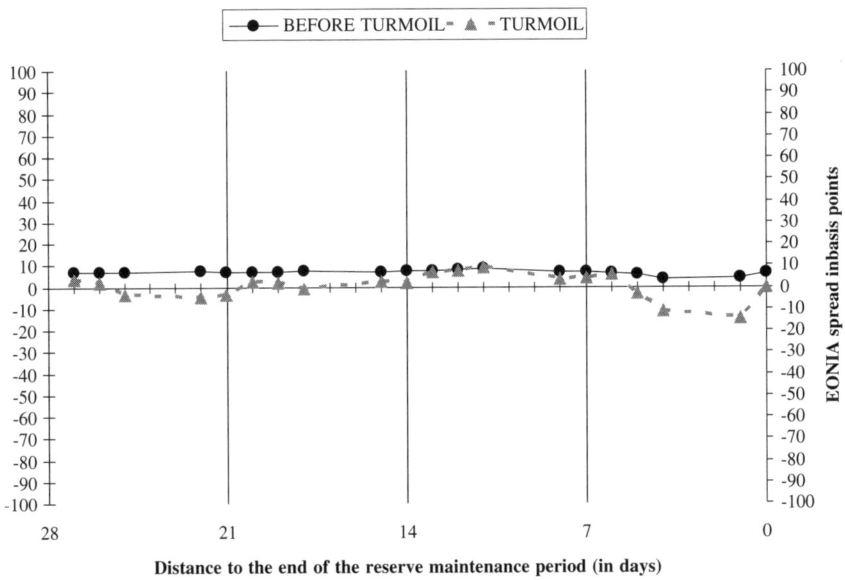

Figure 8. EONIA Spread and Interest Rate Corridor.

Before the turmoil EONIA was very stable at 7 basis points above the policy rate throughout most of the reserve maintenance period, except during the last week when EONIA displayed a smooth U-shape pattern as the overnight rate softened a bit ahead of the last weekend of the reserve maintenance period to increase again until the last day of the reserve maintenance period. During the turmoil, EONIA fluctuated around the policy rate with a more pronounced U-shape pattern after the last MRO of the reserve maintenance period. The frontloading policy appears to have achieved, on average, a reduction in the EONIA spread — virtually eliminating its "natural spread" against the policy rate.

Lowering the EONIA spread has been achieved at the cost of an increase in its volatility. Figure 9 shows the standard deviation of the EONIA spread on each day in the reserve maintenance period. Before the turmoil, EONIA was very stable during most of the reserve main-tenance period, displaying increasing volatility toward the end of the maintenance period and in particular on the last day. During the turmoil, EONIA showed higher volatility throughout the entire

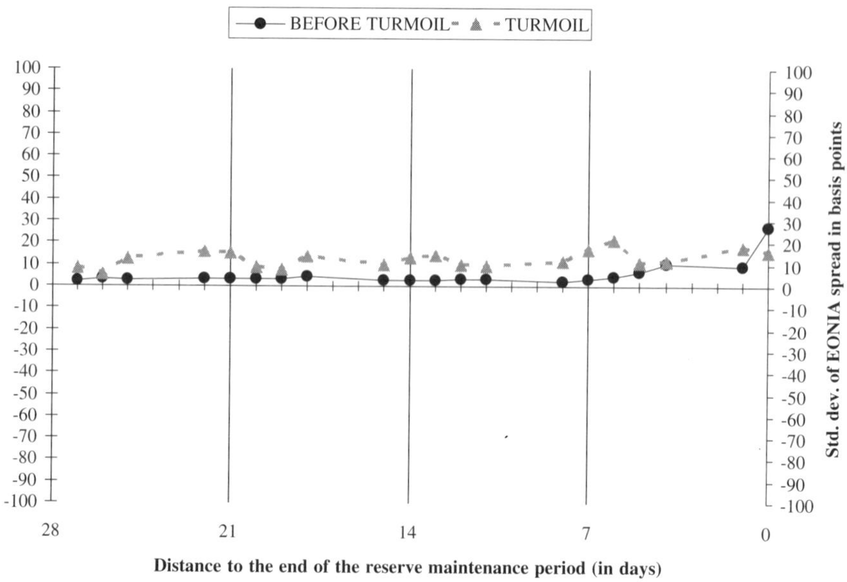

Figure 9. Standard Deviation of EONIA Spread.

maintenance period suggesting some erosion in the efficacy of the averaging mechanism. Whether the increase in volatility was due to the frontloading policy itself (for example, a large deviation from smooth accumulation of reserves) or to the underlying factors (for example, market segmentation, liquidity hoarding, and credit rationing) is an open issue.

The frontloading policy generates volatility in daily aggregate liquidity conditions. Figure 10 shows the daily reserve surplus (defined as the current accounts of banks minus the daily average minimum reserve requirement) on each day of the reserve maintenance period. Before the turmoil, the surplus was very stable and small throughout the reserve maintenance period. During the turmoil, a large surplus has been built during the first week of the reserve maintenance period (€20 billion/day); this has been achieved by MRO allotments (and fine-tuning operations) significantly above benchmark. Banks have been willing to bid for such large amounts. The burden of reducing the surplus then has fallen on the last two weeks of the maintenance period (€ –10 billion/day). Moreover, one-day fine-tuning operations on the last

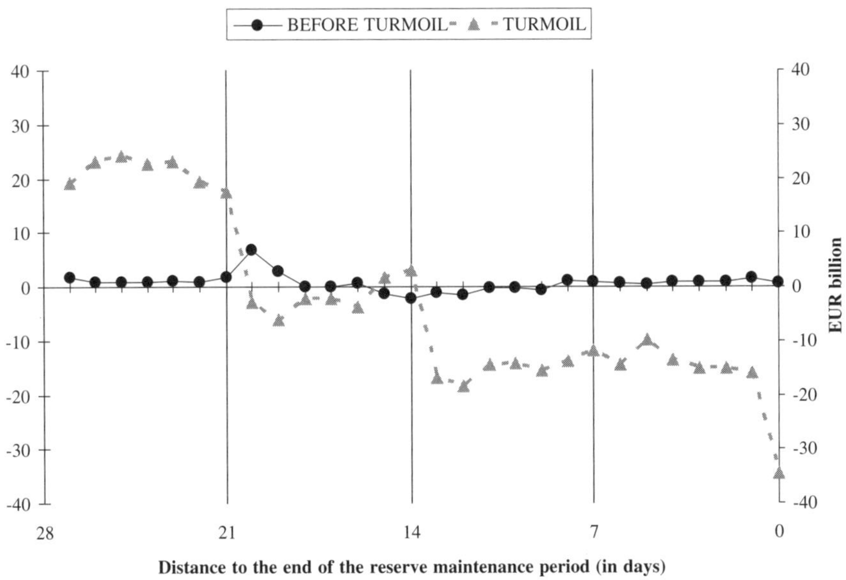

Figure 10. Daily Reserve Surplus.

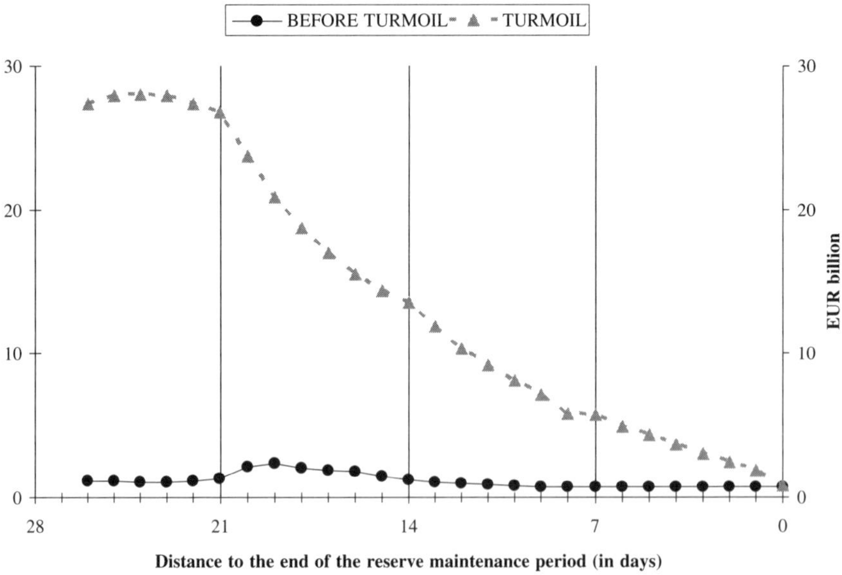

Figure 11. Average Daily Reserve Surplus.

day of the maintenance period have been draining on average about 30 to 40 billion.

Figure 11 shows the average daily reserve surplus on each day in the maintenance period: The average on the last day, after the turmoil, is undistinguishable from the average before the turmoil. This illustrates that the ECB has not increased the supply of reserves; it has merely shifted the time-path of its liquidity provision within each maintenance period.

The large size and variations in the daily reserve surplus documented above seem to be correlated with the level and volatility in the EONIA spread, suggesting the emergence of liquidity effects on a daily basis. Whether those liquidity effects are related to the frontloading policy or are due to other distortions in the functioning of the inter-bank market during the turmoil (that is, market segmentation, liquidity hoarding and credit rationing) is an open issue.

To summarize, the liquidity policy pursued during the first year of the turmoil was able to keep short-term interest rates at levels close to the policy rate and thus managed to counteract the effect of the turmoil on the overnight segment of the money market. However, the EONIA displayed a higher level of day-to-day volatility.

4.2 *Recourse to standing facilities*

Figure 12 shows the net recourse to the standing facilities (marginal lending — deposit facility) of the Eurosystem on each day of the reserve maintenance period. A negative value means a liquidity drain (cash is deposited with the Eurosystem), and a positive value means a liquidity injection (a credit from the Eurosystem). As expected in a regime with averaging and high reserve requirements, the net recourse is negligible under normal market conditions (an exception is that some net usage is observed between observations 8 and 14, coinciding with end-of-month days). Before the turmoil, there was almost zero net recourse and a small positive recourse on the last day (€0.1 billion). During the turmoil, the picture has changed significantly. A net recourse to the deposit facility has emerged which seems persistent,

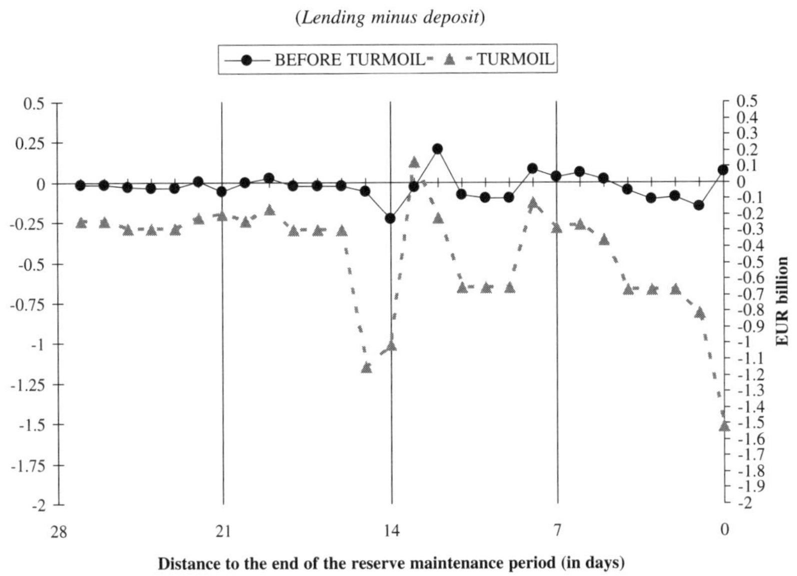

Figure 12. Net Recourse to Standing Facilities.

throughout the reserve maintenance period, with higher volatility around end-of-month days. The net recourse increases rapidly (in absolute terms) during the last week of the maintenance period ending with a net recourse to the deposit facility of about €1.5 billion. The net recourse is mainly due to an increase in the recourse to the deposit facility rather than a decline in marginal lending.

The rapid increase in the deposit facility that occurs on average toward the end of the maintenance period is consistent with the expected impact of the frontloading policy — some banks after the turmoil fulfill their reserve requirements before the last day of the maintenance period. These banks can no longer buffer out daily shocks to their liquidity position and need to deposit all their reserves at the deposit facility. The persistent and steady recourse at around €0.25 billion since the first day of the maintenance period and during most of the time is however difficult to explain with the frontloading policy. Two explanations, not mutually exclusive, seem plausible.

First, banks may be applying, under the turmoil, stricter lending limits in the overnight inter-bank market. The remaining cash is then parked with the Eurosystem — which plays the role of a risk-free counterparty without lending limits. Still, to the extent that banks get refinancing from the ECB, depositing with the Eurosystem implies (at least) a penalty of 100 basis points. That banks are willing to bid up tender rates reveals high degree of funding risk (aversion or premium) and/or market segmentation. In fact, this is equivalent to some form of liquidity hoarding by banks.

Second, instead of frontloading the fulfillment of the reserve requirement (reducing the daily reserve deficiency), banks instead could keep their reserve deficiency on a trajectory which is closer to a smooth fulfillment path — using the deposit facility to control for deviations from the smooth path, rather than interbank lending. This allows banks to keep their current accounts at higher levels without being locked-in and thus reducing the probability of marginal lending. However, this is rational for banks only if there is some stigma attached to, or asymmetry perceived in the cost of marginal lending versus deposit facility. In fact, under symmetry and no stigma "locking-in" and drawing from the marginal lending whenever needed whilst keeping the current account at zero, should be equivalent to not "locking-in," take recourse to the deposit facility and reduce marginal lending to (close to) zero.

4.3 *Limits to the current frontloading policy*

In spite of the success in steering the overnight interest rate close to 4 percent for more than one year, longer-term unsecured money market rates remained elevated and volatile. Figure 13 shows the spreads between EURIBOR (Europe Offered Interbank Rate) deposits and EONIA swap rates for one-week, one-month, and three month maturities. These spreads measure a mix of funding liquidity risk, market risk, counterparty risk, and risk aversion and/or uncertainty. Before the turmoil, those spreads were small and stable, with an essentially flat term structure. During the turmoil, spreads widened sharply and a positively sloped term structure of spreads emerged. In the process, MRO and LTRO tender rates also remained elevated and volatile (see Figure 14 and Figure 15), mimicking developments in the EURIBOR-EONIA swap spreads in terms of size and volatility.

Quite clearly the overnight index swaps spreads and the MRO and LTRO tender spreads have not abated in spite of ECB intervention, suggesting that underlying the apparent resilience of funding liquidity risk

(Daily data: 15/03/2005—10/06/2008)

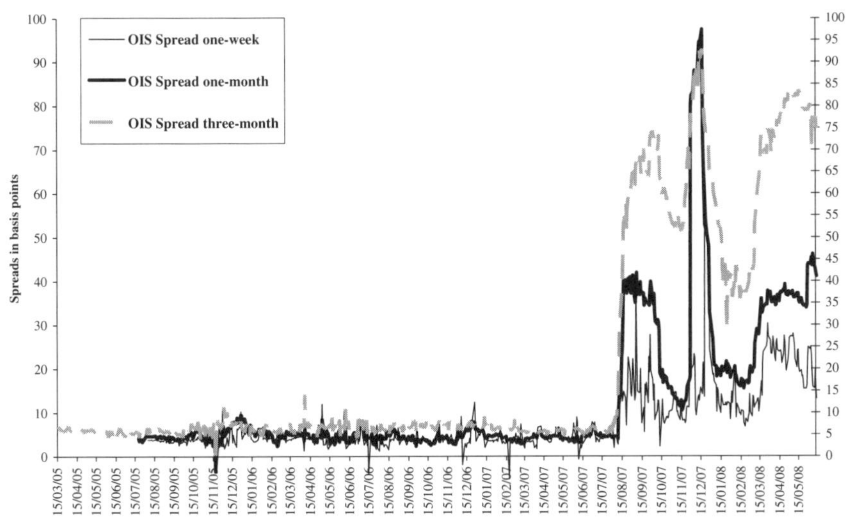

Figure 13. Spreads Between EURIBOR and EONIA Swap Rates.

(Daily data: 15/03/2005—10/06/2008)

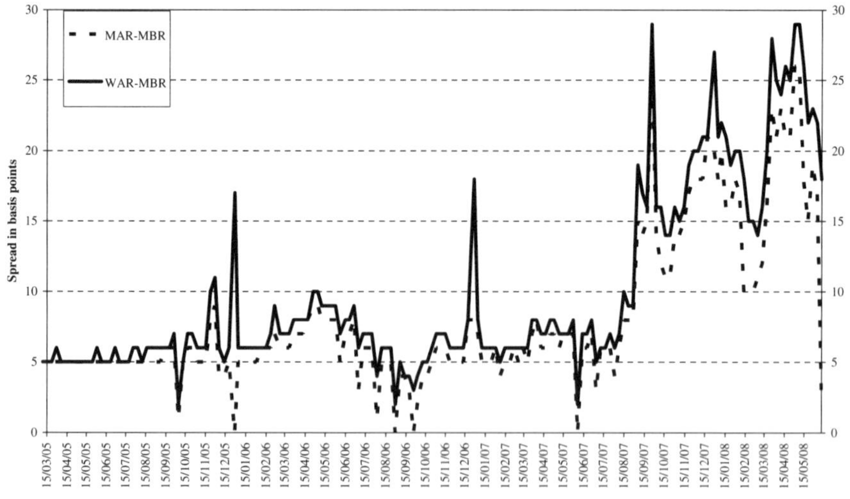

Figure 14. MRO Spreads.

(Daily data: 15/03/2005—10/06/2008)

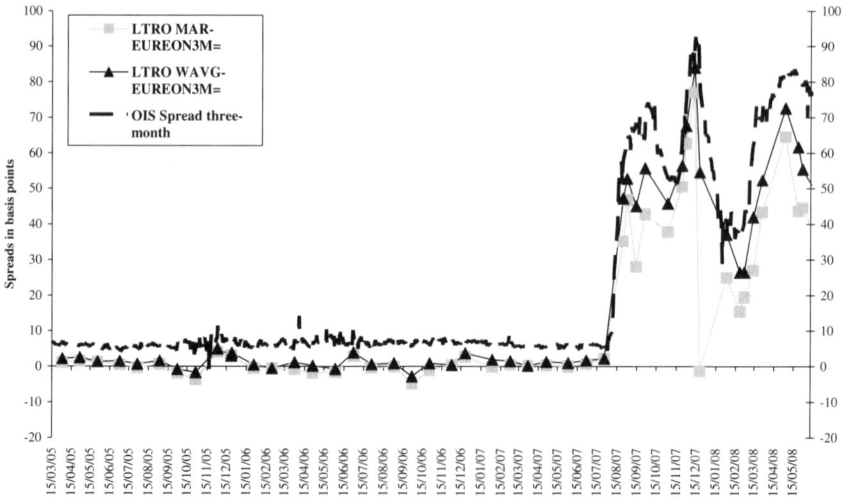

Figure 15. LTRO Spreads.

there has been a persistent concern among investors about the quality of the assets of the banks. The two aspects appear intertwined throughout the August 2007 to June 2008 period.

5. Conclusions and Open Issues

The ECB's operational framework has, at least during the first year, proven to be resilient to the ongoing financial turmoil. Several features that are special to the Eurosystem were particularly helpful. First, in times of market segmentation and very restricted interbank lending, the large number of counterparties to the Eurosystem was particularly important. Second, even in times of rapid changes in asset valuations and breakdown of entire market segments, the broad range of collateral ensured that banks were not restricted to take part in central bank operations by their available assets.

The ECB's liquidity management during the turmoil has gone through several stages. The first phase (after an initial adaptation period), which is also the current one, is characterized by frontloading, in which the central bank changes the time path of its liquidity supply so that banks build up reserves early in the maintenance period. We have argued that the frontloading policy affects short-term market interest rates by influencing the probabilities of having to take recourse to the ECB's standing facilities and by mitigating the funding liquidity risk associated with a downgrade (or collateral shortage) toward the end of the maintenance period. Over the year-end period ECB's liquidity policy effectively put a floor and a ceiling to short-term rates in a way that is similar to implementing a narrow interest rate corridor.

On top of these actions, the ECB participated in the term auction facility (U.S. dollar auctions) together with other major central banks and lengthened the maturity structure of its refinancing operations. These measures had also an indirect impact on conditions in the overnight money market and, thus, contributed further to the stabilization of money market conditions.

Given the ongoing and deepening tensions in global financial markets, the Eurosystem's operational framework will continue to be under pressure. In spite of the success of the liquidity policy in aligning the overnight interest rate with the minimum bid rate, it seems clear that liquidity policy alone cannot solve the underlying asset valuation uncertainties and credit-risk problems, which are the main causes underlying the funding liquidity crisis.

References

Cassola, N. (2008). The reserve fulfillment path of Euro area commercial banks: empirical testing using panel data. *ECB Working Paper 869*, February.

Committee on the Global Financial System (CFGS) (2008). Central bank operations in response to the financial turmoil. *CFGS Papers No 31*. BIS, July.

European Central Bank (2008). The Eurosystem's open market operations during the recent period of financial market volatility. *Monthly Bulletin*, May, 89–104.

European Central Bank (2007). Box 3: The ECB's additional open market operations in the period from 8 August to 5 September 2007. *Monthly Bulletin September*, 30–34.

European Central Bank (2006). T*he Implementation of Monetary Policy in the Euro Area: General Documentation on Eurosystem Monetary Policy Instruments and Procedures*, September.

European Central Bank (2002). The liquidity management of the ECB. *Monthly Bulletin*, May, 41–53.

Gaspar, V., G. Pérez-Quirós, and H. Rodríguez-Mendizábal (2008). Interest rate dispersion and volatility in the market for daily funds. *European Economic Review*, 52(3), 413–440.

Heider, F., M. Hoerova, and C. Holthausen (2008). *Information Asymmetries in the Interbank Market: Theory and Policy Responses*. ECB, mimeograph.

Pérez-Quirós, G. and H. Rodríguez-Mendizábal (2006). The daily market for funds in Europe: what has changed with the EMU? *Journal of Money, Credit, and Banking*, 38(1), 91–118.

Poole, W. (1968). Commercial banks reserve management in a stochastic model: implications for monetary policy. *Journal of Finance*, 23, 769–791.

Välimäki, T. (2003). *Central Bank Tenders: Three Essays on Money Market Liquidity Auctions*. Bank of Finland Studies E26.

Crisis Management and Financial Stability: Some Lessons from the United Kingdom

Nigel Jenkinson*
Bank of England

1. Introduction

I am very grateful for the kind invitation to participate in this important conference. I do not plan this morning to focus on the current acute stress in financial markets, which is well covered by other speakers, but rather to stand back and share some of the experience and initial lessons from the challenges we have faced in the United Kingdom over the past 15 months in managing the financial crisis.

It is helpful to start with a brief reminder of the overall objectives that guide policy decisions and choices. The key objective is to preserve stability of the financial *system* as a whole. That is essential to ensure that the system can continue to fulfil its vital role in supporting the overall economy:

- by facilitating the intermediation of savings into long-term productive investment;
- by supporting the smooth operation of payment and settlement systems and the broader financial infrastructure; and
- by aiding the management of economic and financial risks.

Preserving financial stability consequently requires maintaining confidence in the functions of the overall system. But that in turn does not, and should not, rule out orderly adjustment and consolidation within the financial sector in response to market forces. Moreover, while the

*Nigel Jenkinson is an advisor to the Governor, Bank of England. The author is grateful to Ian Bond for his helpful remarks.

authorities must take immediate action if the stability of the overall financial system comes under serious threat, it is important that the long-term consequences of policy actions are addressed. For example, if policy actions today add to moral hazard by weakening the incentives to manage future risks, it is important that offsetting policy actions are taken over time to mitigate the rise in vulnerability. And recent events clearly demonstrate the importance of policy actions over the medium term to reduce the likelihood and amplitude of costly financial crises, both by lowering the probability of future severe shocks and by strengthening the resilience of the financial system to weather adverse developments.

The origins of the current turmoil have been described well in *Financial Stability Reports*[1] and by other speakers. Summarizing very briefly, financial markets are adjusting to a build up of excess leverage in the system that coincided with a sustained and persistent under-pricing of credit and liquidity risk. Although in the latter stages of the extended global credit boom, many participants were well aware that the compensation for financial risk was likely to prove inadequate, they judged that the increased financial risk was more than outweighed by the business risk that would be borne if the firm stopped writing business in a particular segment of the market. In doing so, participants severely underestimated the build up of *systemic risk*, under-estimating the growing importance of system-wide interactions; for example, that in the event of a shock, many other participants would also wish to exit or hedge positions, thus leading to a sudden evaporation of market liquidity and an amplification of price moves. Defensive actions by banks and market participants to protect their own position have led to a substantial contraction in the supply of credit. As a result, they have increased the risk of a vicious cycle of rising credit losses, as distressed borrowers prove unable to meet their commitments or to refinance them, validating and reinforcing lenders' caution and feeding back into further credit contraction. The very sharp change in financial market conditions, and the likely structural change in financial markets that will result, have increased uncertainty over the viability of some business models that heavily embraced the originate-to-distribute approach or were in other ways dependent on unreliable sources of funding to sustain their business.

---

[1] See, for example, Bank of England, *Financial Stability Reports*, April 2007, October 2007, April 2008.

2. Northern Rock

Northern Rock was one of the early casualties of the current crisis. As seen from Chart 1, the balance sheet of Northern Rock had grown very rapidly in the 10 years running up to the global financial crisis. Indeed, in terms of balance sheet size, Northern Rock had grown from being the 16th largest UK bank[2] in 1997, to number nine by mid-2007. Balance sheet growth was fuelled by a very sharp increase in wholesale funding through the securitization market although, as can be seen from Chart 2, the capital position was in line with the median of large UK banks. Northern Rock had a funding model that depended very heavily on the continuation of sustained liquidity in the securitization market, without adequate contingency arrangements should that source of funding fail. When that market did indeed close, Northern Rock had no alternative source of private funding, and was forced to turn to the Bank of England in early September 2007 to request emergency liquidity support.

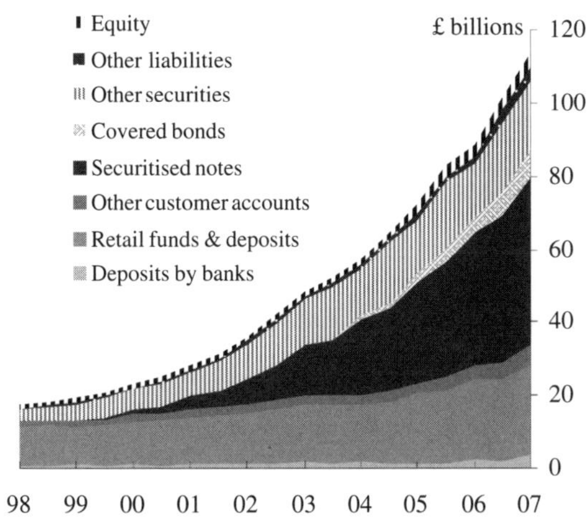

Chart 1. Northern Rock: Balance Sheet Growth and Liability Structure — June 1998–June 2007.
Sources: Northern Rock interim and annual accounts.

[2] Strictly, banks and building societies.

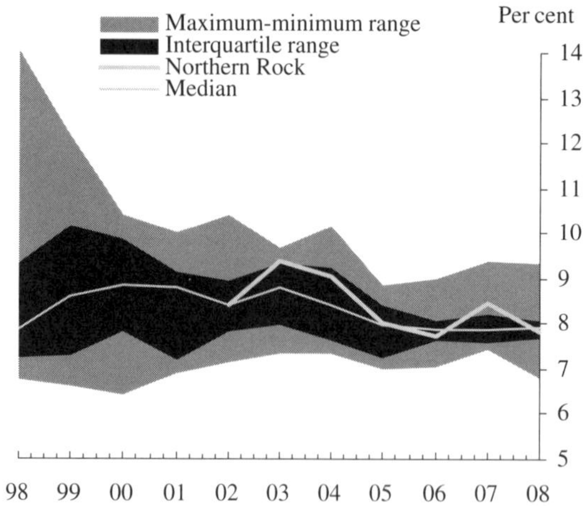

Chart 2. Major UK Banks' Tier 1 Capital Ratios.[a,b]
Sources: Published accounts and Bank calculations.
[a] Tier 1 capital includes ordinary shares associated reserves and retained earnings.
[b] All ratios reported on a Basel 1 basis.

The UK authorities judged that the failure of Northern Rock would pose a severe threat to financial stability given the size of the bank, the febrile conditions in financial markets, and the lack of a legislative framework in the UK to support the orderly resolution of a bank (including its prompt transfer to new owners). An announcement that Northern Rock was receiving Emergency Liquidity Assistance (ELA) from the Bank of England led to an immediate loss of retail depositor confidence given shortcomings in deposit insurance arrangements. The ensuing retail run was halted by a government decision to guarantee the retail and wholesale depositors of the bank. The authorities then tried to engineer a private sector solution. But, after reviewing the options, the government decided that the proposals received did not provide value for money for the taxpayer given the large volume of public funds that had by then been committed. Emergency legislation enacted in February 2008 allowed the government to take Northern Rock into temporary public ownership, in order to preserve financial stability and resolve its future under government control.

Although there are a number of very important broad policy lessons from the current market turmoil that have been highlighted by other speakers and that I will touch on very briefly at the end of my remarks,

I would like to expand a little on four specific areas that were cast into sharp relief by the Northern Rock experience:

- Liquidity risk management and supervision
- Deposit insurance
- Bank resolution
- Central bank operations

3. Liquidity Risk Management and Supervision

One of the major lessons from the recent market turmoil is the need for stronger liquidity risk management by banks and other market participants and for tougher supervision of liquidity risk. Capital markets have grown very strongly in recent years and many banks have increased their dependence on shorter-term wholesale funding and on securitization markets. These developments have led to a marked increase in funding liquidity risks.[3] There was an under-appreciation of the strengthening links between liquidity in capital markets and banks' funding liquidity, and of the rise in *system-wide* liquidity risk as many banks and other market participants adopted similar strategies and increased their exposure to complex, relatively illiquid, securities. And, looking back in the light of the subsequent shock, many banks' contingency funding plans proved deficient: stress tests had been insufficiently severe and cushions of high quality assets were inadequate. As a result, the Basel Committee on Banking Supervision has reviewed the lessons and recently published strengthened principles for liquidity risk management and supervision to raise standards significantly.[4]

4. Deposit Insurance

As noted above, shortcomings in deposit insurance arrangements were among the factors that led to a loss in retail depositor confidence once the

---

[3] See the speech by Nigel Jenkinson "Strengthening regimes for controlling liquidity risk: some lessons from the recent turmoil", 24 April 2008, available at www.bankofengland.co.uk/publications/speeches/2008/index.htm.

[4] Basel Committee for Banking Supervision: *Principles for Sound Liquidity Risk Management and Supervision*, September 2008.

provision of ELA to Northern Rock had been announced. At that time, the UK arrangements relied on co-insurance — the first £2,000 was covered 100 percent, but retail depositors were insured for only 90 percent of the subsequent £33,000. Combined with slow payout of claims, that provided an incentive for retail depositors to seek repayment at the first sign of trouble.

Deposit insurance arrangements were quickly modified in October 2007 to provide 100 percent coverage to a limit of £35,000.[5] Further enhancements are planned to deliver prompt payout of claims to a target of seven days. That will, however, take some time to implement as it requires the pre-identification of eligible accounts and substantial system changes by banks. It is also important to strengthen consumer awareness of deposit insurance arrangements and coverage — a survey undertaken in January 2008 showed that only 1 percent of respondents could correctly identify the limit at that time.[6]

Recent experience has also highlighted the need to ensure that the deposit insurance scheme has sufficient and timely access to funds to support prompt payout. Immediate access to liquidity is essential, but beyond that I see considerable merit in building up a standing fund with risk-based contributions, as in the United States and Canada, in order to contain the moral hazard and adverse incentives associated with deposit insurance. The new banking legislation currently under discussion in the UK contains enabling powers to set up such a fund.

5. Bank Resolution

The lack of a tailor-made regime for resolving failing banks created major challenges in the handling of Northern Rock. The UK regime for resolving failing banks at that time relied on the application of general insolvency law. That proved inadequate for a number of reasons. In particular, the arrangements:

- can only be initiated at insolvency, thus preventing early intervention;

[5] Increased to £50,000 in October 2008.

[6] See "*Financial Stability and Depositor Protection: Strengthening the Framework*", Bank of England, HM Treasury and FSA, CM7308, January 2008.

- do not recognize that banks depend on confidence being sustained and are highly vulnerable to any loss;
- do not recognize the position of key groups of creditors — the retail depositors;
- are not well suited to ensuring continuity of key banking functions; and
- together with the deposit insurance regime described above, inhibit prompt payment to insured depositors and rapid transfer of banking business to sound banks.

The UK authorities have consequently decided to introduce a Special Resolution Regime (SRR) for banks, in line with best practice internationally. The regime will provide the authorities with the powers to take control of and resolve banks in the public interest, with the initiation and implementation under public control. The principal objectives are to ensure that the authorities have the policy tools to undertake an orderly resolution of a bank, preserve financial stability and confidence in the financial system, protect depositors and public funds, and avoid interference with stakeholders' property rights, given the European Convention on Human Rights (ECHR). The regime will repair the deficiencies of the current approach by:

- allowing resolution of a failing bank to be initiated while the bank still has net assets and can meet obligations;
- providing continuity of key banking activities;
- providing a way to protect banking functions and depositors if a bank is closed and, thus;
- removing the need for the authorities to keep a failing bank open.

The new regime is an essential pillar, alongside strengthened regulation and revamped deposit protection, in avoiding another Northern Rock.[7]

A special resolution regime provides the authorities with strong powers to protect financial stability, so safeguards are needed to ensure that the powers are used appropriately. For example, the European Convention on Human Rights requires a fair balance to be struck between the interests of shareholders and the wider public interest — in particular

[7] The Bank of England will be given responsibility for the operation of the special resolution regime.

the shareholders of the bank may be entitled to compensation if the bank is placed into resolution prior to balance-sheet insolvency. A further challenge is to introduce powers to undertake partial solutions (such as various models of good banks that are sold on and bad banks that are closed down) which preserve creditor rankings. To support this process, the UK authorities are planning to introduce a safeguard that would have no creditor worse off than under the counterfactual of an immediate closure and wind-down of assets. A third difficult area is that of financial contacts where counterparties' rights under financial contracts to close out and realize collateral are enshrined in the Financial Collateral Directive and the Settlement Financial Directive. These directives are designed to maintain financial stability by limiting contagion from a failed bank to its counterparties. But, equally if widespread recourse to close out undermines the chances of a successful bank resolution, then the net effect may be to undermine financial stability. To address this, the UK authorities are considering the introduction of safeguards on the netting of contracts and preservation of securities' interests.[8]

Introduction of a special resolution regime will provide the UK authorities with much-needed powers to resolve failing domestic banks. But it remains equally important to improve *international* financial crisis management arrangements, given the continued strong growth of cross-border banking and large international financial groups. Arrangements within Europe have recently been strengthened and a new memorandum of understanding has been introduced across the European Union. A Financial Stability Forum (FSF) working group is developing high-level principles for cross-border crisis management, alongside checklists of information requirements and actions. And the FSF and European Union are also promoting cross-border stability groups that bring together regulators, central banks, and finance ministers to improve international financial crisis planning. It is essential to press ahead with these initiatives.

6. Central Bank Operations

The severe strains on banks' liquidity and funding over the past 15 months have placed considerable pressures on central bank operations. Lending

[8] Bank of England, HM Treasury and FSA, "*Financial Stability and Depositor Protection: Further Consultation*" CM7436 July 2008, and "*Financial Stability and Depositor Protection: Special Resolution Regime*" CM7459 July 2008.

by central banks has increased substantially, and in a number of cases, new facilities have been introduced and old ones adapted or replaced to meet the needs of the market.

Stigma and adverse selection have rendered some tools ineffective. For example, in the UK in August 2007 when one bank experienced a payments glitch late in the day and borrowed from the Bank of England Standing Facility, there was a media witch hunt to identify the bank, followed by a completely erroneous interpretation that the borrowing was a sign of weakness. That experience stigmatized the Standing Facility framework at that time. As a further example, the transparency of Northern Rock's borrowing from the Bank of England helped to precipitate the loss of retail depositor confidence outlined above.

In response, central banks have placed more reliance on facilities where there is a take up by all banks — such as auctions and collateral swap schemes where the behaviour of individual banks is not revealed. In addition, the UK authorities have taken action to modify the disclosure requirements associated with ELA and thus help to avoid it giving rise to severe stigma problems.

Central banks have also in many cases widened collateral and lengthened the maturity of operations to provide additional term liquidity to the market. New schemes have been introduced such as the UK Special Liquidity Scheme (SLS) and a whole range of schemes in the United States. But while such liquidity schemes are essential to support the market and market participants, central banks cannot, through these actions, force banks to lend to each other if perceptions of counterparty risk are high because of concerns of heightened solvency risks. In such circumstances, there are limits to what central banks can do on their own to remedy market failings through the provision of liquidity alone.[9] Over the longer term, there are additional challenges in unwinding central bank liquidity support arrangements and restoring normal market functioning as well as in revising operational frameworks in the light of recent experience.[10]

[9] The recapitalization scheme announced by the UK authorities on 8 October shortly after this talk was given is designed to rectify such solvency concerns, and is supported by an extension of the SLS scheme and a credit guarantee scheme to support bank funding and a lengthening of maturities. Other countries have introduced similar policies. See: Bank of England *Financial Stability Report*, October 2008.

[10] Again, shortly after this paper was presented, the Bank of England published a consultative paper on '*The Development of the Bank of England's Market Operations,*' October 2008.

7. Strengthening Future System Resilience

I have focused above on a number of elements that have featured quite heavily in the United Kingdom over the past year. These, however, form only a small part of the major program of work that is needed internationally to strengthen the resilience of the global financial system and to lower the likelihood of future crises. Many areas have been highlighted by the recent episode: asymmetric information; adverse incentives; excess complexity; over-reliance on ratings; uncertainty of valuations; limited disclosures; inadequate crisis management arrangements; and strengthening of financial infrastructure. Capital and liquidity buffers have proved insufficient. And the procyclicality of the financial system appears to have amplified the economic cycle. A major program of important work is already under way under the auspices of the Financial Stability Forum and the international standard setting bodies to address many of these issues. I strongly support this work program and would encourage participants to be prepared to address thoroughly and from first principles the very difficult questions that the recent turmoil has posed, and take action accordingly.

References

Bank of England (2007). *Financial Stability Report*, April and October.

Bank of England (2008). *Financial Stability Report*, April and October.

Bank of England, HM Treasury and FSA (2008). *Financial Stability and Depositor Protection: Strengthening the Framework*, CM7308, January.

Bank of England, HM Treasury and FSA (2008). *Financial Stability and Depositor Protection: Further Consultation*, CM7346, July.

Bank of England, HM Treasury and FSA (2008). *Financial Stability and Depositor Protection: Special Resolution regime*, CM7459, July.

Basel Committee for Banking Supervision (2008). *Principles for Sound Liquidity Risk Management and Supervision*, Bank for International Settlements, September.

Jenkinson, N. (2008). *Strengthening Regimes for Controlling Liquidity Risk: Some Lessons from the Recent Turmoil*, April, available at www.bankofengland.co.uk/publications/speeches/2008/index.htm.

VI. IMPLICATIONS FOR BASEL II AND BANK CAPITAL REGULATION

Risk Management Failures During the Financial Crisis

Michel Crouhy*
NATIXIS Corporate and Investment Bank

1. Introduction

Many people saw this crisis coming and sounded warning bells ahead of the subprime crisis, but they were ignored. Policymakers as early as 2006 warned of the emerging weaknesses in financial markets and the global economy. But nobody listened. Too many people were busy making money originating mortgages, warehousing assets to be securitized, structuring CDOs, and distributing these structured credit products to investors desperately seeking investments that offer yield enhancement in an environment of low interest rates and low volatility.

The current crisis was thus an accident waiting to happen. The trigger was a series of events that struck out of the blue which were a shock for many market participants:

- In June 2007, the attempt by Bear Stearns to bail out two hedge funds was hurt by subprime mortgage losses. Then, the failed attempt by Merrill Lynch, the prime broker, to liquidate some of the collateral revealed how illiquid the market for such securities has become.
- In July, German regulators first bailout IKB, a German regional bank specialized in lending to small companies and not involved in mortgage lending at all.
- In July also, the French bank BNP Paribas froze three investment funds with assets of two billion euros because the bank could not value the subprime assets in the funds.

* Head of Research & Development, NATIXIS Corporate and Investment Bank.

It seems that all of a sudden the market realized that MBSs, CDOs of ABS and other structured products were mispriced.

As a consequence, during July and August 2007, lenders and investors began to worry not only about risk in mortgage-related securities but also about the extent of the subprime exposure of banks and other financial institutions such as hedge funds, insurance companies and monoline financial guarantors.

This led to information problems and liquidity problems that helped cause markets for important securities to "freeze up" and models to fall apart.[1]

1.1 *Information problems*

- Information was inadequate about the quality of the underlying mortgage loans and the borrowers, especially for subprime mortgages[2] and affordability products that required little or no down-payment, as well as no documentation of the borrower's income. These loans were also known as "liar loans".[3] They accounted for 40 percent of the subprime mortgage issuance in 2006, up from 25 percent in 2001.

---

[1] Here, we emphasize weaknesses in risk models. Most pricing models were fine but useless. In the absence of liquidity, pricing models might give you the "right" hedge ratios, but it does not help if you cannot execute the trades to rebalance your portfolio because trading liquidity has dried out.

[2] "Subprime" mortgages are mortgages to less creditworthy borrowers. A rule of thumb is that a subprime mortgage is a home loan to someone with a credit FICO score of less than 620. Subprime borrowers have limited credit history, or some other form of credit impairment. Some lenders classify a mortgage as subprime when the borrower has a credit score as high as 680 if the down-payment is less than 5 percent. Alt-A borrowers fall between subprime and prime borrowers. They have credit scores sufficient to qualify for a conforming mortgage, but do not have the necessary documentation to substantiate that their assets and income can support the requested loan amount.

Prior to 2005, subprime mortgage loans accounted for approximately 10 percent of outstanding mortgage loans. By 2006, subprime mortgages represented 13 percent of all outstanding mortgage loans with origination of subprime mortgages totaling $420 billion (according to Standard & Poor's), representing 20 percent of new residential mortgages, compared to the historical average of 8 percent. In July 2007, there was an estimated $1.4 trillion of subprime mortgages outstanding.

[3] "Liar loans" is referring to the fact that people could safely lie on their mortgage application because their statement would not be checked. These loans were also called NINJA, referring to applicants who had No Income, No Job and no Assets.

- Market participants lost confidence in the accuracy of the credit ratings of CDO tranches given by the rating agencies as a huge fraction of tranches of CDOs of ABS saw their ratings downgraded, sometimes from AAA to non-investment grade, including default, in one shot.
- Market prices became unavailable or unrealistic for many securities, including those rated triple-A.
- There was a lack of knowledge about the positions and liabilities of the major banks and other players such as hedge funds and insurance companies.

1.2 *Liquidity problems*

- Home buyers could not refinance their loans as they had expected, and they could not make the required payments when their mortgages reset at much higher interest rates.[4]

This phenomenon was aggravated by the incentive compensation system for mortgage brokers based on volume of loans originated and not their performance, with few consequences for the brokers if the loan defaulted within a short period. Originating brokers had little incentive then to perform due diligence and monitor borrowers' creditworthiness, as most of the subprime loans originated by brokers were subsequently securitized. In fact, fraud was also identified among brokers who were inflating the declarations of some applicants for them to obtain the loan.

To some extent this should have been mitigated by originators having to repurchase delinquent loans within a few months of origination ("early payment default" clause). However, as some of the brokers were experiencing financial difficulties and even in some cases filed for bankruptcy, this did not occur, leading to even greater losses on the underlying asset pools. For example, Merrill Lynch demanded in December 2006 that ResMae mortgage Corp., which sold it US$3.5 billion in subprime mortgages, buy back US$308 million of loans where the borrowers had defaulted. ResMae said, in its filing for bankruptcy protection in February 2007, that those demands "crippled" its operations. Accredited Home Lenders Holding reported a loss of US$37.8 million due to repurchase of bad loans (February 2007).

[4] In 2005 and 2006, the most common subprime loans were of the "short-reset" type. They were the "2/28"or "3/27" hybrid ARMs (adjustable rate mortgages) subprime. These loans had a relatively low fixed teaser rate for the first two or three years, and then reset semi-annually to a much higher rate, i.e. an index plus a margin for the remaining period with a typical margin in the order of 400 to 600 bps.

Short-term interest rates began to increase in the U.S. from mid-2004 onwards. However, resets did not begin to translate into higher mortgage rates until sometime later. Debt service burdens for loans eventually increased, which led to financial distress for some of this group of borrowers. In 2008, US$500 billion in mortgages reset.

- Hedge funds could not roll over the financing of their leveraged positions. As their losses increased, they had to sell off securities to meet demands for cash from lenders and investors who were trying to withdraw capital. Compounding the problem was the demand from primary dealers for more collateral. As a result hedge funds were forced to unwind positions in illiquid markets, feeding a downward spiral in asset prices.
- SIVs (Special Investment Vehicules) could not roll over their asset-backed commercial paper (ABCP) as rating agencies started to downgrade these structures. Most sponsoring banks ended up bailing out their SIVs and took over their assets on their balance sheet.[5]
- Some investors, like money market funds, may only hold triple-A rated securities. As these securities, in particular triple-A rated super senior tranches of CDOs, were downgraded, these investors were forced to sell these securities in illiquid markets, putting more downward pressure on the price of structured credit products.

As more and more complex securities, such as MBSs, CDOs of ABS, etc., and later on monolines, were downgraded, banks experienced huge amounts of losses and write-downs, which reached US$700 billion in November 2008. These losses are far in excess of what pricing, rating and risk models would have predicted. Risk measurement models totally underestimated the risks and many risk managers did not see it coming.

In this section, we first analyze what went wrong in risk management and risk modeling, then, we draw some lessons from this fiasco.

2. What Went Wrong in Risk Management and Risk Modeling

Major weaknesses in risk assessment and risk modeling are at the origin of the credit losses in financial institutions worldwide, which mostly originate from over-reliance on:

- misleading ratings from rating agencies;
- unrealistically simple risk models, i.e. models that were not designed to deal with the complexity of structured credit products;

[5] Most sponsoring banks distributed their credit exposures through SIVs in which they retained contractual and reputational liquidity exposures. These vehicules, like banks themselves, were funding longer-term assets with short-term liabilities, and like banks, were subject to a run when their lenders became concerned about the quality of the assets.

- inaccurate data;
- short-term financing with too little consideration for liquidity risk.

2.1 *Over-reliance on misleading ratings from rating agencies*

Rating agencies are at the center of the current crisis as many investors relied on their ratings for many diverse products: mortgage bonds, asset-backed commercial paper (ABCP) issued by the structured investment vehicles (SIVs), Derivative Product Companies (DPCs), and monolines which insure municipal bonds and structured credit products such as tranches of CDOs.

Money market funds are restricted to investing only in triple-A assets; pension funds and municipalities are restricted to investing in investment grade assets and base their investment decision on the rating attributed by the rating agencies.[6] Many of these investors invested in assets that were both complex and contained exposure to subprime assets, mainly because these assets benefited from an investment grade rating and were promising a yield higher than traditional assets, such as corporate and Treasury bonds, with an equivalent rating.

Investors in complex credit products had considerably less information at their disposal to assess the underlying credit quality of the assets they held in their portfolios than the originators. As a result, these end-investors often came to rely heavily on the risk assessments of rating agencies. Implicit in the investment decision is the assumption that ratings are timely and relatively stable. No one was expecting, until recently, a triple-A asset to be downgraded to junk status within a few weeks or even a few days. The argument could be made that as the yields on these instruments exceeded those on equivalently rated corporations, the market knew they were not of the same credit and/or liquidity risk. But investors still misjudged the risk.

Large numbers of rating downgrades on structured credit products, in particular tranches of subprime CDOs, have thus revived the questions

[6] Most of the US$2.5 trillion sitting in money market funds is invested in such assets as U.S. Treasury bills, certificates of deposit, and short-term commercial debt. In the recent low interest rate environment these funds have also invested in triple-A super-senior tranches of CDOs and triple-A rated ABCP, in order to increase the yield generated by these funds.

about the nature of structured finance ratings, their sensitivity to changes in credit fundamentals, the degree to which rating transitions should be expected to differ from those of corporate bonds, and the extent to which ratings can serve as universal measures of credit risk.[7]

In particular, the nature of the risks involved in holding a triple-A rated super-senior tranche of a subprime CDO was completely missed by all the players: rating agencies, regulators, financial institutions, and investors. Subprime CDOs are in fact CDO-squareds, because the underlying pool of assets of the CDO is not constituted of individual mortgages, but instead is composed of subprime RMBS (Residential Mortgage-Backed Securities), or mortgage bonds, that are themselves tranches of individual subprime mortgages (Box 1).

Box 1. Basics of Securitization and the Manufacturing of Triple-A Securities

Securitization is a financing technique whereby a company, the ***originator***, arranges for the issuance of securities whose cash flows are based on the revenues of a segregated pool of assets (e.g. corporate investment grade loans, leveraged loans, mortgages and other asset-backed securities (ABS) such as auto loans, credit card receivables, etc.).[8]

Assets are originated by the originator(s), and funded on the originator's balance sheet. Once a suitably large portfolio of assets has been originated, the assets are analyzed as a portfolio, and then sold or assigned to a bankruptcy-remote company, i.e. a **Special Purpose Vehicle** company (or "**SPV**"), formed for the specific purpose of funding the assets.[9] The pool of loans is therefore taken *off* the originator's *balance sheet*. Alternatively, loans can be bought from other financial institutions.

(*Continued*)

[7] Moody's first took rating action on 2006 vintage subprime loans in November 2006. In 2007, Moody's downgraded 31 percent of all tranches for CDOs of ABS it had rated and 14 percent of those initially rated AAA. This raises questions about the rating methodologies employed by the different agencies. See Ashcraft and Schuermann (2007) for a detailed description of the rating of subprime MBS.

[8] The borrower may be unaware of this, as the lender normally continues to be the loan servicer.

[9] The SPVs are also known as SIVs (Special Investment Vehicles).

Box 1. (*Continued*)

The **SPV** issues tradable "securities" to fund the purchase of the assets. These securities are claims against the underlying pool of assets. The performance of these securities is directly linked to the performance of the assets — and, in principle, there is no recourse back to the originator.[10]

Tranching is the process of creating notes of various seniorities and risk profiles, including senior and mezzanine tranches and an equity (first loss piece). As a result of the prioritization scheme used in the distribution of cash flows to the tranche holders, the most senior tranches are far safer than the average asset in the underlying pool. Senior tranches are insulated from default risk up to the point where credit losses deplete the more junior ones. Losses on the mortgage loan pool are first applied to the most junior tranche until the principal balance of that tranche is completely exhausted. Then, losses are allocated to the most junior tranche remaining, and so on.

This ability of repackaging risks and creating "safe" assets from otherwise risky collateral led to a dramatic expansion in the issuance of structured securities, most of which were viewed by investors to be virtually risk-free and certified as such by the rating agencies (See also Section 2.1.2). Figure 1 gives a graphical representation of the securitization process.

While CDO collateral pools can consist of various forms of debt, such as bonds, loans or synthetic exposures through CDS (credit default swaps), recent structures, such as subprime CDOs, have increasingly been based on other structured credit products such as tranches of mortgage-backed securities (MBS) or of other CDOs. Issuance of these so-called structured credit products increased dramatically since 2004. It represented 49 percent of the $560 billion worth of issuance of CDOs during 2006 up from 40 percent in 2004.[11]

A typical subprime trust is composed of several thousand individual mortgages, typically around three to 5,000 mortgages for a total amount of approximately a billion dollars. The distribution of losses of the

(*Continued*)

---

[10] In practice, it did not work that way for subprime SIVs after the crisis developed. To preserve their reputation, most banks sponsoring subprime SIVs took back the assets on their balance sheet.

[11] See Fender *et al*. (2008).

Box 1. (*Continued*)

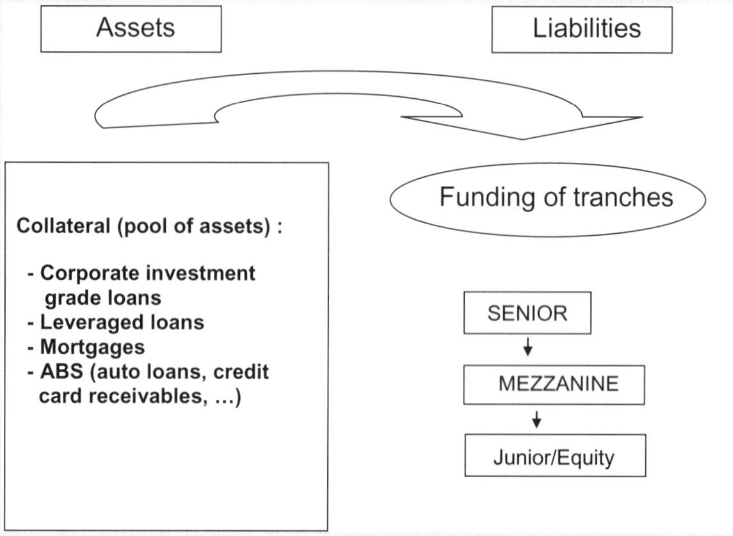

Figure 1. Securitization of Financial Assets.

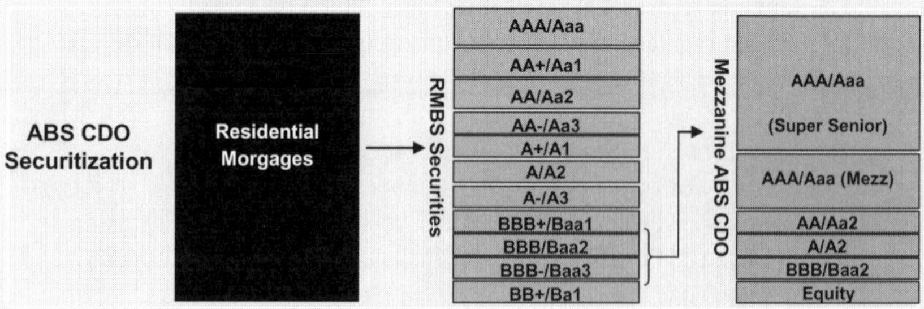

Figure 2. Securitization of Asset-Backed Securities Such as Mortgages.

mortgage pool is tranched into different classes of residential mortgage-backed securities (RMBS) from the equity tranche, typically created through over-collateralization, to the most senior tranche, rated triple-A. A subprime CDO is a CDO-squared with a pool of assets composed of

(*Continued*)

Box 1. (*Continued*)

RMBS rated double-B to double-A, with an average rating of triple-B (Figure 2).[12]

In a typical subprime CDO approximately 75 percent of the tranches benefit from a triple-A rating. On average, the mezzanine part of the capital structure accounts for 20 percent of the securities issued by the SPV and is rated investment grade, the remaining 5 percent is the equity tranche (first loss) and stays unrated.

2.1.1 *"Cliff" effects or nonlinearities in the risk of subprime CDO tranches*

Perhaps one of the biggest failures in the subprime crisis was the failure to understand the binary (zero-one) nature of the senior tranches of subprime CDOs. The problem is that the initial level of subordination for a triple-B mortgage bond is relatively small, between 3 and 5 percent, and the width of the tranche is very thin, 2.5 to 4 percent maximum.

As prepayments occur, the level of subordination of the lower tranches increases, in relative terms, and can reach 10 percent over time. Assuming a recovery of 50 percent on the foreclosed homes, this means that a default rate of 20 percent on subprime mortgages, which is realistic in the current environment, will most likely hit most of the triple-B tranches. Moreover, it is also most likely that in the current downturn in the housing market and recessionary economic environment, the loss correlations across all the triple-B tranches will be close to one. As a consequence, if one triple-B tranche is hit, it is most likely that most of the

[12] As discussed earlier, there was a huge demand by institutional investors for triple-A rated senior and super-senior tranches of CDOs offering a higher yield than traditional securities, such as corporate and Treasury bonds, of equivalent ratings. Hedge funds were the main buyers of the equity tranches which were attractive to them even if there was a high probability for these tranches to be wiped out. The high interest rate paid on these tranches would still make up for the principal over time and pay a good return if defaults of the underlying assets in the pool occur late during the life of the CDO. Mezzanine tranches, with an average rating of triple-B, were harder to distribute so that banks securitized these tranches in new CDOs which are referred to as CDO-squareds.

triple-B tranches will be hit as well during the same period. And, given the thin width of the tranches, it is most likely that if one MBS bond is wiped out, they will all be wiped out at the same time, wiping out the super-senior tranche of the subprime CDO. In other words, we are in a binary situation where either the cumulative default rate of the subprime mortgages remains below the threshold that keeps the underlying RMBS bonds untouched and the super-senior tranches of subprime CDOs would not incur any loss, or the cumulative default rate breaches this threshold and the super-senior tranches of subprime CDOs could all be wiped out.

2.1.2 *Wrong estimates of default rates and default correlations*[13]

Rating agencies based their ratings on wrong estimates of the underlying securities' default risks and how likely defaults were to be correlated in a stressed environment. Rating agencies based their estimates of default rates on a very short history, going back to 2001, characterized by a fairly benign environment for the real estate market. They did not take into account two major changes into their rating model: the rupture in the delinquency statistics starting in 2005 and the inflexion in the real estate market and the economic environment which made defaults on mortgages no longer an isolated phenomenon, but rather a systemic event with borrowers defaulting in clusters in some geographic areas such as parts of California and Florida.

Delinquencies on subprime mortgages rose significantly after mid-2005 for at least four reasons[14]: First, subprime borrowers are typically not very creditworthy, often highly levered with high debt-to-income ratios, and the mortgages extended to them have relatively large loan-to-value ratios. Until recently, most borrowers were expected to make at least a 20 percent down payment on the purchase price of their home. During 2005 and 2006, subprime borrowers were offered "80/20" mortgage products to finance 100 percent of their homes. This option allowed borrowers to take out two mortgages on their homes. In addition to a first mortgage

---

[13] A third factor, i.e. the amount recovered in the event of default, also named recovery rate, affects the expected loss. Very few data are available to calibrate this parameter for subprime loans and it was estimated across the board at 40 percent.

[14] See Crouhy *et al.* (2008).

for 80 percent of the total purchase price, a simultaneous second mortgage, or "piggyback" loan for the remaining 20 percent would be made to the borrower.

Second, in 2005 and 2006, the most common subprime loans were of the "short-reset" type. They were the "2/28"or "3/27" hybrid ARMs subprime. These loans had a relatively low fixed teaser rate for the first two or three years, and then reset semi-annually to a much higher rate, i.e. an index plus a margin for the remaining period with a typical margin in the order of 400 to 600 bps. Short-term interest rates began to increase in the U.S. from mid-2004 onwards. However, resets did not begin to translate into higher mortgage rates until some time later. Debt service burdens for loans eventually increased, which led to financial distress for some of this group of borrowers.

Third, many subprime borrowers had counted on being able to refinance or repay mortgages early through home sales and at the same time produce some equity cushion in a market where home prices kept rising. As the rate of U.S. house price appreciation began to decline after April 2005, it became more difficult for subprime borrowers to refinance and many ended up incurring higher mortgage costs than they expected to bear at the time of taking their mortgage.[15]

Fourth, a decline in credit standards by mortgage originators in underwriting over the last three years was a major factor behind the sharp increase in delinquency rates for mortgages originated during 2005 and 2006. The pressure to increase the supply of subprime mortgages arose because of the demand by investors for higher yielding assets. A major contributor to the crisis was the huge demand by CDOs for BBB mortgage-backed bonds that stimulated a substantial growth in home equity loans. This CDO demand for BBB ABS bonds was due to the fact that the bonds had high yields, and the CDO trust could finance their purchase by

[15] The economy started to change during 2004. First, mortgage rates started to increase, as the Federal Reserve increased the Fed Funds rate and, second, house price appreciation decelerated. There are many factors that cause delinquency in the mortgage markets, major candidates being: job loss, unanticipated medical expenses, divorce, and rising mortgage expenses. House prices can also affect the default decision. If house prices are falling, this can affect the decision in two ways. First, it limits the ability to re-finance and, second, it can cause the home owner's equity to become negative if the initial equity stake was small, as is often the case for subprime mortgages. Since the middle of 2005, the rate of house price appreciation has been continuously decreasing.

issuing AAA rated CDO bonds paying lower yields. This was because the rating agencies assigned AAA ratings to the CDO's senior bond tranches that did not reflect the CDO bond's true credit risk.[16] Because these tranches were mis-priced, the CDO equity holders generated a positive net present value investment from just repackaging cash flows. This process boosted the demand by CDOs for residential mortgage-backed securities (RMBS). Furthermore, this repackaging was so lucrative that it was repeated a second time for CDO-squared trusts. A CDO-squared trust purchased high yield (low rated) bonds and equity issued by other CDOs. To finance the purchase of this collateral, they issued AAA rated CDO-squared bonds with lower yields. This, in turn, created demand for CDOs containing mortgage-backed securities (MBS) and CDO tranches.

This environment encouraged questionable practices by some lenders. Some mortgage borrowers have ended up with subprime mortgages, even though their credit worthiness qualifies them for lower risk types of mortgages, others with mortgages that they were not qualified to have.[17] Some borrowers and mortgage brokers took advantage of the situation and fraud massively increased, but it seems that it was ignored by the rating agencies.

According to rating agencies, ratings assumed a default correlation of 20 percent, which is probably a high estimate in a benign economic environment where defaults are essentially due to idiosyncratic factors: job loss, unanticipated medical expenses, divorce, etc., which are specific to an individual or family and would not affect the other borrowers in the same geography. When a recession hits the economy as it started in 2007, it is a different story. Whole industries are affected; companies are going bankrupt and have to lay off thousands of people, which makes the impact of the recession even more severe in the geographic areas affected by

---

[16] We will subsequently discuss why the CDO tranches were mis-rated. Briefly, the rating methodology did not reflect current market conditions and the sensitivity of losses incurred by senior tranches to errors in delinquency rates and default correlations, without mentioning the incentive problem in the way rating companies were compensated for rating assignments.

[17] Lenders were far too willing to lend as evidenced by the creation of new types of mortgages, known as "affordability products" that required little or no down payment and little or no documentation of a borrower's income, the last ones being known as "liar loans". Liar loans accounted for 40 percent of the subprime mortgage issuance in 2006, up from 25 percent in 2001.

these corporate bankruptcies. Delinquencies occur in waves, and defaults are becoming a systemic phenomenon with defaults becoming highly correlated at least in some locations.

Rating agencies, as well as structurers and investors totally occulted the fact that the securitization process substituted idiosyncratic risks that are largely diversifiable in a benign economic environment for systemic risk, which is not diversifiable during a severe economic downturn.

2.1.3 *Sensitivities of the rating of senior subprime CDO tranches to estimation errors of delinquency rates, recovery rates and default correlations*

Ratings of tranches of CDOs and other credit instruments such as corporate debt, are indicators of default risk based on expected loss (Moody's) or probabilities of default (Standard & Poor's and Fitch Ratings).[18] Rating agencies rely on Monte-Carlo simulation to simulate cash flows and correlated defaults of the assets in the pool and allocate the cash flows to the various tranches according to the waterfall. This simulation produces a loss distribution for the pool and an expected loss for each tranche of the capital structure of the securitization transaction. These expected losses are then mapped into the letter based rating scale. The tranching is structured so that the senior tranches obtain a triple-A rating.

Simple simulations show that small errors in the evaluation of the delinquency rate of the underlying mortgages, recovery rates and default correlations can result in major changes in the expected loss of the senior tranches of a CDO, and consequently their rating.[19] Rating transitions for structured credit products such as tranches of subprime CDOs differ substantially from those of corporate bonds. Therefore, it is misleading to use the same rating scale for bonds and structured credit products. They may have the same expected loss at the time the rating is produced, but their future dynamics may differ substantially.

---

[18] Contrary to a corporate bond, an MBS or a tranche of a CDO does not default in the sense of a corporate default event. Instead, depending on the rate of delinquencies on the underlying pool of assets, these securities will experience cash flow shortfalls and principal write-downs over the life of the transaction.

[19] See Coval *et al.* (2008) and Fender *et al.* (2008).

Rating agencies missed the impact of the leverage imbedded in structured credit products which makes the senior tranches quite sensitive to errors in the evaluation of default rates of the underlying loans and to default correlations.

Small errors in the evaluation of these parameters would not have major consequences for the rating of a corporate bond. On the contrary, tranches of CDOs with their imbedded leverage are much more sensitive to these factors. In addition, the expected loss of senior tranches of CDOs is highly sensitive to the default correlations. As default correlations increase, part of the risk is shifted from the equity to the senior tranches. The expected loss of the equity tranche decreases while the expected loss of the senior tranches increases. This effect is amplified for CDO-squareds, i.e. CDOs of tranches of CDOs, as the leverage effect is more important than for CDOs. During economic crises when the systemic factors become dominant compared to idiosyncratic risks, the senior tranches become much more risky.

From mid-2007, onwards, it has become clear that investors in senior tranches initially rated triple-A have been holding securities much more risky than initially estimated when the impact of systemic risk was totally occulted in the rating and pricing of these tranches. These features, the large sensitivity of expected loss to parameter estimation errors and the exposure to systemic risk of senior tranches, should have demanded much higher risk premia from investors for holding highly rated tranches of CDOs than corporate bonds of the same rating.

This is consistent with the downgrade actions reported by the rating agencies. In February 2007, S&P took the unprecedented step of placing on "credit watch" transactions that had been closed as recently as the previous year. From the first quarter of 2005 to the third quarter of 2007, Standard and Poor's (2008) reports for CDOs of asset backed securities, 66 percent were downgraded and 44 percent were downgraded from investment grade to speculative grade, including default.[20] At the end of 2008 more than 50 percent of the CDO tranches that received initially an A rating or above have been downgraded, compared to 10 percent only for corporate bonds. Most of the corporate bonds that have been downgraded lost one full notch, say from A to

[20] For residential subprime mortgage backed securities, 17 percent were downgraded, and 9.8 percent were downgraded from investment grade to speculative grade, including default.

BBB, while 80 percent of the CDO tranches lost three full notches in one shot.

It is therefore important for rating agencies, investors, and regulators to understand the fundamental difference between the rating of a corporate bond and the rating of tranches of CDOs when it comes to exposure to systemic risk. They cannot be rated on the same scale. It has misled investors seeking safe investments who did not appreciate the risks of highly rated structured products compared to Treasuries or corporate bonds of the same rating. Corporate bonds are mainly exposed to idiosyncratic risks, i.e. risks specific to the firm, the quality of its management, or the positioning of the company within its industry. The risk of a company will be affected by the economic environment but systemic risk is not the dominant factor in assessing the risk of an individual company. On the contrary, a senior tranche of a CDO has the features of a catastrophe bond which is strongly affected in extreme scenarios.[21] Investors in those securities wrote insurance against a major recession but were not properly compensated for the associated risk. In the case of subprime CDOs, the collapse of the real estate market in the context of an economic recession is the extreme scenario characterized by very high default correlations and a transfer of risk from the junior tranches to the senior ones.

2.2 *Over-reliance on unrealistically simple risk models*

Value-at-Risk (VaR) has become the universal risk measure for financial institutions in understanding their sensitivity to changes in market risk drivers such as interest rates, asset prices, correlations, and volatilities. Banks implemented their VaR models in the mid-1990s as a response to the 1996 Amendment to the Basel Accord (implemented in 1998 under the auspices of the Bank for International Settlements and therefore referred to widely as "BIS 98") which extended the initial Accord to include risk-based capital requirements for the market risks that banks incur in their trading book. The authorities recognized the complexity of correctly

---

[21] See Coval *et al.* (2007). According to these authors: "...a triple-A rated tranche of a CDO bears risks that are highly similar to those of a 50 percent out-of-the-money five-year put spread on the S&P 500 index. However, on average, the put spread offers nearly three times more compensation for bearing these risks".

assessing market-risk exposures, especially for derivatives products. The Basel Committee therefore allowed institutions that met certain risk management standards to use their own internal VaR model.

Given the amount of calculations involved in running a VaR model, the pricing of securities within a VaR model requires some shortcuts. One can rely on a closed-form formula for relatively simple products and one should price complex securities based on their first and second order sensitivities (the "Greeks" in the jargon of quants and traders).

At the time, VaR models for market risk, then for credit risk, were designed, structured credit products that are sensitive to changes in credit spreads, default rates, recovery rates, and default correlations did not exist. So far, we are not aware of any full-fledged extension of these models that accounts for the complexity of structured credit products such as tranches of subprime CDOs.

Since structured credit products are rated using the same rating scale as for corporate bonds, banks have naturally taken as proxy for these securities in their VaR models corporate bonds with similar ratings. We have demonstrated in the previous section that this approach is fundamentally flawed and may lead to major underestimation of the risks involved with holding these complex securities.

UBS provides an example of the abysmal losses that can result from not modeling the full complexity of the structured credit products when assessing the risk profile of the bank's portfolio. UBS was the second largest bank in the world by total assets at the end of 2006 and was the winner of Euromoney magazine's "Global Best Risk Management House" award for excellence in 2005. As of August 2008, UBS had written down its assets by $45 billion and had a capital infusion of $28 billion.

A post-mortem shareholder report (UBS, 2008) on UBS's write-downs indicates that "short cuts" were taken to speed up the production of risk reports. But these short cuts were systematically gamed so that risks were structured in such a way they did not show up at all in the risk calculations.[22] Stress tests were carried out but worst case scenarios did not envisage a severe enough real estate crisis. It is reported in the post-mortem report that market fluctuations larger than envisaged in the stress tests were not hedged. In other words, the profits being booked were the

[22] See Honohan (2008) for a detailed discussion.

reward for the assumption of catastrophe risk outside the risk envisaged in the stress tests.

2.3 *Over-reliance on inaccurate data*

For reasons indicated earlier in section 2.1.2 the delinquency rate for subprime mortgages increased significantly after 2004. Statistics in Tables 1 and 2 show that the market experienced a major change of regime in 2004 which was totally occulted in the risk measures, not only by the rating agencies, but also by the banks and other investors holding subprime structured credit products.

These statistics demonstrate clearly that as early as 2004, a change of regime had occurred. Risks should have been assessed for the purpose of both structuring and rating structured credit products based on subprime mortgages, on new estimates of default rates, and default correlations more in line with the new economic environment.

2.4 *Over-reliance on short-term financing with too little consideration for liquidity risk*

Since the beginning of the 1990s, banks have gradually shifted away from the traditional "originate and hold" business model toward the new "originate-to-distribute" business model. Under this new business model, the bank services the loans but the funding of the loans is sourced out to investors, and the risk of default is also transferred out

Table 1. Predicting Losses of Mortgage Products by Vintage and Rating.

Vintage	Subprime (%)	Alt-A (%)	Seconds (%)	Prime (%)	Total (%)
2003	2.7	0.3	4.4	0.1	1.6
2004	3.0	0.5	6.3	0.1	1.7
2005	7.5	1.3	17.2	0.2	4.5
2006	19.3	4.5	43.9	0.3	12.7
2007	22.9	5.4	62.2	0.8	17.4
Total	10.3	2.4	28.5	0.2	6.9

Source: UBS, November 2007.

Table 2. Predicting Losses of Subprime Mortgage Bonds by Vintage and Rating.

Vintage	Aaa (%)	Aa1 (%)	Aa2 (%)	Aa3 (%)	A1 (%)	A2 (%)	A3 (%)	Baa1 (%)	Baa2 (%)	Baa3 (%)	BIG (%)	NA (%)	Total (%)
2003	6		16	81	12	17	20	12	14	18	71	14	16
2004	12	6	8	6	16	9	7	8	12	18	30	29	12
2005	10	4	8	5	8	12	18	28	38	49	68	44	23
2006	22	30	46	59	66	69	80	82	88	91	97	85	69
2007	25	53	55	73	77	72	82	83	84	76	88	70	70
Total	15	17	26	34	41	35	46	45	47	55	76	50	40

Source: UBS, November 2007.

to these investors, without recourse.[23] This new business model was supposed to disperse credit risk throughout the financial system and make financial institutions safer and less sensitive to credit crises, as well as provide banks with additional sources of funding for their lending activities.

This is the theory. In practice, the implementation of this business model was flawed and this crisis demonstrated that the redistribution of credit risk among final investors that it was supposed to achieve was only an illusion.

Banks moved away from their balance sheets the assets to be securitized to locate them into structured investment vehicules (SIVs) that are limited purpose, bankruptcy-remote companies. Their purpose is to fund the purchase of the assets, which are primarily long-term assets, with short-term asset-backed commercial paper (ABCP) and some medium-term notes and capital.

Liquidity risk arises because of the need to refinance due to the maturity mismatch between assets and liabilities. The SIV must demonstrate that apart from the vehicle's cash flows that provide liquidity, it has backstop lines of credit from different institutions and highly liquid assets that can be sold, so that it is able to deal with market disruptions.

The SIVs relied on being able to continuously roll over their short-term funding and, even though they were "bankruptcy remote" from their sponsors, those that were unable to achieve this were able to turn to their sponsoring banks that had undertaken to provide them with backstop liquidity via credit lines in such situations. In fact, these SIVs, akin to "unregulated banks" funding long-term assets with short-term funding resources, have been a contributor to the current credit crisis. As the credit crisis intensified and the mortgage-backed securities held by the SIVs suddenly started to decline in value, some of the ABCP were downgraded, sometimes all the way to default within a few days. An increasing number of SIVs became unable to roll their ABCP, due to concerns about the value of collateral, and turned to their sponsor banks for rescue.

When banks were unable to roll the ABCP funding these SIVs, and market liquidity had totally evaporated for subprime related assets, banks to preserve their reputation had no other alternative but to take back the

[23] See Crouhy *et al.* (2006, Chapter 12).

assets on their balance sheet and face funding liquidity issues that led to the bankruptcy of Lehman and the rescue of Bear Sterns, Merrill Lynch, and AIG in the U.S or Northern Rock in the U.K.

One of the most striking cases of over-reliance on contingent funding liquidity is provided by the German state bank Sachsen, specialized in lending to local small and medium size companies. This bank opened an affiliate in Dublin which only specialized in establishing off-balance sheet vehicles to hold mainly highly rated U.S. mortgage-backed securities in a volume equivalent to one-third of the parent's bank balance sheet. This operation was highly profitable until 2007. It contributed 90 percent of the group's total profit in 2006. The SIVs benefited from a back-up loan facility from the parent bank Sachsen itself for a staggering amount approaching 25 percent of the total balance sheet of the parent bank.[24] It is clear that the size both of the operation and of the commitment was too big relative to the size of the balance sheet and the capital of the parent bank. Subprime related write-downs and losses in 2007 wiped out the capital of the parent bank. In the end, Sachsen was sold to another German state bank.

The risk management system of Sachsen did not consider this funding liquidity commitment as liquidity risk but simply as operational risk, on the argument that only some operational failure could trigger the back-up liquidity facility to be drawn down. As such, it was assigned a very low risk and attracted very little capital.

To revive the "originate-to-distribute" business model we need to find mechanisms that transfer the risk of default, with no recourse, to final investors. Banks need to ensure that when they distribute risks into the market through securitization, the risks really are distributed and will not come back onto their balance sheet later. This supposes that investors do not rely only on risk ratings but also carry out the necessary due diligence to verify the accuracy of the information given by the trust on the quality of the assets being securitized, and that investors carry out their own risk analysis.[25]

[24] See Honohan (2008) for a detailed discussion of this case and others.

[25] The design of the SIVs can be altered to make them less sensitive to market disruptions. There are a number of ways to achieve this. Currently, some of the extant short-term commercial paper gives the vehicle the option to extend the maturity of the debt. Usage of this option could be expanded. Another type of option would be to allow the vehicle to convert the paper into one or two year floating rate debt. The option could be contingent on the event of a market disruption. The cost of the option would be relatively small, given that the probability of a market disruption is small. The cost of these modifications would be to decrease expected profits (See Crouhy *et al.*, 2008).

3. Lessons From This Fiasco

A number of important lessons can be drawn from this post-mortem analysis of the failures of risk management during the crisis.[26]

3.1 *Differentiate the ratings of corporate bonds and structured credit products*

To have confidence in a model, it is necessary to have a clear definition of what a rating means for a particular type of instrument, the factors that an agency considers when assigning a rating, and how well a rating model performs in different economic environments. There is a lack of clarity about what a rating actually measure. Is it a measure of the probability of default or the expected loss over some specified horizon?[27] What is the length of the horizon? Does a rating, say BBB, have the same meaning for asset backed securities as for corporate bonds?

Subprime ABS ratings differ from corporate debt ratings in a number of different dimensions. Corporate bond ratings are largely based on firm-specific risk, while CDO tranches represent claims on cash flows from a portfolio of correlated assets. Thus, the rating of CDO tranches relies heavily on quantitative models while corporate debt ratings rely essentially on the analyst's judgment. While the rating of a CDO tranche should have the same expected loss as a corporate bond for a given rating, the volatility of loss, that is, the unexpected loss, is quite different and strongly depends on the correlation structure of the underlying assets in the pool of the CDO.[28] This in itself warrants the use of different rating scales for corporate bonds and structured credit products.

For structured products, such as ABS collateralized debt obligations, it is necessary to model the cash flows and the loss distribution generated by the asset portfolio over the life of the CDO, implying that it is necessary to model *prepayments*[29] and *default dependence* (correlation) among

---

[26] See also Crouhy *et al.* (2008) for a more exhaustive and detailed analysis of the steps to prevent a repeat of such a crisis.

[27] Moody's ratings are based on expected loss whereas those of Standard & Poor's and Fitch ratings are based on probability of default.

[28] See the discussion in Ashcraft and Schuermann (2007).

[29] Prepayments of principal include both voluntary and involuntary (default) prepayments. Voluntary prepayments depend strongly on the path followed by interest rates. Interest rate risk is a key source of uncertainty in the analysis of cash flows.

the assets in the CDO and to estimate the parameters describing the dependence.[30] Over the life of a CDO, individual defaults may occur at any time, implying that it is necessary to model the loss distribution over time. This necessitates modeling the evolution of the different factors that affect the default process and how these factors evolve together.

It is critical to assess the sensitivity of tranche ratings to a significant deterioration in credit conditions affecting credit worthiness and default clustering. As discussed earlier, the impact of shocks affecting credit worthiness on CDO tranche ratings is very different than for a corporate bond. It depends critically on the magnitude and the clustering of the shocks and it tends to be non-linear.[31]

If default occurs, it is necessary to estimate the resulting loss. Recovery rates depend on the state of the economy, the condition of the obligor, and the value of its assets. Loss rates and the frequency of defaults are dependent (correlated): if the economy goes into recession, the frequency of defaults and loss rates increase. It is necessary to model the factors that affect the loss and the joint dependence between the frequency of default and loss. The level of dependence will vary, in general, with the state of the economy.

To test model predictions against actual outcomes requires data. Unfortunately, for many types of collateralized products, data availability is limited across instruments and does not extend over long periods. Consequently, there is little information about the accuracy and robustness of models over different parts of the credit cycle. To assess the credit risk of structures such as SIVs, it is necessary to consider other risk dimensions, such as market liquidity and valuation of collateral. These factors have been overlooked, though they affect the credit worthiness.

For the last few years, the characteristics of subprime mortgage borrowers were undergoing major changes due to declining underwriting standards and fraud. The failure to explicitly recognize the changing nature of the underlying data used in model estimation implied that the probabilities of default, recovery rates, default dependence and the dependence between default and recovery rates were poorly estimated.

---

[30] There are many different types of factors that influence default dependence. For example, if the local economy deteriorates, then defaults might increase or if a particular sector of the economy deteriorates, then this will adversely affect obligors within the sector.

[31] See Fender *et al.* (2008) and Coval *et al.* (2008).

Models need to capture default contagion that exists in local housing markets.

For collateralized structures, there is the need for more transparency about (a) the types of models used by the agencies; (b) the assumptions about the data used to rate a particular structure; and (c) the accuracy and robustness of the rating methodologies to the underlying assumptions. Current methodologies failed due to the use of inappropriate assumptions derived from historical data for corporate CDOs with tranches much wider than for ABS CDOs. They also failed to appropriately model both default and recovery dependences.

To rate the commercial paper of a SIV, there are additional factors to consider. First is an assessment of the backstop lines of support and other contingent funding in the case of market disruptions. The rating agencies rate the contingent sources of funding available to a vehicle. Second, for an investor to buy asset backed commercial paper (ABCP), they need to know the *nature* of the assets supporting the paper and the *value* of the collateral. The agencies are clear that they make no statement about valuation. Yet if the value of the collateral deteriorates, this adversely affects the credit worthiness of the commercial paper. Thus logically, one must address the issue of the valuation of the collateral, if one is to assess the credit worthiness of the vehicle.

3.2 *Check the quality of the data about the underlying assets and make sure it is complete and timely*

It is essential to perform due diligence on the raw data — neither the rating agencies nor the banks which structured the CDOs have done it.

The rating agencies clearly state that they do not perform due diligence on the raw data. The current situation is analogous to accountants accepting at face value the figures given to them by firms. There is no auditing function. The current situation is problematic. In moving forward, if data auditing is required, then the issue of compensation both for rating and for auditing needs to be addressed. It is not clear that regulating the originators will solve the problem of faulty data unless there is adequate enforcement.

Clarity is required about the data sources used to reach a rating. Is the agency accepting data from a third party and has the agency done anything to check if there have been structural changes in the data sources? Has it checked the data to justify the validity of its distributional assumptions?

For asset backed securities, the government should sponsor an agency that collects information on a timely basis about the collateral pools and make it available to market participants. This will facilitate an independent party's ability to reproduce the credit ratings.

3.3 *Complement the traditional VaR risk measure with worst-case scenario analysis and stress testing*

Value-at-Risk (VaR) is a useful measure of risk in normal market conditions and over a very short-term horizon, say one to 10 days. But it is well documented that VaR does not perform well in exceptional market conditions characterized by unprecedented price moves and significant tail risk. VaR must be complemented by other risk metrics such as "worst-case scenario analysis" and "stress testing" in order to assess the extent of losses consecutive to extreme market conditions that have a very low probability of occurrence but that are still realistic.

When VaR is calculated at a 99 percent confidence level, one exception, on average, is expected every 100 days. A concentration of exceptions, i.e. daily trading losses greater than the daily VaR, over a short period of time, is the signal that the VaR model is failing and does not produce an accurate aggregate risk measure for the trading book of the bank. That is precisely what happened at several banks during the third quarter of 2007, after the start of the subprime crisis. According to a *Risk Magazine* survey published in January 2008, Credit Suisse declared 11 exceptions during the 3rd quarter of 2007, Bear Stearns 10, UBS 16, while Lehman Brothers declared only three exceptions, Goldman Sachs five and Morgan Stanley six, with the VaR of the three last banks being calculated at the 95 percent confidence level.

The subprime crisis introduced new risk features which are not captured in VaR models:

- Liquidity risk, i.e. the fact that trading liquidity dries out suddenly so that traders cannot adjust their hedging portfolios. The disappearance of liquidity is a common feature of financial crises. VaR models are, however, static models which cannot capture the impact of liquidity on asset prices, volatility, and correlations.

- Strong non-linearities in risk for complex structured products such as subprime CDO tranches. We discussed earlier what we called the "cliff" effect for senior tranches of subprime CDOs. This risk is not captured by VaR models.
- Contagion risk also cannot be accounted for in a VaR model.

Shortcuts proposed to deal with these complexities within the framework of VaR have lead to major underestimations of risk. For example, some banks have taken as a proxy for a rated CDO tranche a corporate bond with the same rating. This is flawed for the reasons that we discussed earlier.

If it was not obvious before, this crisis has revealed the necessity to design stress tests and worst case scenarios that include business cycle stresses as well as event specific "tail risks." The methodology must identify and take into account concentration risk, correlation risk, and liquidity risk and cover on-balance sheet as well as off-balance sheet assets. Scenario analysis must be implemented in a dynamic framework with scenarios unfolding over a period of time, say a quarter, during which liquidity is limited and does not allow trading positions to be hedged in a timely manner.

Risk management should also run worst-case scenarios to measure the risk of future collateral calls and write-downs which can have a devastating effect on the finances of the firm. For example, AIG was forced to post about $50 billion in collateral to its trading partners to offset drops in the value of more than $400 billion of securities it insured with credit default swaps, and wrote down several billion dollars. It was reported that no scenario was run at AIG that considered a sharp drop in housing prices and its impact on collateral calls and write-downs.[32]

References

Ashcraft, A. B. and T. Schuermann (2007). *Understanding the Securitization of Subprime Mortgage Credit,* Federal Reserve Bank of New York, Working Paper, December 2007.

Coval, J. D., J. Jurek and E. Stafford (2007). *Economic Catastrophe Bonds*, Harvard Business School, Working Paper 07-102, 2007.

[32] See *Wall Street Journal Europe*, November 3, 2008.

Coval, J. D., J. Jurek and E. Stafford (2008). *The Economics of Structured Finance*, Harvard Business School, Working Paper 09-060.

Crouhy, M. G., D. Galai and R. Mark (2006). *The Essentials of Risk Management.* McGraw-Hill.

Crouhy, M. G., R. A. Jarrow and S. M. Turnbull (2008). The subprime crisis of 2007. *Journal of Derivatives*, 16(1), Fall 2008, 81–110.

Fender, I., N. Tarashev and H. Zhu (2008). Credit fundamentals, ratings and value-at-risk: CDOs versus corporate exposures. *BIS Quarterly Review*, March 2008, 87–101.

Honohan, P. (2008). Bank failures: the limitations of risk modelling. Working Paper, 2008.

Risk Magazine (2008). VaR counts, 288, January, pp. 68–71.

Standard and Poor's (2008). Structured finance rating transitions and default updates as of June 20 2008, June 26.

UBS (2008). *Shareholder Report on UBS' Write-Downs.*

A Supervisor's View of the Current Financial Turmoil

Cathy Lemieux*
Federal Reserve Bank of Chicago

Steven VanBever
Federal Reserve Bank of Chicago

This paper offers some interim reflections on the current financial turmoil, from a supervisor's point of view. To provide perspective, we will begin by briefly surveying the banking crises of the 1980s and early 1990s,[1] including the most important legislative responses to these crises. Next, we will outline some of the ways the current financial turmoil is different from the previous episode. We will continue by summarizing some of the "lessons learned" from the current situation, both for banks and for bank supervisors. Finally, we will survey some of the policy responses to the current financial turmoil, both short-term and longer-term.

Turning to the banking crises of the 1980s and early 1990s, these banking problems were primarily confined to the U.S. A series of severe regional and sectoral recessions that moved from one area of the country to another affected U.S. banks in a number of banking markets and led to a large number of bank failures. These banking crises also unfolded over an extended time period, from approximately 1980 to 1994.

In the last banking crises there was an adequate supply of capital in the U.S. for the banking system as a whole. Banks that failed in one region of the country (for example, the Southwest) could be acquired by banks in other regions. While there were many bank failures, these were able to be

---

* Cathy Lemieux is senior vice president in charge of Supervision and Regulation at the Federal Reserve Bank of Chicago, and Steven VanBever is a lead supervision analyst there. The views expressed are those of the authors and do not necessarily reflect the views of the Federal Reserve Bank of Chicago or the Federal Reserve System.

[1] The standard account of the period is Federal Deposit Insurance Corporation, 1997.

resolved through consolidation of the industry[2] and finding buyers for troubled banks.

The last banking crises involved mostly smaller banks and thrifts. The average asset size of the banks that failed was $128 million.[3] Although there were some larger banks involved, such as Continental Illinois, MCorp, and Bank of New England, the overall scale of the problems was much smaller than it is in the current situation. During the prior period, 1,617 banks and thrifts failed, with total assets of $206.2 billion.[4] By way of comparison, from 1 January 2007, to 24 October 2008, 19 banks have failed, with total assets of $350.7 billion.[5] The current figures include only U.S. banks and thrifts, not the many foreign banks and nonbank financial firms worldwide that have failed. Furthermore, U.S. bank failures are expected to continue to grow, based on the backlog of problem banks that have been identified by regulators but not yet resolved.

Bank commercial real estate lending played a prominent role in the banking crises of the 1980s and early 1990s.[6] By contrast, it was residential real estate lending (specifically subprime mortgages) that triggered the current financial turmoil which, with the help of structured products, spread to other products and markets. Finally, the last banking crises revolved around capital, which was insufficient at many banks to absorb losses on problem assets. Although bank capital ratios improved on average during the period, large banks (banks with assets greater than $1 billion) were on average rather thinly capitalized during much of this period, with equity/assets ratios near or below 6 percent.[7]

Major banking legislation was enacted in response to the banking crises of the 1980s and early 1990s. The most important new laws were the Financial Institutions Reform, Recovery, and Enforcement Act of 1989 (FIRREA) and the Federal Deposit Insurance Corporation

[2] From the end of 1983 through the end of 1994, the number of insured commercial banks declined by 28 percent, from 14,461 to 10,451. Federal Deposit Insurance Corporation, 1997, Chapter 1, p. 8.

[3] Calculated from data in Federal Deposit Insurance Corporation, 1997, Chapter 1, p. 15.

[4] Federal Deposit Insurance Corporation, 1997, Chapter 1, p. 15.

[5] Federal Deposit Insurance Corporation, "Historical Statistics on Banking". This total assets figure includes Washington Mutual Bank, with $307.0 billion in total assets, and IndyMac Bank F.S.B., with $30.7 billion.

[6] An entire chapter of Federal Deposit Insurance Corporation, 1997, Chapter 3, is devoted to commercial real estate.

[7] See graph in Federal Deposit Insurance Corporation, 1997, Chapter 1, p. 6.

Improvement Act of 1991 (FDICIA). We will outline some of the most important provisions of these two laws aimed at preventing or mitigating future banking crises.

FIRREA provided funding for resolving failing thrifts. It also established more stringent thrift capital and regulatory standards and created a new regulatory structure for thrifts with significant FDIC involvement. It increased deposit insurance premiums, allowed bank holding companies to acquire any type of savings association, and expanded supervisory enforcement and resolution powers over depository institutions.[8] FIRREA also expanded membership in the Federal Home Loan Bank System. Originally created to support thrifts, the system was opened to allow many commercial banks to join and obtain funding. Currently, some of the largest borrowers in the FHLB System are commercial banks, such as Citibank and Bank of America, and the system has become a major source of liquidity for the banking system as a whole.

FDICIA represents a highly prescriptive and "rules-based" approach to bank regulation. We will focus on three key areas of that law: prompt corrective action, liquidity support, and least-cost resolution. FDICIA initiated a capital-based supervisory system known as prompt corrective action.[9] This framework consists of mandatory and discretionary supervisory actions that become increasingly severe as an institution's capital ratios decline and it reaches specified capital "tripwires", eventually resulting in closure if a bank's tangible equity becomes 2 percent or less of total assets. These supervisory actions include restrictions on an institution's activities (such as curtailing asset growth or limiting access to high-cost funding) aimed at reducing the institution's risk profile and preventing it from depleting its equity capital. Policymakers believed that regulatory forbearance during the banking crises preceding FDICIA had exacerbated weaknesses at banks and increased the FDIC's resolution costs. As a result, FDICIA reduced the discretion of bank supervisors with regard to institutions whose capital was deteriorating to unsafe levels.

A second key area of FDICIA was liquidity support.[10] It was argued that, during the 1980s, Federal Reserve Discount Window lending to weaker institutions had allowed uninsured depositors to flee and allowed

---

[8] Spong, 2000, Chapter 2, p. 31.
[9] Lemieux, 1993, pp. 2–3.
[10] Lemieux, 1993, pp. 3–7.

these banks to remain open longer than they would otherwise, thereby increasing losses to the deposit insurance fund. Therefore, FDICIA placed limitations on Federal Reserve lending. If a bank is considered "undercapitalized", the Fed cannot lend to it for more than 60 days in any 120-day period. When a bank reaches the "critically undercapitalized" stage, lending is essentially limited to five days. FDICIA also prevents troubled banks from shifting to volatile funds to meet liquidity needs. Specifically, "adequately capitalized" banks must obtain a waiver from the FDIC to accept brokered deposits. Furthermore, undercapitalized banks may not accept brokered deposits at all or pay deposit interest rates that exceed prevailing market rates.

FDICIA also introduced the requirement of least-cost resolution.[11] Prior to FDICIA, the FDIC, when resolving problem banks, typically protected uninsured as well as insured depositors, although it was not legally required to protect the former. FDICIA requires that the FDIC choose the resolution alternative that results in the least cost to the deposit insurance fund. The FDIC may not take any action that would increase losses to the insurance fund by protecting uninsured depositors or creditors other than depositors. However, an exception to these principles was allowed for situations in which severe adverse effects on the economy or financial stability could result from adhering to the principles.

Least-cost resolution sounds like an attractive idea, especially for taxpayers. However, we are finding that there are significant practical obstacles to implementing it, particularly at larger banks. Until recently there was no easy way to determine who the uninsured depositors were; it was a very manual process.[12] In addition, it is not a simple matter to determine which portion of a deposit is insured and which is not. This is also a manual, time-consuming process. Other complicating factors related to least-cost resolution are the treatment of corporate transaction accounts and foreign depositors, maintaining the franchise value of the organization for later sale by the FDIC, and the use of sweep accounts to circumvent deposit insurance.

An additional legislative solution to the last crises was the adoption of national depositor preference. Before the enactment of the Depositor

[11] Lemieux, 1993, pp. 7–9.

[12] To aid the FDIC and other supervisors in the resolution of problem banks, beginning with the March 2002 Call Report, all banks were required to report the estimated amount of their uninsured deposits.

Preference Act in 1993, subordinated debt holders were generally treated as general creditors with equal standing in liquidation with the FDIC. In attempting to close banks during the last crises there was often difficulty in determining who was covered by deposit insurance and who was not. Consequently, all depositors were often covered. Now the priority of claims has been clearly laid out. One major consequence of this is that parties with lower priority are quick to leave banks at signs of trouble, which, on the positive side, is an example of market discipline but can also increase stress on the banking system.

Now we will outline some of the ways the current financial turmoil is different from the banking crises of the 1980s and the early 1990s. The first difference is the much greater dispersion of risk. Geography is much less important this time. The current financial turmoil has spread from one product to another, not from one region of the U.S. to another. The current financial turmoil is truly global is scope. The assets that triggered the current turmoil (subprime mortgages) were originally concentrated in certain U.S. markets. However, due to financial innovation (especially securitization), the credit risks of these assets have been dispersed throughout the global financial system, affecting entities such as regional savings banks in Germany and pension funds in Norway. In addition, problems this time are not limited to commercial banks and thrifts. Government-sponsored entities Fannie Mae and Freddie Mac, the large U.S. investment banks, and insurance companies (most prominently American International Group, Inc.) are among the entities that have been affected most dramatically.

Finding sufficient capital to resolve banking problems is more difficult this time around. Compared to the 1980s, the U.S. banking industry as a whole had a solid capital base going into the current problems. As of June 30, 2007, the average leverage, Tier 1 risk-based, and total risk-based capital ratios for insured depository institutions were 8.18 percent, 10.38 percent, and 12.87 percent, respectively — well above the levels specified for well-capitalized banks.[13] However, actual and prospective losses are so large that raising sufficient capital to offset them will be a major challenge. The IMF estimates that aggregate write-downs based on global holdings of U.S.-originated and securitized mortgage, consumer, and corporate debt will total $1.4 trillion.[14] By way of contrast, banking

[13] Federal Deposit Insurance Corporation, 2007.

[14] International Monetary Fund, 2008, Chapter 1, p. 14.

losses during the U.S. savings and loan crisis were $273 billion.[15] So far, raising new capital has significantly lagged behind losses. Through September 2008, global write-downs at banking institutions have totaled roughly $580 billion, while only $430 billion of new capital has been raised.[16]

Raising capital has become extremely difficult in recent months.[17] It is estimated that, because of the weak market for bank stocks, new investors in bank stocks lost 29 percent of their investment, on average, from April through September 2008.[18] (Some investments have performed even worse. The investment by private equity firm TPG Capital LLP in Washington Mutual, Inc. in April 2008 has been virtually wiped out by the seizure of the latter's banking assets in September 2008.)[19] As a result, potential new sources of capital for the banking industry, such as sovereign wealth funds and private equity funds, appear to have become less willing to provide funds than they were earlier in the financial turmoil. The Treasury Department's Capital Purchase Program, announced on October 14, 2008, is a response to the current difficulty of raising capital.

As opposed to the previous crises, when capital was (or was perceived to be) the main cause of bank failures, it is liquidity pressures that have precipitated the largest bank failures this time around, such as IndyMac Bank F.S.B. and Washington Mutual Bank. Another aspect of liquidity is the increased reliance on wholesale funding, even at the smallest banks. Banks have been increasingly unable to fund their loan growth through (more-stable) deposits, so they turn to wholesale funding. The average loan-to-deposit ratio as of June 30, 2008, was 92.2 percent for insured institutions with total assets over $1 billion and 87.9 percent for those under $1 billion.[20] It is not uncommon to see loan-to-deposit ratios over 100 percent.

In addition to being primarily driven by liquidity, bank failures are playing out differently in the current situation, due to the changes in laws and regulations outlined earlier. Prompt corrective action has substantially reshaped the treatment and timing of failing banks where capital is the issue, since regulators intervene at a much earlier stage than used to

[15] International Monetary Fund, 2008, Chapter 1, p. 16.
[16] International Monetary Fund, 2008, Chapter 1, p. 23.
[17] International Monetary Fund, 2008, Chapter I, p. 22.
[18] Goldman Sachs, 2008, p. 2.
[19] Davis, 2008.
[20] Federal Deposit Insurance Corporation, 2008.

be the case.[21] Limitations on the use of brokered deposits are also having an effect. As indicated earlier, banks that are only "adequately capitalized" can only accept these deposits with FDIC approval. Brokered deposits have become a very important part of the funding structure of most banks, and the FDIC has granted very few waivers. The result is that dropping even to "adequately capitalized" status puts significant funding pressure on banks. In addition, bank regulators now find themselves under great scrutiny, often before Congressional committees, when banks fail. This gives them a strong incentive to find private-sector resolutions of troubled banks.[22] In the current situation, the FDIC has used a variety of different approaches to resolution other than depositor payouts, including conservatorship, receivership, and open-bank assistance.[23] Uninsured depositors have not always been protected, and this has led retail depositors in general to become more concerned than before about the safety of their particular bank and of the banking system as a whole. Finally, although FDICIA has constrained Federal Reserve Discount Window lending to troubled institutions in the current situation, the Fed has been highly innovative in introducing temporary lending programs to enhance liquidity in specific areas of the financial system that have come under strain.

Many private- and public-sector groups have been mining the financial crisis for lessons learned.[24] We will briefly touch on some of the findings of these exercises. Beginning with lessons learned for banks, "overconfidence and complacency must be continually battled, especially during an extended period of good times".[25] Unfortunately, the long period of stellar banking conditions made many bankers and other market participants overconfident. This led them to underestimate risks and to expect the good times to last forever. For example, many players expected housing prices to go up indefinitely and did not properly assess what might happen if prices leveled off or fell.

Second, "if risks are to be successfully managed, they must first be properly identified, measured, and understood."[26] Unfortunately, many

---

[21] Vartanian, 2008.
[22] Vartanian, 2008.
[23] Adler, 2008.
[24] See, especially, Financial Stability Forum, 2008, and Senior Supervisors Group, 2008.
[25] Kohn, 2008.
[26] Kohn, 2008.

banks underestimated the credit risk of subprime mortgages. Many also had a poor understanding of the particular market-risk characteristics of structured credit products. Some banks relied completely on third-party assessments of risk that turned out to be overly optimistic. Other banks did not fully consider the linkages between the various types of risk, such as how reputational risk can turn into credit, liquidity, or market risk when previously off-balance-sheet assets are taken back on the books to protect the name of the firm.

Finally, "financial institutions must understand their liquidity needs at an enterprise-wide level and be prepared for the possibility that market liquidity may erode quickly and unexpectedly".[27] For example, many banks' contingency funding plans did not adequately anticipate the current freeze in the interbank funding markets or the possibility that certain off-balance-sheet exposures might have to be brought back onto the balance sheet.

What are some of the things bank supervisors have learned from recent events? First, "the increased complexity and linkage within and among increasingly globalized markets presents greater challenges not just for bankers but also for supervisors".[28] Supervisors need a better understanding of the direct and indirect relationships among markets and market participants, and their impact on the banking system. They also need a better grasp of how those relationships can change over time and how they behave in times of stress. Supervisors need to understand not only banks but also other financial firms that play key roles in financial markets and have an important impact on financial stability.

Second, "supervisors need to enhance their focus on consumer compliance issues at the point of contact between lenders and households and on the linkages between weaknesses in consumer lending practices and safety and soundness, such as occurred with subprime mortgages".[29] To promote stronger compliance risk management, the Federal Reserve has recently published supervisory guidance to clarify expectations for compliance risk, specifically firm-wide compliance risk management for large, complex organizations.[30]

---

[27] Kohn, 2008.

[28] Kohn, 2008.

[29] Kohn, 2008.

[30] Board of Governors of the Federal Reserve System, 2008a.

Third, "the current U.S. regulatory structure, with multiple supervisory agencies, has a number of strengths and benefits, but challenges can arise in assessing risk profiles of large, complex financial institutions operating across financial sectors ..."[31] The Federal Reserve has been designated the consolidated supervisor for bank holding companies and financial holding companies. This consolidated supervision process works well overall, due to the strong, cooperative relationships that exist between the Federal Reserve and the other bank and functional regulators. But as institutions grow larger and more complex (as is happening at a very rapid pace during the current crisis), supervisors need to ensure that the system of consolidated supervision keeps pace. So the Fed has recently enhanced its supervisory guidance on consolidated supervision.[32]

Fourth and last, as part of promoting better risk management at banks, supervisors need to reinforce the need for financial institutions "to maintain sizable and more reliable liquidity and capital cushions, given the inherent uncertainty in financial markets".[33] Recent events clearly demonstrated weaknesses in managing liquidity and capital at a number of banks. In response to this, the Federal Reserve has helped to develop the Basel Committee's enhanced guidance on managing liquidity risk,[34] and it is also heavily involved in continually refining the Basel II capital framework.

In addition, here are a few "lessons learned" from our own recent experience that we offer as food for thought:

- What goes on in the marketplace matters (even if it is not in the entities supervised by a particular regulator). To promote financial stability, it is necessary for bank supervisors (particularly the Federal Reserve) to understand potential risks to the financial system, regardless of where they originate. In the current crisis, investment banks (including their securitization function), insurance companies, and the government sponsored enterprises have played critical roles and have had an enormous impact on the banking system.

---

[31] Kohn, 2008.

[32] Board of Governors of the Federal Reserve System, 2008b.

[33] Kohn, 2008.

[34] Basel Committee on Banking Supervision, 2008.

- Sometimes Adam Smith needs some help. For example, if every market participant operates in its own interest, the end result can be the absence of counterparty trading and the liquidity hoarding that characterize the present situation.
- Accounting drives behavior. For example, the use of off-balance-sheet structures created the illusion that risk did not lie with the arrangers of these structures and led market participants to underestimate banks' risk exposures.[35] Also, there has been much debate about whether fair value accounting may have exacerbated the current crisis.
- Incentives matter. For example, under the originate-to-distribute model, originators and distributors lacked sufficient incentives to monitor credit quality. Also, compensation schemes at many banks encouraged excessive risk-taking, with insufficient regard to longer-term risks.[36]
- Sometimes the skill in using models is in knowing when to turn them off. Financial firms that performed better in the current crisis effectively balanced the use of quantitative models with qualitative assessments. This addition of human judgment to the use of models helped these firms reduce exposures when risks became excessive and helped them pursue positive opportunities as they emerged.[37]
- Under stressed conditions, all correlations go to one. Because of the interconnectedness of markets and market participants, when panic sets in (as it did after Lehman Brothers was allowed to fail), everyone heads for the exits at the same time. Presently, risk aversion has become so extreme that the preferred counterparty for many market participants seems to be the U.S. government.
- Market disclosures require informed readers. Banks' public disclosures often failed to accurately portray their on- and off-balance-sheet risks, especially for structured products. Where information was disclosed, it was often not easily accessible or usable.[38] On the retail side as well, the required disclosures for subprime mortgage products may have been too voluminous and complex for the intended audience.
- Bad news travels fast. This is even more true in the Internet age. For example, the FDIC's website contains links to companies that rate

---

[35] Financial Stability Forum, 2008, p. 25.
[36] Financial Stability Forum, 2008, p. 8.
[37] Senior Supervisors Group, 2008, p. 4.
[38] Financial Stability Forum, 2008, p. 8.

banks. So anyone can find out what the market thinks of their bank. Also, for most larger banks there are blogs where anyone can log on and find the latest chatter about the bank's financial condition, including any hot rumors. It is important at all times for banks to maintain the value of their reputation, but especially so in highly stressed periods like the present.

How have policymakers responded to the current financial turmoil? The Federal Reserve has taken a number of steps to increase liquidity and stabilize markets. It has used open market operations. It has created a wide range of innovative new lending programs, including support for money market funds and commercial paper markets. It has also entered into reciprocal currency arrangements with foreign central banks.

Policy has also sought to promote confidence in key market participants. With Federal Reserve consultation and support, the Federal Housing Finance Agency placed Fannie Mae and Freddie Mac into conservatorship, and the Treasury provided financial support to the two firms. The Federal Reserve provided an emergency credit line to the large insurance firm American International Group (AIG) to facilitate an orderly resolution of its problems. In doing so, it ensured that the credit terms to AIG imposed significant costs and constraints on the firms' owners, managers, and creditors. The Fed also approved applications by Goldman Sachs and Morgan Stanley to become bank holding companies. In performing these interventions, policymakers have put existing equity holders in these firms at risk, although this is not always acknowledged in the public debates about "bailouts". In the cases of Fannie Mae, Freddie Mac, and AIG (and also Bear Stearns and Lehman Brothers), equity holders have definitely suffered significant losses.

Despite the efforts of the Federal Reserve, the Treasury, and other agencies, global financial markets (as of late September 2008) remained under extraordinary stress. Some of the key concerns were frozen interbank markets, asset valuations severely distorted by markets that have seized up, and the ever-increasing threat of a generalized "credit crunch".

Finally, with regard to longer-term, structural reforms, many proposals have been put forth. The Treasury Department provided a focal point for these discussions in March 2008 when it released its policy blueprint.[39]

[39] U.S. Department of the Treasury, 2008.

In addition, policymakers will have to consider whether to extend any of the liquidity programs that the Federal Reserve has created during the current crisis.

So far, Chairman Bernanke has weighed in on several important structural issues.[40] For example, he has called attention to the joint private/public sector efforts to strengthen the financial infrastructure, including clearing and settling over-the-counter derivatives and the market for tri-party repurchase agreements. He has also suggested that the Fed may need more explicit oversight authority for critical payment and settlement systems. Finally, he pointed out that new tools may be needed for the orderly liquidation of a systemically important securities firm (such as Bear Stearns).

The future nature and role of investment banks remains an open question. Just recently, many were arguing that investment banks needed a stronger, consolidated framework for prudential supervision, but market developments since then have overtaken that debate.

We want to conclude with a few brief reflections about the longer term:

- Activities need to be regulated similarly, regardless of where they are conducted. The current regulatory structure, based on type of legal entity rather than type of activity, produces gaps, inefficiencies, and opportunities for regulatory arbitrage. For example, regulation of subprime mortgages varied widely, depending on the type of legal entity and charter involved.
- Financial stability, prudential supervision, market-conduct regulation, and providing deposit insurance have different objectives and require different approaches and skills.[41] That does not mean that more than one function could not be combined in a single agency, but the differences have to be kept in mind.
- How supervision is funded matters. Some regulators derive a large percentage of their revenue from a few large institutions. When supervision is funded by institutions that have chosen a particular charter, this creates the potential for conflicts of interest.
- Risk management and incentives are key. Supervisors have been encouraging better risk management for years, but this crisis pointed

---

[40] Bernanke, 2008.

[41] For an overview of these concepts and the Treasury blueprint's recommendations, see U.S. Department of the Treasury, 2008, Chapter I, pp. 13–21.

out deficiencies on a scale no one expected. A key theme of the Senior Supervisors Group report is that firms that have performed relatively well during the current crisis had much better risk management than firms that have performed relatively poorly.[42]

- Financial stability is crucial for macroeconomic well-being. This is a key theme in academic discussions of prior episodes of a "credit crunch", as well as in current anxieties about an impending global downturn triggered by the current financial crisis.

In conclusion, the current financial crisis possesses a scope and a scale that policymakers have not seen for decades, perhaps since the 1930s. In addition to the issues touched on in this paper, public policy needs to address many other weaknesses. These include poor investor due diligence, poor performance by the credit rating agencies with regard to structured credit products, incentive distortions (for example, in the originate-to-distribute model), weaknesses in disclosures, and vulnerabilities in the settlement infrastructure for over-the-counter derivatives. Both the analysis of lessons learned and the ongoing attempts at crisis management are still works in progress, and the jury is still out on many issues, including the long-term shape of the financial industry and its regulation.

References

Adler, J. (2008). Wachovia deal forces FDIC to use systemic tool. *American Banker*, September 30.

Basel Committee on Banking Supervision (2008). *Principles for Sound Liquidity Risk Management and Supervision.* September. http://www.bis.org/publ/bcbs144.pdf?noframes=1

Bernanke, B. S. (2008). Regulatory restructuring. *Testimony before the Committee on Financial Services, U.S. House of Representatives*, July 10. http://www.federalreserve.gov/newsevents/testimony/bernanke20080710a.htm

Board of Governors of the Federal Reserve System (2008a). Compliance risk management programs and oversight at large banking organizations with complex compliance profiles. *Supervisory Letter SR 08-8/CA 08-11*, October 16. http://www.federalreserve.gov/boarddocs/srletters/2008/SR0808.htm

Board of Governors of the Federal Reserve System (2008b). Consolidated supervision of bank holding companies and the combined U.S. operations of foreign

[42] See Senior Supervisors Group, 2008, Transmittal letter.

banking organizations. *Supervisory Letter SR 08-9 / CA 08-12*, October 16. http://www.federalreserve.gov/boarddocs/srletters/2008/SR0809.htm

Davis, P. (2008). Capital's available, but it will cost you … *American Banker*, September 29.

Federal Deposit Insurance Corporation (1997). *History of the Eighties — Lessons for the Future*. http://www.fdic.gov/bank/historical/history/index.html

Federal Deposit Insurance Corporation (2007). *Quarterly Banking Profile*. Second Quarter. http://www2.fdic.gov/qbp/qbpSelect.asp?menuItem=QBP

Federal Deposit Insurance Corporation (2008). *Quarterly Banking Profile*. Second Quarter. http://www2.fdic.gov/qbp/qbpSelect.asp?menuItem=QBP

Federal Deposit Insurance Corporation. *Historical Statistics on Banking — Bank and Thrift Failure Reports*. http://www.fdic.gov/bank/individual/failed/index.html

Financial Stability Forum (2008). Report of the Financial Stability Forum on Enhancing Market and Institutional Resilience. April 7. http://www.fsforum.org/publications/r_0804.pdf

The Goldman Sachs Group, Inc. (2008). *United States: Banks*, September 29.

International Monetary Fund (2008). *Global Financial Stability Report*, October. http://www.imf.org/external/pubs/ft/gfsr/2008/02/index.htm

Kohn, D. L. (2008). Condition of the banking system. *Testimony before the Committee on Banking, Housing, and Urban Affairs*, U.S. Senate, June 5. http://www.federalreserve.gov/newsevents/testimony/kohn20080605a.htm

Lemieux, C. M. (1993). FDICIA: where did it come from and where will it take us? *Financial Industry Perspectives*, Federal Reserve Bank of Kansas City, November.

Senior Supervisors Group (2008). *Observations on Risk Management Practices During the Recent Market Turbulence*, March 6. http://www.newyorkfed.org/newsevents/news/banking/2008/ssg_risk_mgt_doc_final.pdf

Spong, K. (2000). *Banking Regulation: Its Purposes, Implementation, and Effects*, Federal Reserve Bank of Kansas City.

U.S. Department of the Treasury (2008). *Blueprint for a Modernized Financial Regulatory Structure*, March. http://www.treas.gov/press/releases/reports/Blueprint.pdf

Vartanian, T. P. with R. H. Ledig (2008). Viewpoint: some new dynamics for troubled institutions. *American Banker*, July 18.

The Subprime Crisis: Lessons About Market Discipline

Mark J. Flannery*
University of Florida

Abstract

During the subprime crisis, market forces have not generally led firms to follow prudent operational procedures. Market prices (CDS spreads) differentiated stronger from weaker firms, but provided no advance indication of large risk concentrations in specific firms. Poor government supervision also contributed to the crisis. The information provided by market prices can be used effectively to hasten supervisory actions, which will reduce the social cost of financial failures.

From amidst the most serious financial crisis in 70 years, I have been asked to evaluate how the current situation should affect our assessment of market discipline as an aid to supervision of financial firms. I start with a brief overview of recent events to motivate my comments about market discipline. Because other scholars and market participants have provided cogent accounts of the subprime crisis and its sources, this overview can be brief.[1] Section 2 reviews the principles of market discipline, and Section 3 discusses some lessons. The fourth section suggests two near-term policy reforms, and the final section offers a brief conclusion on the continued efficacy of market discipline for financial firms.

---

* Mark J. Flannery is the Bank of America Professor of Finance, University of Florida. Email: flannery@ufl.edu. The author thanks the Markit Group for providing the data underlying Figures 1–6 and 8. Doug Evanoff, Bob Litan, and Wayne Archer provided helpful comments on an earlier version of this paper. Remaining errors are the author's own.

[1] For example, Gorton (2008) or Greenlaw *et al.* (2008).

1. The Crisis

1.1 *What happened?*

The federal government has long offered incentives to help citizens purchase a home. Earlier in this decade, mortgage lenders innovated a series of new contracts, which were designed to facilitate mortgage lending to a broader range of households. By reducing down payments, providing flexible repayment schedules, and permitting frequent "cash out" renegotiations (albeit for a fee), mortgages were made available to Alt-A and subprime borrowers. These innovations were correlated with a relatively sharp rise in homeownership. For example, Doms and Krainer (2007) report an unusually rapid increase in homeownership rates (from 64 percent to 69 percent) between 1994 and 2004 and attribute it to "several innovations in mortgage markets, such as the lowering of down payment requirements, the increased flexibility in repayment schedules, and the reduction of costs associated with extracting equity from homes" (pp. 22–23). Some observers argue that "easy lending" contributed to a housing price bubble, but this is difficult to prove. However, many subprime borrowers could only repay lenders if housing prices continued their rise. As housing prices in fact declined across much of the country, mortgage delinquencies and foreclosures rose beyond anything previously observed. Some borrowers defaulted on loans whose balance came to exceed their house's value. Other borrowers had purchased houses beyond their means, and could not continue to carry the mortgage without tapping expanding house equity.

The majority of these "innovative" mortgage loans were securitized. On its face, this appeared merely to extend a decades-long trend in the U.S. market. Traditional securitization structures, however, had been "brain dead." That is, they required no further funding over their lives and the servicers had limited ability to renegotiate the loan's initial terms. In contrast, many of the early-2000s' subprime mortgages found their way into structured investment vehicles (SIVs) or asset-backed commercial paper (ABCP) conduits, which required continual access to new funding in order to roll over their short-term debt. Although these vehicles included interest rate swaps that protected them against shifts in the riskless term structure, they had no defense against increases in default risk premiums. Moreover, the value of renegotiations increased with the number of defaults, but servicers still had severely limited flexibility in this dimension.

The rating agencies (Moody's, Standard and Poor's, Fitch) also played a central role in the securitization process. Their projected mortgage default rates determined how much junior debt each securitization structure required in order for the senior tranche (including the ABCP) to be rated AAA. Comforted by these ratings, many relatively uninformed investors purchased ABCPs that offered a rate premium exceeding what AAA paper "usually" offered. As the market became more comfortable with these structures, ABCP funding rose to as much as 90 percent of the total package.

It turned out that the rating agencies' models did not extrapolate well from historical data. The nationwide housing price collapse that began in 2006 lay well outside of historical experience, and this eliminated the diversification benefits traditionally provided by mortgage-backed securities (MBS). Because many subprime borrowers' repayments depended on continued house appreciation, securitization structures included loans whose values became highly correlated when house prices fell (Coval *et al.*, 2008). The situation was further exacerbated by "Rampant fraud in the mortgage industry [which] has increased so sharply that the FBI warned Friday of an 'epidemic' of financial crimes which, if not curtailed, could become 'the next S&L crisis'". (CNN.com, 2004).

In the financial industry, the first signs of trouble emerged early in 2007 (Gorton, 2008).

- February: HSBC announced a $1.76 billion loan loss provision related to its American subprime lending.
- March 13: The Mortgage Bankers Association announced that 13.3 percent of all subprime mortgages had late or missed payments during the last quarter of 2006.
- May 3: UBS closed two subprime-related hedge funds.
- June 10–12: Rating agencies downgraded or placed on credit watch a large number of MBS and CDOs tied to subprime loans.
- June 20: Bear Stearns closed two subprime-related funds.
- August 9: BNP Paribas froze withdrawals from three hedge funds, citing its inability to establish prices for some of the subprime securities held in the funds.

Some firms quite promptly wrote down their mortgage portfolio values and many of the same firms raised substantial amounts of new equity capital. However, a widespread suspicion remains that many large financial firms continue to hold unrecognized losses sufficient to wipe out their recorded equity. Uncertainty about firms' exposures and the value of subprime assets has caused serious problems within the financial sector. Financial firms are reluctant to lend to one another, even with collateral, and a system-wide demand for liquidity has resulted in higher lending standards for real-sector customers.

1.2 *Why did it happen?*

Many observers have argued that the origination and dissemination of subprime mortgages, particularly in 2005–7, reflected widespread agency problems in the investment chain. Others contend that top executives simply erred by overlooking the possibility that a fall in house prices would generate catastrophic default rates. One's view on this question largely determines one's conclusion about the role of market discipline in the crisis. "Who knew what, and when?"

1.2.1 *Underwriters*

Loan brokers (or other originators) have been accused of misrepresenting applicant information or accepting questionable documentation from loan applicants.[2] Originating firms also decided to accept applications without "full" documentation and lent with higher loan-to-value (LTV) ratios than had historically been common. They then sold the loans, without recourse, to MBS arrangers. With no residual stake in the loan's credit quality, underwriters' earnings varied directly with the number of loans originated. Did the underwriters — consciously or otherwise — make riskier loans that subsequently generated extraordinary losses? Some analysts maintain that lending standards did not decline (Bhardwaj and Sengupta, 2008). However, the raw data indicate that between 2004 and 2007, subprime loans had less complete documentation, higher LTV ratios, and lower FICO scores. In addition, the FBI had detected substantial mortgage-industry fraud by 2004 (CNN.com, 2004).

[2] Ashcraft and Schuerrmann (2008) evaluate the "frictions" that might arise in a mortgage securitization deal. For purposes of assessing market discipline, the question is whether those frictions were purposeful, consciously ignored, or just the result of bad luck.

Loan originators may also have offered inappropriate loan amounts or structures to individuals who did not fully understand the implications of their mortgage loan agreements. Brokers had no fiduciary responsibility to their mortgage customers, leaving them free to maximize their own fee income with little danger of legal retribution. The Federal Reserve addressed some of these issues by revising Regulation Z in July 2008.

1.2.2 *Investors*

Self-dealing or sloppy underwriting at the origination stage could not have succeeded unless investors subsequently purchased the resulting loans. Theory and practice clearly specify that the originators of opaque loans should retain a first loss piece of the resulting securitization (Diamond, 1984; Pennacchi, 1988). But this became less common as the housing boom proceeded. With the originator taken out of the deal, investment managers should have undertaken extensive due diligence of their own before committing clients' money. Yet many investors apparently paid little attention to MBS features beyond their ratings and continued to purchase subprime-backed securities as lending standards deteriorated.[3] In the end, investment managers with large subprime holdings suffered substantial losses for their customers. Is this outcome consistent with responsible due diligence?

In the absence of a "smoking gun" or intra-firm emails, we cannot conclude that "all" or "most" financial actors exercised insufficient care in originating and holding subprime mortgage claims. These were new instruments, and opinions could reasonably differ about their value. Many market participants probably recognized the sensitivity of subprime mortgages to widespread house price declines, but few put much weight on such an unprecedented possibility.[4] In many cases, investors' choices were encouraged (abetted) by high credit ratings from the Nationally

[3] Hansell (2008) reports that investment companies may have chosen model parameters or specifications deliberately to make subprime mortgage claims appear less risky.

[4] Gorton (2008) argues that this collective oversight explains events preceding and during the crisis. He contends that investors were not aware of the subprime mortgage payoffs' correlations until 2006, when the (new) ABX default swap first combined investors' atomistic information sets into a single, more relevant security price.

Recognized Statistical Rating Organizations (NRSROs, which in the U.S. presently include Moody's, Standard and Poor's, and Fitch). Even if some investors truly believed that subprime MBS were solid investments, one must wonder why so many "sophisticated" investors were willing to take on large exposures to a single event. It appears likely that agency problems were responsible for much of the subprime investment patterns. Investment managers served their customers poorly, perhaps in part because the firm's goals were badly transmitted to frontline actors via compensation mechanisms.

1.2.3 *Rating agencies*

The credit rating agencies (NRSROs) played an important role in the subprime mortgage securitization process. Many ratings proved to be vastly over-optimistic. (E.g., total dollar losses on AAA-rated tranches have exceeded all losses on lower-rated tranches.) Why were they so optimistic? One possibility is that honest assessments were derived from faulty models. New default information arrived rapidly after July 2007, and it was not obvious how to incorporate the new information into models based on historical experience. Another plausible possibility is that the agencies competed for deal flow by offering lenient rating standards.

The SEC (2008) notes that the "insurer pays" model of ratings has raised questions since it appeared around 1970. The flow of mortgage securitization deals early in the decade may have overwhelmed the rating agencies' prior incentives to protect their reputations.

> The combination of the arrangers' influence in determining the choice of rating agencies and the high concentration of arrangers with this influence appear to have heightened the inherent conflicts of interest that exist in the "issuer pays" compensation model. (SEC, 2008, p. 32).

SEC (2008) reports cases in which a rating agency had new data that raised projected default rates, but delayed updating their models until an important client's issue had been rated. During this period, the agencies were somewhat overwhelmed with the volume of business. However, they chose to handle all requests despite their inability to do a careful analysis of all the deals. Emails uncovered by SEC staff indicate that the rating agencies' staffs were aware of and uncomfortable with the situation.[5]

2. What is "Market Discipline"?[6]

"Market discipline" can be divided into two components, monitoring and influence (Bliss and Flannery, 2002). "Market monitoring" asserts that investors impound accurate information about a financial firm's condition into its security prices. "Market influence" describes mechanisms by which those market assessments "influence" the firm's behavior, *ex ante* or *ex post*.

The earliest market discipline proponents conjectured that market prices would reflect information unknown to supervisory personnel. Empirical tests failed to provide much support for this conjecture. Market and supervisory information generally overlapped substantially (Berger *et al.*, 2000, Gropp *et al.*, 2006, Krainer and Lopez, 2004), and it appears that market prices do not add greatly to supervisors' information sets about the condition of regulated firms. Nevertheless, market prices can still influence a regulated financial firms' behavior indirectly.

Influence can occur *directly* if market price changes induce firm managers to take (or avoid) specific actions. If investors monitor firm risk exposures accurately, managers will understand that taking on riskier investments will raise their borrowing costs. When they evaluate new opportunities, they will accept only those promising enough return to compensate for the cost of higher risk. This "direct" market influence constitutes the standard explanation of how markets affect firm behavior. Despite the general acceptance of this governance mechanism, its importance is very difficult to observe in the data.[7]

---

[5] For example, an analytical manager wrote that the rating agencies were creating an "even bigger monster — the CDO market. Let's hope we are all wealthy and retired by the time this house of cards falters)". (SEC, 2008, footnote 8, p. 12)

[6] Market discipline is defined and discussed more extensively in Flannery (2009).

[7] Bliss and Flannery (2002) tested whether increased debenture spreads were followed by bank actions consistent with reducing debenture default risks. Rajan (2002) points out that spread changes reflect both exogenous firm developments and investors' expectations about firm responses. See also Bond *et al.* (forthcoming) for information about how to interpret a regulated firm's security price changes. Berger *et al.* (2008) and Flannery and Rangan (2008) interpret large U.S. banks' "excess" capital holding as a response to counterparty (market) pressures.

Regulation provides another, "indirect" channel by which market opinions can influence firm behavior: supervisors can use market price signals to motivate intervention in a firm's activities (Kwast *et al.*, 1999). Supervisors suffer from an oft-cited tendency to forbear. Laws and regulations restrict government supervisors' ability to act quickly in most circumstances, and human nature itself tends to delay decisions based on bad news. Requiring that supervisors comment publicly about negative changes in a firm's market prices (equity prices, deposit or debt rates, or CDS premiums) may counteract forbearance — regardless of whether market prices impound information supervisors do not know (DeYoung *et al.*, 2001). The available evidence indicates that indirect influence is the most promising channel through which market prices can influence regulated firms' behavior.

3. Viewing Market Discipline Through a Subprime Lens

Proponents of market discipline contend that actors with their own money involved will investigate a firm more aggressively than a third-party monitor with no financial involvement. The subprime crisis provides abundant support for this hypothesis: SIVs and ABCP conduits constituted a parallel banking system, free from "excessive" supervisory restrictions. These pseudo-banks funded opaque, long-term portfolios substantially with short-term funds. Although they appeared to be a simple extension of past (successful) securitization devices, these appearances were deceiving. In fact, the SIVs' asset-liability maturity mismatches made them more like 1980s-style thrift institutions. SIVs were created during a period of historically low risk premiums and steep yield curves, which made maturity mismatching appear relatively benign. SIVs could hedge pure interest rate changes with interest rate swaps, but they had no protection against a change in risk premiums. The sharp increase in credit risk premiums in 2007 reduced the SIVs' asset value, leaving the "senior" tranches of a subprime pool with substantially less credit risk protection.

The fact that this crisis occurred outside the banking system (narrowly defined) highlights the problem with regulating financial *institutions* — as opposed to financial *functions*. Market forces displayed initiative and flexibility, while the regulatory structure was not organized to respond to those (partially unobserved) changes.

3.1 *Lessons about market monitoring*

An important feature of market monitoring is that market investors have "their own" funds at risk and hence carefully evaluate each security's risk-return tradeoff at its current price. Changes in a firm's security prices should therefore indicate changes in its asset values, asset risk, or leverage. During the subprime crisis, visual inspection of credit default swap (CDS) premiums indicates that market investors successfully identified the weakest firms, although not very far ahead of events.

Figures 1 and 2 report CDS spreads for five investment banks and five commercial banks, respectively, from the start of 2006 through August 12, 2008.[8] Strikingly, no meaningful fluctuations appear in the data before August 2007, despite some initial signs of trouble brewing in the subprime sector. (See above.) During the 19 months from January 2006 through July 2007, the most noteworthy feature of these figures is that the investment banks' spreads exceeded those of the commercial bank holding companies

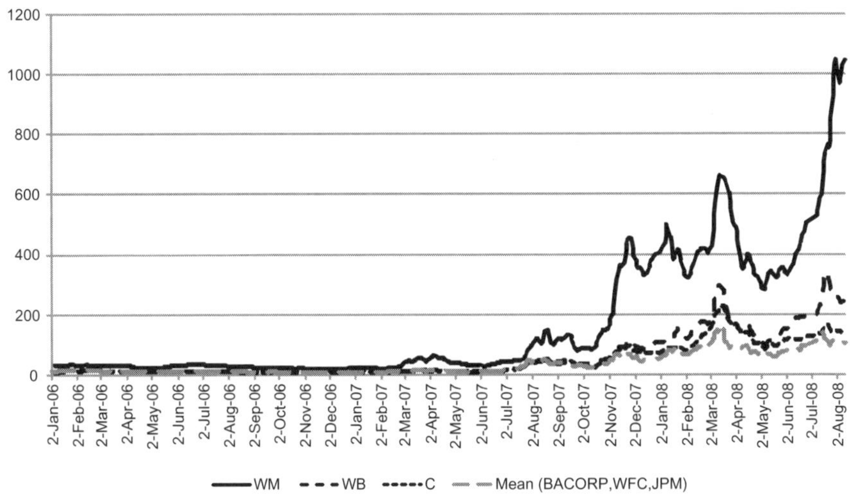

Figure 1. "Commercial" Banks' Credit Spreads.

[8] The reported data have been smoothed by plotting 5-day trailing averages of daily premiums on 5-year, single-name CDS contracts.

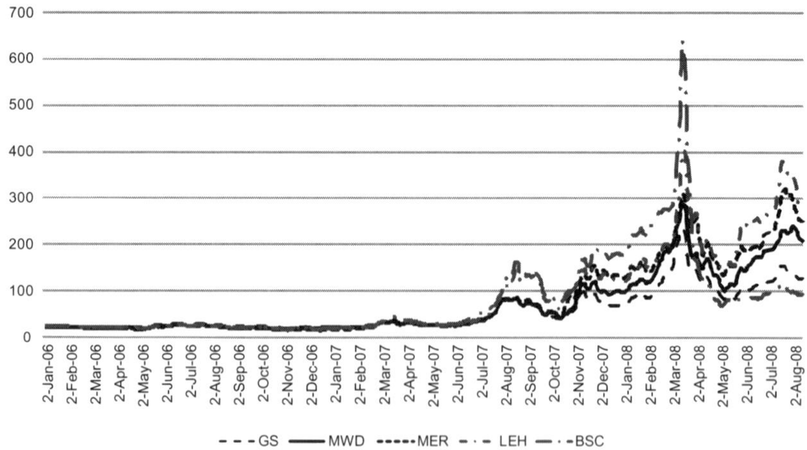

Figure 2. "Investment" Banks' Credit Spreads.

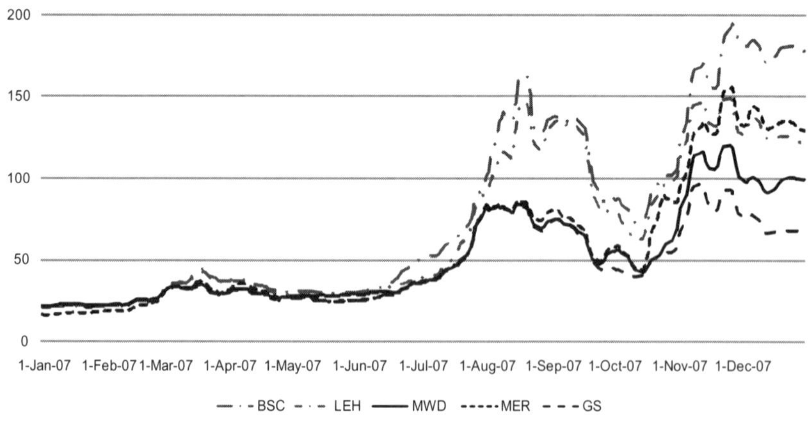

Figure 3. "Investment" Banks' Credit Spreads, 2007.

(26 basis points (bp) vs. 13 bp).[9] Figures 3 and 4 provide greater detail about the initial market disruptions by reporting only 2007 data.

After the first large shock in August 2007, CDS premiums became larger and the divergence of firms' premiums increased markedly. Figure 3

[9] Indeed, over the entire sample period shown in Figures 1 and 2, the investment banks' premia exceeded the bank holdings companies' premia (a mean of 72 bp vs. 41).

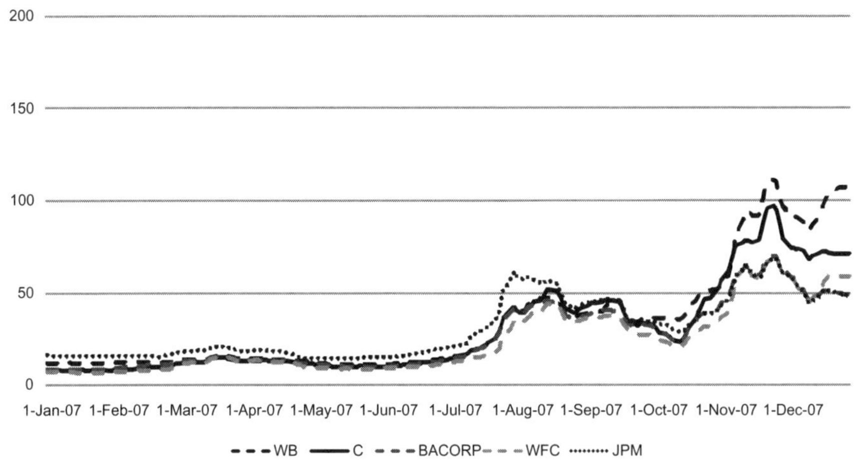

Figure 4. "Commercial" Banks' Credit Spreads, 2007.

indicates that the investment banks' default risk increased slightly during June and July of 2007, but only Bear Stearns (BSC) separated itself visibly from the other investment banks. By the middle of August, CDS premiums for Bear Stearns and Lehman (LEH) had risen to twice those of their three peer investment banks. Some calm returned in September and October of 2007, but by November we see four distinct tiers of CDS premiums, spanning 111 bp. The market considered Bear and Lehman the weakest among this group. Figure 4 indicates that the commercial banks' credit spreads also widened somewhat in August. Yet a distinct tiering emerged only in November 2007, when Wachovia (WB) and Citibank (C) stood above Wells Fargo (WFC) and JPMorgan-Chase (JPM).

Figures 5 and 6 plot data for the calendar year 2008 (through August 12), when the financial system experienced even more severe shocks. The distinct ranking among banks persisted, with Bear's (truncated) CDS premium exploding to 737 bp on March 14 when JPMorgan-Chase agreed to lend it funds with Fed support. Two days later, JPMorgan agreed to purchase Bear Stearns outright and its CDS premium rapidly fell to coincide with JPMorgan's premium through the end of the period. By mid-August we see qualitatively the same sort of dispersion among investment banks as existed at the end of 2007, with two differences. First, the spread is larger, at 180 bp. Second, Lehman Brothers is now considered the most likely to fail, followed by Morgan Stanley (MWD) and Merrill-Lynch (MER).

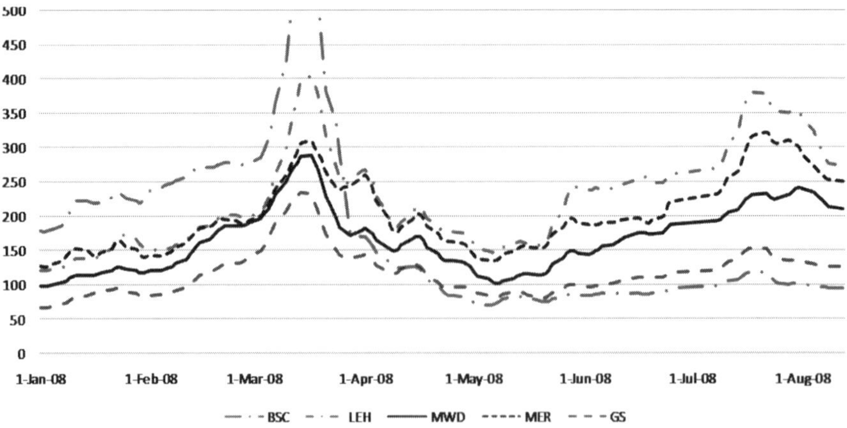

Figure 5. "Investment" Banks' Credit Spreads, 2008 (Through August 12).

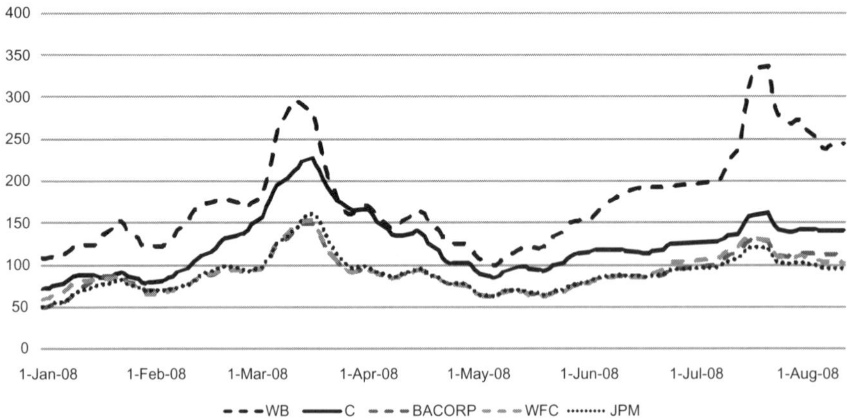

Figure 6. "Commercial" Banks' Credit Spreads, 2008 (Through August 12).

The commercial bank sub-period data in Table 6 exhibits the same general pattern. The banks' CDS spreads generally jumped up around the time of Bear Stearns' takeover. Wachovia (WB) showed the highest premium, followed by Citigroup (C). The other three spreads (BAC, WFC, and JPM) were lower and indistinguishable from one another. This general pattern persisted through mid-August, except that Wachovia's premium rose both absolutely and relative to the other banks while CitiGroup's premium fell closer to those of the other three.

Overall, the evidence shows that market prices indicated distinct quality differences among large financial firms, but provided little advance warning before the problems became apparent in August 2007. The volume of outstanding asset-backed commercial paper (ABCP) shows a similar pattern in Figure 7. ABCP volume rose very rapidly until August 2007, and then fell precipitously. Investors were monitoring effectively, perhaps, but failed to predict serious problems.

One exception to this conclusion comes from inspecting CDS prices for Washington Mutual (WM). Figure 8 adds WM to the banks shown in Figures 1, 4, and 6. The CDS market reflected a predominantly rising probability of default for WM from the initial crisis event (August 2007) through the Bear Stearns resolution. All CDS spreads fell sharply after mid-March, but WM's spread remained substantially above the others. Events during the summer of 2008 raised the premium on WM CDS very substantially above those of the other banks and, of course, WM failed on September 25.

A different lesson about market monitoring emerged after the crisis had begun. Sometimes, market prices provide only a crude estimate of an asset's value. Under normal financial market conditions, even opaque financial

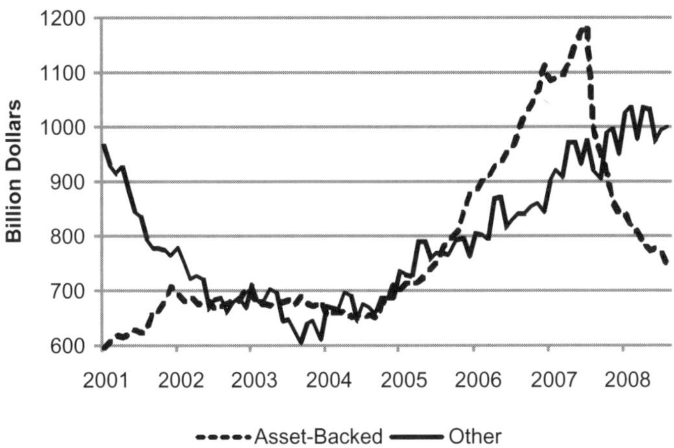

Figure 7. Commercial Paper Outstanding.
Source: Federal Reserve Board.

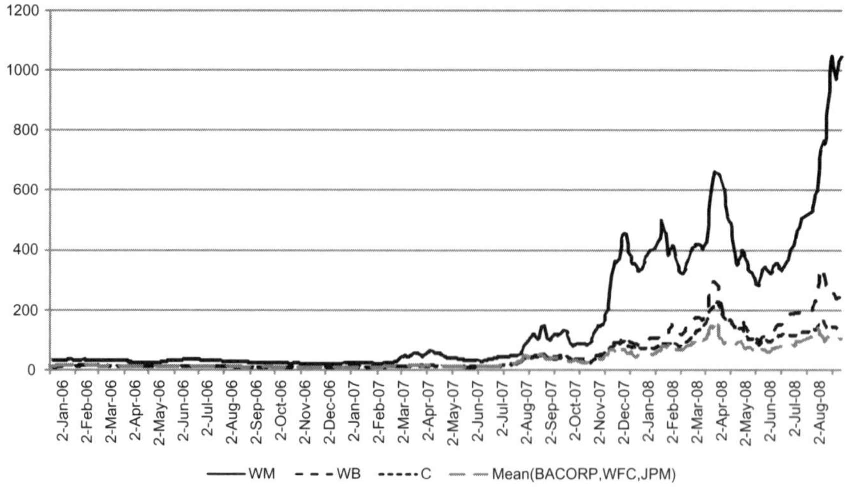

Figure 8. Commercial Banks Plus WaMu (WM).

institutions can be valued by outside investors.[10] Discussions of market monitoring also tend to interpret prices as general (shared) assessments of asset value. Substantial differences of opinion emerged during the subprime crisis, causing market prices to diverge widely from some investors' assessments of true value. Akerlof (1970) evaluated how such differences of opinion could lead to market failure, but he provided little guidance about the impact of a market's failure on potential buyers and sellers.

The subprime crisis has thus shown that highly diffuse market valuations can have detrimental effects even if prices reflect the expected asset value (Mishkin, 1992). Unusually wide bid-ask spreads can raise doubt about a firm's solvency. To determine the implications of these market monitoring problems for optimal supervision, we must determine whether supervisors' assessments of firms' values were more or less accurate than what the market was producing.

3.2 *Lessons about market influence*

The lessons about market influence are mixed, but overall rather negative.

[10] See Flannery, Kwan, and Nimalendran (2004). Contradictory evidence is presented by Morgan (2002) and Iannotta (2006).

3.2.1 *Agency and incentive problems*

A firm operating under appropriate "market influence" will organize itself to maximize the shareholders' risk-adjusted returns. The extensive literature on CEO compensation implicitly assumes that properly motivating the CEO (or a small number of executives) will trickle down to generate other pay-for-performance relationships that maximize firm value. Yet the subprime crisis is replete with stories about bankers or brokers who were so keen to "get a deal done" that they cut some important corners. Ashcraft and Schuermann (2008) list numerous places in a securitization deal where agency problems or conflicts of interest could affect financing decisions.

On the sell side, mortgage brokers often earned immediate commissions for making mortgage loans, regardless of the loans' ultimate performance.[11] Mortgage portfolio arrangers were interested in selling securities, sometimes without complete knowledge of their characteristics. On the buy side, investment managers seemed enamored of opportunities to earn "better than AAA" yields on "AAA" risk, and consequently performed less due diligence than would (in hindsight) have been optimal. In its Report to Shareholders, the UBS Board of Directors (2008) admitted that their information systems were inadequate for identifying and managing subprime-related risks on a company-wide basis![12]

Operating under uncertainty, investors cannot precisely identify the most lucrative assets. In a multi-segment investment firm, however, power

---

[11] A lengthy *New York Times* story (Morgenstern, 2007) reports that Countrywide mortgage brokers were primarily encouraged (and given incentives) to make loans that would be most profitable for resale in the market, with much less consideration about underwriting standards or the borrower's ability to afford the loan. Even if Countrywide was extreme in this regard, it was not a complete exception to normal practice in the industry.

[12] For example: "there was no comprehensive view available of the gross notional holdings with Subprime exposure across the IB. This was principally due to incomplete data capture and the effects of hedging. Hedging resulted in positions being netted off and therefore not showing up in the overall position data." (UBS Board of Directors, 2008, p. 21);
"There were not however any Operational Limits on the CDO Warehouse, nor was there an umbrella Operational Limit across the IB ("investment bank") ... or the combination of IB and DRCM ("Dillon Read Capital Management") that limited overall exposure to the Subprime sector (securities, derivatives and loans)." (UBS Board of Directors, 2008, p. 20).

tends to flow to the people whose lines of business have been most successful. When one line of business continuously delivers large profits, it becomes more difficult to argue that the business contains large, as yet unobserved, risks. Concerned risk managers become viewed as Cassandras, and the institution can lose objectivity. Investors who have seen subprime mortgage paper earn "excess" returns for several years become less vigilant in examining the terms of subsequent issues. In short, executive behavior reflects current beliefs, and recent profits affect those beliefs. When information is imperfect, corporate governance cannot be expected to resist strong forces of the sort that emerged during the run-up to the subprime crisis.

Agency theory clearly predicts that managers will seek perquisites, and that agents will tend to deliver the things for which they are compensated most highly. However, principal-agent contracting was apparently much weaker among subprime originators and arrangers than in other parts of the financial marketplace. The dismal science (economics) is sometimes criticized as "seeing something work in practice and wondering if it can work in theory." Economic theory indicates that underwriting decisions and loan monitoring should be undertaken by agents who will be affected by the loan's repayment (e.g. Diamond, 1984; Pennacchi, 1988). From this perspective, the puzzle is not that the subprime sector caused a crisis. Rather, the puzzle is that subprime lending and securitization worked so well even based on institutional arrangements that are so clearly inconsistent with what we know about financial intermediation theory: If monitoring a loan is important, why did downstream investors purchase assets for which the originating institutions bore virtually no responsibility and no risk of default?

3.2.2 *Raising capital*

The institutional arrangements that facilitated the origination and securitization of subprime mortgages must be considered a failure of market influence. However, the large banks' treatment of equity capital during the crisis has been aggressive (by historical standards) and surprisingly quick. Greenlaw *et al.* (2008, p. 34) report that by May 8, 2008, U.S. firms had written off \$162 billion in assets and raised \$138 billion in new equity. (60 banks and brokerages worldwide (including those in the U.S.) wrote off \$381 billion while raising \$266 billion.) This rapid recapitalization is particularly striking because the banks substantially exceeded Basel I capital standards as they entered the crisis. With so much "excess" regulatory capital, the banks could have postponed equity issues if their primary goal was to satisfy supervisory standards. The fact that they moved so quickly suggests that market-related pressures were the predominant motivation.[13]

3.2.3 *Lessons about rating agencies*

Rating agencies contribute to the market monitoring process. They also exert potential influence on market participants.[14] In addition, the rating agencies operate under a rather extreme form of the "reputational" incentives that also affect other firms in the financial sector. When John Moody began evaluating railroad bonds more than a century ago, he sold his opinions to investors. Investors who found Moody's opinions informative paid for them, and he needed to sell enough subscriptions to break even. This payment scheme broke down around 1970 as technology reduced the cost of quickly sharing a rating agency's opinions. Amid extensive debate, the rating agencies began to collect most of their revenue from the companies they were rating. As noted above, the SEC staff recently conjectured that competition for new MBS rating business probably affected at least some assigned subprime-related ratings:

> Some observers have indicated that while conflicts of interest due to the 'issuer pays' model exist with respect to all asset classes that receive ratings, the conflicts created from the 'issuer pays' model in rating structured finance products, particularly RMBS and related-CDOs (sic), may be exacerbated for a number of reasons. First, the arranger is often the primary designer of the deal and as such, has more flexibility to adjust the deal structure to obtain a desired credit rating as compared to arrangers of non-structured asset classes (SEC, 2008, p. 31).

---

[13] The additional capital might have been required to restore a bank's credit rating, or to provide "dry powder" to be deployed in a troubled environment. Either way, the capital additions clearly strengthened the financial sector.

[14] For example, Kisgen (2006) and Hovakimian *et al.* (2008) conclude that firms target specific credit ratings, which require them to observe certain leverage and operating characteristics.

A growing reliance on ratings for setting supervisory capital standards has further complicated the rating agencies' incentives. In 1995, an executive vice president and director of Moody's Corporate Department told the Securities and Exchange Commission that by

> using securities ratings as a tool of regulation, governments *fundamentally change the nature of the product* agencies sell. Issuers pay ratings fees to purchase . . . a license from the government . . . if present trends of regulatory use of ratings are not arrested, the *credibility and integrity of the ratings system itself will inevitably be eroded.* (McGuire, 1995, emphasis added).

Both the "issuer pays" and "regulatory license" aspects of ratings hit the subprime rating segment hard. We expect that normally an agency's incentive to provide a sloppy (cheap) rating will be counteracted by the damage to its reputation if its carelessness becomes known. This equilibrium obtains if the present value of future quasi-rents exceeds the immediate gain from poor performance. The last few years before 2007 included an unusually large flow of deals to be rated, which increased the dollar gains (savings) from doing poor credit evaluations. Quite possibly, these near-term savings came to exceed the value of future rents, critically compromising the value of a credit rating. The credit rating industry is not unique in this regard. The opinions of stock analysts and auditors, whose values also derive from reputation, have been questioned extensively in the past decade.

3.2.4 *Summary*

To summarize, what have we learned about the various components of market discipline from the subprime crisis? First, financial firms' security prices provided no advance warning that they were undertaking large risks, but they effectively distinguished among firms once the subprime crisis got underway. Second, asset (subprime loan) prices became much noisier during the crisis due to asymmetric information and increased risk aversion. The (presumably) simple relationship between prices and value became more complex. Third, incentive contracts within originators, investment advisers, and the rating agencies probably went awry in a regime with limited accountability for bad loans. Finally, on the "plus" side, banking firms quickly raised large amounts of new equity capital to replace reported losses.

Although "market discipline" has not performed very well in the current crisis, the *ex ante* advantages of market vs. government oversight remain effectively unchanged from the period before 2007. Market monitoring and influence are flexible and forward-looking. While government personnel tend to react to financial innovation, investors make their living by forecasting future developments. Government oversight must follow explicit rules. Legal challenges can postpone effective action. In contrast, market prices owe no explanation to anyone. Combining market monitoring with government monitoring and influencing capabilities still seems like the best approach to financial system regulation.

4. Where Should We Go From Here?

Currently, government has an unusual opportunity to rationalize some of the rules of the financial game. It should seize this opportunity for two near-term purposes.

First, some collective action is needed to rationalize the world's massive OTC securities markets, which initially emerged as bilateral deals designed to accommodate idiosyncratic needs. However, many OTC contracts now take a standard form: the five-year CDS swap, fixed-floating interest rate swaps, etc. In an OTC market, an investor must offset her initial position by originating a second contract. This potentially doubles the system's counterparty risk and reduces the transparency of an investor's credit risk exposures. Trading these standardized contracts on an exchange would increase transparency, simplify the settlement process, and eliminate the potential for one hedge to involve multiple counterparties and notional amounts. An informed regulator could encourage the private cooperation required to implement a shared settlement system. By reducing opacity, supervisors could understand a firm's true condition more readily, and could worry less (at least, not so much as they recently have) about the knock-on effects of a large derivative player's demise.

A second role for government concerns subprime lending, but the general principles apply more broadly. By 2006, mortgage brokers were originating 60–70 percent of all new loans. Such brokers have a significant informational advantage vis-à-vis many loan applicants. Yet outside of California, Ohio, and New York, neither federal nor state law assigns a duty of fiduciary care to the broker on behalf of the borrower. Just as SIVs evolved into a shadowy, less-regulated banking system, mortgage brokers may have evolved as a less-accountable way of dealing with consumer lending laws. A classic government responsibility is to set the rules within which contracting can occur. While it would be inappropriate for government to specify what sort of loans can be made to an individual, it is quite appropriate to impose upon mortgage brokers some fiduciary obligation to borrowers. I applaud the Fed's amendments to Regulation Z (July 2008), which explicitly assigned such responsibility to brokers.

Finally, I'd like to call attention to the government's decision to outsource some important evaluations of a bank's asset quality to the credit rating agencies. This process began with revisions to Basel I, and continues in both the Standardized and Risk-Based approaches to capital adequacy calculation under Basel II. Two "quantitative impact studies" (QIS) undertaken by the Basel Committee on Bank Supervision confirm that Basel II requires less capital than Basel I, in part because of capital concessions for highly rated securities. Given the demonstrated incentive conflicts under which rating agencies operate, an expanded reliance on their opinions makes me nervous. At the same time, I am not sure (exactly) how to change things for the better.

5. Summary

The subprime crisis has taught us some valuable lessons about prices, portfolio opaqueness, and the value of reputation-based implicit contracts. Market discipline has performed poorly in leading firms to follow prudent operational procedures. Market prices (CDS spreads) have differentiated stronger from weaker firms, but provided no advance indication of large risk concentrations in specific firms. Yet poor government supervision also contributed to the crisis. The information provided by market prices can be used effectively to hasten supervisory actions, which will reduce the social cost of financial failures. Rather than assert that market discipline is perfect, I would defend it the same way Winston Churchill defended democracy in a 1947 speech before the House of Commons:

> No one pretends that democracy is perfect or all-wise. Indeed, it has been said that democracy is the worst form of government except all

those other forms that have been tried from time to time. (http://en.wikiquote.org/wiki/Winston_Churchill).

References

Akerlof, G. A. (1970). The market for 'lemons': quality and the market mechanism. *Quarterly Journal of Economics*, 84, August, 488–500.

Ashcraft, A. B. and T. Schuermann (2008). Understanding the securitization of subprime mortgage credit. *Federal Reserve Bank of New York Staff Report 318.*

Berger, A. N., Davies, M. Sally and M. J. Flannery (2000). Comparing market and regulatory assessments of bank performance: who knows what when? *Journal of Money, Credit and Banking*, 32, August, 641–670.

Berger, A., R. DeYoung, M. J. Flannery, O. Oztekin, and D. Lee (2008). Why do large banking organizations hold so much capital? *Journal of Financial Services Research*, 34(2/3).

Bhardwaj, G. and R. Sengupta, Where's the smoking gun? A study of underwriting standards for U.S. subprime mortgages. *Federal Reserve Bank of St. Louis working paper.*

Bliss, R. R. and M. J. Flannery (2002). Market discipline in the governance of U.S. bank holding companies: monitoring vs. influencing. *European Finance Review*, 6, January, 361–395.

Bond, P., I. Goldstein and E. S. Prescott (forthcoming). Market-based regulation and the informational content of prices. *Review of Financial Studies.*

CNN.com, FBI warns of mortgage fraud 'epidemic', (September 17, 2004) International Edition.

Coval, J. D., J. W. Jurek, and E. Stafford (2008). Economic catastrophe bonds. HBS Finance Working Paper No. 07-102, April.

DeYoung, R., M. Flannery, W. Lang, and S. Sorescu (2001), The information content of bank exam ratings and subordinated debt prices, *Journal of Money, Credit and Banking*, 33, 900–925.

Diamond, D. W. (1984). Financial intermediation and delegated monitoring, *Review of Economic Studies*, 51, July, 393–414.

Doms, M. E. and K. John (2007). Innovations in Mortgage Markets and Increase Spending on Housing. Federal Reserve Bank of San Francisco Working Paper No. 2007–05, August.

Flannery, M. J. (2009). *Market Discipline in Bank Supervision*, Oxford Handbook on Banking, (forthcoming).

Flannery, M. J., S. Kwan, and M. Nimalendran (2004). Market evidence on the opaqueness of banking firms' assets. *Journal of Financial Economics*, 71, March, 419–460.

Flannery, M. J. and Rangan, P. Kasturi (2008). What caused the bank capital build-up of the 1990s? *Review of Finance*, 12(2), 391–429.

Gorton, G. (2008). The Panic of 2007, Yale School of Management working paper, August 25.

Greenlaw, D., J. Hatzius, A. K. Kashyap, and H. S. Shin (2008). Leveraged Losses: Lessons from the Mortgage Market Meltdown, U.S. Monetary Policy Forum, Rosenburg Institute, Brandeis International Business School and Initiative on Global Markets. University of Chicago Graduate School of Business.

Gropp, R., J. Vesala, and G. Vulpes (2006). Equity and bond market signals as leading indicators of bank fragility, *Journal of Money, Credit and Banking*, 38, March, 399–428.

Hansell, S. (2008). *How Wall Street Lied to Its Computers*. New York Times, September 18.

Hovakimian, A. G., A. Kayhan, and S. Titman (2008). How Do Managers Target Their Credit Ratings? A Study of Credit Ratings and Managerial Discretion, University of Texas working paper, March.

Iannotta, G. (2006). Testing for opaqueness in the European banking industry: evidence from bond credit ratings. *Journal of Financial Services Research*, 30, May, 287–309.

Kisgen, D. J. (2006). Credit ratings and capital structure. *Journal of Finance*, 61(3), June, 1035–1072.

Krainer, J., and J. A. Lopez, (2004). Incorporating equity market information into supervisory monitoring models. *Journal of Money, Credit and Banking*, 36, December, 1043–1067.

Kwast, M. *et al.*, (1999). Using Subordinated Debt as an Instrument of Market Discipline, Study Group on Subordinated Notes and Debentures, Federal Reserve Board of Governors Staff Study 172, December.

McGuire, T. J. (1995). Ratings in Regulation: A Petition to the Gorillas, Speech by Thomas J. McGuire, executive vice president and director of Moody's Corporate Department, before the U.S. Securities and Exchange Commission, April 28.

Mishkin, Frederic, Anatomy of a financial crisis. *Evolutionary Economics*, 2, 115–130.

Morgan, D. P. (2002). Rating banks: risk and uncertainty in an opaque industry. *American Economic Review*, 92, September, 874–888.

Morgenson, G. (2007). Inside the Countrywide Lending Spree *New York Times*, August 26.

Pennacchi, G. G.. (1988). Loan sales and the cost of bank capital. *Journal of Finance*, 43, June, 375–396.

Rajan, R. G. (2001). Comment on Market Discipline in the Governance of U.S. Bank Holding Companies: Monitoring vs. Influencing, in *Prudential*

Supervision: What Works and What Doesn't (F. Mishkin (ed.)), The University of Chicago Press, Chicago, Illinois, Chapter 4, pp. 143–146.
UBS Board of Directors (2008). Shareholder Report on UBS's Write-Downs, 18 April, 2008.
United States Securities Exchange Commission, "Summary Report of Issues Identified in the Commission Staff's Examinations of Select Credit Rating Agencies By the Staff of the Office of Compliance Inspections and Examinations Division of Trading and Markets and Office of Economic Analysis," July 2008.

Comments: Implications for Bank Capital Standards/Regulation

Robert E. Litan*
The Kauffman Foundation and The Brookings Institution

The papers prepared for this panel are excellent. In my comments, I will focus specifically on how the recent and ongoing (as of this writing) financial crisis should affect bank capital standards.

I will not mince words. Our current capital standards — those developed by the Basel Committee — have failed miserably. They took far too long to refine, roughly 10 years. By the time the Basel II standards were ready to implement, we were already in the early stages of this crisis.

The Basel standards were also too easily circumvented. As we know now, many of the largest banks for whom they were intended ran around them by creating supposedly off-balance sheet "Structured Investment Vehicles" (SIVs), largely to purchase the mortgage and other asset-backed securities they originated. When the crisis first become evident during the summer of 2007, the SIVs could not roll over the commercial paper they had issued to fund the securities. After some initial attempts to avoid this fate, the bank sponsors of the SIVs eventually took their assets and liabilities, and their embedded loses, back on the banks' balance sheets. As it turned out, the losses proved so great that, about one year later, governments in the United States and Europe felt compelled to provide massive injections of capital to keep many of the remaining large banks alive (and, in the case of the United States, smaller banks too).

* Robert E. Litan is Vice President for Research and Policy, The Kauffman Foundation, and Senior Fellow, Economic Studies and Global Economics Programs, The Brookings Institution.

The financial turmoil has unmasked other problems with the Basel standards. In focusing heavily on bank capital, they overlooked the importance of liquidity. The standards unwisely delegated too much authority to the credit rating agencies to define the risks of different types of assets. Likewise, letting the large and apparently sophisticated banks use their own internal models to determine the appropriate amount of risk-weighted capital these institutions should have had also clearly was mistaken (totally apart from the banks' use of SIVs to circumvent the capital requirements).

Although the magnitude of the problems among the banks of developed countries has been surprising, the disappointment with the Basel standards should not be unexpected. For years, a number of academic scholars have been severely critical of the Basel process, arguing that in lieu of the 400-plus pages of complexity in the revised standards, banks and financial systems would have been safer had the Basel participants agreed on a relatively simple requirement that large banking organizations back a set percentage, say 2 percent, of their assets (perhaps plus their off-balance-sheet liabilities) with uninsured subordinated debt. The Shadow Financial Regulatory Committee, of which I am a member, has long called for this requirement. So have a number of former Governors of the Federal Reserve Board.

To be sure, the Basel II standards (as did their predecessors) *allowed* banks to count subordinated debt as Tier II capital, but a set percentage has never been *required.* The arguments for a mandate are straightforward.

Subordinated debt holders are naturally risk averse, since they earn only a fixed interest rate on their investment and have no upside benefit from a bank's risk-taking. Moreover, because debt instruments are not deposits, their holders cannot demand repayment, even with a penalty, and cannot "run" like depositors. Accordingly, there is no reason why regulators concerned with preventing systemic risk ever need to extend government guarantees to subordinated debt. These considerations make the holders of subordinated debt ideal sources of market discipline that need not be undermined by government bailouts.

A subordinated debt requirement could also have the added plus of providing earlier market-driven signals to regulators about potential problems in given banks. Admittedly, there is some debate on this subject in the literature, and indeed some evidence that holders of subordinated debt are no more clairvoyant than other creditors or regulators.[1] Nonetheless, existing studies of effectiveness of subordinated debt in providing early warning are limited by the fact that the issuance of such debt currently is voluntary. It is possible that the subordinated debt market would provide better signaling if banks were required to issue such instruments regularly, as their balance sheets expand. The inability of a bank to sell subordinated debt in the open market clearly would provide a strong signal of a bank's looming difficulties. Indeed, knowing this, managers who know their banks are weak would avoid expanding their assets and thus their risks for precisely this reason.

Might banks be able to use off-balance-sheet entities and perhaps other not-yet-born devices to circumvent a subordinated debt requirement, much as a number of them did in forming SIVs to circumvent the current bank capital rules? This is always possible, but much less likely with mandated subordinated debt. Precisely because they do not benefit from any upside associated with financial games, subordinated debt holders (who tend primarily to be institutional investors) have strong incentives to ask bank management what risks they are taking that may not be reflected in their published financial statements.

Recent events have demonstrated one possible weakness with a subordinated debt requirement, but it is one that can be cured, in my view. We have just discovered that in times of crisis, bank problems come in bunches, not just in "one-offs". In such environments, retail and institutional investors can become so highly risk averse that they run to 'safe havens' like Treasury bills and notes and forsake investments carrying any kind of risk, including such instruments as subordinated debt. If regulators were to insist in such a time of crisis that banks meet a mandatory minimum percentage of subordinated debt, they would not be in a position to accept bank deposits, and thus to fund new loans. The financial system itself could be put at risk.

For this reason, bank regulators, in consultation with the central bank, must be able to include a "systemic risk" exception in any subordinated debt requirement. In extreme circumstances where the market for bank subordinated debt in general has dried up, regulators should be able to suspend the requirement.

In short, in an ideal world, I would vastly streamline the Basel bank capital standards by eliminating each of the three pillars and replacing

---

[1] See, for example the paper by Mark Flannery for this conference.

them with a leverage ratio applanded by a subordinated debt requirement, with a systemic risk exception. It is possible that such a requirement would also eliminate the need for a separate liquidity requirement, although I would be open to considering one. I would also retain the Basel Committee itself to continue to provide a forum in which bank supervisors from the member countries can regularly meet to discuss institution-specific and overall system-wide risks.

I recognize, of course, that we do not live in an ideal world. Too many governments and financial regulators who work for them may have too much of an interest in retaining and indeed continuing to refine the current Basel II standards, rather than adopting the suggestion I have just outlined.

In that event, I would counsel U.S. bank regulators, at least, to supplement the Basel standards with a sub-debt requirement that applies to banks chartered in this country. This financial crisis has demonstrated that the safety of our banks is too important to be entrusted to a set of standards that are ineffective at best, and potentially counter-productive at worst. Even though policy makers seem to temporarily have thrown market discipline out the window in rescuing banks and other financial institutions, it is not only possible but necessary to find a way to restore market discipline for our largest banks going forward. A subordinated debt requirement is a good answer to this challenge.

VII. IMPLICATIONS FOR REGULATION OF FINANCIAL MARKETS AND INSTRUMENTS

Implications of the Crisis for Regulation

Mark Carey*
Board of Governors of the Federal Reserve System

1. Introduction

In this essay, I offer perspective about the relative importance of causes of the current financial crisis and about ways forward. Most of the causes discussed below have been mentioned in the popular press, but most press reports and public discussion have given too much weight to a single cause, credit losses on subprime mortgage loans to U.S. borrowers, and too little weight to incentive conflicts and to the nature of the incompleteness in the regulatory paradigm that exists today. It is a truism among economists that policy actions should be targeted to mitigate specific market failures that lead to undesirable outcomes. Thus, the actions and reforms that are implemented over the next few years are less likely to be effective if their design is based on an unrealistic weighting of the causes of the crisis.

This essay, and the conference remarks upon which it is based, is not intended to provide a rigorous analysis, nor does it provide much in the way of supporting evidence. Instead, it makes assertions about the consistency of causes with facts. Such assertions merely represent my own opinions as an experienced observer, which clearly are not a sufficient basis for action. Thus, this essay should be viewed mainly as a suggestion of topics for research.

---

* Mark Carey is an Advisor in the Division of International Finance at the Board of Governors of the Federal Reserve System in Washington, DC. This essay represents the opinions of the author, not those of the Board of Governors or the Federal Reserve System.

I begin by suggesting that six popularly cited causes are not important enough to be viewed as dominant causes, although each contributed to some extent. They are as follows:

- Financial engineering;
- Bad risk-management models;
- Subprime mortgage credit losses;
- Inadequate capital at major financial institutions;
- Inept prudential supervision; and
- Moral hazard from government safety nets (deposit insurance, too-big-to-fail, and other implicit and explicit guarantees).

I then suggest that two problems that have received less attention are central to the crisis:

- Asymmetric incentive-compensation and career profiles in the financial industry; and
- A failure to appreciate the importance to aggregate liquidity of bank-run-type behavior by market participants, combined with a regulatory model that focused too much on solvency and not enough on liquidity and runs.

2. Not Financial Engineering

Financial engineering has been a favorite target of many who worry about financial crises for at least 20 years. Early worries about instability arising from popular use of interest rate swaps has given way to similar concerns about credit derivatives, securitization, and other innovations. Such activities have indeed been used by some to take on risk (but others shed risk at the same time). And it is true that a casual inspection of the history of the last two decades identifies more periods of financial turbulence in the advanced economies that in the preceding decades (turbulence not associated with macroeconomic or monetary imbalances). But correlation is not causality, and many instruments that have imposed losses on financial institutions in the current episode have been around for a long time (for example, residential mortgages, corporate loans, and municipal bonds). Moreover, viewed as broad asset classes, the most frequently mentioned innovations have functioned as intended: Credit derivatives written on reference entities that experienced contractually specified credit events have settled (and relatively smoothly). Securitization vehicles have mostly continued to allocate cash flows, and new issuance of some types of asset-backed securities has continued (such as credit-card securitizations), though other new-issue securitization markets are closed at least for the moment. Some hedge funds have failed and more will do so, but a significant fraction of hedge funds fail each year.

None of this is to say that the aforementioned instruments and institutions are trading near par or are not stressed. But as I argue below, the problem is not so much with the innovations themselves, but rather how they have interacted with the incentives of agents in the financial industry. Substantially restricting such innovations is not likely to substantially reduce the likelihood of future crises.

3. Not Bad Risk-Management Models

Every financial institution's risk-management models and procedures failed to adequately allow for the systematic and systemic volatility of funding and market liquidity that has been observed since August 2007. In that sense, the current crisis could indeed be viewed as a failure of risk-management technology. However, most who point to risk-management failures have credit risk in mind.[1]

Risk management is thought to have failed because it failed to properly capture the risks that materialized or, in a more extreme view, is thought to be an amplifier of turbulence because too many financial entities use the same models and end up holding the same positions (see Persaud, 2000). Recent research has offered no support for the amplification view (Berkowitz and O'Brien, 2006; and Jorion, 2006). I believe that the fact that many financial institutions took positions that imposed large losses is due not so much to a fundamental failure of risk-management and modeling technology, but rather to its improper use.

Effective management of risk at the level of a large financial institution requires application of a number of different tools and exercise of good judgment. For example, it is well known in the risk-management community that value-at-risk and similar models do a poor job of measuring the

[1] Credit losses can show up not only as loss provisions or other write-offs but also as market-value losses of assets held in trading or available-for-sale accounts.

risk of very infrequent but very bad loss events. Variants of well-designed stress tests are more useful for measuring such risks. At the very least, such tests should 1) employ asset price and quantity changes at least as large as have been observed historically; 2) extrapolate to larger changes; and 3) be attentive to the higher correlations of price and quantity movements that occur during periods of market stress. Moreover, financial institutions must take stress test results seriously in managing exposures. In addition, where the usable historical record is short, for example in the case of new instruments, financial institutions' exposure must be limited (or economic capital allocations must be large) because risk cannot be measured well.

In the past few years, the senior management of too many financial institutions did not use risk-management technology properly, either deliberately or accidentally. For example, in a public report on the losses of UBS that echoes UBS's own report, the Swiss Federal Banking Commission writes, "UBS was not aware of the extent and the nature of its risk exposure to the Subprime mortgage and related markets until the beginning of August 2007, and was thus unable to take appropriate measures in a timely manner".[2] Of course, if UBS did not even track its exposure, it could not possibly measure or manage the risk associated with the exposure. Such failures of exposure tracking were not limited to UBS. These and other failings were not failures of risk-management technology but they were failures of the senior management of financial institutions to use the technology property and to govern their firms properly.

4. Not Subprime Mortgage-Related Credit Losses

Many estimates of mortgage credit losses have appeared in the absence of Lehmen's failure, I believe that ultimate credit losses from mid-2007, cumulated over the next few years, on all U.S. residential mortgages (not just subprime) will be around $600 billion.[3] Although it is a substantial amount, $600 billion is far too small to threaten solvency of the financial

[2] Swiss Federal Banking Commission (2008), p. 2.

[3] By "ultimate" loss I mean the eventual loss of principal net of recoveries. At the moment, secondary market prices of most mortgages and related financial instruments are trading below their "fundamental" value, meaning prices embed substantial illiquidity and uncertainty discounts, so current mark-to-market losses on such instruments are surely larger than ultimate losses.

system as a whole. For example, U.S. chartered commercial banks alone had over $1 trillion of equity capital at mid-2007. The nonbank portions of U.S. bank holding companies, U.S. investment banks, and European banks and related entities had far more capital than chartered U.S. banks, and this leaves aside insurance companies, pension funds, and other entities that will absorb some of the ultimate losses. Moreover, ongoing operating income of financial institutions, though lower than in good times, will cover a significant share of the credit losses during the next few years.

Of course, losses are not spread evenly across the financial system, and some entities with concentrated mortgage exposure have already failed or been acquired, such as IndyMac. But the identities of large entities with large exposure concentrations were pretty well known by early 2008 at the latest, so it is difficult to believe that uncertainty about ultimate loss concentrations was responsible for the continuing crisis during 2008. (Of course, as the crisis worsened, secondary market trading prices of many instruments fell by far more than reasonable estimates of ultimate loss rates imply. But the dynamics of such price fluctuations should not be attributed to fundamental credit risk.)

As another reality check, ultimate credit losses on the debt of a subset of large U.S. corporations that defaulted during the years 2000 through 2003 were about $180 billion.[4] The holders of such debt were mostly banks and other leveraged investors, and the broader financial system barely burped as a result of such losses.[5] $180 billion is less than $600 billion, but not enormously less.

Rather than being the primary problem, subprime credit losses might better be described as a hand grenade thrown into a room full of (liquidity) dynamite. The grenade is damaging, but the major problem is the dynamite and the explosion of the dynamite itself amplifies mortgage losses well beyond the amount of the original mortgage shock.

5. Not Inadequate Capitalization of Banks

A common prescription for prevention of future crisis is that banks should be better capitalized. But as I have just argued, global banking system

[4] Author's calculations based on S&P's Creditpro database.

[5] The widespread financial distress at the time was driven by other factors, especially the pop of an equity price bubble, but very few banks failed and credit continued to be available to creditworthy entities.

capital at the start of the crisis was adequate to protect solvency. Moreover, the steady stream of write-offs by major financial institutions that has been witnessed over the past 15 months has been accompanied by inflows of new capital. As of this writing, over $600 billion has been written off globally (approximately the amount of my estimate of ultimate subprime mortgage credit losses) and over $600 billion of capital has been raised. The latter does not include the portion of net earnings that was retained over the same period.[6] Even though capital plus retained earnings kept up with ongoing write-offs and, in the aggregate, a portion of the write-offs may ultimately be reversed, the crisis grew more severe through mid-October 2008. These gross facts seem inconsistent with a shortage of capital as the core problem in the current episode.

6. Not Inept Prudential Supervision

Inadequate prudential supervision by the authorities has frequently been suggested as a primary cause of the crisis. Of course, in one sense, this must be correct: If the authorities had only recognized the risks and acted to prevent them, no crisis would have occurred. A more useful question is whether supervisory authorities could have been expected to do better. In my opinion, the answer is generally "no" for two reasons.

First, regardless of the degree of their organizational independence, supervisory authorities operate under political constraints. They can constrain individual entities that stray from the herd toward excessive risk-taking, but if enough of the herd of financial institutions increases risk-taking, it is rarely possible for the authorities to apply broadly effective restraints (an exception is countries in which the public memory of a financial system problem and associated recession is recent and painful enough to support a broad political consensus in favor of restraint). Often the risk-taking involves an element of financial innovation, and an argument that is usually effective with the public and its elected representatives is that "it's different this time". Supervisory entities understand the pattern very well, but they are not empowered to prevent its recurrence.

Second, at large financial institutions, supervisory staff depend on the institutions' own risk-management system when they make assessments

[6] Source: Bloomberg (WDCI page).

of risk posture. At large institutions, the number of exposures is huge. It is effectively impossible for (an always relatively small number of) examiners to make their own bottom-up assessments. They can only make spot checks, and even these may be ineffective if the bank's own systems do not adequately reflect exposures. They can ask banks to improve risk-management systems that they perceive as inadequate, but such improvements are expensive and time-consuming. As a practical matter, if a financial institution does not know its own risk posture, the ability of supervisory entities to recognize and restrain risk-taking is quite limited. This is especially the case if the institution's senior management is not interested in knowing the institution's exposure to bad-tail risks, which are harder to detect than day-to-day risks.

To summarize, although official-sector bank supervision activity might be effective in an ideal world, it is unlikely to be effective in preventing systemic excessive risk-taking. By analogy, one might blame maintainers of beaches for not sweeping back the tide, but it is more apt to focus on the circumstances in which it is possible to sweep back the tide. None of this is to say that financial supervision and regulation should not be strengthened — that will surely be worthwhile — but only that such strengthening is not likely to be enough by itself to prevent future crises.

7. Not Moral Hazard from the Safety Net

Since the U.S. thrift and banking crises of the 1980s and early 1990s, the intellectual foundation of financial regulation and supervision and analysis of crises has been that "government is the problem". One branch of this view, most often applied to crises in some emerging-market economies, focuses on corruption and on distortions from direct government ownership or government pressure to allocate credit. The more relevant branch for the current crisis notes that government safety nets for financial institutions give them incentives to take excessive risk. If only the safety net could be weakened sufficiently, market discipline would appropriately determine an optimal level of risk-taking and material crises would not occur.

The details of the supporting argument matter. The conventional argument is that because at least some holders of financial institution debt expect to bear no losses in most bad states of the world (due to deposit insurance, too-big-to-fail guarantees, or lenient failure-resolution procedures), they accept returns on the debt that are low relative to those in the free-market equilibrium. With cheap financing, the *equity holders* of financial institutions, who are presumed to be in control of such institutions, naturally cause managers to move farther out on the risk dimension of the risk–return tradeoff than is socially optimal. The magnitude of incentives to take more risk is importantly related to capitalization: For a given safety net, the more leveraged the institution, the greater the increase in risk-taking due to the safety net.

This argument has three major weaknesses when applied to the current crisis. First, given that almost all major financial institutions were well capitalized during the period when they inflated their risk postures (especially in the United States), the size of the tail risks that institutions took seems to me to be too large to be attributable to the safety net distortion.[7] Second, in the United States, the FDIC Improvement Act of 1991 materially restricted the U.S. safety net. Though the number of bank failures from 1993 through 2006 was relatively small, uninsured depositors and holders of other liabilities of failed banks took losses, which should have established a presumption that the safety net was limited to insured deposits, thus making the distortion much smaller than before 1991. Indeed, as I argue below, market participants did have such a presumption and it worsened the crisis.

Third, it seems unlikely that outside equity holders actually control major financial institutions. Especially in the United States, large block holders are relatively rare, and the corporate governance literature offers evidence that diffuse equity holders rarely have much impact on the managers of large firms. It seems much more likely that the senior managers of major financial institutions are in effective control. I argue below that moral hazard associated with their incentives is a key problem. But this is different than moral hazard from the safety net, and policies targeted on the safety net distortion may be ineffective or even counterproductive if the safety net is not the only problem.

---

[7] The magnitude of the distortion should be amenable to simulation, but I have not myself done such simulations.

8. Asymmetric Financial Services Industry Compensation Profiles Did Contribute to the Crisis

It has been said that "there are no principals — everybody is an agent".[8] In the usual view of the role of the financial system, households and firms (the principals) delegate aspects of their saving and investment activity to financial firms (the agents), which then allocate capital to the highest and best uses in a faithful attempt to optimize portfolio risk and return for final savers. Motivating the agents to act in the interests of the principals is key.

As at other corporations, financial firms have designed compensation packages for senior executives (and some other employees, especially star traders and business line managers) that are tied to accounting and stock price measures and that confer relatively large rewards in good times. In bad times, the probability of such employees being fired is fairly high. However, unlike 40 or more years ago, the costs of being fired are often not large relative to the good-time gains.[9] Moreover, because the risk postures of financial institutions are opaque, outsiders have a limited ability to separate good short- and medium-term earnings performance that is due to skill and effort from that which is due to excessive risk-taking. That is, the principals (households and firms) have little ability to monitor the agents, and the agents' compensation setup offers powerful incentives for them to cause their financial institution to take on opaque risk.

There are exceptions: Incentives are different at firms with a partnership structure and unlimited liability (but few such firms remain). Sufficiently wealthy individuals would seem to have both the means and the incentive to monitor their financial service providers. Employees of university endowments may self-regulate because their social network depends somewhat on the financial health of the university.

Two standard mechanisms for controlling the principal-agent problem do not work well in the context of large U.S. financial institutions. One is

---

[8] Jeremy Stein, December 2007.

[9] Decades ago, major financial institutions were largely closed organizations that promoted from within, so expected returns to a fired employee's human capital were relatively low. Now, such employees routinely find jobs in the industry again, perhaps after some time off. CEOs are a special case in that the probability of finding another CEO job is relatively small. As compensation, their severance packages are often quite generous.

corporate governance pressure by holders of large blocks of the institution's equity.[10] However, most major financial institutions have few large blockholders, and where such blocks exist, they are controlled by other financial institutions, which in turn are run by "agents". A second potential control mechanism is "exit:"[11] If a firm does not serve the interests of its clients well, the clients will move their business to a different firm. By extension, if the financial services industry does not serve savers and investors well, they might purchase few or no services from the industry. But in reality, doing so is very difficult because saving and investing outside the financial system imposes large fixed and variable costs on savers and investors.

Given these facts, households and firms implicitly depend upon the government to monitor and discipline financial institution managers. However, its ability to do so is limited, as discussed previously.

Financial engineering has amplified the impact of asymmetric incentives in the financial services industry by making it easier for senior executives of financial institutions to lay on large risk positions that are difficult for outsiders to detect (most insiders at an individual institution are also likely to be unaware of tail risk positions). Restricting financial engineering is not likely to be a constructive step. Financial engineering taken alone is welfare-improving, and restricting it is not likely to remove the incentive problem.

9. An Incomplete Regulatory Model Did Contribute to the Crisis

At least since the early 1990s, financial supervision and regulation have been increasingly focused on limiting the moral hazard associated with the safety net, and have been driven by a view that bank insolvency is the main source of systemic risk. The notion was that moral hazard would be reduced enough not to be a major systemic threat by higher levels of bank capitalization. Moreover, the United States placed legal restrictions on how regulators could resolve bank failures and implemented a prompt-corrective-action (PCA) regime of supervisory penalties associated with capital triggers. It was presumed that solvent banks that

[10] Many small U.S. commercial banks are family-owned or controlled by a few individuals, so in principle governance might be effective.

[11] See Hirschman (1970).

encountered liquidity problems would be able to borrow at their central bank's primary credit facility until liquidity problems dissipated. Bank runs as a threat to systemic stability were implicitly thought to be a thing of the past.

By implicitly targeting only conventional moral hazard associated with the safety net, the current regulatory regime was not focused on the distortions that were central to the current crisis. Moreover, casual observation has convinced me that the higher capitalization of banks that followed implementation of Basel 1 did little to prevent the crisis and that the crisis was amplified by PCA and least-cost failure resolution methods.

Rather than viewing the U.S. "well-capitalized" Basel risk-based capital ratio of 10 percent of total assets as a minor tripwire, market participants seem to have viewed it as something similar to an insolvency point.[12] And because resolutions of bank failures in the U.S. since the early 1990s had demonstrated that uninsured depositors and other claimants were exposed to loss in event of failure, wholesale funding market participants ran from any bank that was rumored to "need capital" (one rumored to have plans to write off enough losses to move their ratio even a little bit below 10 percent).[13] Such banks would not borrow from their central bank's primary credit facility because the circumstances surrounding the failure of Northern Rock in the United Kingdom had taught bankers that the market would view any such borrowing as a sign of further weakness and would intensify their run.[14]

Thus, runs led to a classic fire-sale-of-assets scenario in which the bank experiencing the run would desperately try to raise funds by selling assets at discounts and by paying very high rates in wholesale and retail funding markets (both of which would reduce solvency). As the crisis continued, central banks altered operating procedures and some introduced

---

[12] Pressure applied over the years by rating agencies caused most European banks to have ratios above 10 percent as well, even though U.S. regulations did not apply to them.

[13] In Diamond and Dybvig's (1983) model of runs, "sunspots" (meaning random exogenous events) trigger runs. Though the runs seen recently are often viewed as being driven by concerns about solvency, it is also reasonable to think of them as sunspot runs in that the validity of the solvency concerns did not matter.

[14] Northern Rock's intention to borrow from the Bank of England was leaked around 7:00 p.m. on a Wednesday night. An official announcement followed the next day. Over the ensuing four days, about one-quarter of Northern Rock's retail deposits were withdrawn, and virtually all maturing wholesale liabilities were not rolled over. A blanket guarantee by the U.K. government followed.

novel facilities for providing liquidity, but many of these are not perfectly suited for providing medium-term funding to a solvent bank experiencing a run. Moreover, most central banks are not comfortable being the primary source of a bank's funding for any length of time, so banks experiencing a run come under heavy pressure to sell themselves at a steeply discounted price to another entity.

As it became clearer that any institution in the U.S. or Europe could experience a major run triggered by rumors (even if unfounded), and that the consequences of a run would be devastating, banks found it more and more difficult to raise capital. A potential investor could examine the bank's books and determine that it was in fact solvent and likely to remain so, but this provided little assurance because runs were not necessarily associated with insolvency. Eventually, so many major institutions were experiencing wholesale funding runs that money market pressures became gargantuan and the official sector was forced to respond with broad-based guarantees and capital injections. These have a good chance of working because they address run risks, and such risks are central to the current crisis, whereas the *ex ante* regulatory regime, with its focus on solvency and market discipline, not only did not effectively address run risks, it actually amplified them. A complete solution is difficult to see at the moment.

10. Ways Forward

Many commonly mentioned reforms have little prospect of reducing the probability that similar crises will recur in the future.

- More market discipline is unlikely to help, as the discipline would be applied largely by "agents" with distorted incentives.
- Higher capital requirements are unlikely to help. They will only set the implicit run trigger point at a higher level of capital to assets. Even the efficacy of countercyclical capital buffers (extra capital above the well-capitalized minimum that can be drawn down in bad times) is questionable if market participants interpret a drawdown of buffer capital as a signal to run.
- Preventive government intervention as systemic risks are building up is unlikely to be effective because senior financial industry executives will use the political process to apply pressure to weaken such intervention and will attempt to hide the risks they take.

One might hope to constrain incentive compensation in the financial services industry. But incentive compensation does serve useful purposes, and any attempt to regulate it would amount to very unusual interference with labor market operation. Moreover, how would the set of firms and executives to which such regulations would apply be determined? Would they apply to a manufacturing company with a major finance subsidiary, such as General Electric? What about to hedge fund managers? Regulating compensation at some firms might simply cause financial activity to migrate into other types of firm.

Central banks can redesign their facilities for providing liquidity to financial institutions, and formal and informal failure-resolution procedures can be redesigned to deal more flexibly with institutions in different circumstances and with systemic episodes. My impression is that the official sector in the United States and Europe is already grappling with how to do so. Such improvements in crisis management capabilities will be helpful. But it is not clear that they will be enough to substantially reduce the probability of future crises if the core incentive conflicts are not mitigated.

11. Concluding Remarks

I have argued that risk-taking incentives rooted in asymmetric financial industry compensation schemes, as well as supervisory, regulatory, and central bank liquidity-provision models that did not fit recent circumstances, are the most important sources of the current crisis. I have argued that other commonly cited causes are less important, though they may have contributed. These include subprime mortgage credit losses, the standard moral hazard associated with official safety nets, financial engineering, bad risk-management technology, inept prudential supervision, and inadequate financial institution capital.

A conventionally ideal path toward reforms designed to limit future crises would target the fundamental problems. Taking as given that there is little prospect of putting "principals" in charge of financial services firms, ways forward might include the following: 1) greatly reduce the asymmetry in incentive compensation in the financial services industry (but this might be costly in other ways); 2) develop a more complete model of financial services industry distortions that supports clearer thinking about the tradeoffs between controlling conventional moral hazard, principal-agent problems, and runs; and 3) alter supervision, regulation, central bank liquidity facilities, as well as crisis management procedures, to better reflect such tradeoffs.

Some such changes appear more challenging to implement effectively than others. But the first step toward doing so is a burst of research that will help us clarify our thinking. Such research may reveal new reform strategies. Thus, this essay should be viewed not so much as a diagnosis of the crisis nor as a confident prediction of the proper way forward, but rather as a call for research that tries to start researchers off with the idea that all may not have been as conventional wisdom has so far portrayed it to have been.

References

Diamond, D. W. and P. H. Dybvig (1983). Bank runs, deposit insurance, and liquidity. *Journal of Political Economy*, 91, 401–19.

Hirschman, A. (1970). *Exit, Voice, and Loyalty: Responses to Decline in Firms, Organizations, and States*. Cambridge, MA: Harvard University Press.

Jorion, P. (2006). Bank trading risk and systemic risk. In Carey, Mark, and Rene M. Stulz (eds.). *The Risks of Financial Institutions*, pp. 29–57.

O'Brien, J. and J. Berkowitz (2006). Estimating bank trading risk: a factor model approach. In Carey, Mark, and Rene M. Stulz (eds.). *The Risks of Financial Institutions*, pp. 59–91.

Persaud, A. (2000). Sending the herd off the cliff edge. Institute of International Finance. Available at http://www.erisk.com/ResourceCenter/ERM/persaud.pdf.

Swiss Federal Banking Commission (2008). Subprime crisis: SFBC investigation into the causes of the write-downs of UBS AG. Report, September 30. Available at www.ebk.admin.ch/e/publik/medienmit/20081016/ubs-subprime-bericht-ebk-e.pdf.

The Seven Deadly Frictions of Subprime Mortgage Credit Securitization

Adam B. Ashcraft*
Federal Reserve Bank of New York

Til Schuermann†
Federal Reserve Bank of New York and Wharton Financial Institutions Center

The securitization of mortgage loans is a complex process that involves a number of different players. Figure 1 provides an overview of the players, their responsibilities, the important frictions that exist between the players, and the mechanisms used in order to mitigate these frictions. An overarching friction which plagues every step in the process is asymmetric information: usually one party has more information about the asset than another. We think that understanding these frictions and evaluating the mechanisms designed to mitigate their importance is essential to understanding how the securitization of subprime loans could generate bad outcomes.[1]

1. Frictions Between the Mortgagor and Originator: Predatory Lending

The process starts with the mortgagor or borrower, who applies for a mortgage in order to purchase a property or to refinance an existing mortgage. The originator, possibly through a broker (yet another intermediary

*Research Officer, Financial Intermediation, Federal Reserve Bank of New York; email adam.ashcraft@ny.frb.org.
†Vice-President, Financial Intermediation, Federal Reserve Bank of New York and Wharton Financial Institutions Center; email til.schuermann@ny.frb.org.
[1] A recent piece in *The Economist* (September 20, 2007) provides a nice description of some of the frictions described here.

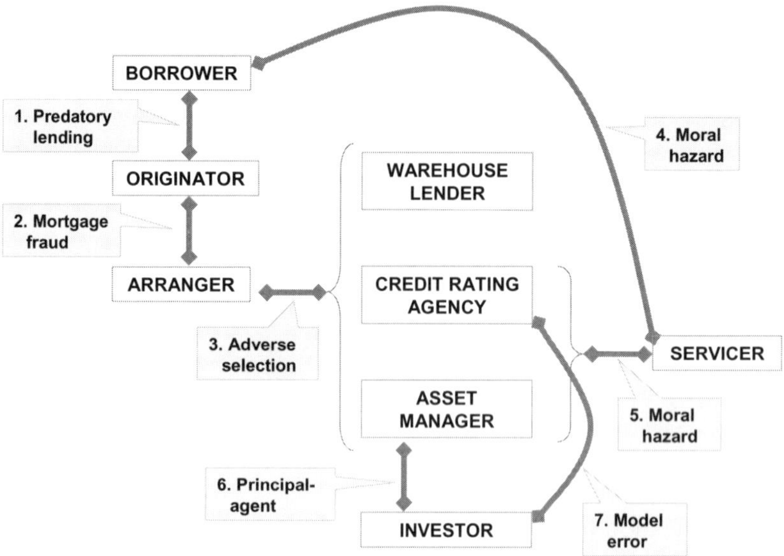

Figure 1. Key players and frictions in subprime mortgage credit securitization.

in this process), underwrites and initially funds and services the mortgage loans. Table 1 documents the top 10 subprime originators in 2006, which are a healthy mix of commercial banks and non-depository specialized mono-line lenders. The originator is compensated through fees paid by the borrower (points and closing costs), and by the proceeds of the sale of the mortgage loans. For example, the originator might sell a portfolio of loans with an initial principal balance of \$100 million for \$102 million, corresponding to a gain on sale of \$2 million. The buyer is willing to pay this premium because of anticipated interest payments on the principal as well as prepayment penalties.

The first friction in securitization is between the borrower and the originator. In particular, subprime borrowers can be financially unsophisticated. For example, a borrower might be unaware of all of the best interest rates for a particular type of loan. Moreover, even if this is known, the borrower might be unable to make the best choice between different financial options. This friction leads to the possibility of being taken advantage of by a lender or mortgage broker. This friction obviously becomes more acute as loans become more complex and the true cost of

Table 1. Top subprime mortgage originators.

		2006		2005	
Rank	Lender	Volume ($b)	Share (%)	Volume ($b)	Change (%)
1	HSBC	52.8	8.8	58.6	–9.9
2	New Century Financial	51.6	8.6	52.7	–2.1
3	Countrywide	40.6	6.8	44.6	–9.1
4	CitiGroup	38.0	6.3	20.5	85.5
5	WMC Mortgage	33.2	5.5	31.8	4.3
6	Fremont	32.3	5.4	36.2	–10.9
7	Ameriquest Mortgage	29.5	4.9	75.6	–61.0
8	Option One	28.8	4.8	40.3	–28.6
9	Wells Fargo	27.9	4.6	30.3	–8.1
10	First Franklin	27.7	4.6	29.3	–5.7
	Top 25	543.2	90.5	604.9	–10.2
	Total	600.0	100.0	664.0	–9.8

Source: Inside Mortgage Finance (2007).

credit is obscured.[2] Predatory lending is defined by Morgan (2007) as the welfare-reducing provision of credit, and typically involves the steering of a borrower into a product which is more profitable for the lender and/or mortgage broker.

A recent study by Ernst, Bocian, and Li (2008) documents that otherwise similar loans that were originated by mortgage brokers carried interest rates which were on average 130 basis points higher than loans originated directly by lenders. This difference is larger for borrowers with low credit scores or high leverage, and positive or close to zero for borrowers with high credit scores or low leverage. In the presence of prepayment penalties, these high interest rates are essentially locked in after origination. The authors attribute this effect to the common practice of lenders who pay mortgage brokers a bonus called a Yield Spread Premium (YSP) for getting the borrower to agree to a higher interest rate.

[2] However, this view ignores the possibility that mortgage brokers used part of the yield premium spread (YSP) to defray borrowers' closing costs, which could explain at least part of the higher interest rate on brokered loans.

Moreover, the authors estimate that between 63 and 81 percent of all subprime loans were originated through mortgage brokers in 2006. These estimates appear consistent with a claim by Lewi Ranieri that as much as 50 percent of recent subprime origination could have been done by the government-sponsored enterprises (GSEs) at a lower interest rate. The authors conclude by arguing that YSP and pre-prepayment penalties should be banned on subprime loans, that lenders and investors should be held accountable for mortgage broker behavior, and that mortgage brokers should have a fiduciary duty to serve borrowers.

However, it is important not to throw the proverbial baby out with the bathwater, as prepayment penalties serve an important purpose, especially for subprime borrowers. A recent study by Mayer *et al.* (2007) documents that otherwise similar borrowers with prepayment penalties receive interest rates that are on average 80 basis points lower, with larger reductions for more risky borrowers. More importantly, borrowers with prepayment penalties default at a lower rate. This result is driven by the fact that risky borrowers without a prepayment penalty are more likely to repay their mortgage in response to a positive shock to home prices.

Finally, note that the discussion of predatory lending in subprime mortgage lending has a parallel to a similar policy debate about payday lending. A payday loan is typically a small loan (i.e. $300) made for short maturity (i.e. two weeks). The Center for Responsible Lending (2006) reports that 90 percent of payday lending revenues are based on fees stripped from trapped borrowers who refinance instead of repaying their loans, and that the typical payday borrower pays back $793 for a $325 loan. While these are extremely high interest rates, research by Flannery and Samolynk (2005) suggests that this is because the loan size is small relative to the costs of originating and default rates are quite high. Moreover, borrowers are willing to pay these high rates because the cost of the alternative — typically a bounced check or overdraft protection — has even greater costs. Interestingly, a recent academic study by Morse (2007) documents that the presence of payday lending makes communities more resilient to natural disasters, finding an impact on foreclosures, births, deaths, and even alcohol and drug treatment.

This friction is mitigated through federal, state, and local laws prohibiting certain lending practices and requiring certain disclosures of fees and interest rates, as well as the recent regulatory guidance on subprime lending.

2. Frictions Between the Originator and the Arranger: Predatory Lending and Borrowing

The pool of mortgage loans is typically purchased from the originator by an institution known as the arranger or issuer. The first responsibility of the arranger is to conduct due diligence on the originator. This review includes but is not limited to financial statements, underwriting guidelines, discussions with senior management, and background checks. The arranger is responsible for bringing together all the elements for the deal to close. In particular, the arranger creates a bankruptcy-remote trust that will purchase the mortgage loans, consults with the credit rating agencies in order to finalize the details about deal structure, makes necessary filings with the SEC, and underwrites the issuance of securities by the trust to investors. Table 2 documents the list of the 10 largest subprime mortgage-backed security (MBS) issuers in 2006. In addition to institutions which both originate and issue on their own, the list of issuers also includes investment banks that purchase mortgages from originators and issue their own securities. The arranger is typically compensated through

Table 2. Top subprime mortgage-backed security issuers.

		2006		2005	
Rank	Lender	Volume ($b)	Share (%)	Volume ($b)	Change (%)
1	Countrywide	38.5	8.6	38.1	1.1
2	New Century	33.9	7.6	32.4	4.8
3	Option One	31.3	7.0	27.2	15.1
4	Fremont	29.8	6.6	19.4	53.9
5	Washington Mutual	28.8	6.4	18.5	65.1
6	First Franklin	28.3	6.3	19.4	45.7
7	Residential Funding Corp	25.9	5.8	28.7	−9.5
8	Lehman Brothers	24.4	5.4	35.3	−30.7
9	WMC Mortgage	21.6	4.8	19.6	10.5
10	Ameriquest	21.4	4.8	54.2	−60.5
	Top 25	427.6	95.3	417.6	2.4
	Total	448.6	100.0	508.0	−11.7

Source: Inside Mortgage Finance (2007).

fees charged to investors and through any premium that investors pay on the issued securities over their par value.

The second friction in the process of securitization involves an information problem between the originator and arranger. In particular, the originator has an information advantage over the arranger with regard to the quality of the borrower. Without adequate safeguards in place, an originator can have the incentive to collaborate with a borrower in order to make significant misrepresentations on the loan application, which, depending on the situation, could be either construed as predatory lending (the lender convinces the borrower to borrow "too much") or predatory borrowing (the borrower convinces the lender to lend "too much").

While mortgage fraud has been around as long as the mortgage loan, it is important to understand that fraud becomes more prevalent in an environment of high and increasing home prices. In particular, when home prices are high relative to income, borrowers unwilling to accept a low standard of living can be tempted into lying on a mortgage loan application. When prices are high and rapidly increasing, there is an even greater incentive to commit fraud given that the cost of waiting is an even lower standard of living. Rapid home price appreciation also increases the return to speculative and criminal activity. Moreover, while benefits of fraud are increasing, the costs of fraud decline as expectations of higher future prices create equity that reduces the probability of default and severity of loss in the event of default.

It is clear that mortgage fraud was an important part of the story. A recent report by Fitch (2007) conducted an autopsy of 45 early payment defaults from late 2006. Early payment defaults occur when a borrower becomes seriously delinquent shortly after origination. In its study, Fitch investigated the loan files, finding widespread evidence of fraud that was ignored by the underwriting process: occupancy misrepresentation, suspicious items on credit reports, incorrect calculation of debt-to-income ratios, poor underwriting of stated income for reasonability, first-time homebuyers with questionable credit and income. In addition, research by Ben-David (2007) documents how sellers provided cash back to buyers at closing in a fashion that was neither detected nor priced by lenders. Buyers of properties where the seller hinted about giving cash back paid more for those properties and were more likely to be foreclosed upon. These effects were stronger when borrower leverage was higher. A paper by Seru *et al.* (2007) documents the lender's participation by focusing on loans near a 620 FICO score. In particular, it is easier for a lender to sell loans with a FICO score just above 620. To the extent that being able to sell loans reduces incentives for screening and monitoring, one might expect that loans just above 620 would perform worse than loans just below 620, and this is exactly what the authors document. Moreover, this effect is largest for low documentation loans where the lender has the greatest scope to help the borrower misrepresent income.

There are several important checks designed to prevent mortgage fraud, the first being the due diligence of the arranger. In addition, the originator typically makes a number of representations and warranties (R&W) about the borrower and the underwriting process. When these are violated, the originator generally must repurchase the problem loans. However, in order for these promises to have a meaningful impact on the friction, the originator must have adequate capital to buy back those problem loans. Moreover, when an arranger does not conduct or routinely ignores its own due diligence, as suggested in a recent Reuters piece by Rucker (Aug 1 2007), there is little to stop the originator from committing widespread mortgage fraud.

3. Frictions Between the Arranger and Third Parties: Adverse Selection

The pool of mortgage loans is sold by the arranger to a bankruptcy-remote trust, which is a special-purpose vehicle that issues debt to investors. This trust is an essential component of credit risk transfer, as it protects investors from bankruptcy of the originator or arranger. Moreover, the sale of loans to the trust protects both the originator and arranger from losses on the mortgage loans, provided that there have been no breaches of representations and warranties made by the originator.

There is an important information asymmetry between the arranger and third parties concerning the quality of mortgage loans. In particular, the fact that the arranger has more information about the quality of the mortgage loans creates an adverse selection problem: the arranger can securitize bad loans (the lemons) and keep the good ones (or securitize them elsewhere). This third friction in the securitization of subprime loans affects the relationship that the arranger has with the warehouse lender, the credit rating agency (CRA), and the asset manager. We discuss how each of these parties responds to this classic lemons problem.

3.1 *Adverse selection and the warehouse lender*

The arranger is responsible for funding the mortgage loans until all of the details of the securitization deal can be finalized. When the arranger is a depository institution, this can be done easily with internal funds. However, mono-line arrangers typically require funding from a third-party lender for loans kept in the "warehouse" until they can be sold. Since the lender is uncertain about the value of the mortgage loans, it must take steps to protect itself against overvaluing their worth as collateral. This is accomplished through due diligence by the lender, haircuts to the value of collateral, and credit spreads. The use of haircuts to the value of collateral implies that the bank loan is over-collateralized (o/c) — it might extend a $9 million loan against collateral of $10 million of underlying mortgages — forcing the arranger to assume a funded equity position — in this case $1 million — in the loans while they remain on its balance sheet.

We emphasize this friction because an adverse change in the warehouse lender's view of the value of the underlying loans can bring an originator to its knees. The failure of dozens of mono-line originators in the first half of 2007 can be explained in large part by the inability of these firms to respond to increased demands for collateral by warehouse lenders (Wei, 2007; Sichelman, 2007).

3.2 *Adverse selection and the asset manager*

The arranger underwrites the sale of securities secured by the pool of subprime mortgage loans to an asset manager, who is an agent for the ultimate investor. However, the information advantage of the arranger creates a standard lemons problem. This problem is traditionally mitigated by the market through the following means: reputation of the arranger, the arranger providing a credit enhancement to the securities with its own funding, any due diligence conducted by the portfolio manager on the arranger and originator, and through the use of short-term funding.

While this latter mechanism is an effective device in resolving the information problem between unsophisticated investors and informationally-advantaged arrangers, it makes the financial system fragile. In particular, this lemons problem became acute in August 2007 when investors in

Asset-backed Commercial Paper (ABCP) became nervous about mortgage exposure. This concern was aggravated in part by the decision by mortgage originators who relied on ABCP for funding to exercise the option to extend the maturities of outstanding paper. The subsequent run for the exits resulted in a significant decline in the amount of ABCP outstanding, putting stress on the balance sheets of banks that provided explicit or implicit liquidity support for sponsored ABCP conduits and Structured Investment Vehicles (SIVs).

This friction became important again in March 2008 as secured funding markets seized up in response to repo market lenders becoming nervous about their exposure to investment banks, ultimately forcing the shareholders of Bear Stearns to accept a rescue by JP Morgan Chase in order to avoid filing for bankruptcy protection.

3.3 *Adverse selection and credit rating agencies*

The rating agencies assign credit ratings on mortgage-backed securities issued by the trust. These opinions about credit quality are determined using publicly available rating criteria which map the characteristics of the pool of mortgage loans into an estimated loss distribution. From this loss distribution, the rating agencies calculate the amount of credit enhancement that a security requires in order for it to attain a given credit rating. The opinion of the rating agencies is vulnerable to the lemons problem (the arranger likely knows more) because they only conduct limited due diligence on the arranger and originator.

4. Frictions Between the Servicer and the Mortgagor: Moral Hazard

The trust employs a servicer who is responsible for collection and remittance of loan payments, making advances of unpaid interest by borrowers to the trust, accounting for principal and interest, customer service to the mortgagors, holding escrow or impounding funds related to payment of taxes and insurance, contacting delinquent borrowers, and supervising foreclosures and property dispositions. The servicer is compensated through a periodic fee paid by the trust. Table 3 documents the 10 largest

Table 3. Top subprime mortgage servicers.

		2006		2005	
Rank	**Lender**	**Volume ($b)**	**Share (%)**	**Volume ($b)**	**Change (%)**
1	Countrywide	119.1	9.6	120.6	−1.3
2	JP MorganChase	83.8	6.8	67.8	23.6
3	CitiGroup	80.1	6.5	47.3	39.8
4	Option One	69.0	5.6	79.5	−13.2
5	Ameriquest	60.0	4.8	75.4	−20.4
6	Ocwen Financial Corp	52.2	4.2	42.0	24.2
7	Wells Fargo	51.3	4.1	44.7	14.8
8	Homecomings Financial	49.5	4.0	55.2	−10.4
9	HSBC	49.5	4.0	43.8	13.0
10	Litton Loan Servicing	47.0	4.0	42.0	16.7
	Top 30	1,105.7	89.2	1,057.8	4.5
	Total	1,240	100.0	1,200	3.3

Source: Inside Mortgage Finance (2007).

subprime servicers in 2006, a mix of depository institutions and specialty non-depository mono-line servicing companies.

Moral hazard refers to changes in behavior in response to redistribution of risk, e.g., insurance may induce risk-taking behavior if the insured does not bear the full consequences of bad outcomes. Here, we have a problem where one party (the mortgagor) has unobserved costly effort that affects the distribution over cash flows which are shared with another party (the servicer), and the first party has limited liability (it does not share in downside risk).

An important moral hazard problem is the option of borrowers to walk away. In particular, with significant declines in home prices, millions of borrowers could find themselves underwater in their homes. Performing but underwater borrowers could find it difficult to sell their homes without bringing cash to closing, which limits their ability to move. Borrowers without this cash may find it in their interest to exercise the option to simply walk away from their homes. Moreover, this option to walk away can give borrowers significant bargaining power over lenders who do not want to foreclose in a difficult home price environment. A recent report by Experian (2007) provides some evidence that this is more than just conjecture, as there appear to have been changes to the pecking order of payments. Traditionally, borrowers paid their mortgages first and credit cards next. However, the credit score agency reports some evidence of borrowers making their credit card payments before their mortgages. Another piece of evidence is the existence of the web site www.youwalkaway.com, which asks underwater borrowers if they want to live in their homes for free for eight months and claims that foreclosure can be removed from a credit report.[3]

This friction is typically resolved through the down payment, which limits borrower leverage *ex ante*, and through modification of principal, which reduces borrower leverage *ex post*. An important challenge going forward is that frictions between the servicer and investor (discussed in the next section) put constraints on the ability of the servicer to modify the principal. The inability of investors to respond to the increased bargaining power of borrowers created by lower home prices through reductions of principal could result in unprecedented levels of foreclosure and loss as borrowers walk away.

5. Frictions Between the Servicer and Third Parties: Moral Hazard

The servicer can have a significantly positive or negative effect on the losses realized from the mortgage pool. Moody's estimates that servicer quality can affect the realized level of losses by plus or minus 10 percent. In this case, we have a similar problem as in the fourth friction, namely where one party (here the servicer) has unobserved costly effort that affects the distribution over cash flows which are shared with other

[3] The recent bankruptcy reform law has also adversely affected the bargaining power of mortgage lenders vis-à-vis other lenders. In particular, borrowers could previously file Chapter 7, have their credit card debts discharged, and keep their home. However, by making it more difficult for borrowers to file Chapter 7, the law has made mortgage lending more risky. A recent study by Morgan *et al.* (2008) documents that subprime foreclosures have increased more in states where the home equity exemptions are higher, which is where the impact of bankruptcy reform in limiting Chapter 7 filings is greatest.

parties, and the first party has limited liability (it does not share in downside risk).[4]

The servicing fee is a flat percentage of the outstanding principal balance of mortgage loans. The servicer is paid first out of receipts each month before any funds are advanced to investors. Since mortgage payments are generally received at the beginning of the month and investors receive their distributions near the end of the month, the servicer benefits from being able to earn interest on float.[5] In the event of a delinquency, the servicer must advance unpaid interest (and sometimes principal) to the trust as long as it is deemed collectable, which typically means that the loan is less than 90 days delinquent. In addition to advancing unpaid interest, the servicer must also keep paying property taxes and insurance premiums as long as it has a mortgage on the property. In the event of foreclosure, the servicer must pay all expenses out of pocket until the property is liquidated, at which point it is reimbursed for advances and expenses.

Note that the un-reimbursable expenses of the servicer are largely fixed and front-loaded: registering the loan in the servicing system, getting the initial notices out, doing the initial escrow analysis and tax setups, etc. At the same time, the income of the servicer is increasing in the amount of time that the loan is serviced. It follows that the servicer would prefer to keep the loan on its books for as long as possible. This means it has a strong preference to modify the terms of a delinquent loan and to delay foreclosure.

Resolving this problem involves a delicate balance. On the one hand, one can put hard rules into the pooling and servicing agreement limiting loan modifications, and an investor can invest effort into actively monitoring the servicer's expenses. On the other hand, the investor wants to give the servicer flexibility to act in the investor's best interest and does not want to incur too much expense in monitoring. This latter point is especially true since other investors will free-ride off of any one investor's effort. It is not surprising that the credit rating agencies play an

---

[4] Several points raised in this section were first raised in a February 20, 2007 post on the blog http://calculatedrisk.blogspot.com/ entitled "Mortgage Servicing for Ubernerds."

[5] In addition to the monthly fee, the servicer generally gets to keep late fees. This can tempt a servicer to post payments in a tardy fashion or not make collection calls until late fees are assessed.

important role in resolving this collective action problem through servicer quality ratings.[6]

In addition to monitoring effort by investors, servicer quality ratings, and rules about loan modifications, there are two other important ways to mitigate this friction: servicer reputation and the master servicer. As the servicing business is an important counter-cyclical source of income for banks, one would think that these institutions would work hard on their own to minimize this friction. The master servicer is responsible for monitoring the performance of the servicer under the pooling and servicing agreement. It validates data reported by the servicer, reviews the servicing of defaulted loans, and enforces remedies of servicer default on behalf of the trust.

6. Frictions Between the Asset Manager and Investor: Principal-Agent

The investor provides the funding for the purchase of the mortgage-backed security. As the investor is typically financially unsophisticated, an agent is employed to formulate an investment strategy, conduct due diligence on potential investments, and find the best price for trades. Given differences in the degree of financial sophistication between the investor and an asset manager, there is an obvious information problem between the investor and portfolio manager that gives rise to the sixth friction.[7]

---

[6] Servicer quality ratings are intended to be an unbiased benchmark of a loan servicer's ability to prevent or mitigate pool losses across changing market conditions. This evaluation includes an assessment of collections/customer service, loss mitigation, foreclosure timeline management, management, staffing & training, financial stability, technology and disaster recovery, legal compliance and oversight and financial strength. In constructing these quality ratings, the rating agency attempts to break out the actual historical loss experience of the servicer into an amount attributable to the underlying credit risk of the loans and an amount attributable to the servicer's collection and default management ability.

[7] Most subprime MBS tranches issued in 2005–07 were re-packaged in new structures called ABS CDOs. A significant fraction of the exposure to ABS CDO was either retained by CDO-issuing banks or was hedged with the mono-line bond insurance companies. Both of these groups have suffered devastating losses related to this exposure in late 2007 and early 2008. A recent note by Adelson and Jacob (2007) argues that underwriting standards in subprime did not deteriorate until ABS CDOs became the marginal investor. This line of argument suggests that the largest risk management failures were by large sophisticated investors who likely over-relied on the credit rating agency's view of the underlying RMBS bonds in managing the risk of these exposures.

In particular, the investor will not fully understand the investment strategy of the manager, has uncertainty about the manager's ability, and does not observe any effort that the manager makes to conduct due diligence. This principal (investor)-agent (manager) problem is mitigated through the use of investment mandates, and the evaluation of manager performance relative to a peer benchmark or its peers.

As one example, a public pension might restrict the investments of an asset manager to debt securities with an investment grade credit rating and evaluate the performance of an asset manager relative to a benchmark index. However, there are other relevant examples. The FDIC, which is an implicit investor in commercial banks through the provision of deposit insurance, prevents insured banks from investing in speculative-grade securities or enforces risk-based capital requirements that use credit ratings to assess risk-weights. An actively managed collateralized debt obligation (CDO) imposes covenants on the weighted average rating of securities in an actively managed portfolio as well as the fraction of securities with a low credit rating.

As investment mandates typically involve credit ratings, it should be clear that this is another point where the credit rating agencies play an important role in the securitization process. By presenting an opinion on the riskiness of offered securities, the rating agencies help resolve the information frictions that exist between the investor and the portfolio manager. Credit ratings are intended to capture the expectations about the long-run or through-the-cycle performance of a debt security. A credit rating is fundamentally a statement about the suitability of an instrument to be included in a risk class, but importantly, it is an opinion only about credit risk. It follows that the opinion of credit rating agencies is a crucial part of securitization, because in the end the rating is the means through which much of the funding by investors finds its way into the deal.

However, recent events have demonstrated that the resolution of this friction does not end with the rating agencies. In particular, a recent report by the Senior Supervisors Group (March 2008) details significant differences in the risk management practices of large financial institutions with regard to structured credit exposures in the trading book. In general, institutions with better outcomes questioned the accuracy of credit ratings.

7. Frictions Between the Investor and the Credit Rating Agencies: Model Error

The rating agencies are paid by the arranger and not investors for their opinion, which creates a potential conflict of interest. Since an investor is not able to assess the efficacy of rating agency models, they are susceptible to both honest and dishonest errors on the agencies' part. The information asymmetry between investors and the credit rating agencies is the seventh and final friction in the securitization process. Honest errors are a natural byproduct of rapid financial innovation and complexity. On the other hand, dishonest errors could be driven by the dependence of rating agencies on fees paid by the arranger (the conflict of interest).

Some critics claim that the rating agencies are unable to objectively rate structured products due to conflicts of interest created by issuer-paid fees. Moody's, for example, made 44 percent of its revenue last year from structured finance deals (Tomlinson and Evans, 2007). Such assessments also command more than double the fee rates of simpler corporate ratings, helping to keep Moody's operating margins above 50 percent (*The Economist*, 2007). Despite these concerns, a SEC investigation (July 2008) of this issue recently concluded that there was "no evidence that decisions about rating methodology or models were based on attracting or losing market share." In other words, credit ratings analysts were exposed to but did not succumb to pressure.

If there were no conflicts of interest, then what were the dishonest errors? A recent report by the Committee on the Global Financial System (March 2008) tackles this question, concluding that the major mistakes included: underestimating the severity of the housing downturn, usage of limited historical data, and ignoring differences in the quality of originator underwriting practices across firms and over time.

This friction is minimized through two devices: the reputation of the rating agencies and the public disclosure of ratings and downgrade criteria. For the rating agencies, their business is their reputation, so it is difficult — though not impossible — to imagine that they would risk deliberately inflating credit ratings in order to earn structuring fees, thus jeopardizing their franchise. Moreover, with public rating and downgrade criteria, any deviations in credit ratings from their models are easily observed by the public.[8]

8. Five Frictions that Caused the Subprime Crisis

We believe that five of the seven frictions discussed above help to explain the breakdown in the subprime mortgage market.

The problem starts with friction #1: many products offered to subprime borrowers are very complex and subject to misunderstanding and/or misrepresentation. This opened the possibility of both excessive borrowing (predatory borrowing) and excessive lending (predatory lending).

At the other end of the process, we have the principal-agent problem between the investor and asset manager (friction #6). In particular, it seems that investment mandates do not adequately distinguish between structured and corporate credit ratings. This is a problem because asset manager performance is evaluated relative to peers or relative to a benchmark index. It follows that asset managers have an incentive to reach for yield by purchasing structured debt issues with the same credit rating but higher coupons than corporate debt issues.[9]

Initially, this portfolio shift was likely led by asset managers with the ability to conduct their own due diligence, recognizing value in the wide pricing of subprime mortgage-backed securities. However, once the other asset managers started to underperform their peers, they likely made similar portfolio shifts, but did not invest the same effort into due diligence of the arranger and originator.

This phenomenon worsened the friction between the arranger and the asset manager (friction #3). In particular, without due diligence by the asset manager, the arranger's incentives to conduct its own due diligence

---

[8] We think that there are two ways these errors could emerge. One, the rating agency builds its model honestly, but then applies judgment in a fashion consistent with its economic interest. The average deal is structured appropriately, but the agency gives certain issuers better terms. Two, the model itself is knowingly aggressive. The average deal is structured inadequately.

[9] The fact that the market demands a higher yield for similarly rated structured products than for straight corporate bonds ought to provide a clue to the potential of higher risk.

are reduced. Moreover, as the market for credit derivatives developed, including but not limited to the ABX, the arranger was able to limit its funded exposure to securitizations of risky loans in a fashion unknown to investors. Together, these considerations worsened the friction between the originator and arranger, opening the door for predatory borrowing and providing incentives for predatory lending (friction #2). In the end, the only constraint on underwriting standards was the opinion of the rating agencies. With limited capital backing representations and warranties, an originator could easily arbitrage rating agency models, exploit the weak historical relationship between aggressive underwriting and losses in the data used to calibrate required credit enhancement.

The inability of the rating agencies to recognize this arbitrage by originators and respond appropriately meant that credit ratings were assigned to subprime mortgage-backed securities with significant error. The friction between investors and the rating agencies is the final nail in the coffin (friction #7). Even though the rating agencies publicly disclosed their rating criteria for subprime, investors lacked the ability to evaluate the efficacy of these models.

While we have identified seven frictions in the mortgage securitization process, there are mechanisms in place to mitigate or even resolve each of these frictions, including for example anti-predatory lending laws and regulations. As we have seen, some of these mechanisms have failed to deliver as promised. Is it hard to fix this process? We believe not, and we think the solution might start with investment mandates. Investors should realize the incentives of asset managers to push for yield. Investments in structured products should be compared to a benchmark index of investments in the same asset class. When investors or asset managers are forced to conduct their own due diligence in order to outperform the index, the incentives of the arranger and originator are restored. Moreover, investors should demand that either the arranger or originator — or even both — retain the first-loss or equity tranche of every securitization, and disclose all hedges of this position. At the end of the production chain, originators need to be adequately capitalized so that their representations and warranties have value. Finally, the rating agencies could evaluate originators with the same rigor that they evaluate servicers, including perhaps the designation of originator ratings.

It is not clear to us that any of these solutions require additional regulation, and note that the market is already taking steps in the right direction. For example, the credit rating agencies have already responded with greater transparency and have announced significant changes in the rating process.[10] In addition, the demand for structured credit products generally and subprime mortgage securitizations in particular has declined significantly as investors have started to re-assess their own views of the risk in these products. Along these lines, it may be advisable for policymakers to give the market a chance to self-correct.

That being said, it does appear to us that the tranching of subprime mortgage credit risk has made it challenging for servicers to implement loan modifications which reduce principal balance. While such modifications might benefit both the borrower and average tranche, especially in a market of declining home prices, they require the most junior tranche to absorb loss. The threat of litigation by these junior investors, or the outright ownership of these junior tranches by servicers, may prevent the market from achieving a socially desirable outcome. Going forward, it might make sense for the public sector to require these securitization structures manage these conflicts in a socially optimal fashion, possibly through provisions in the tax code which prevent the double-taxation of interest income collected from borrowers and remitted to investors.

References

Adelson and Jacob (2008). The subprime problem: causes and lessons. *Journal of Structured Finance*, 14(1) (Spring).

Ben-David, I. (2008). Manipulation of collateral values by borrowers and intermediaries. Unpublished working paper. Available at http://home.uchicago.edu/~ibendavi/manipulation.pdf.

Center for Responsible Lending (2006). *Financial Quicksand: Payday Lending Sinks Borrowers in Debt.*

Committee on the Global Financial System (2008). *Ratings in structured finance: what went wrong and what can be done to address shortcomings?* Available at http://www.bis.org/publ/cgfs32.htm, January.

The Economist (2007). *Measuring the Measurers.* May 31.

[10] Moody's updated its subprime RMBS surveillance criteria in October 2007, putting originators into different tiers, recognizing the impact that different underwriting practices have had on performance.

The Economist (2007). *Securitization: When it Goes Wrong....* September 20.

Ernst, K., D. Bocian, and W. Li (2008). *Steered Wrong: Brokers, Borrowers, and Subprime Loans.* Available at http://www.responsiblelending.org/research/steered-wrong-brokers-borrowers-and-subprime-l-oans.html.

Flannery and Samolynk (2005). Payday lending: do costs justify the price? *FDIC Center for Financial Research Working Paper No. 2005/09.* Available at SSRN: http://ssrn.com/abstract=771624.

King, U., L. Parrish, and O. Tanik. *Financial Quicksand: Payday Lending Sinks Borrowers in Debt.* Available at http://www.responsiblelending.org/pdfs/rr012-Financial_Quicksand-1106.pdf.

Mayer, C. J., T. Piskorski, and A. Tchistyi (2007). The Inefficiency of Refinancing: Why Prepayment Penalties are Good for Risky Borrowers. Unpublished working paper, available at http://papers.ssrn.com/sol3/papers.cfm?abstract_id=1108528.

Moody's Investors Services (2007). Update on 2005 and 2006 vintage U.S. subprime RMBS Rating Actions: October 2007. *Moody's Special Report*, New York, October 26.

Morgan, D. (2007). Defining and detecting predatory lending. *Staff Report #273*, Federal Reserve Bank of New York.

Morgan, D., B. Iverson, and M. Botsch (2008). Subprime foreclosures and bankruptcy reform. *Unpublished Federal Reserve Bank of New York working paper*. Available from the authors upon request.

Morse, A. (2007). Payday lenders: heroes or villains? Unpublished Working Paper. Available at http://www.clevelandfed.org/research/conferences/2007/october2/morse_payday061125.pdf.

Securities and Exchange Commission (2008). *Report of Issues Identified in the Commission Staff's Examinations of Select Credit Rating Agencies*. Available at http://www.sec.gov/news/studies/2008/craexamination070808.pdf.

Senior Supervisors Group (2008). Observations on Risk Management Practices during the Recent Market Turbulence. Available at http://www.newyorkfed.org/newsevents/news/banking/2008/SSG_Risk_Mgt_doc_final.pdf.

Keys, B. J., T. K. Mukherjee, A. Seru, and V. Vig (2008). *Did Securitization Lead to Lax Screening? Evidence from Subprime Loans*? Available at SSRN: http://ssrn.com/abstract=1093137.

Sichelman, L. (2007). Tighter underwriting stymies refinancing of subprime loans. *Mortgage Servicing News*, May 1.

Tomlinson, R. and D. Evans (2007). CDO boom masks subprime losses, abetted by S&P, Moody's, Fitch. *Bloomberg News*, May 31.

Wei, L. (2007). Subprime lenders may face funding crisis. *Wall Street Journal*, 10 January.

VIII. POLICY PANEL: WHERE TO FROM HERE?

Where to From Here?: Lessons for Research, Policy and the Industry

Philipp Hartmann*
European Central Bank

The market turmoil that is ongoing while we are meeting here in Chicago has illustrated a fundamental problem in economic policy. There are two views on financial systems. In one view, financial systems are an indispensable engine of growth and development. They distribute savings and idle funds to productive real investments and consumption. By reallocating funds from less promising firms and industries to firms and industries with good growth prospects they contribute to the Schumpeterian process of "creative destruction". In the other view, financial systems are inherently fragile. Stricken by maturity mismatches, asymmetric information, strong interconnectedness, leverage, and governance problems they are prone to recurrent crises often with severe adverse consequences for the real economy.

The past one or two centuries have featured many episodes of booms followed by busts. In many cases financial systems have played a driving, or at least, a contributing role to the boom which paved the way for the subsequent bust. It is stunning for me that neither research nor policy have been able, over such a long time, to reconcile the two perspectives. We simply don't know how to harness efficient and dynamic financial systems promoting growth and prosperity and at the same time preventing costly financial crises. I think the events of the last year have abundantly demonstrated that major efforts have to be made to finally align with each

---

* Philipp Hartmann is the head of the Financial Research Division at the European Central Bank (ECB). The views expressed in this comment are only the ones of the author and do not necessarily correspond to the views of the ECB or the Eurosystem.

other the two "faces" of financial systems. In other words, we need to develop a financial architecture that supports a dynamic, innovative, and growing economy without an "end in tears".

In the remainder of my remarks, I would like to draw some lessons from the market turbulences that have happened so far. In so doing, I will cover lessons for research, for policy, and for the industry. Of course in the available time, I have to be highly selective. So, I decided to make a few points that have been less often mentioned recently. The conference of which we are all part in this room today has perfectly outlined all the issues that are on the table, so many I do not need to repeat.

Let me start with lessons for **research**, an area I am representing in the European Central Bank. The design of new financial instruments that made credit risk tradable have played an important role in the build up of imbalances and in the transmission of instability. So, a first step would be to look at the evidence on major wholesale financial innovations more generally. This should be done from two perspectives. First, did the introduction of options, futures, swaps, and, lately, structured finance instruments contribute to financial efficiency and the performance of the real economy? Second, have the same instruments played any material role in financial instabilities and how? I assume that you will be as surprised as I was to learn that these "benefits and costs" of financial innovation are not well documented. From research, we simply know very few hard facts about the value of wholesale financial innovations. I think we all in the research community, both in academia and in research departments of policy institutions, need to rectify this urgently.

My second point about research that is less often made relates to macroeconomic forecasting. I hope my academic colleagues will forgive me for being a bit provocative here. The phenomenon of "herding" may sometimes be as relevant a feature in academic research as it is in financial markets. There are strong disincentives for scholars to deviate from an established modeling paradigm, as it makes the publication of their work much more difficult. One of the more recent trends is the use of Dynamic Stochastic General Equilibrium (DSGE) models. The DSGE models are the current "state of the art" in macroeconomic modeling and most larger policy institutions, where a strong research staff was available made the development of such a model a priority for their forecasting activities. Many resources went into these models and few resources were available for alternatives. Problems with these elegant but complicated models, however, are that at least until the time of the present conference 1) DSGE modelers failed to integrate financial sectors in them, and 2) because of their linearized structure they are not well designed to address crisis situations.[1] As a consequence, most policy institutions found themselves in the turmoil with an important part of their forecasting infrastructure being of limited use in assessing the impact of financial instability on the real economy. I hope I was not the only one who more than five years ago suggested that the development of a new generation of forecasting models in central banks needed to involve as a priority a good representation of the financial sector and credit. If the current "work horse" of academic research cannot represent an important aspect of central banks' work well, then one needs to have less elegant models alongside with it capturing the missing features.[2]

Let me come to **policy** lessons now. We as researchers have the tendency to look for the single most important cause of a problem. And then we compete with our fellow scholars who have an alternative explanation. One characterizing feature of the current episode is, however, its multifaceted nature. Many factors, both macro and micro, have contributed to it: ample liquidity, low interest rates, features of new credit instruments, low underwriting standards for mortgage credit, incentives for herding in financial markets, compensation schemes fostering risk taking, conflicts of interest in rating agencies, bank business models, regulatory arbitrage, etc. (Over the last two days our conference has addressed all of them.) The turmoil has laid bare weaknesses at virtually all levels of the financial architecture of industrial countries. This is well reflected in the "road map" by the Financial Stability Forum (2008) about how to make financial systems more resilient, which comes to an impressive list of 67 recommendations, all of which were subsequently approved by the Group of Seven (G-7) ministers and central bank governors and currently pursued rigorously by the competent authorities. We should not have the illusion that the problems can be fixed with a small number of measures.

[1] One DSGE model that has a financial sector is discussed in Christiano, Motto, and Rostagno (2003), but it is not a model designed for forecasting.

[2] To be fair, most central banks, including the ECB, actually use a multiplicity of models. We have for example a tradition of cross-checking economic projections with results from smaller models based on money and credit aggregates. My point is more one of relative balance in research efforts and of generally paying enough attention to the financial sector.

It is a rather Herculean task. And a major issue — in particular in times of daily crisis management — is how to perform it while preserving some consistent Ordnungspolitik framework in establishing, what some call the New Financial Architecture.

While regulatory reforms are necessary, I do not believe that they will be sufficient. As is well known, regulators cannot lead markets or be permanently eye to eye with markets. By the very nature of their role, they will always lag behind: sometimes more, sometimes less. But given the increased sizes and importance of financial systems (see for example, Ferguson *et al.*, 2007), I am concerned with the resources that regulatory and supervisory authorities have at their disposal. In order to reduce the regulatory lag, jobs in these policy institutions need to be more attractive for people with market experience. Moreover, staff composition needs to shift from legal and accounting experts toward a greater share of economists (and researchers). Finally, in some countries the number of supervision experts is probably too low. I am saying this with the aim to achieve better regulation and supervision, reducing the regulatory lags, and enhancing supervisors' understanding of banks' newest business techniques and not to create more or necessarily heavier regulation.

Last, since September/October 2007, I have represented the view that to attempt to contain the instabilities we observe the policymakers need to pay careful attention to the consequences of asymmetric information, notably to adverse selection phenomena. One major reason why the interbank market, the Asset-Backed Commercial Paper (ABCP) market, and other important markets became dysfunctional was such adverse selection phenomena. I have described the intuition for them in an ECB Research Bulletin article (see Cassola *et al.*, 2008). For example, the enormous uncertainties about valuation of securitization products and about the risks on or off banks' balance sheets (for example, through the complexity and opaqueness of structured finance products) that emerged in the summer of 2007 made it very difficult for banks to assess the health of their counterparts. While some banks are in better shape and others are in worse shape, the inability of them to distinguish one from the other led to general hesitations to lend in the interbank market. So, lending dried up or became prohibitively expensive for all players in this market. Similarly, ABCP investors could not distinguish any more good from bad instruments, as the description of the collateral used in them or its valuation were unclear. And as a consequence, they withdrew from this market and thereby removed the possibility for off-balance-sheet vehicles to roll over their funding. Banks, which had sponsored the vehicles, had to take the assets back on their balance sheets, incurring additional risks difficult to value. It is important that these problems caused by asymmetric information can be fought, inter alia, by increasing transparency about who holds which risks and by improving valuation. This will lead the healthy players to resume lending to each other. But such information policies need to be accompanied by strategies how to deal with the "bad" (failing) banks and how to dispose of the "toxic" assets. These tasks can ultimately only be fulfilled by governments in conjunction with their supervisory authorities.

Let me close with the lessons for the **industry**. I do not believe that even the best policy reforms will be sufficient to attenuate the inherent procyclicality of financial systems described at the start of my remarks. The present episode convinced me that something has to change in the business governance and ethics in the financial sector. You may be surprised to hear this from an economist, who usually accepts the rational self-interested behavior of individuals. But I really believe that if the industry is not managing to control and change certain behaviors, then it risks a major popular backlash after the present episode or, at the latest, after the next crisis. In a democracy, this may lead to heavy regulation and ultimately a modern form of financial repression. In the long term, the industry has therefore all the interest in putting its own house in order. And it must find ways to avoid the present incentives for their management and staff to engage in immense risk taking, potentially making a lot of money in a short period of time and not being held fully accountable when investments turn sour. Initiatives like the ones by the Institute of International Finance (2008) go in the right direction and many of the proposals need to be enforced in financial institutions.

References

Cassola, N., M. Drehmann, P. Hartmann, M. Lo Duca, and M. Scheicher (2008). A research perspective on the propagation of the credit market turmoil. *ECB Research Bulletin*, 7, June.

Christiano, L., R. Motto, and M. Rostagno (2003). The great depression and the Friedman-Schwartz hypothesis. *Journal of Money, Credit and Banking*, 35, 1119–1179.

Ferguson, R., P. Hartmann, F. Panetta, and R. Portes (2007). International Financial Stability, *9th Geneva Report on the World Economy*, November.
Financial Stability Forum (2008). Enhancing Market and Institutional Resilience, 7 April.
Institute of International Finance (2008). Final Report of the IIF committee on Market Best Practice: Principles of Conduct and Best Practice Recommendations, Washington (DC), July.

Tarp Version 1: A Turning Point in Crisis Management

Richard J. Herring*
The Wharton School, University of Pennsylvania

By chance, this conference took place at an especially critical point in the current crisis. Indeed, I was asked at the last minute to substitute for a European regulator who was faced with a crisis in a major domestic institution and could not leave his post. This week also proved the end of a concerted effort by the US regulators to portray the subprime debacle as a liquidity crisis. I will begin by reviewing the outbreak of the crisis and indicate why it quickly spread from the relatively small sub-prime related sector of the market for securitized debt to engulf other markets that seemed only tangentially related and quickly spread round the world. Then I will review some of the policy improvisation by the US authorities leading to the two-and-one half page proposal for a $700 billion Troubled Asset Relief Program (TARP).

1. Securitization and the Outbreak of the Crisis

Securitizations began with the Government Sponsored Enterprises (GSEs) — Fannie Mae and Freddie Mac — as a way of reducing the cost and increasing the flow of funding to the housing industry. Securitization permitted financial institutions to use capital more efficiently in an originate-and-distribute approach in which mortgages were pooled and securities were issued against the pool of mortgages to fit the particular preferences of various clienteles in the capital market. Although holders of securitized claims had to concern themselves with interest rate risk and

* Richard J. Herring is the Jacob Safra Professor of International Banking at The Wharton School, University of Pennsylvania.

pre-payment risk, they did not need to worry about credit risk. They could rely on guarantees from the GSEs.

Private securitizations began to grow as market participants found ways to substitute for the guarantees against credit risk supplied by the GSEs. Three main props replaced the GSEs: (1) Statistical models that were sufficiently reliable to predict the excess servicing, over-collateralization, performance triggers, subordination and residual tranching necessary to achieve the desired degree of safety; (2) Ratings of asset-backed securities by Nationally Recognized Statistical Ratings Organizations (NRSROs) — mainly Standard & Poors, Moodys' and Fitch; (3) Insurance issued by monoline insurers. Private securitizations were very innovative and increasingly complex, leading to a virtual alphabet soup of new instruments such as CDOs, CDO^2, CLOs, ABCP, SIVs and SIV-Lites. These innovations were so successful that they constituted a virtual off-balance sheet banking system amounting to nearly $12 trillion worldwide.

In part this growth was driven by the fact that the demand for high-quality assets greatly exceeded the supply of investment grade corporate and sovereign bonds. Partly this was a consequence of the use of ratings in the regulation of insurers, some mutual funds, pension funds, and various other investors subject to the prudent man rule. The implementation of the Standardized variant of Pillar 1 of the Basel II further adds to the demand for highly rated securities by reducing capital charges for banks that hold these securities. Private securitizations provided a way to synthesize investment grade securities that served to fill the gap.

This increasingly elaborate structure of private securitizations was shaken to its foundations when confronted with the brute fact that the quality of subprime mortgages in recent years was inconsistent with the optimistic ratings assigned to securities based on these subprime mortgage pools. The peak in delinquencies in this kind of lending is generally expected two to three years after origination when low, initial teaser rates are replaced by adjustable rates set at substantial margins above some benchmark market rate. It was widely assumed that the worst likely performance was the cohort of subprime mortgages underwritten in 2000, just before the recession of 2001–02. But mortgages underwritten in 2005, 2006, and 2007 showed signs of deteriorating far more rapidly and at much higher rates than the 2000 cohort. Indeed, an astonishing proportion of subprime mortgages underwritten in 2007 became 60-days delinquent within 60 days.

This undermined confidence in the three principal supports for private securitizations. Many of the institutions that had played a leading role in underwriting subprime-related debt and should therefore have had the most sophisticated and accurate statistical models suffered substantial losses from the declining value of subprime mortgages in the pipeline to be securitized and from subprime securities which they held. Since these institutions also played a central role in over-the-counter markets and interbank markets, concerns about counterparty risk mounted.

Confidence in the NRSROs was undermined by the realization that subprime-related securities were much more vulnerable to multi-notch downgrades than corporate bonds with similar ratings. Three notch downgrades are comparatively rare among corporate bonds and confined mainly to bonds that were initially rated as less than investment grade. In contrast, 68% of BBB rated subprime-related securities were downgraded at least three notches. This removed the investment grade imprimatur from these securities and forced some institutions to sell the securities into thin and declining markets. More broadly, loss of confidence in the NRSROs led to a marked decline in demand for other kinds of asset-backed securities in which investors relied heavily on ratings issued by the NRSROs.

Finally, when it appeared that the monoline insurers might have to make good on their guarantees, markets doubted that they would be able to support the $800bn in structured finance obligations they supported at yearend 2006. The average equity price of the monoline insurers fell precipitately and the average credit default swap rose to nearly 1000 basis points by the end of January 2008. Loss of confidence in the monoline insurers spread the crisis to other insured borrowers, especially some municipal obligations that had no relationship whatsoever to subprime mortgages.

Thus, by undermining confidence in the three main supports for private securitizations, the subprime problem led to a loss of confidence in other kinds of securitizations, a drying up of new issues and a collapse of secondary market activity. Subprime-related losses heightened concerns about counterparty risk that led to a sharp decline in interbank lending and a hoarding of liquidity.

2. The Authorities View the Problem as a Liquidity Crisis

By August 2007, it should have been clear that the financial system was faced with the prospect of insolvencies at many of the Large Complex Financial Institutions (LCFIs) that were heavily involved in the securitization process. Indeed in recent years, some had earned nearly half their profits from this source. (See Table 1 for a list of the 16 LCFIs.) But it was clear that some of these institutions were now facing massive losses. These included looses from holding downgraded securities and losses

Table 1. Overview of Large Complex Financial Institutions.*

LCFIs	Total assets (Billions of $, Year End 2006)[1]	Total Subsidiaries[1]	Foreign Subsidiaries (%)
UBS AG	1,964	417	96
Barclays Plc	1,957	1,003	43
BNP Paribas	1,897	1,170	61
Citi	1,884	2,435	50
HSBC Holdings Plc	1,861	1,234	61
The Royal Bank of Scotland Group Plc	1,711	1,161	11
Deutsche Bank AG	1,483	1,954	77
Bank of America Corporation	1,460	1,407	28
JP Morgan Chase & Co.	1,352	804	51
ABN AMRO Holding NV**	1,300	670	63
Société Générale	1,260	844	56
Morgan Stanley	1,121	1,052	47
Credit Suisse Group	1,029	290	93
Merrill Lynch & Co., Inc.	841	267	64
Goldman Sachs Group, Inc.	838	371	51
Lehman Brothers Holdings Inc.	504	433	45

* Year end 2007 (unless otherwise specified). **After the most recent list of LCFIs (Bank of England, 2007b) was published, a consortium of three banks (RBS, Fortis and Santander) acquired ABN AMRO.

[1] *Source*: Bankscope. Data on subsidiaries refer to majority-owned subsidiaries for which the LFCI is the ultimate owner with a minimum control path of 50.01%. This and the following tables are extracted from Herring and Carmassi (2009).

from honoring implicit guarantees backing-up off balance sheet vehicles, money market mutual funds, and sometimes even hedge funds. They also included losses from funding a pipeline of assets that could no longer be securitized and the loss of an important component of bank revenue. Several institutions faced a challenge to replace lost capital and, indeed, to increase capital as a precaution against loss of access to funding. Table 2 shows that, although some institutions succeeded in raising capital, the amounts raised fell short of the losses incurred. Nonetheless, the US authorities framed this problem as a liquidity crisis. There was without doubt a lack of liquidity in many markets, but the reason was concern over counterparty risk. It was known that large losses were overhanging the system, but the precise allocation of those losses was and remains unclear.

The Fed responded not only with a series of aggressive cuts in the discount rate, but also with a series of innovative attempts to inject liquidity into the system through extending auctions to a broader range of institutions and accepting lower quality collateral. During March, the Fed crossed a regulatory Rubicon without the appropriate weapons. Its hastily improvised rescue of Bear Stearns set precedents that may have contributed to future damage.

Traditionally, the US has taken the view that investment banks do not pose systemic risk. They are unlikely to be subject to a run by their

Table 2. Bank Losses Relative to Capital Injections.

Bank Losses/Capital Injections

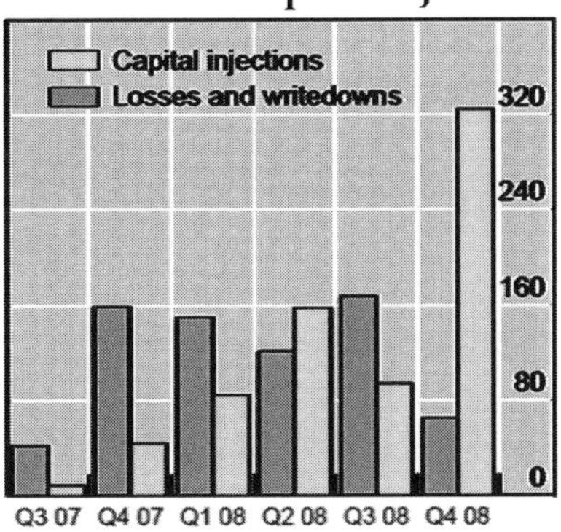

Source: BIS Quarterly Review, Dec. 2008.

customers, since customer funds are strictly segregated from the firm's own funds and could be easily transferred to another firm in the event of a failure. In addition, investment banks hold mainly marketable securities and should be able to deleverage rapidly without suffering illiquidity losses in the event of a funding shock. Finally, access to systemically important, large payment clearing and settlement systems was through large banks. The demise of Drexel Burnham Lambert (DBL) in 1990 tended to confirm this view. The Fed and Bank of England acted as honest brokers to unwind the positions of DBL, but there was no bailout. Spillovers were so minimal that the stock market rose the day that Drexel declared bankruptcy.

In the meanwhile, the nature of investment banking changed markedly. Investment bank portfolios shifted in favor of lower quality, less liquid assets which made it much more difficult to deleverage in the event of a funding shock. The leading investment banks became increasingly global with funding operations in the US, the UK, and Japan. While this diversified the funding base, it also increased coordination costs in the event of a shock since each local regulator would need to ensure that local residents were protected. In addition, net leverage increased sharply from 2000 to 2007, with Bear Stearns the most leveraged of the big five investment banks. There was also a growing reliance on third-party repos to fund the balance sheet. Since 1990, the repo market has grown markedly. In 1990 secured repo credit was 13% of federally insured deposits. By 2007 it had become 60% of federally insured deposits. Two-thirds of the repos mature or must be rolled over overnight. For third-party term repos where values might fluctuate substantially, counterparties must have confidence that the firm can provide additional margin when necessary. Investment banks became increasingly involved in over-the-counter derivatives markets, especially the booming credit default swap market.

After the collapse of its two subprime-related hedge funds in June of 2007, Bear Stearns was viewed with increasing concern. Its share price plummeted and credit default swap premium rose sharply. Nonetheless, regulators and the management of Bear Stearns claimed to have been stunned by the speed of its collapse and claimed that it was the victim of a run. By the end of the week, 14 March 2008, the authorities were faced with the unpleasant choice of watching Bear Stearns apply for bankruptcy or bailing it out.

The authorities feared the spillover consequences of a declaration of bankruptcy. Stays, which are central to the bankruptcy process for non-banks, can cause severe systemic spillovers when applied to a firm like Bear that trades actively in global markets. Stays may cause clients and counterparties to lose access to funds. Viable borrowers may lose access to collateral and undrawn credit lines. More fundamentally, lack of clarity regarding position vis-à-vis the insolvent bank may inflict possible damage on counterparties which are unable to hedge their uncertain positions and cause dislocations in interbank markets as traders attempt to assess the ultimate damage. One key concern for the authorities was damage to primary dealers who facilitate government borrowing.

The authorities chose instead to improvise a bailout in which the Fed engineered a sale of Bear to JPMorgan Chase facilitated by the purchase of $30 billion in investment grade Bear assets by an SPE financed by a $29 billion loan from the Fed and $1 billion in subordinated debt from JPMorgan Chase. Although there was considerable public debate over whether Bear shareholders would receive $2 or $10 per share and whether it constituted sufficient market discipline, less attention was paid to the fact that all creditors and counterparties, the entities which should have the strongest incentives to discipline risk-taking by Bear, were protected from loss. This could not help but encourage more risk-taking in the future. Moreover, having made this kind of intervention once, any similar firm that encounters stress will want to bargain for similar aid from the Fed. This is likely to delay and complicate private sector solutions in the future.

If Bear had been a bank, the Fed would have had a much more attractive range of options. In particular, it could have relied on Prompt Corrective Action measures with mandatory triggers for regulatory intervention to ensure that Bear would seek a market solution before its situation became desperate. The authorities would have had the power to act quickly and decisively before insolvency, and the FDIC could have established a bridge institution to continue systemically important services.

Unfortunately, the authorities lack the authority to enforce Prompt Corrective Action measures and establish a bridge bank for investment banks. But a similar model could be devised. A number of issues would need to be resolved. Should least cost resolution principles apply with a parallel process for determining systemic risk exceptions? What authority should underwrite the costs of establishing a bridge institution for investment banks? How should that authority be reimbursed? What authority should serve a prudential regulator to oversee a prompt corrective action regime? What authority should make the decision to take control rights from the shareholders and establish a bridge institution? What authority should act as a receiver to oversee the bridge institution? These are difficult questions, but surely not insoluble. Answers have been found in the case of commercial banks and should have been devised for subsequent troubles at non-bank financial institutions.

There was one significant exception, however, to the general trend of hastily improvised bailouts. After trying to broker a merger of Lehman Brothers (LB) with other, stronger institutions, the US authorities declined to bail it out and sent the holding company, Lehman Brothers Holdings International (LBHI) to the bankruptcy courts for protection under Chapter 11 of the US bankruptcy code, the largest bankruptcy in US history. Although LB was by far the smallest and one of the least complex institutions on the list of Large Complex Financial Institutions (LCFIs), it was nonetheless of sufficient systemic importance that its collapse led to substantial spillovers on global capital markets. Credit risk spreads rose to record highs, equity prices fell by 4% worldwide when the bankruptcy was announced, and government bond yields declined sharply as foreign exchange carry trades were unwound.

Understandably, after the US government had subsidized the merger of Bear Stearns, a much smaller, less complex investment bank, the market expected that when Lehman Brothers (LB) began to show a similar weakness (see Table 3), it would receive similar treatment. Why then was LB permitted to fail? The Fed and the Treasury claimed they lacked authority to bail it out. It is also likely that they wished to limit moral hazard by engaging in a bit of "constructive ambiguity". Moreover, since the Fed had had a team of examiners in LB ever since the collapse of Bear Stearns, they knew much more about the condition of LB and may have believed they could predict and control the spillover costs. They may have thought that counterparties and creditors had sufficient warning about LB's weakening condition to take precautionary measures. But, of course, in a complex and integrated financial system, regulatory action or inaction can have unintended consequence through indirect exposures and linkages that are apparent only after the fact.

Lehman's total reported assets were roughly $700 billion. Table 4 shows its corporate structure at the end of 2007. It included 433

Table 3. 5 Year CDS for Morgan Stanley, Lehman Brothers, and Bear Stearns.

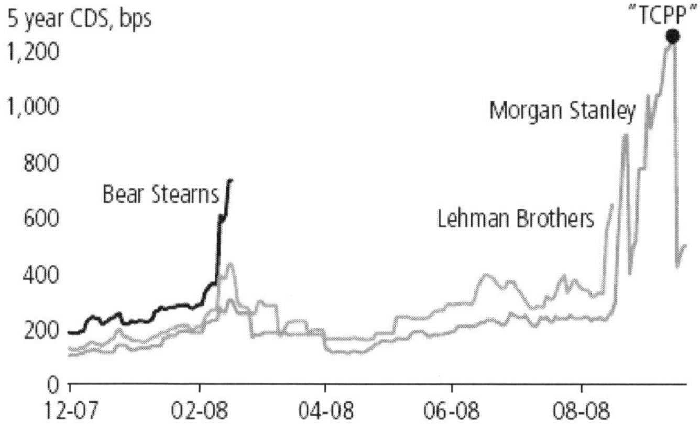

Source: Bloomberg. Data as of 10/17/2008.
Note: By August 2008 CDS Spreads for Lehman Brothers were as high as they had been for Bear Stearns. TCPP is the date of the Treasury Capital Purchase Program.

subsidiaries in 20 countries. This corporate complexity greatly impeded the orderly resolution of the firm, created significant spillovers to other institutions and markets, and led the Group of 7 finance ministers to pledge (Guha, 2008) "to do everything in their power to prevent any more Lehman Brothers-style failures of systemically important financial institutions".

One of the major concerns was that LB was the sixth largest counterparty in over-the-counter derivatives markets. But back offices succeeded in processing billions of dollars of contracts and the International Swap Dealers Association organized an auction to determine settlement prices. Because derivatives contracts in which LB was a counterparty were usually marked to market daily and collateral was adjusted each evening to reflect changes in market prices, losses were relatively light. Losses were much greater, however, with regard to credit default swap contracts written on LB. Those selling protection on LB are in a similar position to bondholders and received a similar price. Buyers of $100 of default protection will receive $91.375, a substantial loss for sellers of protection.

Table 4. Corporate Structure of Lehman Brothers (Year End 2007).

Lehman Brothers Holdings Inc (Year End 2007)	
Country	**Majority-Owned Subsidiaries**
USA	238
United Kingdom	120
Cayman Islands	18
Australia	9
Luxembourg	6
Ireland	5
Netherlands	5
Bermuda	4
France	4
Hong Kong	4
Japan	4
Korea Rep. of	4
Germany	3
Singapore	2
Thailand	2
Argentina	1
Canada	1
Switzerland	1
India	1
Mauritius	1
Total	433
Number of Countries	20

Source: Bankscope. Majority-owned subsidiaries.

A second major concern was LB's key role in the Repo market, which roughly totals $11 trillion and is the short-term, collateralized lending market that banks, broker/dealers, and hedge funds use to finance securities positions. The Fed attempted to address the risk that the market would seize up by allowing broader use of the Primary Dealer Credit Facility through expanding the list of eligible securities. In addition a group of global banks announced plans to use their own capital to establish a $70 billion private sector credit facility for those securities not eligible for the Fed facility. The Fed also announced an increase in its Treasury Securities Lending Facility to $200 billion.

What turned out to be more disruptive, however, were the traditional exposures to LB's outstanding debt. Among the largest unsecured creditors were the US federal government's Pension Benefit Guaranty Corp., the German government's deposit-insurance arm (McCracken, 2008), and money market mutual funds. The latter proved to be one of the most important channels of contagion. One of the oldest money market funds, the Reserve Primary Fund, was forced to write off $785 million of short- and medium-term notes and became the first money market mutual fund to "break the buck" in 14 years. This triggered $184 billion in money market mutual fund redemptions and forced fund managers to sell assets into illiquid markets. This spilled over into commercial paper markets including not only asset-backed commercial paper, but also non-asset backed commercial paper that had held up reasonably well and was a key means of financing corporations and banks. The interbank market seized up entirely with the almost complete collapse of confidence in counterparties in money markets. Spreads between the euro-dollar interbank rate and the comparable US Treasury rate rose to nearly 450 basis points, more than double the already high spreads that prevailed before the LB bankruptcy.

In addition, failed trades proved particularly disruptive. Prior to LB's bankruptcy, portfolio managers placed thousands of trades with LB's broker dealer (LBI), many of which were subsequently transferred for settlement to LBI affiliates throughout the world. After the bankruptcy, these failed to settle and this has led to civil proceedings on three continents. The UK administrator said that about 43,000 trading deals were still "live" in the London subsidiaries alone and would need to be negotiated with each counterparty (Hughes, 2008).

But the fundamental problem was that LB was managed as an integrated entity with minimal regard for the legal entities that would need to be taken through the bankruptcy process. LBHI issued the vast majority of unsecured debt and invested the funds in most of its regulated and unregulated subsidiaries. This is a common approach to managing a global corporation, designed to facilitate control over global operations, while reducing funding, capital and tax costs. LBHI, in effect, served as banker for its affiliates, running a zero balance cash management system. LBHI lent to its operating subsidiaries at the beginning of each day and then swept the cash back to LBHI at the end of each day. The bankruptcy petition was filed before most of the subsidiaries had been funded on September 15th and so most of the cash was tied up in court proceedings in the US.

Lehman also centralized its information technology so that data for different products and different subsidiaries were comingled. This was an efficient way of running the business as a going concern, but presents an enormous challenge in global bankruptcy proceedings. LB stored data in 26,666 servers, 20,000 of which contained accumulated emails, files, voice mail messages, instant messages and recorded calls. The largest data centers were in New York, London, Tokyo, Hong Kong and Mumbai. Moreover, LB used approximately 2,700 proprietary, third-party and off-the-shelf programs, each of which interacted with or created transactions data. The bankruptcy administrators must preserve, extract, store and analyze data relevant to the entities they are dealing with. This problem was made more difficult by the success of the administrators of LBHI in selling two important entities that were rapidly declining in value because of loss of human capital: its investment banking operations and its asset management business.

Most of the US investment banking operations — the assets, not the legal entities — were sold to Barclays. This necessitated bringing a Securities Investor Protection Corporation (SIPC) proceeding, which put all LBI accounts under the control of the SIPC Trustee and permitted the broker-dealer to be liquidated. Nomura bought most of the investment banking business in Asia and continental Europe, and LB's asset management business was sold in a management buyout. But this meant that the data was owned by Barclays, Nomura and the now independent asset management division and so bankruptcy administrators are dependent on the new owners for access to data to determine the assets and liabilities of each legal entity. The administrator of the four London subsidiaries complained that nine weeks after the bankruptcy, he has yet to receive a confirmation of the assets owned by these subsidiaries.

The US administrators expressed the optimistic view that they would be able to complete the resolution within 18 to 24 months, but the presiding judge reminded the administrator that the biggest impediments to a timely completion of the administration are the timetables of the other insolvency fiduciaries around the world. The administrators in London warned that it may take years for creditors to get their money back, noting that they were continuing to work on Enron, which failed seven years ago, which was about one-tenth the size and complexity of Lehman (Hughes, 2008).

The conclusion I would draw from the LB experiment is not that all systemically important institutions should be bailed out, but rather than regulators and supervisors should focus on devising orderly resolution plans that will enable them to unwind even the largest most complex institution with minimal spillover to the rest of the financial system. A useful first step would be to require that each institution create and maintain a plan for winding down the institution just as they now maintain plans for business continuity. (The bankruptcy administrator of LBIH has claimed that the hastily prepared bankruptcy filing has cost as much as $75 billion in lost value (McCracken, 2008).) If the regulators deem the plan unworkable, the institution may be required to reduce its complexity or set aside a higher capital charge. An institution that is too complex to fail is simply too complex and presents too great a threat to the rest of the financial system.

The TARP version 1 response to this near financial collapse revealed a fundamental failure to understand the true nature of the problem and a blatant disregard for basic standards of public policy. Sound public policy should: (1) start from a clear diagnosis of the problem; (2) have clear goals that address the problem; (3) be efficient both in the sense of accomplishing the goals at least cost and minimizing distortion of incentives; and (4) be equitable both in the sense of treating similar entities comparably (horizontal equity) and in the sense of not exacerbating the income distribution (vertical equity); and (5) minimize costs to taxpayers. TARP version 1 was deficient in each respect.

A year into the crisis, US Treasury Secretary Paulson continued to characterize the crisis as a liquidity problem caused by illiquid mortgage assets choking off the flow of credit. While it is certainly true the subprime-related mortgage assets have become illiquid, that cannot explain the breakdown in other markets. Concern over counterparty risk is the key problem.

Paulson's proposal was to spend $700 billion to buy these illiquid mortgage assets. The effect of this approach all depends on the price that is paid. But many of these securities are illiquid because it is very difficult to determine the price. Indeed, without a credible guarantee, a liquid secondary market for these securities is unlikely to be restored. On close inspection, many of the securities are simply too heterogeneous and require too much analysis to be easily traded. In principle the current price of subprime-related debt reflects current defaults, anticipated future defaults, a risk premium for uncertainty and an illiquidity discount. But it is very difficult to disentangle and quantify these factors, and the Treasury is almost certain to suffer from adverse selection in such purchases since the seller will inevitably be better informed. Moreover, the Treasury was very unclear about the price it intended to offer.

If the purchases were to be made at "fair value" somehow determined, then this does not address the capital shortage problem that is the underlying cause for the breakdown of interbank markets. Moreover, if participation in the Treasury auction forces institutions to accept write-downs, whether their assets are purchased or not, many institutions will simply not participate.

If the purchases are made at a premium, it would address the capital problem, but in a way that is inefficient and inequitable, although it would address (at least indirectly) the capital problem by providing a subsidy. But the subsidies would be distributed without making an assessment of which institutions are viable and might be wasted on many firms that do not require a subsidy. In addition, distributing subsidies in this way will tend to reward some of the most imprudent, incompetent investors at the expense of taxpayers who are generally much less well-off than the executives and traders who made the crucial errors. And it would distort incentives for taking risk in the future.

Luckily, Congress bulked at the first version of TARP and the Treasury has changed its focus. There is now an emphasis on recapitalizing institutions, although there is still no clear strategy for protecting taxpayers and ensuring that the capital subsidies restore health to the banking system. But giving up the assumption that the crisis is merely a liquidity problem ends a year of what amounted to forbearance and may signal the start of a more effective approach.

References

Guha, K. (2008). G7 pledge 'no more Lehmans'. *Financial Times*, October 12.

Herring, R. and J. Carmassi (2009). "The Corporate Structure of International Financial Conglomerates: Complexity and Implications for Safety & Soundness," in The Oxford Handbook of Banking, edited by A. N. Berger, P. Molyneux and J. Wilson, Oxford University Press, pp. 172–203.

Hughes, J. (2008). Lehman creditors to face years of waiting. *Financial Times,* November 14.

McCracken, J. (2008). Lehman's chaotic bankruptcy filing destroyed billions in value. *Wall Street Journal*, December 29.

Financial Crises: Seeing Patterns, Limiting Risks

Henry Kaufman*
Henry Kaufman & Co., Inc.

1. Introduction

I am delighted to participate in this conference on a subject of vital importance. I have been asked to comment on the analogies in recent financial history to the current market turbulence, and to suggest ways to limit credit crises in the future.

Since the end of the Second World War, approximately 15 credit crises have roiled U.S. financial markets, beginning in the late 1960s and continuing through every decade since. Some centered on events and institutions in the U.S.; others affected U.S. markets and institutions through their international ties. Some originated chiefly with individual institutions, while others were more systemic.

Several common threads run through these financial upheavals. First, with the exception of the 1966 credit crunch, all involved the *excessive* use of credit. Second, each was accompanied by a noticeable lowering of credit standards. Third, borrowers had come to rely heavily on leverage prior to each postwar crisis. Fourth, most of the crises were preceded by a period of market euphoria. Fifth, although each postwar financial crisis inspired some modest regulatory reforms, the overall trend in the last half-century has been toward the greater and greater liberalization of financial markets in ways that encourage greater risk taking.

In the current situation, the various agencies deemed guardians of our financial institutions have not seemed up to the task, perhaps more so than in the past. Private credit rating agencies seem overwhelmed by the enormity of their task, and far too many are infused with conflicts of interest. Federal financial regulators have been too passive. The primary guardian

* Henry Kaufman is the President of Henry Kaufman & Co., Inc.

of our financial system — the Federal Reserve — has failed to appreciate how major structural changes in financial markets demand a new regime of monetary policies and practices. Federal regulators seldom probe deeply enough to unearth dangerous credit and risk practices.

Whereas most previous credit crises involved non-tradable assets, the current one is driven by tradable financial instruments. The greater liquidity of instruments at the center of the present crisis has, in turn, increased the threat of contagion throughout the global economy. And, indeed, the current crisis — unlike many of its predecessors — is centered in the world's leading financial centers, especially in the United States and Europe, rather than in emerging markets.

Ironically, boosters of the more free-wheeling financial environment claim that excesses will be held in check by growing transparency. But the opposite has been happening. The growing complexity and interconnectedness of financial markets worldwide has fostered greater financial market opacity. That, in turn, makes it more and more difficult to assess the true scale and scope of the current crisis.

2. A New Regulatory Authority

How can we limit the dangerous loosening of credit creation and market behavior in order to repair the current damage and reduce the chances of another credit crisis of equal or greater magnitude? For many years, I have proposed the creation of a new kind of regulatory body that I have provisionally named the Federal Financial Oversight Authority (FFOA). This new authority would monitor and supervise the activities of our economy's largest financial conglomerates. It would assess the soundness of their trading practices, the adequacy of their capital, their conflicts of interest with customers and competitors, and other measures of their soundness and stability.

The key distinction between the new FFOA and existing regulatory bodies is that it would oversee only the upper-tier financial giants. I am proposing comprehensive supervision of them, not of all or most financial firms. This is a relatively small number of firms. In the United States, for instance, the top fifteen financial firms dominate many key areas of trading, underwriting, and investment management, and possess combined assets of roughly $13 trillion. Some also are leaders in derivatives and in other esoteric financial instruments that have become so popular in recent years. Therefore, closer oversight of these top-tier firms would do much to assure the smooth functioning of financial markets. For smaller financial institutions, which are not too big to fail, the current system of oversight can continue to operate.

Let me outline the structure and functions of the new Federal Financial Oversight Authority. Its board should be bipartisan, staffed by members with recognized expertise across a broad range of financial services. The FFOA should operate under the auspices of, and cooperate closely with, the Federal Reserve System. To insure that the nation's monetary authorities are apprised of the status and health of leading financial institutions, the chairman of the FFOA should serve as a voting member of the Federal Open Market Committee. Finally, both chairmen — at the Federal Reserve and at the Federal Financial Oversight Authority — each year should co-sign a report to Congress that documents the safety and soundness of the financial institutions under their jurisdiction.

Clues to the current financial crisis can be found in the background and training of many of those who manage leading financial corporations. Therefore, the FFOA should work to insure that board members at those institutions are well qualified. Directors need to understand quantitative risk analysis, information technology, and accounting, at minimum. The board as a whole should possess expertise across the full range of the institution's major financial services.

The new FFOA also should collaborate closely with new corporate board members, through regular meetings. Initial meetings should be devoted to making sure that new directors of financial institutions understand their responsibilities as they are understood, in turn, by the supervising authorities. New directors then will take part in periodic meetings between FFOA representatives and all board members — meetings when the results of examinations are reviewed, as are regulators' recommendations and directives. It seems fitting that independent directors should be given special attention: separate, periodic meetings, chaired by a designated lead director, that include outside legal counsel, and are guided by prepared agendas that address critical issues including the firm's risk policies, growth aspirations, and succession planning.

Another weak link in financial institution oversight has been credit ratings. The Fed already rates quite a few of the institutions under its supervision, issuing what is called a "CAMEL rating" (for Capital, Assets, Management, Earnings, and Liquidity). The weak link in credit ratings has been the private agencies, which, as I've noted, seem overwhelmed with the challenge of garnering enough information to render timely and meaningful ratings. The challenge is the greatest — and the stakes highest — when it comes to leading, integrated financial conglomerates. If a new supervisory authority is created to oversee those key institutions, one of its tasks should be to rate their credit rather than outsourcing the function to private agencies.

Given the pace and reach of globalization, other leading economies also would benefit from creating their own versions of the FFOA to oversee their top-tier financial firms. The European Union, Canada, and Japan are the best candidates. There, as in the United States, regulators in each country would need to oversee only the largest 5–30 financial conglomerates to achieve the desired results. Transnational cooperation and coordination would be essential, and would go a long way toward achieving the kind of unified supervision that currently is not possible under the Basel Agreements.

3. Concluding Remarks

Finally, I'd like to say a few words about one of the most pressing and controversial issues of our day, in finance as well as many other sectors of the economy — management compensation. First, when stock options are given as awards, they should have long maturities. Second, corporate America should consider changing its stock option plans to elongate the period over which a deputy manager can exercise his options. Third, companies should consider whether cash settlements payable on termination should not be paid in full immediately.

Several decades ago, here at the Economic Club of Chicago, I warned that we may well be moving into an environment where credit has no guardian. In the current crisis — in large part because of the strategies, policies, and philosophies of large, integrated financial institutions — we seem to have come close to that risky state of affairs. It is time to reverse direction, or risk even greater turmoil in the future.

Addressing the Credit Market Turmoil of 2007–08

Sam Peltzman*
University of Chicago

At this writing in early October 2008, it appears that the first phase of the financial crisis is ending and the second is about to or has begun. The phase that is ending entails flushing the worst assets created during the subprime lending boom out of the financial system. It has been accomplished by massive writedowns and government actions of various kinds culminating in the creation of a taxpayer financed buyout fund for these assets. The phase that is beginning will be driven by the broader deterioration in bank balance sheets and income streams emanating from the ongoing decline in real estate values. This decline has already created negative equity for many prime mortgage holders. Were plain vanilla, held-to-maturity prime mortgages marked to market or to some realistic approximation thereof, it is likely that significant chunks of the banking system would be or will shortly be insolvent. We should expect this underlying economic reality to roll through the banking system in 2009 and 2010. It will create more demands on the Federal Deposit Insurance Corporation's (FDIC) insurance fund and, ultimately, the federal Treasury.

There is little we can do now to avoid this painful unraveling, though wise policy may mitigate the pain. The policy question that will shortly move to the fore is how to avoid or contain a repeat of the kind of system meltdown we are currently embroiled in. My remarks will focus on this question, and I will sketch a modest proposal that I think would make the financial system less fragile.

A widespread view among academic economists is that we should rely more on market forces to restrain excessive risks. On this view, suppliers

---

*Sam Peltzman is the Ralph and Dorothy Distinguished Service Professor Emeritus of Economics in the Booth School of Business at the University of Chicago.

of funds should bear losses from risky asset purchases. Then they will exert pressure on management to restrain risks, or they will move their funds to safer institutions. This market discipline should be supplemented by risk-based deposit insurance fees or capital requirements, because insured depositors have no incentive to monitor risk. There is, I think, some intellectual merit to some of this academic orthodoxy. To some degree, we are today reaping the whirlwind spawned by overriding the market signals in the cases of Continental Illinois, the era of regulatory forbearance of zombie savings and loans, Long-Term Capital Management, and most recently Bear Stearns.

On the other side, I have become less optimistic about the efficacy of balance-sheet regulation or risk-based insurance fees in reducing systemic risk. Such regulation creates incentives for offsetting responses that strike me as too powerful for regulators to adequately overcome. Thus, the current meltdown began when large banks were called to make good on guarantees to investors in Special Investment Vehicles (SIVs). The SIVs were a response to Basel capital requirements which effectively took the liability off the banks' books. The Basel requirements, themselves enacted in the wake of a previous crisis, arguably made the underlying problem worse, because the SIVs hid the banks' liability and thereby weakened corrective market forces. Suppliers of funds to the banks were being led to believe — by the regulatory treatment accorded the SIVs, by their AAA ratings, by the banks' silence on their residual liability — that the SIVs posed no threat.

While the kind of policy that relies on market forces, possibly complemented by regulation, to avoid excessive risk has some intellectual merit, I have concluded that it is wrong. The reason for this conclusion is that such a policy has become irrelevant, so it is a waste of time to discuss it. We must contend with two facts, which have crystallized during the current crisis:

1. The Federal Reserve and the Treasury will always be in the grip of a world view that it is they alone who stand between the rest of us and the abyss.

   The large participants in the markets they regulate, who often supply the leadership of these agencies, share this world view.

2. Much more importantly, these agencies have the demonstrated ability to act on this belief system without serious democratic restraint.

How else can one interpret the sudden revelation that $29 billion of the full faith and credit of the U.S. Treasury had been committed to the Bear Stearns transaction, or the equally sudden undebated and unvoted announcement that $85 billion of government funds had been loaned to AIG? If there is any principle that emerges from these announcements — and non-announcements like the decision not to rescue Lehman Brothers — it seems to be that amounts at least as large as $85 billion can be appropriated, or not, at the discretion of official Washington. Significantly greater amounts will require the assent of a Congress rushed into action by officially sanctioned fear of the consequences of delay. Exactly where the border between $85 billion and that larger amount is remains utterly unclear.

No intelligent policy response to the current crisis can ignore these two facts. They seem entirely unalterable. The policy problem that they create is that, if left unchecked, they will lead to recurrent crises or, at least, to an ever lengthening line of potential supplicants. That prospect will likely evoke some response, either from Congress or the agencies or from both. Most likely the response will be another round of tougher regulation: higher capital requirements, more balance-sheet restrictions, and the like. For reasons I have already indicated, this kind of response is unlikely to work well in the long run. Just as Basel led to the SIVs, so will the next round of regulation have to contend with the ingenuity unleashed by the incentives to find a way around them. The likely outcome of tougher regulation is a short-run success that is eroded over time.

Another policy approach would seek a broad realignment and redirection of the institutionalized moral hazard incentives emanating from the Washington/Wall Street world view. Proposals to attach warrants to any financial aid or to exchange the aid for preferred stock are a move in this direction. They capture some of the upside from what would otherwise be a heads, you win–tails, I lose kind of bet. However, such proposals are wholly ex post. They cannot change any of the behavior that got us here. We need to think about ex ante mechanisms, which can affect future decisions in a world where there is no realistic hope of avoiding potential future claims on government funds. Such mechanisms would, I think, have two desirable properties: They would shorten the number of claimants on the government; and they would mitigate the taxpayer burden. I will sketch out a mechanism that I think has these properties. It is designed to deter the kind of behavior that leads government to ride to the world's rescue and to provide a self-funding mechanism for the rescues that do occur. I will be deliberately vague about details.

I would begin by institutionalizing government bailouts. Once we understand that they will happen, whether we like it or not or whether voted by Congress or not, we should regularize them so that they do not, as they do now, engender further panic. For example, the Federal Reserve Act institutionalizes liquidity provision by allowing eligible institutions to borrow against good collateral. I would extend this to provision of funds not secured by good collateral, without an artificial distinction between liquidity and capital funding. An eligible institution should be able to be accommodated by the Fed whether or not it is able or willing to post eligible collateral. In return for any unsecured credit, however, the institution would be required to give the Fed a convertible bond, with the following properties:

- A fixed term, say, due in five years;
- Pay interest at the Treasury rate, plus a hefty premium;
- Senior to all other liabilities not already insured by the federal government; and
- Convertible to equity at the market price on the issue date if not paid back at maturity.

I leave open thorny issues, like whether the funding comes at the request of the bank, or the Fed itself, or some other regulator. Suffice it to say that, even if we keep the current system whereby only the government can commandeer the aid, it makes sense to impose the ex ante restriction that any aid be paid for by a convertible bond along the lines just described. This would be so if the aid comes in the form of a capital injection, a loan, a loan guarantee, or any other form.

An ex ante requirement for exchanging government assistance for the convertible bond would have several desirable properties:

1. Deterrence. The conversion feature creates the prospect of dilution or transfer of control to the government. The force of this threat is enhanced by the presumably low conversion price, which is set at a time when the recipient has already experienced bad news. It is further enhanced by the penalty interest rate and the senior status of the bond. All of this should create a disincentive for management to

make decisions that will raise the likelihood of requiring government assistance. Or, it will create an incentive to take actions that allow the bond to be paid off before its due date.

2. Reduced taxpayer exposure. Presumably the deterrence will reduce the occasions that require taxpayer exposure. Any exposure that does occur will either result either in repayment in full or the acquisition of some valuable assets that can cushion the taxpayer loss. There is currently no institutionalized mechanism whereby government assistance requires some promise of repayment. For example, the Bear Stearns loan guarantees came at no cost to the beneficiaries. The just enacted program to buy bad bank assets has no charge for the benefits it will grant. This willingness to grant benefits without cost to the beneficiaries has poor deterrence characteristics, and it leaves taxpayers exposed to all the resulting costs.
3. Avoidance of capital structure distortions. The strict priority of the government's claim is an important part of this proposal. The imposition of large losses on equity holders in Bear Stearns and AIG (not to mention Fannie and Freddie) is sometimes pointed to as an offset to moral hazard. Surely the prospect of future equity wipeouts will deter excessive risk taking in the future, according to this view. This view is incorrect. My late colleague, Merton Miller, and Franco Modigliani taught us to be skeptical about artificial distinctions between equity and debt. In the aforementioned cases, if your claim on a firm's assets was called "equity", you lost, but if it was called "debt", you gained. In the Washington/Wall Street world view a wipe out of equity is merely unfortunate, but any loss to debt holders threatens to push us into the abyss. This is dangerous foolishness, because it threatens to multiply the number of crises. It does so by providing an incentive for suppliers of funds to get their claims classified as debt rather than equity. This increases the financial system's leverage and its vulnerability to shocks that threaten debt values. The priority rule for the proposed convertible bond eliminates this source of instability by making it clear ex-ante that government assistance will not be biased in favor of one kind of claimant over another.

The kind of incentive mechanism I have just sketched obviously needs to be fleshed out. Perhaps it can be improved upon, or replaced by something much better. But it is important to begin discussing such mechanisms before we are engulfed by, or preferably to head off, the next crisis. There is a need to create institutional incentives for not getting rescued even if, as I think is likely, we rely heavily on tougher regulation going forward. We need a hedge against the failure of that regulation to produce more stability than similar moves have in the past. But that hedge needs to be put in place now, before the decisions that lead to the next crisis are taken.

Where to From Here?

Lawrence R. Uhlick*
Institute of International Bankers

1. Introduction

I am pleased to have this opportunity to offer some private-sector thoughts on the regulatory and supervisory reforms under discussion to address the current market turmoil and make the U.S. financial system more resilient to future shocks as well as make it more competitive internationally. Since the topic of our panel is "Where to From Here?" — as opposed to "What Got Us Here in the First Place" — I will try to take a forward looking approach in my remarks in terms of the policy remedies under consideration.

Cleary, there is broad agreement in both the public and private sectors that our balkanized financial regulatory structure — designed during the Great Depression — is hardly ideal to meet the challenges posed by today's highly complex, interconnected global marketplace.

As is so often the case, however, the devil is in the details. And while many important ad hoc initiatives have already been undertaken, particularly by the Treasury and the Fed, as well as by private-sector groups, it will be

* Lawrence R. Uhlick is Chief Executive Officer of the Institute of International Bankers, which represents the interests of the international banking community in the United States. The views expressed in this paper are the personal views of the author and do not necessarily represent the views of the Institute. Richard Coffman, General Counsel of the Institute, provided extensive comments and editorial assistance in the preparation of this paper. Note: This paper reflects developments through September 17, 2008. Subsequent market/regulatory developments, including the conversion of Goldman Sachs and Morgan Stanley to bank holding companies and the termination of the SEC's Consolidated Supervised Entities (CSE) program, were anticipated in the paper but had not yet taken place.

up to the new Congress and Administration to work out necessary definitive statutory changes. This will involve a number of difficult and conflicting policy choices and trade-offs. It is very easy to imagine that the process could get quite contentious and time-consuming regardless of who wins the presidential election this November.

Many of these issues were framed in July during the first two in a series of hearings being held by House Financial Services Committee Chairman Barney Frank, whom I applaud for his forward-thinking efforts to examine these critical issues. The separate testimony by Treasury Secretary Paulson, Fed Chairman Bernanke, New York Fed President Geithner and SEC Chairman Cox provide a good preview of the policy debates that will start in earnest in January with a new Congress and Administration on a major overhaul of our regulatory system, as well as a longer-term plan for Fannie Mae and Freddie Mac. My remarks will focus on regulatory reorganization and not the complex subject of Government-Sponsored Enterprises (GSEs).

2. Prudential Oversight of Large, Complex Financial Institutions

One of the more interesting — and problematic — issues to be hashed out involves prudential umbrella oversight of investment banks and whether such responsibility should reside with the SEC, be handed over to the Fed, or somehow shared by both. Depending on how the issue is resolved, there could be fundamental implications for the very nature of the investment banking business model in this country, as well as for hedge funds and other unregulated but systemically important financial players.

Once the Fed opened its discount window in March to investment banks, following the near collapse of Bear Stearns, it seemed inevitable that a more robust umbrella regulatory framework for investment banks and other large securities dealers would necessarily follow. Fed examiners, of course, have indeed been inside the major investment banks since last spring as part of the Fed's liquidity initiatives, but those institutions are not subject to statutorily mandated umbrella oversight.

In his July 24th testimony before the Financial Services Committee, Tim Geithner made the point that as the financial system's lender of last resort, the Fed should play an "important role" in the consolidated supervision of firms that borrow from the Fed. Appearing before the Committee two weeks earlier, Fed Chairman Ben Bernanke called on Congress to consider requiring consolidated supervision of investment banks, while at the same time taking care not to unduly inhibit innovation or risk-taking.

The SEC currently provides umbrella supervision of investment banks on a voluntary basis under its Consolidated Supervised Entities (CSE) program. Originally, five firms were participating in this program — Goldman Sachs, Morgan Stanley, Merrill Lynch, Lehman Brothers, and Bear Stearns. Now, of course, only two independent Wall Street investment banks are still standing — and who knows how long that will remain the case. In any event, a principal inducement for firms to subject themselves to consolidated umbrella supervision by the SEC is to become eligible for the favorable risk-based Alternative Net Capital rule for their registered broker-dealers. The other key benefit, of course, is to be able to qualify under the European Union's (EU) Conglomerates Directive as a firm that is subject to "equivalent" umbrella oversight.

It is understood that Citigroup also participates in the CSE program — and gets the benefit of the risk-based capital rule for its broker-dealer — but it is unclear exactly what kind of arrangement has been worked out between the Fed and the SEC regarding umbrella supervision of the holding company, since that role is already performed by the Fed. Where there is already an umbrella supervisor of the ultimate holding company — as is the case with Citigroup — the SEC's CSE rules call for substantially less direct SEC oversight of the holding company, and one can only assume that the SEC defers enough to the Fed to make the arrangement sufficiently attractive to Citi. Similar issues will also arise in connection with Bank of America's acquisition of Merrill Lynch. Nevertheless, the SEC apparently insists on receiving full holding company financial information and retains umbrella authority over Citi even if it generally relies on the Fed.

On the other hand, it should be noted that internationally headquartered banks have not received the same favorable risk-based capital treatment for their U.S. broker-dealers, because they have been unwilling to subject themselves to at least a theoretical third layer of umbrella supervision of their global operations by the SEC, rather than qualifying on the basis of equivalent umbrella supervision provided by their home-country regulator and the Fed. Moreover, the SEC imposes on the group's U.S. broker-dealer subsidiary a $5 billion "tentative net capital" threshold in order to qualify for the CSE program. One could make the argument that a more appropriate threshold would be based on a broker-dealer's risk-based capital.

It is worth noting that the big U.S. securities firms do not receive duplicative umbrella supervision under the EU's Conglomerates Directive because the EU defers to the umbrella supervision provided by their home country regulators, including the Fed and SEC. In all candor, the lack of reciprocal deference by the SEC has rankled our friends in Europe — and rightly so.

Both the Fed and the SEC appear to agree that consolidated supervision of investment banks should be statutorily mandated by Congress, but they also seem to part company over the question of who should be given the statutory mandate to perform this function. Not surprisingly, Chairman Cox argued in his July Congressional testimony that it should be given to the SEC.

At this point, I would say that the betting in the private sector is that Congress will side largely with the Fed.

If, indeed, the Fed is given the mandate to provide consolidated supervision of investment banks, the availability of the SEC's risk-based Alternative Net Capital rule to broker-dealers would presumably continue, even as the CSE program itself would cease.

Under this scenario, the unequal treatment of U.S. broker-dealer subsidiaries of international banks should be resolved, since the issue of a third layer of SEC umbrella supervision would no longer be an issue. And no doubt Citi — and presumably Bank of America with respect to Merrill Lynch — will benefit from being exempted from the SEC umbrella oversight in the future.

3. International Competitiveness

It is worth recalling that the Treasury's Blueprint, unveiled in March 2008, was initially conceived before the subprime mortgage meltdown as part of Secretary Paulson's initiative to enhance the international competitiveness of U.S. financial markets. Correcting the competitive imbalance posed by the existing CSE program would be one way to help achieve that goal.

More broadly, the policy debates to come on restructuring the U.S. financial regulatory system must take into account how such regulatory restructuring will affect not just U.S. domestic firms, but also their internationally headquartered counterparts operating in the United States. After all, nearly one-quarter of the total assets in America's banking system are held by the U.S. operations of internationally headquartered financial institutions.

Treasury's Blueprint — which in fairness was billed by Secretary Paulson himself as a set of "long-term ideas" requiring further extensive debate — is completely silent on how U.S. branches and agencies of international banks would be treated under the proposed "optimal regulatory structure," which envisions three federal supervisory authorities with different purposes, including the Fed as market stability regulator, but not the actual supervisor of individual institutions.

4. Conclusion

In conclusion, where do we go from here? It is always dangerous to make predictions about outcomes in the legislative process, but when the dust settles, the U.S. financial regulatory system probably will not look radically different than it does today. The Fed will most likely retain its existing supervisory function with broader authority over systemically important institutions, including not only investment banks, but also hedge funds and insurance companies, particularly in view of the AIG bailout. The dual banking system will also likely remain in place and one could expect a continued separation of banking and commerce. And while there very well may be some consolidation of federal agencies, we are not moving toward the single financial regulator model, as there appears to be an emerging consensus that it would be an unmanageable organization burdened with some of the perceived shortcomings of the U.S. Department of Homeland Security.

The overarching goal should be to achieve a system that is more cohesive and rigorous, while less cumbersome and needlessly burdensome, particularly for large systemically important institutions. I would expect a continued willingness to leave alone the regulatory pattern as it applies to the many smaller institutions that operate throughout the U.S.

Conference Agenda

Thursday, September 25

9:00 a.m. **Registration and Continental Breakfast**

9:40 a.m. **Welcoming Remarks**

Charles L. Evans, *President and Chief Executive Officer, Federal Reserve Bank of Chicago*

José Manuel González-Páramo, *Board Member, European Central Bank*

10:00 a.m. **Session I: What Happened, Where?**

Moderator

Douglas D. Evanoff, *Federal Reserve Bank of Chicago*

United States

Robert DiClemente, *Citigroup*

Europe

Jesús Saurina, *Banco de España*

Rest of the World

Laura E. Kodres, *International Monetary Fund*

Discussant and Commentator

John P. C. Fell, *European Central Bank*

12:00 p.m. **Luncheon and Keynote Address**

Introduction

Charles L. Evans, *President and Chief Executive Officer, Federal Reserve Bank of Chicago*

Speaker
Paola Sapienza, *Zell Center Faculty Fellow, Kellogg School of Management, Northwestern University*

2:00 p.m. **Session II: How Serious is the Damage?**

Moderator
Philipp Hartmann, *European Central Bank*

Major Losses and Failures
Patrick Honohan, *Trinity College, Dublin*

Damage to Financial Markets
S. (Vish) Viswanathan, *Duke University*

Effects to Real Economy
David Greenlaw, *Morgan Stanley*

Discussant and Commentator
Christopher Kent, *Reserve Bank of Australia*

3:45 p.m. **Break**

4:00 p.m. **Session III: Why Did It Go Undetected/ Underestimated for So Long?**

Moderator
Garry J. Schinasi, *International Monetary Fund*

Pricing Risk
Joseph R. Mason, *Louisiana State University*

Securities Spillovers and Complexity
John C. Hull, *University of Toronto*

The Role of Rating Agencies
Frank Partnoy, *University of San Diego School of Law*

Discussant and Commentator
Mark Zandi, *Moody's Economy.com*

5:45 p.m. **Reception**

6:45 p.m. **Dinner and Keynote Address**

Introduction
Charles I. Plosser, *President and Chief Executive Officer, Federal Reserve Bank of Philadelphia*

Speaker
José Manuel González-Páramo, *Board Member, European Central Bank*

Friday, September 26

7:30 a.m. **Registration and Continental Breakfast**

8:15 a.m. **Session IV: Experience with Crisis Management**

Moderator
Richard J. Rosen, *Federal Reserve Bank of Chicago*

Euro Area
Nuno Cassola, *European Central Bank*
Cornelia Holthausen, *European Central Bank*
Flemming Würtz, *European Central Bank*

United Kingdom
Nigel Jenkinson, *Bank of England*

United States
Richard J. Rosen, *Federal Reserve Bank of Chicago*

10:00 a.m. **Break**

10:15 a.m. **Session V: Implications for Basel II and Bank Capital Regulation**

Moderator
Harald A. Benink, *Tilburg University (Netherlands)*

Role of Risk Models
Michel Crouhy, *NATIXIS Corporate and Investment Bank*

Role of Supervision
Cathy Lemieux, *Federal Reserve Bank of Chicago*

Role of Market Discipline
Mark J. Flannery, *University of Florida*

Discussant and Commentator
Robert E. Litan, *Kauffman Foundation*

12:15 p.m. **Luncheon and Keynote Address**

Introduction
José Manuel González-Páramo, *Board Member, European Central Bank*

Speaker
Kenneth W. Dam, *Max Pam Professor Emeritus of American and Foreign Law, University of Chicago Law School*

2:15 p.m. **Session VI: Implications for Regulation of Financial Markets and Instruments**

Moderator
Olli Castrén, *European Central Bank*

Role of Financial Engineering
Mark Carey, *Board of Governors of the Federal Reserve System*

Complex Securities
Markus K. Brunnermeier, *Princeton University*
Martin Oehmke, *Columbia University*

Aligning Incentives
Adam B. Ashcraft, *Federal Reserve Bank of New York*

Discussant and Commentator
James Overdahl, *U.S. Securities and Exchange Commission*

4:00 p.m. **Break**

4:15 p.m. **Session VII: Policy Panel: Where to from Here?**

Moderator
George G. Kaufman, *Loyola University Chicago and Federal Reserve Bank of Chicago*

Panelist
Philipp Hartmann, *European Central Bank*
Richard Herring, *University of Pennsylvania*
Takatoshi Ito, *University of Tokyo*
Henry Kaufman, *Henry Kaufman & Company*
Sam Peltzman, *University of Chicago*
Lawrence R. Uhlick, *Institute of International Bankers*

6:00 p.m. **Reception**

6:45 p.m. **Dinner and Keynote Address**

Introduction

Douglas D. Evanoff, *Federal Reserve Bank of Chicago*

Speaker

Charles H. Dallara, *Managing Director, Institute of International Finance*

Index